GENEALOGY

OF THE

TENNANT FAMILY

Their Ancestors and Descendants Through
Many Generations

BY

Rev. Albert Milton Tennant

WITH

Contributions From Other Members of the Family

1915
DUNKIRK PRINTING COMPANY
DUNKIRK, NEW YORK

DEDICATION.

In Loving Remembrance of My Dear Sainted Father and Mother, Moses Asel and Delinda Tennant, this Book is Most Affectionately Dedicated by their Son, Albert Milton.

MOSES ASEL TENNANT
Born December 23, 1801   Died November 1, 1876

MRS. DELINDA TENNANT

Born April 18, 1802   Died February 3, 1893

INTRODUCTION.

The author of this Genealogy makes no pretensions to any special literary ability. His sole object in its composition and publication is to furnish the living members of the Tennant families a correct account of the relationship of the various branches of the family to each other, and to their ancestors and descendants. The facts herein gathered have been furnished the author by living members through an extensive correspondence. The author wishes to acknowledge his indebtedness to all the relatives who have sent him their family records. Without this aid this Genealogy could not have been written. Special mention is due those who have written for him quite extensive family histories, giving records of births, marriages and deaths of parents, grandparents and children. The following have contributed very much to aid the author.

Prof. Frank D. Shaver of Benedict College, North Carolina, who sent in the names of the ancestors of Elizabeth Loomis, wife of John Tennant; Ernest Hollenbeck; Ralph Waldo Champion; Rev. Eli S. Way; Solon Clough; George Sawin; Jewett Tennant; Cassius Gay; Selden David Tennant; Augustus Tennant; Herbert C. DeHart; Holden Phillips; Mrs. Orlando Bunnell; Mrs. Cora McLeod; Mrs. Josephine Tennant; Mrs. Elizabeth Hastings; Mrs. Ida Phillips; Mrs. James Phillips; Mrs. Alice Shaw; Mrs. Blanche Wattles; Mrs. Henry Baisley; Mrs. William DeHart; Mrs. Lucy E. Doolittle; Mrs. Juliette Sawin Smith, and very many others too numerous to mention. Indeed, the author has done but little more than to compile the facts sent to him, and write them into a connected readable form. Of the author's father's family, the family record was sufficient to furnish a good portion of the facts needed to complete their history.

Many facts herein mentioned are recollections of the author. To these he has added some remembrances of his paternal grandmother, Mrs. Sarah Jewett (Tennant) Morse and of his maternal grandfather, John Tennant.

The author believed it would add much value to his book to mention the families into which his brothers and sisters, his uncles, aunts and cousins have married. As his mother was a Tennant by birth and had two brothers and four sisters, these and their descendants must be considered branches of the Tennant family. As the author's father, Moses Asel Tennant, had two half-brothers and four half-sisters, these and their descendants must be included in any complete genealogy of the Tennant family.

For the convenience of reading and reference, the author divides this Genealogy into five parts, and a supplement, each part being subdivided into Chapters.

The first three parts comprises the body of the work, each part containing the history and records of a single great branch of the Tennant Family. The Fourth Part contains Memorial Tributes written by the author, except one written by Prof. Frank D. Shaver concerning his mother, the author's sister, Julia Emma Tennant, wife of David Shaver. The facts contained in the Memorials have been contributed by near relatives, and written into readable form by the author. This Fourth Part contains an autobiography of Miss Helen Potter, and of the author of this book.

A list of all the descendants of the three Great Branches closes the book and constitutes the supplement.

All poems in the book are original with the author, except those duly credited to other persons.

There must of necessity creep into the work errors of facts, errors of dates and ages, and errors of spelling, especially of names. To avoid errors, the author has gone over and over again every part of the work up to June, 1915. He has labored upon it for four years, less by two months. This Genealogy is not written for the public to purchase or read. Sufficient number of copies will be printed to supply each family descendant with one copy, a second edition will never be published.

Before I close this Introduction, I wish to thank all my dear cousins, over and over again, for the hearty and generous response I have received in my call for aid to complete this work. Hundreds of letters have been written to me, and always most gladly received.

I trust the religious sentiment which prevails throughout the book, all of which is designed by the author, will enlighten minds that may be in darkness, encourage those in despondency, and comfort the bereaved and sorrowing. No teaching of doctrines is intended in any poem or article found in this work .

Most sincerely,

A. M. TENNANT.

P. S.—At my request the Hon. Willis H. Tennant has written an article relating to the early settlement of the Tennants.

—A. M. T.

CONTENTS.

CHAPTER V.

CHAPTER VI.

CHAPTER VII.

CHAPTER VIII.

PART II.

CHAPTER FIRST.

CHAPTER II.

CHAPTER III.

CHAPTER IV.

CHAPTER V.

PART III.

CHAPTER I.

CHAPTER V.

In Three Divisions.

CHAPTER VI.

MISS ESTHER TENNANT.

PART IV.

In Two Divisions

DIVISION FIRST.

DIVISION SECOND.

MEMORIAL TRIBUTES.

PART V.

SUPPLEMENT.

FIRST PART

ELIZABETH LOOMIS

AND HER

ANCESTORS and DESCENDANTS

Deacon John Loomis, Samuel Loomis,
Daniel Loomis and John Loomis
Her Husband

John Tennant and Her Children
Alfred Tennant, Betsey Tennant, Orrel Tennant
Olive Eliza Tennant, Alvin Loomis Tennant
Delinda Tennant
and Clarise Tennant

Sarah Tennant Daughter of John Tennant
by Second Marriage

PART FIRST.

CHAPTER I.

MISS ELIZABETH LOOMIS—Importance of Family Records—Her Ancestors, Brothers and Sisters—Four Centuries of History—Great Evolution of Events— Her Marriage to John Tennant. His ancestry unknown—Veteran of the War of 1812—Wounded and Honorably Discharged—Mrs. Loomis Tennant's Death and Burial—Sketch of his Life—His Death and Burial—A Poem by the Author.

IT IS greatly to be regretted that so many families in our own and other countries have been so indifferent and neglectful in preserving their family history. Generation after generation lives, dies and passes away leaving no reliable record of the names of ancestors and descendants, of the age in which they lived, of the scenes through which they passed, of the positions which they occupied in society, of the works which they have wrought and the influences for good or evil which they have exerted upon the communities and nations among which they have lived. The individual is the unit of the family and the family the unit of the nation. A single family has oft times risen to such a degree of power and influence as to shape the character and determine the destiny of nations. Indeed, an entire generation of men, women and children have been uplifted or depressed by the powerful influence of a single individual. How great was the influence of Moses, of David and Solomon, of Caesar Augustus, of Alexander the Great, of Napoleon Bonaparte, of Washington, Lincoln and Grant. Warriors, statesmen, poets, historians, inventors, philosophers, scientists and great financiers may be said to rule the world and determine the destiny of the race. These facts are mentioned only to emphasize the great importance of preserving a history of families.

A History of all the families is a history of all nations and generations of mankind. If it is important to preserve a history of the most distinguished and influential families, no less is the importance of preserving a genealogy of families of the middle and lower classes, as oft times from these will arise the most distinguished individuals of a nation or race.

In this Genealogy of the Tennant family we may not discover among their ancestors or descendants living or dead, any great or especially distinguished men or women, however, we shall learn that their ancestry extends back near to the middle of the sixteenth century; that they have connections with the ancestry

of other families of distinguished characters and that here and
there among the descendants are persons of excellent natural
gifts who have risen to positions of trust and wide influence in
society and the Christian Church.

In this genealogy we include only the Tennants which are
known by the author to be connected by consanguinity with his
parents.   In a broader view the families bearing the name Tennant are very numerous in this country, in Canada and England.
Families by this name were early settlers in Connecticut, New
Hampshire, Rhode Island, New Jersey, Virginia and New York.
These early settlers lived in the period of the Revolutionary
War and of the formation of the American Republic.   How
many took an active part in the great revolution is not known
by the writer.   This fact, that one of the ancestors had an active part in the War of 1812, is positively known by the writer
and will be mentioned later.

It is proper that we begin this genealogical history by men-
tioning first that line of ancestry which can be traced the farth-
est back in the by-gone centuries.   This leads us to trace first
the ancestry of the author's beloved mother, Delinda Tennant,
daughter of ELIZABETH LOOMIS.

DELINDA TENNANT'S ANCESTORS.

DELINDA TENNANT was her maiden name.   She was the
daughter of John Tennant and Elizabeth Loomis.   Nothing is
known by the writer of the ancestry of John Tennant except
that his father's given name was Daniel, and that he (the father)
came to this country in an early day and settled in Rhode Island.
Here we begin to realize the importance of family records for
the maiden sur-name of the mother of John Tennant, is lost.
Her given name was Sarah.

We now follow the line of the

ANCESTORS OF ELIZABETH LOOMIS.

ELIZABETH LOOMIS was born in Connecticut March 15, 1767.
She married John Tennant in Connecticut in 1788.   Between
the years 1788 and 1789 they moved to Springfield, N. Y.
The time of this movement can only be determined approximately from the fact that her second child, Betsey, was born in 1789
at Springfield.   John Tennant was born in Rhode Island, June
1762.   He was a little less than 5 years older than his wife.

We now give the ancestors of ELIZABETH LOOMIS and names
of her brothers and sisters.   We begin with the first known generation.

DEACON JOHN LOOMIS, born in England in 1622, and died in
1688.   He was the great-great-grand-father of Elizabeth
Loomis.

SAMUEL LOOMIS, born in Colchester, Connecticut in 1666, and died in 1754, was a son of Deacon John Loomis and great grandfather of Elizabeth Loomis.

DANIEL LOOMIS, son of Samuel Loomis, was born at Colchester, Connecticut in 1729 and died in 1784. He was grand father of Elizabeth Loomis.

JOHN LOOMIS, son of Daniel Loomis, was born Jan. 6, 1741 and died May 4, 1811. He was the father of Elizabeth Loomis and the grand-father of Delinda Tennant and, of course, of her two brothers and four sisters, Alfred, Betsey, Orrel, Alvin, Olive-Eliza and Clarissa, hereafter to be mentioned with their descendants in the order of their ages.

We could pause here in our record of facts and suffer our imagination to take wings and fly back over the intervening centuries from 1622, the year of the birth of Deacon John Loomis, our great-great-great-great-grandfather and try to recall the marvelous events which have transpired since this very great grandfather of ours was born. Suffice it to say, that at that period of the world's history the American continent was a vast howling wilderness. What few settlements there were only dotted here and there the shores of the Atlantic, the Gulf of Mexico and the Pacific coast. The natives and the wild beasts roamed over the land, struggling with each other for existence. What are now known as modern improvements have, for the most part, sprung into existence since the days of the earliest of the above mentioned fore-fathers.

Steamboats, telegraphs, telephones, and many thousand kinds of implements of war and of industry have been invented and brought into practical use. During these past four centuries there has been a revival of learning. Science and philosophy have advanced with marvelous speed. Educational institutions of all grades have been established, and great libraries founded in our own and the European countries. In history, literature, art and law, marvelous advancements have been made. These changes, and many more than we have space to mention, have taken place within the period of the lives of these ancestors and their descendants.

ELIZABETH LOOMIS' mother's maiden name was Rachel Harris, born as we are informed, about the year 1740. There were born to her and her husband, John Loomis, eight children, five sons and three daughters. We give their names in the order of their ages with the year of their births and deaths, beginning with the oldest.

Jacob	-	-	born in 1761 died in 1838
John	-	-	born in 1763 died in 1830

Rachel	-	-	born in 1765 died in 1807
Elizabeth	-		born in 1767 died in 1808
Elsie	-	-	born in 1769 died in 1841
Harris	-		born in 1770 died in 1806
Joel	-	-	- born in 1773 died in 1867
Hubbel		-	born in 1775 died in 1872

The writer is indebted to his nephew Prof. Frank Shaver for this genealogy of the Loomis family. Joel is mentioned as having been an Assemblyman and Probate Judge. Elias, a son of Hubbel Loomis, was a Professor in Yale University. His father was a distinguished Christian Minister who served as pastor of one church for twenty-four years.

The above named brothers and sisters, except Elizabeth, were uncles and aunts of Delinda Tennant and her brothers and sisters. Prof. Elias Loomis was a first cousin.

The mind grows dizzy with its own thoughts, when it attempts to call up in its imagery the scenes, the personal experiences of joy and sorrow, the labors and associations, the possible defeats and many victories, through which these beloved ancestors passed. Their united lives lapped over periods of marvelous events in the evolution of the old and the new world. The changes and events of this life soon pass away. Happy is that soul whose hopes perish not with material things, but are anchored "within the veil" of heavenly and eternal things. This dear grand-mother whom the writer has never seen, and knows not the place where the beautiful temple of her body has found its peaceful resting place, he must believe, received in her dying moments, the comforts and triumphs of a christian faith and hope, and is now, while he is writing these lines, waving the palm of victory and casting her crown of glory at the feet of Him who has washed her robe and made it white in His cleansing blood.

TO ELIZABETH LOOMIS

My Mother's Mother.

By her Grand-son.

We never have met in this earthly life,
  You were gone ere life dawned upon me;
But if ever I see your dear face up in Heaven,
  How happy and blest I will be.

My mother has told me some things about you,
  In my boy-hood days long ago;
Their memory still lingers within my fond heart,
  To brighten my life as I go.

The years are now passing most swiftly away,
  Your grand-son would hasten their flight;
He longs for the union of loved ones above,
  In that home most celestial and bright.

He is lingering and waiting for the Master's call,
  His mother has gone on before;
He stands near the end of his earthly career,
  And looks toward the golden shore.

Ah! soon, very soon, the glad hour will come,
  When grand-mother, mother and son,
Will join the bright angels in the far-away home,
  Life's battles all fought and its victories won.

1 Cor. 15:57.
"But thanks be to God who giveth us the
victory through our Lord Jesus Christ."

ELIZABETH LOOMIS TENNANT entered into her eternal rest at Springfield, Otsego Co., N. Y., May 4th, 1808, six years after the birth of her daughter, Delinda. She left to mourn their loss her husband, one son and five daughters. Her burial was in the cemetery of the Village of Springfield. As there was no durable monument left to mark her grave its exact place cannot be found.

Her husband, John Tennant, was a man of sterling qualities, of great physical strength, a good neighbor and a loyal citizen. He enlisted when a young man in the war of 1812. The writer does not know in how many battles he was engaged, but remembers a deep scar on his grand-father's wrist, the effects of a wound made by a minnie ball shot through his arm. The loss of his wife, ELIZABETH LOOMIS, and the sudden death of his son, Alfred by accident, greatly depressed his spirits and almost unbalanced his mind. The story in part of his subsequent life will be related in connection with that of his daughter, Sarah Tennant, found in this book following the records of his other children and their families. (See Part I Chapter VII).

Grandfather Tennant spent his last years with his daughters who lived on Ripley Hill in the Wattlesberg district, County of Chautauqua, N. Y. He was a cabinet maker and left with some of his children samples of his handicraft. He led a very quiet and simple life toward the last. The writer has seen his grandfather roast a slice of salt pork held on the sharp end of a long stick before a bed of hot coals, and this with a potato roasted in the hot ashes of the fireplace and a good slice of bread without any butter, made this veteran of the war of 1812 a most enjoyable meal.

His very last days were spent with his daughter, Delinda. In the old log house on Ripley Hill, with his children and grandchildren near his bedside, his spirit passed out of the body, after a short illness, on the 20th of Feb. 1846. The temple of mortal flesh in which he lived and fought life's battles being broken and falling to decay, was buried by loving hands in its last resting place in the cemetery at Ripley Village in the family lot upon which, in subsequent years, was placed by his son-in-law. Moses Asel Tennant and his grand-sons, Alvin, Delos, Albert and John Tennant, a large and beautiful monument of Scotch granite. Beneath the shadow of this monument rest the mortal remains of our father's mother, Sarah Selden Jewett, and our mother's father, John Tennant, to await the resurrection of the just.

> The battle of life is ended
> And the victory is won;
> The Captain of their salvation
> Has said to His soldiers, "Well done."
>
> With Him do they reign in glory,
> Before and near the white throne;
> Clothed in robes of His righteousness,
> They stand in that and in that alone.
>
> As the years go on, we shall meet them;
> We shall see them and know who they are;
> For the God that forms earthly relations,
> In some way will continue them there.

PART I.

CHAPTER II.

ALFRED TENNANT, the oldest child of John Tennant and Elizabeth Loomis Tennant, his wife, was born at Springfield, Otsego Co., N. Y., in 1791. He had a common school education such as farmers' sons received at that time. At the early age of seventeen, while riding on a load of lumber, in going down a steep hill, the load was jolted forward against the horses, they commenced to run, and Alfred, who was driving the team, was thrown from the wagon and a wheel passed over him and he was killed. His death was such a shock to his mother that it caused a permature birth of her child which resulted in the death of both the mother and the child. This occurred in the year 1808. The mother's death was on the 24th day of May. The effect of this double bereavement on the husband and father is mentioned in the history of his daughter, Sarah Tennant recorded in Part III, Chapter VII. From the date of the birth of their oldest child, Alfred, in 1791, we conclude that the marriage of John Tennant and Elizabeth Loomis occurred in the year 1789 or 1790, or possibly a short time before this. As Miss Loomis was born March 15th, 1767, she was about 22 years old at the time of her marriage, and her husband, who was born in June, 1767, was about 26 years old at their marriage.

PART I.

CHAPTER III.

Containing records of the Descendants of BETSEY TENNANT and her husband, Rev. George Sawin; Olive Eliza (Sawin) Webster; Maria Edna (Sawin) Shrove, Orlando Sawin, Helen and Emma Webster; Frank, Bernice and George Sawin; Nellie Ruth, William, Arnold, Bernice, Milton, and Grace Sawin.

BETSEY TENNANT, oldest daughter of John Tennant and Elizabeth Loomis Tennant, was born at Springfield, Otsego Co., N. Y., May 31, 1789. She married Rev. George Sawin at Starkville, Herkimer Co., N. Y., on the 19th of March, 1812. Mr. Sawin entered the Baptist ministry and was ordained Pastor of the Baptist church at Springfield, N. Y. He was born in Herkimer Co., N. Y., June 6, 1787. He was a brother of Rev. John Sawin.

Rev. George Sawin and family moved from Springfield, N. Y. in 1832 to Chautauqua Co., N. Y., and settled in the town of Ripley in the district known as Wattlesberg. Here he purchased a farm on which he lived till the time of his death, Sept. 19, 1860. His beloved wife died May 31, 1860, which was her 71st birthday. Mr. Sawin was 73 years, 3 months and 13 days old at the time of his death.

Further mention of the life and service of Rev. Sawin will be mentioned in a Memorial Tribute found in Part IV, Section Second, Article First.

CHILDREN AND GRANDCHILDREN
OF
REV. GEORGE AND BETSEY TENNANT SAWIN.

There were born to Rev. and Mrs. Sawin, three children, named Olive Eliza, Maria Edna and William Orlando.

OLIVE ELIZA, the oldest child, was born at Starkville, Herkimer Co., N. Y., Nov. 23rd, 1815. She came with the family to Chautauqua County, N. Y., in 1832. She married Platt Webster at Ripley, Chautauqua Co., N. Y., May 26, 1836. They settled on a farm just east of Palmer's Gulf formerly occupied by Rev. John Sawin and family. Here they lived for many years. Mr. Webster was born in Madison Co., N. Y., April 27, 1805. He died at Brooklyn, Green Co., Wisc., May 14, 1883, being at his death 78 years and 17 days old. His beloved wife died at Ripley, Jan. 9th, 1877, being at her death 61 years, 1 month and 16 days old. She preceded her husband in death about 6 years.

There were born to Mr. and Mrs. Webster, two children, Helen and Emma.

1. HELEN M. WEBSTER was born in the Town of Ripley, N. Y., August, 1837. She married Lorenzo Sawin, son of Rev. John Sawin at Ripley, Nov. 7, 1860. Immediately after marriage they went to Evansville, Green Co., Wisc.,where Mr. Sawin had a farm. There were born to them two children, named Iola Adell and Emma Grace. Their record may be found under their father's name in the genealogy of the family of Rev. John Sawin and Orrel Tennant Sawin.

2. MARIA EMMA WEBSTER, second daughter of Platt and Olive Sawin Webster, was born in Ripley, N. Y., Mar. 4, 1845. She married James Henry Green of Gowanda, Erie Co., N. Y., at Evansville, Wisc., Mar. 4, 1891. They settled on his farm at Gowanda where they lived to the time of his death which took place at his home in Gowanda May 24, 1905. They had no children.

After a few years Mrs. Green married Adelbert Newbury, son of Deacon John Newbury, as his second wife. He was of the town of Ripley and was born and lived in his early days in the same district as his wife, and they attended the same school. This marriage took place at Hanover Center, Chautauqua County, N. Y., Feb. 25, 1909. Mr. and Mrs. Newbury lived in their pleasant home at Ripley Village for about three years and seven months when he was taken suddenly ill and died at his home Oct. 11, 1912. He was a noble christian man, and influential citizen, whose death was deeply mourned by his family, his relatives and the entire community.

II. MARIA EDNA SAWIN, second daughter of Rev. George and Betsey Tennant Sawin, was born at Starkville, Herkimer Co., N. Y., May 20, 1818. She came with the family to Chautauqua County, N. Y., in 1832. She married Eli Shrove at Ripley, N. Y., the 7th of March, 1839. Mr. Shrove was born Aug. 8, 1812. He died Feb. 27, 1842 at Ripley, N. Y. His beloved wife survived him for a few days over three years and died at Ripley, March 26, 1845, being at her death 26 years, 10 months and 6 days old.

The writer remembers well hearing told, in later years, of the remarkable vision that Mrs. Shrove had just before her death. Her mind was perfectly clear and rational up to the moment she breathed for the last time. Just before her death came, she began to exclaim: "See, see, see the angels! Why, don't you see them? There is a great many of them." There is no doubt in the mind of the writer, but that this cousin was permitted to have a pre-vision of the heavenly world, before death separated her enraptured spirit from the body. He stood by the bedside of

a young woman who had a similar vision a few moments before
her death.   This was during his pastoral service at Clymer, N.
Y.

She said to me after the vision had passed, "So you think, Mr.
Tennant, that God will let me die in darkness after he has shown
me his glory?"   I replied: "I believe not."   In a few moments
her beautiful spirit took its flight to the realms of celestial glory.
Let us not be skeptical when "All things are possible with God."
This young woman was Miss Emma Knowlton.

III.   WILLIAM ORLANDO SAWIN, only son of Rev. George
and Betsey Tennant Sawin, was born at Starkville, Herkimer
Co., N. Y., Dec. 9, 1827.   He also came with the family to
Chautauqua Co., N. Y., in 1832.   He married Miss Jane Eli-
zabeth Bacon, oldest child of James Bacon, at Ripley, N. Y.,
Oct. 23, 1850.

For the first twelve years of their married life, up to the time
of the death of Mr. Sawin's father and mother, they made their
home with them at the old farm on Ripley Hill.   After the
parents' death, Mr. Sawin sold the hill farm and bought land
in the town of Westfield, Chautauqua Co., N. Y., located on
what is known at this date, 1912, as the Prospect road.   This
farm is now owned and occupied by his son, George and family.

The story of the early life of Mrs. Jane Bacon Sawin would
make interesting reading could it all be told in writing.   She was
born in Westfield, Chautauqua Co., N. Y., Dec. 22, 1828.   When
she was only two or three years old, her mother died. Subsequently
her father moved on to a farm now owned by Mrs. Jane Farrington on the Main or Buffalo road.   Across the street from
their house, was a forest of heavy timber.   It is a singular providence that Mrs. Sawin was buried in the Farrington cemetery
on the field where in early childhood she plucked and filled her
hands with wild flowers.

Mr. Sawin purchased a home on Spring Street in the Village
of Westfield.   Here he and his wife lived for a number of years,
his son, George and family occupying the farm.   Here he died,
after a brief illness, May 1, 1898.   His widow still continued her
residence at her home on Spring St. till age and infirmity compelled her to break up house-keeping, when she went to her son's
home on the old farm to spend her last days.   After a sickness
which continued for a few weeks, she entered into her eternal
rest Aug. 9, 1907.   Both husband and wife were buried in Farrington cemetery and a beautiful monument erected by their son,
George, marks the resting place of their mortal remains.

Mr. and Mrs. Sawin were worthy members of the Baptist
Church of Westfield, N. Y., for many years.   He served the
church as deacon and trustee up to the time of his death.   His

influence in the church and the community was that of a worthy and honored Christian citizen. He favored all worthy reform movements. His judgment was always calm and well balanced. He could look upon all sides of important questions which might arise in business, church, community or political affairs. His opinions were deliberately formed and firmly fixed. In the main, he was conservative and not radical, and hence his influence was strong for the right and his views on many subjects commanded respect. His taking away was a great loss to the church and the community. Mrs. Sawin heartily sympathized and co-operated with her husband in all his purposes and labors. In unity of faith and labor they lived and died, and together they are now receiving the eternal rewards.

THEIR CHILDREN AND GRANDCHILDREN.

There were born to Orlando and Jane Bacon Sawin three children, Frank, Bernice and George.

I. FRANK BENJAMIN SAWIN was born at Ripley, N. Y., Aug. 8, 1851. He was a very bright and promising young man with high ideals and bright hopes. But these were all blasted in the morning of life, for at the age of 19 past, he died Mar. 3, 1870. The death of this son was a great sorrow to the family.

II. BERNICE AUGUSTA SAWIN was born at Ripley, N. Y., June 9, 1857. She married George W. Douglas at Westfield, N. Y., Sept. 3, 1884. Mr. Douglas was a native of New Brunswick, born at St. Johns, March 8, 1859.

For nearly six years after their marriage their home was in Westfield, N. Y. In May, 1890, the family moved to Omaha, Neb. At this city he took up the trade in hard-wood lumber in which he is now engaged, 1912. For a number of years he was alone in the business, but finally took in a partner and they are doing business under the firm name of Douglas & Field. Their purchases are made in western, northwestern and southern states. A considerable part of the lumber is shipped by rail to Omaha, but when sales are made before shipment, the lumber goes to different places to the buyers. They have a large and flourishing business, with but little local competition.

To Mr. and Mrs. Douglas was born one child, a son, named Donald Sawin Douglas, born at Westfield, N. Y., Feb. 19, 1888. He married Miss Stella Leonora Gordon of Chicago, Ill., at Chicago, March 27, 1909. They have a son, Lloyd Lyman Douglas, born at Hamilton, N. Y., Feb. 1, 1910.

Miss Gordon was born at Chicago, May 14, 1882. She has been an active worker in her home church, a devoted and self-sacrificing christian young woman, of excellent culture and earnest piety that fits her well for the position to which by Providence she is called by her marriage to a young man who is preparing to enter the christian ministry or professorship. The young couple were married while her husband was pursuing his college course .

Young Douglas was reared at Omaha, Neb., receiving his elementary and High School training there, graduating in 1905. For two years he took a post-graduate study, and entered Colgate University at Madison, N. Y., in Sept. 1907, from which he was graduated in 1911, receiving the degree of A. B., ranking third in his class, and with a Phi Beta Kappi membership. He writes the author June 10, 1912 "I have just completed one year of graduate study, leading to the degree of Master of Arts, completing the required work, all but a thesis, which will be written in the near future."

Mr. Douglas entered the Theological Seminary of Colgate University in Sept. 1912, and pursued the regular course outlined for the degree of Bachelor of Divinity. His course of study has been Greek language and literature, preparing himself for textual criticism of the New Testament. He is not yet ordained, (1913).

The author has heard Mr. Douglas preach at a service in the Baptist Church of Westfield, N. Y., the place of his birth, and marked him as a young man of more than ordinary ability. If his health is preserved, he has promise of success in the high calling to which he has consecrated his talents, his acquisitions and his life.

III.   GEORGE WILLIAM SAWIN, third child and second son of Orlando and Jane Bacon Sawin, was born at Westfield, N. Y., Dec. 31, 1863.   He married Miss Margaret Taylor Wilson at Westfield, Nov. 27, 1883.   Miss Wilson was born in Westfield, N. Y., July 2, 1861.   They settled on the farm purchased by his father, located on the Prospect Road, where he now lives at this date, 1913, in the Town of Westfield, N. Y.

There were born to them three children, Nellie, William and Ruth, all born in Westfield, Chautauqua Co., N. Y.

1.   NELLIE SAWIN was born Aug. 21, 1884.   She was graduated from the Westfield Academy in the Spring of 1906.   She took a normal course as a preparation for teaching.   She closed in June, 1912, her third year of teaching.   Her success in this occupation has given her an excellent reputation and her services are in much demand.

She married Mr. Lewis Delos Lull at her home in Westfield, N. Y., June 11th, 1913.   Mr. Lull was born at Chatsworth, Burlington Co., N. Y., March 24th, 1879.   He is the son of Andrew D. and Annie Elberson Lull.   Mr. and Mrs. Lull, soon after their marriage, went to their home, already prepared for them, located on Prospect road in the town of Westfield. This home is on a farm of 40 acres, well located, and has a full bearing vineyard. These young people started in married life under very favorable circumstances. At their home on Prospect Road in the Township of Westfield. N. Y., there was born to them March 22nd, 1914, a son, named Raymond Sawin Lull.

2. WILLIAM WILSON SAWIN was born Aug. 25th, 1888. He was graduated from the Westfield High School in the summer of 1909. He prepared himself for teaching and closed his first year in this work in the spring of 1912. He has since taken a course in Bible Study in New York City. He was granted a license to preach by the Baptist Church of Westfield, N. Y., at a meeting called for that purpose.

3. MARGARET RUTH SAWIN was born Dec. 7th, 1892. She has taken a course of study in the Westfield, N. Y. High School. She was united in marriage to Byron James Kester at her home in Westfield on Wednesday evening, August 12th, 1914. Mr. Kester was born at Collins Center, N. Y., Sept. 25th, 1893. He is the son of Amos Parker Kester and Hattie Maud Abbey, his wife. Mr. Kester is employed by the Welch Grape Juice Co. at Westfield. After marriage, Mr. and Mrs. Kester commenced house-keeping at No. 39 Spring Street, Westfield. This place had long been the home of Mrs. Kester's grand-father and grand-mother, Mr. and Mrs. Orlando and Jane (Bacon) Sawin. They built a home later.

The mother of the above named children died at her home on the old farm Dec. 14, 1892, a short time after the birth of her baby Ruth. Mr. Sawin, left with the care of three small children and a large farm, his parents came immediately back to the farm, and his mother took care of the children until their son's second marriage which took place at Bear Lake, Pa., on the 28th day of March, 1894. The bride was Miss Mary Maud Carr, born March 15, 1870, at Conneaut, Ohio.

By this second marriage, Mr. Sawin has four children, named Arland, Bernice, Milton and Grace, all born at Westfield, N. Y.

4. GEORGE ARLAND SAWIN was born Feb. 25, 1895. He is at this date (1912) in attendance at the Westfield High School.

5. BERNICE HELEN SAWIN was born July 6, 1897. She is also in attendance at the Westfield High School.

6. MILTON ORLANDO SAWIN was born Dec. 11, 1900. He is in attendance at the District School.

7. MARY GRACE SAWIN was born May 2, 1904. She is in attendance at the District School taught by her brother, William.

In justice to the memory of his cousin, Orlando Sawin and his family, the writer would say, that Mr. Sawin and his entire family of children and grand-children have maintained and presented to the world a high and beautiful type of an active, devoted and self-sacrificing christian household. Mrs. Sawin was baptized into the fellowship of the Baptist church of Ripley, N. Y., Apr. 7, 1865. Her husband joined the Baptist church of Westfield, N. Y., Feb. 25, 1877. Both have been faithful in all things to their christian and church covenant. Their son, George and his family have followed in their footsteps and have likewise been strong supporters of the christian church and the cause of Christ. Such commendations may be lightly esteemed by irreligious minds, but judged by the Divine Standards of human life they confer the highest honors that man can attain in his earthly state.

Since writing above the grand-son, William Wilson Sawin, has commenced a course of study for a position as secretary of a Young Men's Christian Association. His success may be safely predicted from the beginning, as in mind and heart and temperament he is so well adapted for such christian work.

The descendants of Rev. George and Betsey Tennant Sawin, number as follows: Children 3, grand-children 5, great-grand-children 10, great-great grand-children 3, total nineteen. With the parents and grand-parents they comprise six generations.

REV. JOHN SAWIN

Born August 10, 1786   Died March 19, 1866

MRS. ORREL TENNANT SAWIN
Born April 28, 1793   Died August 5 1873

PART I.

CHAPTER IV.

MISS ORREL TENNANT, her marriage to Rev. John Sawin. Their settlement at Ripley, Chautauqua Co., N. Y. Their migration to Green Co., Wisconsin. Their descendants by family names, Gott, Erdly, Mayhew, Logan, Crawford, Tillinghast, Rickenbrode, Edward Gott, Hayne, Ellis, Tupper, Wattles, Montgomery, Baldwin, Cole, Hatfield and Smith.

ORREL TENNANT, the third child and 2nd daughter of John and Elizabeth Loomis Tennant, was born at Springfield,Otsego Co., N. Y., Apr. 28, 1793. She married Rev. John Sawin at Starkville, Herkimer Co., N. Y., June 25, 1813. He became a Baptist minister. He was born in the town of Willington, Tolland Co., Conn., April 10, 1786. His father's family moved from Connecticut to Washington Co., N. Y. when his son, John was eleven years old, and afterwards to Herkimer Co., N. Y. Some time after their marriage, Mr. Sawin and his wife moved and settled at Springfield, N. Y., where they lived till they moved to Ripley, Chautauqua Co., N. Y. in 1832. All of their large family of thirteen children were born in New York State. At Ripley they settled upon a farm just south and east of what was known as Palmer's Gulf. Here they resided until the Summer of 1846 when they moved west and made for themselves a home in Green Co., Wisconsin territory.

A further history of the family will be given in a Memorial Tribute to Rev. John Sawin and wife to be found in Part IV, Division 2nd, Article 2nd.

There were born to Rev. John and Orrel Tennant Sawin thirteen children named as follows: Aurilla, Ann Eliza, Alvin, Clarissa, David M., Ethan, Lucinda, Lorenzo, Mary Jane, Maranda, Marinda, Eleanor, and Juliette.

I. AURILLA SAWIN was born at Minden, Chenango Co., N. Y. July 28, 1814. She came with the family to Chautauqua Co., N .Y. and went with them when they moved to Wisconsin. She was never married, and spent the early part of her life in assisting her mother in the care of her younger brothers and sisters. She died at Evansville, Wisc., January 3, 1902.

II. ANN ELIZA SAWIN, the second child was born at Minden, Herkimer Co., N. Y., Feb. 18, 1816. She came with the family in 1832 to Ripley, N. Y. She married Nathaniel William Gott at Ripley, N. Y. June 4, 1844. She was his second wife, his first wife's maiden name being Cornelia Johnson. Immediately after their marriage they went to Bloomfield, Walworth Co.. Wisc. and settled upon a farm. Mr. Gott was a prosperous farmer who accumulated a good fortune, lived well, and brought up his family giving his children a good liberal education that they might become useful citizens and honorable members of society. Mrs. Gott died at Burlington, Racine Co., Wisc. March 3, 1895.

There were born to Mr. and Mrs. Gott two children named Emma Augusta and William Watson.

1. EMMA AUGUSTA GOTT was born at Spring Prairie, Walworth Co., Wis. May 3, 1847. She married Henry Erdly at Lyons, Walworth Co.. Wisc. Oct. 5, 1871. They have one child, a daughter, named Emma Eliza.

1. EMMA ELIZA ERDLY was born at Spring Prairie ,Wisc., Jan. 26, 1877. She married Chester Mayhew at Spring Prairie, Wisc. June 21, 1902.

There were born to them three children named as follows Henry, Wallace and Willard.

1. HENRY MILTON MAYHEW was born at Spring Prairie July 14, 1903.

2. WALLACE CHESTER MAYHEW was born at Burlington, Racine Co.. Wisc., June 7, 1909.

3. WILLARD EUGENE MAYHEW was born at Burlington, Wisc.. March 21st, 1911.

2. WILLIAM WATSON GOTT, second child and first son of William and Ann Eliza Sawin Gott, was born at Spring Prairie, Wisc. May 13, 1849. He married Emma Hicks at Lyons, Wisc., on Oct. 24, 1872. There were born to them four children named Mabel, Irene, Nina Belle, and Ellis.

1. MABEL ELIZABETH GOTT was born in Lyons, Walworth Co., Wisc. She married Rev. Harland Chester Logan at Elkhorn, Wisc. Aug. 16, 1905. There were born to them four children named Eveline, Ruth, Margaret and Gordon.

- 1. EVELINE IRENE LOGAN was born at Milwaukee, Wis. Nov. 30, 1906.

2. RUTH F. LOGAN was born at Milwaukee, Wisc. Oct. 3, 1908.

3. MARGARET LUCILE LOGAN was born at Beaver Dam, Dodge Co., Wisc. Nov. 24, 1910.

4. GORDON DONALD LOGAN was born at Beaver Dam. Dodge Co., Wisc. Aug. 20, 1912.

2. IRENE GOTT, second daughter of William and Emma Gott, was born at Lyons, Walworth Co.. Wis., March 8, 1880. She is unmarried and lives at home at this date, 1912, assisting her father in his office as an insurance agent.

MRS. CLARISA SAWIN TILLINGHAST
Born March 12, 1827
Daughter of Rev. John Sawin and Mrs. Orrel Tennant Sawin

3. NINA BELLE GOTT was born at Lyons, Wis., Feb. 19, 1882. She married Leroy John Crawford at Elkhorn, Walworth Co., Wis., April 27, 1904. They have no children. Their present residence, 1912, is in Burlington, Wis. Mr. Crawford is a successful business man in the jewelry business. His wife as may be known by the above family record, is a great-granddaughter of Rev. John Sawin and his wife, Orrel Tennant Sawin.

4. ELLIS GOTT was born at Lyons, Wis. Aug. 8, 1883. At this date, 1912, he is unmarried. He is the youngest child and only son of William Watson Gott.

III. ALVIN J. SAWIN, third child and oldest son, was born at German, Chenango Co., N. Y., Feb. 19, 1819. He never married. He was a true and noble man and rendered great assistance to his parents in support of their large family. He died at Evansville, Rock Co., Wis. Nov. 1, 1902, being at his death 83 years, 8 months and 12 days old.

IV. CLARISSA SAWIN, the fourth child and third daughter was born in German Township, Chenango Co., N. Y., March 12, 1821. She married Albert Tillinghast at Rutland, Wisc. Sept. 6, 1848. Her husband was a prosperous farmer. His farm was located in the east part of the town of Ripley, N. Y. He died at Ripley Nov. 17, 1868. His beloved wife has survived him for many years. At this date, April, 1915, she lives at Ripley Village having passed her 94th birthday. Her mental faculties as well as bodily strength are remarkably well preserved. She keeps her own house, lives by herself, does all her own housework, attends church, visits her relatives and friends. She is a member of the Baptist church at Ripley Village and made a large contribution to this body to assist in lifting a heavy indebtedness incurred in building. She is loyal to her Master and His cause. At this date, 1915, she is living with her daughter, Mrs. Rickenbrode in Ripley Village.

There was born to Albert and Clarissa Tillinghast a daughter named Ella Florine.

1. ELLA FLORINE TILLINGHAST was born at Westfield, N. Y. May 10, 1863. She married Franklin Webster Rickenbrode at Ripley, N. Y., June 5, 1884. They have one daughter, an only child, born at Ripley, Sept. 4, 1890, and named May Alice. Mr. Rickenbrode is a prosperous farmer located at the west end of the Village of Ripley, on a farm formerly owned by George Goodrich, Sr.

V. DAVID M. H. SAWIN, fifth child and second son, was born in Cincinnatus, Cortland Co., N. Y. Feb. 3, 1823. He died at Cincinnatus, N. Y. Aug. 2, 1823 at the age of six months.

VI. ETHAN PHILANDER SAWIN, sixth child and third son,

was born at Cana, Otsego Co., N. Y., Sept. 10, 1823. He married Harriet Lucina Tupper at Union, Rock Co., Wis. Jan. 4th, 1853. Miss Tupper was born at Ripley, Chautauqua Co., N. Y., June 8, 1833.

Mr. Sawin died at Evansville, Rock Co., Wis. April 18, 1903 being at his death 78 years 7 months and 8 days old. His beloved wife died at Evansville, Sept. 16th, 1911, being 78 years old at her death. There were born to them two sons named Albert and Charles.

1. ALBERT MONROE SAWIN was born April 3, 1858 at Union, Rock Co., Wis. He married Miss Josephine Alice Hull at Evansville, Wis., June 23, 1885. Miss Hull was born at Attica, Wis. Sept. 19, 1861. There were born to them four children, named Lester, Genevieve, Ruth and Ethel.

1. LESTER MONROE SAWIN was born at Evansville, Wis., Nov. 6, 1886. He is a commission merchant doing business at 501 Plymouth Building, Minneapolis, Minn.

2. GENEVIEVE SAWIN was born at Laramie, Wyoming Co., Dec. 19, 1891. She is a milliner at Rochelle, Ill.

3. RUTH SAWIN was born at Brooklyn, N. Y. Jan. 18, 1902.

4. ETHEL SAWIN was born at Evanston, Ill., July 2, 1903. She died in infancy.

Mr. Albert Sawin was ambitious to obtain an education. After a preparatory course he entered the Wisconsin State University and was graduated in 1883 at the age of twenty-five, taking the degrees of B. S. and M. S. In 1884 he took the Professorship of Mathematics in the Minnesota State Normal School and served for two years. From 1887 to 1892 he was Professor of Mathematics in the Wyoming State University. After this work as a teacher he took a two year course of study in the Northwestern University of Ill., at Evanston, taking the degree of B. D. in 1894. Following this he was Professor of Mathematics in the Northwestern University Academy, 1894-1895, two years in the same professorship in the Clark University of Atlanta, Georgia, and one year in the Syracuse University of N. Y. State during 1899 and 1900. His studies and teaching had continued for about 25 years down to 1900. At this date, 1915, he and his brother, Charles, reside at Hermiston, Oregon.

2. CHARLES ELLSWORTH SAWIN, youngest son of Ethan and Harriet Tupper Sawin, was born at Union, Rock Co., Wis. April 3, 1863. He resides at this date, Jan. 1915, at Hermiston, Oregon. He is a farmer engaged in the raising of fruit. He has never married up to the date of this writing. His brother, Albert is interested somewhat in the same business.

VII. LUCINDA M. SAWIN, the seventh child and fourth daughter of Rev. John and Orrel Tennant Sawin, was born in

Exeter Township, Otsego Co., N. Y. March 10, 1827. She married Edward Gott, a brother of William Gott, her sister's husband, at Troy, Wis. Feb. 13, 1859. They had no children. She died at Burlington, Wis. Nov. 26, 1900.

VIII. LORENZO SAWIN was born at Springfield, N. Y. Aug. 6, 1829. He married Miss Helen Webster at Ripley, N. Y., Nov. 7, 1860. She was the daughter of Olive (Sawin) Webster, a first cousin of Lorenzo. They made thier home at Evansville, Rock Co., Wis. He was a prosperous farmer. The writer was five years younger than this cousin, yet we used to play together and enjoyed each other's company very much. Lorenzo was a pleasant jovial boy, always trying to make other boys enjoy life as well as himself. When he left Ripley with the family for the far west, his absence made a great vacancy in my boy-life. His memory is precious today though many years have passed since we were separated.

Mr. Sawin died at Evansville, Wis., July 25, 1907. His beloved wife survived him for a number of years and died at the homestead in Evansville, Wis. March 1, 1911. They had two children, Ida and Grace.

1. IDA ADELL SAWIN was born at Brooklyn, Green Co., Wis., April 27, 1863. She married Frank Hyne at Brooklyn, Wis. Feb. 28, 1884. They had three children named Ray, Hugh and Grace.

1. RAY S. HYNE was born in Brooklyn, Wis., May 6, 1885.

2. HUGH P. HYNE was born in Evansville, Wis. March 13, 1895.

3. GRACE WINIFRED HYNE was born at Evansville, Wis. June 26, 1896. She died at the same place Feb. 17, 1897, being seven months and twenty-one days old.

> "Little children, little children,
>   Saved by their Redeemer,
> Are His jewels, precious jewels,
>   His loved and his own.
> Like the stars of the borning,
>   His bright crown adorning,
> They shall shine in their beauty,
>   Bright gems for his crown."
>   —Selected.

3. EMMA GRACE SAWIN was born at Brooklyn, Green Co., Wis. Aug. 16, 1866. She married John Fay Ellis Dec. 13, 1888. Mr. Ellis died and Mrs. Ellis married for her second husband Jay B. Wattles of Buffalo, N. Y. at Evansville, Wis Jan. 29, 1896. Mrs. Wattles had no children by either husband. Mr. Wattles is the youngest son of Erbin and Wealthy Tennant Wat-

tles.   His business career is mentioned in the record of their family.

EMMA GRACE in a few months over three years after her second marriage died at Buffalo, N. Y. July 28, 1899.   She was a beautiful and lovely character.   Her death was a severe grief to all the family.   How precious is the hope that in the coming years our loved ones will be restored to us when the mysteries of life and death are solved and death and the grave have given up their human treasures and eternal life has gained a glorious victory.

"Thanks be to God who giveth us the victory through our Lord Jesus Christ."   1 Cor. 15th Chap. 57 V.

IX.   MARY JANE SAWIN, the ninth child and fifth daughter, was born at Springfield, Otsego Co., N. Y. Aug. 15, 1831.   She married John J. Montgomery at Brooklyn, Green Co., Wis., Apr. 3, 1854.   There were born to them three children named Orrel Marie, John Eugene and Kittie Adell.

1.   ORREL MARIE MONTGOMERY was born at Brooklyn, Wis. Oct. 28, 1855.   She died in 1864 at the place of her birth.   She was between 8 and 9 years of age at her death.

2.   JOHN EUGENE MONTGOMERY was born at Brooklyn, Green Co., Wis., March 15, 1858.   He married Kate S. Starkweather, daughter of Harvey Price Starkweather and his wife, Sarah Ryan Starkweather, Nov. 26, 1896.   Miss Starkweather was born in Brooklyn, Green Co., Wis. June 6, 1864.   There were born to Mr. and Mrs. Montgomery three children named Alvin, Caryl and Lyell, all born in Brooklyn township, Green Co., Wis.

1.   ALVIN EUGENE MONTGOMERY was born Sept. 24, 1898.

2.   CARYL KATHRYN MONTGOMERY was born Jan. 24, 1900.

3.   LYELL STARKWEATHER MONTGOMERY was born June 12, 1903.

3.   KITTIE ADELL MONTGOMERY was born at Brooklyn, Green Co. Wis. Sept. 19, 1861.   She married Edward R. Ellis at Brooklyn, Wis. Apr. 14, 1881.   They had one child, a daughter named Mary Adell Ellis, who was born Dec. 8, 1883, at Evansville, Wis.

1.   MARY ADELL ELLIS married Harry Wall Dec. 7, 1905. at Porter, Rock Co., Wis.   They have one child, a son named Fred Ellis Wall, born at Union, Rock Co., Wis., Oct. 24, 1906.

Mr. Edward R. Ellis died at Evansville, Wis. Dec. 14, 1883. After his death his widow, who was Kittie Adell Montgomery Ellis, married Mr. Frank Tupper at Evansville, Wis. Sept. 11, 1894.   No children born of this marriage.

X.   MARANDA SAWIN was born at Ripley, N. Y. Feb. 24, 1834.   When a young woman she died on the 21st of June

1850 at Brooklyn, Green Co. Wis., being at her death 16 years, 3 months and 27 days old. She was a twin sister of Marinda.

XI. MARINDA, the twin sister, born at the same date, lived till the 43rd year of her age and died at Brooklyn, Wis. Sept. 28, 1886. She never married.

These twin sisters, cousins of the writer, are well remembered by him. Born in the same year, our ages differed only from Feb. 24th to Aug. 7th. We had many happy days playing together. They were the first children of their family born after the family moved to Chautauqua Co., N. Y. and the writer was the first-born of his family in Chautauqua. These twin sisters never married. As the family moved to Wis. in June, 1846, they were past twelve years of age the February before they went west with the family.

XII. ELEANOR MATILDA SAWIN, the twelfth child and eighth daughter of Rev. John and Orrel Tennant Sawin, was born at Ripley, Chautauqua Co. N. Y. April 19, 1836. She married Anson Baldwin Nov. 28, 1860 at Brooklyn, Wis. Mr. Baldwin was born at Clearville, Kent Co., Ontario, Canada July 11, 1836. Mr. Baldwin was a farmer. There were born to them six children named as follows: David, Myrtle, Lewellyn, Jay, Jennie and Zala.

1. DAVID JOHN BALDWIN was born at Oregon, Dane Co., Wis. Apr. 30, 1862. He died July 31, 1862, being three months old at death.

2. MYRTLE MAY BALDWIN was born at Union, Rock Co., Wis. Apr. 2, 1880. She married Edgar Meyers Cole at Evansville, Wis. June 17, 1903. Mr. Cole was born at Winterset, Madison Co., Iowa, May 29, 1877. He is a machinist. They have a son named Donald Baldwin Cole, born at Evansville, Rock Co., Wis. May 2, 1905.

3. LEWELLYN ANSON BALDWIN, third child and second son, was born at Oregon, Dane Co., Wis. Oct. 10, 1863. He married Janet Ann Peach July 10, 1899 at Porter, Rock Co., Wis. Miss Peach was born at Porter, Rock Co., Wis., July 10, 1869. Mr. Baldwin is engaged in the mill and grain elevator industry. No children reported.

4. JAY BURDETTE BALDWIN, fourth child and third son of Anson and Eleanor Sawin Baldwin, was born in Union Tp. Rock Co., Wis. Nov. 16, 1876. He married Meta Charlotte Selle at Poynette, Columbia Co., Wis. Aug. 21, 1900. Miss Selle was born in Leeds, Columbia Co., Wis. Dec. 23, 1878. Mr. Baldwni is a traveling salesman for the Laurel Book Company. No children reported.

5. JENNIE ELLA BALDWIN was born in Brooklyn, Green Co., Wis. Feb. 10, 1870. She married Fred Burr Hatfield Apr. 16,

1895.   Mr. Hatfield was born in Union Tp., Rock Co., Wis.
Aug. 16, 1872.   He is a merchant and deals in general merchandise.   Mr. and Mrs. Hatfield have a daughter named Hazel May,
born at Evansville, Wis., Sept. 23, 1898.   The family moved to
Palmer, Iowa where Mr. Hatfield has been engaged in mercantile business.

6.   ZALA SAWIN BALDWIN, the youngest child and fourth son
of Anson and Eleanor Sawin Baldwin, was born in Oregon Tp.,
Dane Co., Wis. May 31, 1867.   He married Nora Y. Haynes at
Brooklyn, Wis. Feb. 10, 1892.   Mr. Baldwin is general manager
of an Eastern company.

Mrs. Baldwin was born in Rutland, Tp., Dane Co., Wis. Nov.
3, 1871.   There were born to them three children named Percy, Eunice and Esther, all born at Madison, Dane Co., Wis.

1.   PERCY HAYNES BALDWIN was born Apr. 2, 1896.
2.   EUNICE IRENE BALDWIN was born July 23, 1901.
3.   ESTHER ELEANOR BALDWIN was born Aug. 4, 1904.

Since writing the above record of Mrs. Baldwin and family
the writer has received notice of the death of both husband and
wife; the husband died on Wednesday, Feb. 4th, 1914 and the
wife the day following.

Mrs. Baldwin was 77 years, 9 months and 15 days old at her
death, and Mr. Baldwin 77 years, 6 months and 23 days old.
There was but one month and 22 days difference in their ages,
Mrs. Baldwin being the older.   Their married life extended
through 53 years, 2 months and 6 days.   All these years they had
lived in Wisconsin.   They were a prosperous family.

From an extended obituary notice the writer gathers the following facts:

Mr. Anson Baldwin passed away quietly at his home in Evansville, Wis.   His health had been failing for the last few years,
so the end was not unexpected.   He retained consciousness till
the very last.   His wife was ill in an adjoining room, and his
last words were inquiries concerning her.   He was the youngest
of thirteen children.   After their marriage, Mr. Baldwin and
wife made their home at the old homestead in the town of Oregon, Dane Co., Wis. for seven years; afterwards they purchased
land in the town of Brooklyn, Green Co., Wis. where they resided for twenty seven years.   They moved to Evansville,
Green Co., Wis., where they spent the last years of their lives.
We quote from the obituary: "From their home there has quietly radicated an influence that has been beneficial and helpful to
many.   Their golden wedding, they said, was the happiest day
of their life together.   Each had seemed to live with and for the
other.   So it is beautiful to think of them as not being separated even by death."

Mrs. Baldwin, when about ten years of age, in 1846, went with the family to Racine, Wis., then overland to Green Co., Wis. where they located and where Mrs. Baldwin was educated, and where she lived with her parents till she was married in 1860.

The writer of this Genealogy remembers well this cousin, when the family lived on old Ripley Hill in Chautauqua Co., N. Y. He was older than his cousin by 1 year, 8 months and 12 days. We attended the same school for about 3 years. How little did I then know that I should live to record her life and death and to join with other relatives to lament her passing away.

THE RIVER OF LIFE.

On the banks of the river of life we shall meet,
  When the scenes and conflicts of this life are all o'er,
T'will be joy unspeakable then to greet,
  Our loved ones on that ever-green shore.

Flow on thou river of Life, flow long,
  We hail you from earths every land;
On thy banks we will gather in joyful song,
  A redeemed and a blood-washed band.

No more shall sorrow or sin blight our lives,
  When we stand by thy pure flowing tide;
Gathered there in sweet union, are husbands and wives,
  Children, neighbors and friends to ever abide.

We are waiting Blest River to see thy bright waves,
  When the Garden of death we have passed,
Then, rising to life from our earthly graves,
  We'll bathe in Thy waters forever at last.

By the Author.

XIII. JULIA ETTE SAWIN, the thirteenth and youngest child of Rev. John and Orrel Tennant Sawin, was born at Ripley, Chautauqua Co., N. Y. Sept. 3, 1839. She married Charles Mortimer Smith, M. D., in Brooklyn, Wis. May 16, 1861. Mr. Smith was born in Cattaraugus, N. Y., June 25, 1834. He was a physician and surgeon and had a good practice we are informed.

There were born to Mr. and Mrs. Smith two children, Flora and Charles.

1. FLORA D. SMITH was born at Fortville, Wis., Dec. 9, 1863. She married George O. Gordon in Evansville, Wis. June 18, 1889. Mr. Gordon was born at Grand Rapids, Wis. Oct. 3, 1864. He was a pharmacist at Lodi, Columbia Co., Wis. They had a daughter named Doris Mildred Gordon, born at Lodi, Co-

lumbia Co., Wis. Nov. 6, 1895.   She is a great-grand-daughter
of Rev. John and Orrel Tennant Sawin.

2.   Dr. CHARLES MORTIMER SMITH, JR.,son of Dr.Charles M.
and Julia Sawin Smith, was born in Evansville. Rock Co., Wis.
March 23, 1866.   He is a physician and surgeon.   He married
Jennie M. Frantz at Evansville, June 3, 1903.   Miss Frantz was
born in Evansville, Wis. June 15, 1879.

There was born to Mr. and Mrs. Dr. Smith, Jr., a daughter
named Ruth E. Smith, born in Evansville, Wis. Jan. 13, 1912.

Dr. CHARLES M. SMITH, SR., died at Evansville, Wis. Apr. 1,
1912.   At this date, January. 1913, his widow is living at Evansville, Wis.

This large family, descendants of Rev. John Sawin and Orrel
(Tennant) Sawin is composed as follows:

Children 13
Grand Children 21
Great-Grand Children 19
Great-great-grand Children 9

Total Descendants 62

With the parents and grand parents, these descendants include
six generations.

These descendants are now living for the most part in the
following states: New York. Wisconsin, Michigan, Iowa and
Oregon.   The business men of the family, for the most part, are
farmers, but the learned professions have a goodly representation.   Certainly the Rev. Sawin and his wife have not lived in
vain.   A numerous posterity lives to perpetuate their memory,
and to continue the good work they began on earth.

Truly, the godly men and women, through their children, do
in reality inherit the earth.   Their religious education gave them
a strong attachment to the christian faith.   Their fore-fathers
and mothers were Baptists in their beliefs and church relations.
However, there was a safe rational liberalism in their belief.
The entire family were firm believers in the divine authority,
authenticity and inspiration of the christian scriptures.   In this
faith the children of all the families were educated; and none
went astray into immoral and disreputable practices.

At this date, May, 1914, only three of the thirteen children
are now living: there are Clarissa (Mrs. Tillinghast) and Mary
Jane (Mrs. Montgomery) and Julia Ette (Mrs. Dr. Smith.)

ALVIN LOOMIS TENNANT

Born June 18, 1797   Died July 7, 1875

PART I.

CHAPTER V.

ALVIN LOOMIS TENNANT, his birth; his settlement
at Lockport, N. Y.; his 1st and 2nd marriage; his children, Harriet Amanda, Alfred, Milton and Eliza; his
grand-children, Alice Tennant, and William, Cora,
Nora and Charley Plate.

ALVIN LOOMIS TENNANT, fourth child and oldest son of John
and Elizabeth (Loomis) Tennant, was born at Springfield,
Otsego Co., N. Y., June 18, 1797. He married Miss Eliza Ann
Thompson at Cambria, Niagara Co., N. Y. Oct. 14th, 1824.
Miss Thompson was born at Swanzy, Cheshire Co., New Hamp-
shire, Nov. 20th, 1806.

Mr. Tennant moved from Otsego Co., N. Y. to Niagara Co.,
N. Y. in 1820. He was not married at this time. He went into
the mercantile business at Lockport, which he followed for a
few years. He then turned his attention to farming and purchased a farm in Cambria township, Niagara Co., N. Y., of one
hundred acres, located west of Lockport City. He added to this
purchase other lands until the whole amounted to two hundred
and twenty acres all in the same township.

Notwithstanding his prosperity, a great sorrow came upon him
in the loss of the wife of his first marriage. Mrs. Tennant died
in Cambria, April 25th, 1842, being at the time of her death 35
years, 5 months and 5 days old. She was in the prime of her
life. She had been a faithful wife, a devoted mother, and worthy member of the Presbyterian church of Cambria. She was
buried in the beautiful rural cemetery of Cambria.

Mr. Tennant married for his second wife Sophronia G. Kelley,
June 11th, 1843. Miss Kelley was born at Henrietta, Monroe
Co., N. Y., April 17th, 1816.

Good fortune had crowned all his business activities. He had
built him a fine home where he lived for many years. His prosperity continued until another sorrow overshadowed his heart
and life, this was the loss of his second wife by death, which occurred at Cambria, Niagara Co., N. Y. Oct. 2nd, 1863, she being
at her death 47 years, 5 months, and 15 days old. Mr. Tennant
and his second wife had lived together some over twenty years.
She was also buried at Cambria, N. Y.

At the death of his second wife, MR. TENNANT was in his
67th year. At this time he had an unmarried daughter some
over 18 years of age to care for and comfort him. His two

sons, hereafter to be mentioned in the family record, had always lived at home and assisted on the farm. MR. TENNANT began now to anticipate his retirement from farm cares and labor. In the next few years he divided between his sons all his farm property except thirty acres where his home was located. He gave 100 acres to his oldest son Alfred, 90 acres to his son Milton, and kept 30 acres and his home for himself. After the marriage of his daughter, Eliza, to Mr. Plate, he sold the 30 acres and his home for $3000.00. The proceeds of this sale he gave to his daughter. After her marriage, Mrs. Plate and her husband moved to Utica, Macomb Co., Mich. Her father made her an extended visit at this place, then returned to Niagara Co., N. Y., and spent the remainder of his days with his two sons and their families.

MR. TENNANT had been a lifelong member of the Presbyterian church of Cambria. He was a regular attendant upon the services of the church and helped in its finances. He was highly esteemed by his neighbors and friends. Being of a gentle and quiet disposition, he aroused no antagonism in his business or social life.

The author of this genealogy knew him well, and can testify to his excellent life and character. Having served his allotted time he died at Cambria, Niagara Co., N. Y. on the 7th of July, 1873, being at his death 78 years and 19 days old. He was buried in the beautiful rural cemetery of Cambria township near the old church edifice where he worshipped for so many years.

CHILDREN OF ALVIN TENNANT BY HIS FIRST MARRIAGE.

There were born to Alvin and Eliza Ann (Thompson) Tennant three children named Harriet Amanda, Alfred and Milton.

I. HARRIET AMANDA TENNANT was born at Lockport, Niagara Co., N. Y., July 12th, 1825 and died at the same place Sept. 25th, 1825, being at her death one month and thirteen days old.

> Sometime we shall know
>   Why those little ones go
> To their heavenly home in such early years;
>   Let us wait, and them see,
>   What their future will be,
> God's love for the children should quiet our fears.

II. ALFRED LOOMIS TENNANT, the older son, was born in Lockport, N. Y., July 26th, 1826. He married Miss Cornelia Hixon in Cambria, Niagara Co., N. Y. Oct. 20th, 1858. Miss

ALFRED TENNANT

Born July 26, 1826   Died September 4, 1898

Hixon was born in Lockport. N. Y. Jan. 26th, 1833. They had but one child, a daughter, born in Cambria, Sept. 26th, 1863, and named Alice Tennant.

MR. TENNANT commenced his business life on a farm in Cambria township west of Lockport. Upon the division of his father's farm between his two sons, Alfred had a splendid possession. He occupied the old home of his father, built a beautiful and costly barn with all modern improvements. Thinking of living a more congenial life than that of the farmer, he moved into Lockport and started a factory for the manufacture of shirt-fronts. In this business he was quite successful. He became so well-to-do that he built one of the most costly brick dwelling houses in the city, located north of the Erie canal, a beautiful ornament to th city, and stands today, 1912, as a tangible proof of the fine taste, ambition, and pride of the owner.

MR. TENNANT was well known by his cousin, the author of this work. He can speak of him as a man of a gentle, kind nature, quiet and unpretentious in his ways, a husband and father most devoted to his family, and a citizen highly esteemed by all who knew him. It seemed befitting that the life of such a man should be prolonged to the fullness of man's appointed time, but the angel of death visited his home and called him to a higher life on Sept. 4th, 1898. His remains lie buried in the cemetery at Cambria. He was 72 years, 8 months and 8 days old at his death.

His daughter, Alice, outlived her father only one year and three months and ten days when she died at Lockport, Dec. 14, 1899 and was buried in Cold Spring cemetery in the city of Lockport.

She was past thirty-six years of age at her death. She was never married. She was a member of the Presbyterian church at Cambria. Under date of March 11th, 1906, her mother wrote to the author these tender and loving words, "Alice liked to travel. She visited Chicago and Michigan. She was a close observer and learned much in that way. She could not stand close confinement in school—she always attended a Select School. She had taught in the High School, and was prepared to teach a Select School. She had pleasant associations among the teachers who visited her during her last illness. Alice was a good girl; how I miss her! She was so much to me after her father's death. I live and trust from day to day, and try to make the best of life."

What words could express a more befitting tribute to the memory of a beloved daughter than the above lines! How precious is the memory of the beautiful and the true!

Dear Alice, in visions that memory brings
To our hearts of the days that are past;
We see thy sweet face, and hear thy glad voice,
As if shadows between us had never been cast.

We roam o'er earth's fields and woodlands so bright,
Forgetting that really thy footsteps are not there;
Yet, by faith we do know that thou livest still,
In the realm of the blest, so glorious and fair.

In that land of the pure and home of the blest,
We are hoping to meet you at some future day;
And then, with the saints before the Great Throne
We'll cast down our crowns and chant our glad lays.

After the deaths of her husband and daughter, Mrs. Tennant made her home with her brother, Phillip Hixon, at Barker, Niagara Co., N. Y. This brother moved to Lockport, N. Y., Mrs. Tennant going with the family. Here she lived up to the time of her death.

Mrs. Tennant was in many respects a remarkable woman. Misfortunes had overtaken the family sufficient to crush any spirit that was not strongly fortified against adversity, by natural qualities of mind and heart, supported by an abiding trust in God. She was one of those gentle, even tempered persons, who make but never alienate friends; who shed only light and comfort in the family, and her christian experience, and example were a steady glowing light that shines more and more to the perfect day. The author had abundant opportunity to become acquainted with her, as he was entertained in his cousin's family for nine weeks, while he was assisting the acting pastor of the Baptist church of Lockport in a series of revival meetings, held in January, February and March, 1874. Mrs. Tennant was an active members of the Presbyterian church, and a firm believer in Christian doctrines. She fell asleep in the full hope of immortality and eternal life. Her death took place at her brother's home in Lockport, Aug. 5th, 1909. She was buried in Cold Spring Cemetery at Lockport beside the resting place of her beloved daughter.

III. MILTON TENNANT, the third child and second son of Alvin and Eliza Ann Tennant, was born in Cambria, Niagara Co., N. Y., Feb. 19th, 1832. He married Miss Isabelle Martha Sage at Pekin, Niagara Co., N. Y., Oct. 18th, 1865. She was the daughter of Mr. Sparrow Smith Sage whose wife's maiden name was Kathrine C. DeFoe.

Mr. and Mrs. Tennant never had any children. After their marriage they settled on a farm in Cambria township. They

MILTON TENNANT

Born February 19, 1832   Died September 8, 1913

had a nice home and a beautiful farm, where they lived and labored for many years. Retiring from the farm the family moved into the city of Lockport. Here they resided for a number of years. Circumstances in life changing, they moved to Pekin, where they resided in the old home that Mrs. Tennant received as a gift from her mother, Mrs. Sage. Both husband and wife were members of the Presbyterian Church.

In this home Mr. and Mrs. Tennant lived for many years. On account of lameness, Mr. Tennant was not able to do only the lightest manual labor. He was naturally a jovial and happy disposition and was fond of congenial society, to which he could always contribute a large share of pleasant entertainment. In all respects, he lived a good moral and christian life. He was a firm believer in the inspiration and authority of the christian scriptures.

During the last months of his life, he suffered much from weakness and nervousness caused by a weak action of the heart induced by old age. For several days before the end came, he was much better and was able, the Sabbath before his death, to attend church at Cambria to partake of the Lord's Supper and to visit the grave of his father and mother. On Monday morning of Sept. 8th, 1913, after bringing into the kitchen of his home a pail of water, he dropped to the floor and instantly expired. He was 81 years, 5 months and 19 days old at his death. His funeral was held at his home on Wednesday, the 10th, the Methodist pastor, Rev. Wm. Swail conducting the services. His remains were buried in the cemetery at Pekin, Niagara Co., N. Y.

VICTORY AT LAST.

The battle of life is now ended,
  The victory surely is won;
To His servant the Master has spoken
  The cheerful and hopeful "Well done."

The billows of trouble are rested,
  The clouds have all passed away;
The peace of his soul is perfected,
  In the glow of an eternal day.

Shall we call him back to our presence?
  To this earthly home again?
Nay: let him rest on the bosom of Love,
  Where the saints in glory reign.

Be it ours to pursue life's journey,
  With patience and courage withall;
Till we shall have finished our work,
  And go at the Master's call.

CHILD AND GRAND CHILDREN OF SECOND MARRIAGE.

ELIZA ANN TENNANT, a daughter of Alvin Tennant by his second marriage, was born in Cambria, Niagara Co., N. Y., on the 8th of November, 1844. She married Willard H. Plate at Cambria Nov. 14th, 1867. Soon after their marriage they moved to Michigan and located at Utica, Macomb County. Mr. Plate was born in Cambria, N. Y., May 1st, 1845.

There were born to Mr. and Mrs. Plate four children named Willard, Cora, Nora, and Charley.

1. WILLARD F. PLATE was born at Utica, Macomb Co., Mich. Aug. 21st, 1869. He married Miss Lillie Belle Dilvend Dec. 9th, 1886. Miss Dilvend was a native of Missouri, but lived at Fresno, Cala. at the time of her marriage.

2. CORA E. PLATE, second child and first daughter, was born at Utica, Mich. Nov. 11th, 1872. She is at this date, 1912, unmarried. In Oct. 1910, the writer visited his cousin, Mrs. Plate, and her family at Fresno, Cala. MISS CORA was then employed as chief book-keeper in a large grocery and crockery store where she had been engaged for a number of years. MISS CORA is by nature and choice a talented business woman. She receives an excellent salary because of her trust worthy and business ability. She is not masculine in her temper, speech, tastes or manners. She is a business woman and womanly in her business.

3. NORA L. PLATE was born at Fresno, Fresno Co., Cala., Jan. 1st, 1879. She married Fred E. Barr of San Francisco, Cala., Dec. 11th, 1901. Mr. Barr was born in 1910, at the time of the writer's visit to his cousins at Fresno. Mr. Barr and family were located at Tracy, Cala.

4. CHARLES F. PLATE was born in Boise Co., Idaho, May 1st, 1882. He is the youngest but in stature the largest of the family. He is unmarried and in 1913 is proprietor of a large meat-market in San Francisco, Cala.

SUMMARY OF FAMILY RECORD.

Parents—three—children four, grand-children five—total twelve persons in the family and descendants nine.

Parents 3
Children 4
Grand children 5
                                                    —
Total of the family 12

These include with parents and grand parents four generations.

PART I.

CHAPTER VI.

Containing a record of the birth of OLIVE ELIZABETH TENNANT, and her sister, DELINDA TENNANT.

OLIVE ELIZABETH TENNANT.

MISS OLIVE ELIZABETH TENNANT, the fifth child and third daughter of John Tennant and his wife Elizabeth (Loomis) Tennant. was born in Springfield, Otsego Co., N. Y. Sept. 27th, 1795. She had only a common school education such as daughters of that early day obtained. At he age of nineteen, in 1814, at Springfield, N. Y., she married Rev. David Tennant, son of Moses Tennant, Sr., and his wife whose maiden name was Betsey Tennant. At the time of her marriage,her husband had not entered upon the work of the christian ministry. It will be seen by the record of her husband's life found in Part II Chapter V of this work that her husband was a very promising young man of more than ordinary ability. We can only imagine what ardent love, what bright hopes filled the heart of this young woman, when she was led to the altar of marriage and paid her solemn vows to "forsake all others" and to unite her life with the man she devotedly loved, to share in his fortunes or misfortunes, as Providence might determine their future. At the beginning of their married life not a sign nor intimation was given to them of the dark shadow of misfortune, trial, disappointment and sorrow, that was in store for them. The period of their unclouded happiness can only be determined approximately by the records of the Baptist Church of Springfield, which called Rev. Tennant to become their pastor. He was first granted a license to preach on the 6th of May, 1819, about five years after their marriage. On the first Wednesday in March, 1823, he was ordained. They had then been married about nine years. Up to this date, 1823, there were no indications, so far as known, of the approaching calamity. He served the church as pastor, as near as can be determined, three years from 1823 to 1826. This makes a period of about twelve years after their marriage, when Rev. Tennant was forced by mental dementia to stop preaching. The story of this great affliction has been told by the writer in a sketch of his uncle's life found in another chapter of this book. (See Part II, Chapter 5th.)

The writer has no desire to portray in words the woes and sorrows of this devoted wife. His mother said "Your aunt Olive died of a broken heart."

During these years of married life, she bore to her husband two sons and two daughters. Her death took place at Springfield in or near the year 1824. All her family survived her. She was buried in the cemetery at Springfield. The record of her family may be found included in that of her husband, Rev. David Tennant, in Part II, Chapter V of this book.

DELINDA TENNANT.

Delinda Tennant, the sixth child and fourth daughter of John Tennant and Elizabeth (Loomis) Tennant, was born at Springfield, Otsego Co., N. Y. Apr. 18th, 1802. She had only a common school education such as the State schools of that day afforded the children. From early life she was forced to such labor as she was able to do and endure. She read books and papers as her pastime, taking but little interest in social affairs. Indeed her life was so filled with home duties that it was impossible for her to give much time or attention to recreations or pleasures of any kind. Her mother died when she was a few days over six years of age. She remembered her in later years, but at that age, could not realize the great loss she suffered. In advancing years she learned from her older sisters much about her mother, and always cherished sweet and precious memories of the dear one who nursed her in babyhood and tenderly cared for her during the first six years of her life. Her mother died at Springfield, Otsego Co., N. Y. May 4th, 1808. Her oldest sister, Betsey Tennant, was 19 years old the month their mother died. Of course, at that age, she would naturally become the housekeeper and the head of the family. Betsey was not married until four years after her mother's death. Her marriage took place on the 19th of March, 1812.

The writer regrets that he is unable to give more fully in detail the incidents of the early life of his mother. Her father did not marry to bring to their home a step-mother. Where she found a home, after the marriage of her oldest sister, the writer has never been informed.

On Dec. 19th, 1820, she married Moses Asel Tennant. She was four months past eighteen years of age when married. Her husband was only about two years older. His father, Moses Tennant, Sr., had married Sarah Seldon Jewett (Baker) Shaw as his second wife, in 1792 or 1793. This marriage provided no home for Delinda Tennant, who was of another branch of the Tennant family. Now, however, after marriage, she had a home she could call her own. She went to her husband's home, which was on a side hill farm not far from Springfield Village, Otsego Co., N. Y.

At the time of her marriage she had four sisters living and one brother, her husband had two half-brothers and four half-sisters, and three full sisters, all living at this time. Their history is in part related in other parts of this work. Her father was living, her mother was dead. Her husband's mother was living, but his father died about the year 1808. The four husbands of Sarah Selden Jewett were all dead before her son Moses Asel Tennant was married. Deacon Daniel Morse, her fourth and last husband, lived only a few years after their marriage. His widow, Mrs. Sarah Selden Jewett Morse, left without a home, came to her son, Moses Asel for an asylum and a home.

This large Tennant family of two branches, in a few years were all married, and most of them and their children were moved from N. Y. state to Pennsylvania, Ohio, Michigan and Wisconsin. The life of Delinda Tennant may be divided into three periods, the first, the period of her childhood from her birth to her marriage in 1820, a period of eighteen years: the second, the early period of her married life, extending to the Spring of 1833, when she and her family moved from Otsego Co., N. Y. to Chautauqua Co., N. Y., a period of twelve years. During this second period six children were born into her family, Alvin, Delos, Selden, Eliza, Julia and Wealthy Tennant. The third period extended from the time of the settlement of the family in Chautauqua Co. in 1833, to the time of her death on Feb. 3rd, 1893, a period of sixty years.

During the early part of this third period, four more children were added to the family, Albert, Ellen, Fannie and John.

The writer will relate the story of this third period of his mother's life in a memorial article found in the chapter of this book containing Memorial Tributes. (See Part IV, Division 2nd).

The record of her descendants will be found in Part III, Chapter V of this work. She spent the last years of her life with her youngest son, John Asel, and his wife. She had the most tender and loving care that a son and daughter could give her. She became feeble in body and mind before death came to release her from the thraldom of the flesh. She died at the old home in Ripley Village, Chautauqua Co., N. Y. Feb. 3rd, 1893. She was buried in the beautiful Ripley Cemetery, there to await the resurrection of the just.

OUR MOTHER.

I see in the heavens a vision most bright,
　'Tis the name of our mother in letters of light;
No clouds intervene to hide the clear rays
　That shine through the nights as well as the days.

I read in that name a life story dear ,
   Full of deeds of great kindness and radiant cheer;
I pray that the vision may never depart,
   But brighten with age as it shines in my heart.

When shadows of earth are all faded away,
   And heavenly realities bring in their glad day;
Then "face to face" we surely shall see
   The forms of our loved one forever to be.

When we rise to the realms where bright angels are,
   No more shall we need a mother's kind care;
The Shepherd of Israel will then be our guide,
   He will lead to "green pastures" by "still waters' " side.

HENRY GAY

Born October 16, 1827   Died August —, 1892

Husband of Clarisa Tennant

PART I.

CHAPTER VII.

MISS CLARISSA TENNANT, her birth, her marriage to Henry Gay; her descendants by family names, Palmer, Sawin, Phillips, Newbury, Ruch, Philpott, Bartlett, Rice, Smith and Bright.

CLARISSA TENNANT, youngest daughter of John and Elizabeth Loomis Tennant, was born at Springfield, N. Y., June 5, 1804. She married Henry Gay in Herkimer Co., N. Y. Oct. 16, 1827. They came to Chautauqua Co., N. Y. in 1834 and purchased a farm on Ripley Hill. Mr. Gay was born in Herkimer Co., N. Y. Apr. 4, 1805. He was a wide-awake business farmer. He combined energy, industry and economy with good business tact, which compelled success in making money and providing well for his family. His wife was equally industrious and frugal, of a mild even temperament and became a zealous and devoted christian. She and her husband united with the Methodist Episcopal church of Ripley Village.

Their farm on Ripley Hill was sold and they purchased a farm on the Main road near Northville, N. Y., where they labored for a number of years and where they both died, the husband in August, 1892, being 87 years old and the wife died Jan. 29, 1891, being 86 years, 7 months and 24 days old.

There was born to them four children named Laura Ann, Ira, Francis and Alonzo.

I. LAURA ANN GAY, only daughter and oldest child of Henry and Clarissa Tennant Gay, was born in Herkimer Co., N. Y., Aug. 6, 1828. She was well educated in all the common school branches and having received a certificate from the Town Superintendent of Schools for the town of Ripley, Chautauqua Co., N. Y. she commenced teaching while young in years. The writer remembers her as his teacher during the first years of his attendance at the district school. She had a gentle spirit, was kind yet firm and dignified in her manner, and gained at once the love and respect of the students under her instruction.

Having closed her work as a teacher she married Isaac Palmer, a son of Israel Palmer of Ripley Township, at Ripley, Sept. 14, 1848. The writer remembers Mr. Palmer very well as we attended the same winter school. He was an athlete in the real sense of the term. In wrestling, jumping, and running matches, he usually carried off the honors as victor. He was as kind of heart as he was strong in nerve and muscle. He never engaged in fighting scraps, as he was too genial and social in his nature to provoke hostilities and gain enemies. For a number of years after their marriage Mr. and Mrs. Palmer made their home in Ripley, N. Y. Their first three children were born there. After their birth the family moved to Illinois and settled at Cortland.

Mr. Palmer was a prosperous farmer. After the birth of all his children he died at Cortland, Ill., March 26, 1865. Mrs. Palmer was left a widow with her family of five children to support and educate.

Six years intervened when on June 16, 1871, at Maple Park, Ill., Mrs. Palmer married Mr. John Ward. By this marriage there were no children born. Mr. and Mrs. Ward lived together in the marriage relation for over twenty-four years from the date of their marriage to Sept. 9, 1895, when at Cortland, Ill. Mr. Ward died. Again widowed for over ten years, Mrs. Ward died at Elgin, Ill. Feb. 8, 1906, being at her death 77 years, 6 months and 2 days old.

How strange are the vicissitudes of life. Is life worth living? Yes, most assuredly! Life is divine and eternal. Even in the earthly state, the lives of parents are perpetuated in the lives of their children and grand-children generation after generation. So, viewed in its true light, life is eternal in the spirit world, and may continue, in a numerous posterity on earth to the end of time. Thanks be to God for the unspeakable gift of life!

There were born to Mr. and Mrs. Palmer five children named as follows: Galen, Alice, Clara, Frank and Etta.

I. GALEN EUGENE PALMER was born at Ripley, Chautauqua Co., N. Y. Aug. 12, 1849. He married Martha Cook at Hinckley, Ill. in the year 1874. There were born to them six children named as follows: Grace, Earl, Ira, Frank, Ray and Norris.

CHILDREN.

1. GRACE E. PALMER was born at Hinckley,Ill. Oct. 30, 1875. She died at Aurora, Ill. March 18, 1888, being at her death 12 years, 4 months and 18 days old.

2. EARL EUGENE PALMER was born at Hinckley, Ill. March 16, 1877. He married Miss Emma Jane Porter at her home in DeKalb, Ill. Oct. 9, 1897.

There were born to them three children named as follows: Floyd, Ira and Ray. These children are great grand-children of Isaac and Laura Ann Gay Palmer.

1. FLOYD ALLEN PALMER was born at Kellog, Kan. Oct. 10, 1898.

2. IRA WILLIAM PALMER was born at Winfield, Kan. July 26, 1900.

3. RAY AURORE PALMER was born at Farm Hill, Kan. May 19, 1903.

Earl Eugene was the only grandson of Isaac and Laura Ann Gay Palmer that has married, as the writer is informed up to this date, 1912. His children are the only great-grand children who bear the name Palmer.

3. IRA N. PALMER was born at Ellsworth, Kan., Jan. 20, 1879. He died at Winfield, Kan., Aug. 16, 1900, being at his death 21 years, 6 months and 26 days old.

4. FRANK C. PALMER was born at Ellsworth, Kan., Sept. 18, 1887.

5. RAY A. PALMER was born at Aurora, Ill., Feb. 24, 1891. He died at Winfield, Kan., on the 10th day of April.

6. NORRIS O. PALMER was born at Waterman, Ill., Dec. 9, 1897.

II. ALICE ELIZABETH PALMER, second child and first daughter of Isaac and Laura Ann Gay Palmer, was born at Ripley, N. Y. Aug. 1, 1850. She married Horace Eugene Sawin, only son of Horace Sawin, and a grandson of Col. Ethan Sawin, at Ripley, N. Y. Oct. 18, 1869. His mother's maiden name was Maria Osterman.

Mr. Sawin was a farmer but engaged also in other lines of business. For his honesty, uprightness and business ability he was trusted and patronized in trade by many of his fellow citizens. Although of large and strong physical frame, a subtle and long continued disease brought him under the shadow of death and his spirit passed out of the body at Ripley, N. Y., Jan. 5, 1905. Mrs. Sawin's second marriage made her the wife of Mr. Daniel Shaw, on Nov. 22, 1907 at Ripley, N. Y. where they have since resided. There were no children by the 2nd marriage.

Two children were born of the 1st marriage, named Laura and Lee.

1. LAURA MAY SAWIN was born at Ripley, N. Y. Apr. 10, 1872. She married Burdette Phillips of Thornton, N. Y. Dec. 24, 1900. There were born to them two children, Alice and Raymond.

1. ALICE LARINDA PHILLIPS was born at Brooklyn, N. Y. May 22, 1905.

2. RAYMOND BURDETTE PHILLIPS was born at Brooklyn, N. Y. Nov. 22, 1907.

2. LEE WILLIS SAWIN, only son of Eugene and Alice Palmer Sawin, was born at Ripley, N. Y. Apr. 14, 1873. He married Emma Morgan of Ripley, N. Y. Oct. 3, 1894. There were born to them four children named Albert, Jennie, Laura and Frederic. These were grand children of Isaac and Laura Ann Gay Palmer. All were born at Ripley, N. Y.

1.   ALBERT LEE SAWIN was born June 27, 1896.

2.   JENNIE MARIA SAWIN was born June 3, 1903.

3.   LAURA MAY SAWIN was born Dec. 7, 1906.   Her given name was the same as that of her grand-mother.

4.   FREDERIC BURDETTE SAWIN· was born Apr. 10, 1909.

III.   CLARA AUGUSTA PALMER, third child and second daughter of Isaac and Laura Ann Gay Palmer, was born at Ripley, N. Y. June 1, 1853.   She married John Newburg of Ripley, N. Y. at Ripley Sept. 21, 1870. She died at Ripley, July 1, 1890 at the age of 37 years and one month.   After a little over twenty years of married life she entered into a rest from all earthly cares, labor and trial, having performed her duties as wife and mother with love and loyalty, and left as a sacred inheritance to her children an example and an influence that will linger in memory as a beacon light to guide and a protecting angel to shield them as they pass onward through life.   It may be truthfully said of her in the words of Solomon,

"She openeth her mouth with wisdom; and in her tongue is the law of kindness.

She looketh well to the ways of her household, and eateth not the bread of idleness.

Her children rise up and call her blessed;

Her husband also, and he praiseth her."

Proverbs XXXI, 26, 27 & 28.

There were born to Mr. and Mrs. Newbury four children, named as follows: Bertha, Julia, Rush and Alice.

1.   BERTHA ALICE NEWBURY was born at Ripley, N. Y., Nov. 10, 1873.   She married George R. Russell at Ripley, Sept. 10th, 1891.   They have one child, a daughter, named Velma Jessie Russell, born in Elgin, Ill., Dec. 22, 1905, a great grand-child of Isaac and Laura Ann Gay Palmer.

2.   JULIA ETTA NEWBURY was born at Ripley, N. Y. Sept 29, 1877.   She married Herman Ruch at Elgin, Ill., March 6, 1893. There were born to them two children named Clara and John.

1.   CLARA MARGUERITE RUCH was born in Elgin, Ill., Nov. 10, 1895.

2.   JOHN CLIFFORD RUCH was born in the town of Ripley, N. Y. March 26, 1899.

3.   RUSH BROWN NEWBURY, third child and only son of John and Clara Palmer Newbury, was born in Ripley Tp. Jan. 30, 1879.   He married Miss Elsie Needham in the town of Clifton, Kan. Aug. 30, 1904.   Mrs. Newbury died Oct. 28, 1904.   Mr. Newbury married the second wife at Phillipsburg, Kan., Aug. 31, 1907.   Her name was Lulu Hanencratt.

4. ALICE MARGUERITE NEWBURY was born at Ripley, N. Y., Aug. 12, 1888.

IV. FRANK HENRY PALMER, fourth child and second son of Isaac and Laura Ann Gay Palmer, was born in Cortland Township, Ill. Nov. 4, 1862. He married Miss Nellie Lentz at Kindston, Ill. Aug. 24, 1892. They have a daughter named Laura E. Palmer born at Pecatonica, Ill. Oct. 29, 1895.

V. ETTA ESTELLA PALMER, fifth child and fourth daughter of Isaac and Laura Ann Gay Palmer, was born in Cortland Tp., Ill., Nov. 28, 1864. She married John Philpott at Cortland, Ill. May 4, 1885. Mr. Philpott died at Cortland, June 30, 1898.

There were born to Mr. and Mrs. Philpott five children named Chester, Frank, an infant son (name not given), John and Myrtle.

1. CHESTER ARTHUR PHILPOTT was born at Cortland, Ill. Aug. 5, 1886. He died at the same place Jan. 23, 1887, being at his death 4 months and 18 days old.

2. FRANK ESMOND PHILPOTT was born at Rose Creek, Minn., Dec. 13, 1887.

3. INFANT SON, name not given, was born at Dixon, Ill., Dec. 28, 1890, and died Jan. 4, 1891.

4. JOHN EZRA PHILPOTT was born at Cortland, Ill., Sept. 9, 1894.

5. MYRTLE NAOMI PHILPOTT was born at Maple Park, Ill., Nov. 9, 1898.

This closes the genealogy of the descendants of Mrs. Laura Ann Gay Palmer. We add to this record the dwelling places at this date, 1912, of a few of the descendants.

Mr. Galen Palmer and his family live at Greensburg, Kan.

Mrs. Alice Shaw lives in the Township of Ripley, Chautauqua Co., N. Y.

Laura May Sawin Phillips and her family have a home at Flushing, L. I.

Bertha Newbury Russell and her family reside in Ripley, N. Y.

Julia Newbury Ruch and her family live at Fort Wayne, Ind.

Rush Brown Newbury and wife live at Mankato, Kan.

Alice Marguerite Newbury lives at Los Angeles, Cal., with an aunt, Mrs. Julia Newbury Griffin, as an adopted daughter.

Frank Palmer and his family and Mrs. Etta Palmer Philpott and her family live at Elgin, Ill.

The descendants of Isaac Palmer and Laura Ann Gay Palmer, number as follows: children, 5; grand children, 17; great-grandchildren 14.

II. IRA GAY, oldest son of Henry and Clarissa Tennant Gay, was born at Stark, Herkimer Co., N. Y. May 5, 1830. He came with the family to Chautauqua County in 1832. He mar-

ried Diana Mason, daughter of Hezekiah and Rosina Mason, at
Ripley, Nov. 6, 1851. Their first settlement was on a farm on
Ripley Hill. In 1858 he purchased a farm in the eastern part
of North East Township, Erie Co., Pa., where the family made
their home till 1876 when they moved into the gulf of the Twenty Mile Creek where he owned and run a mill until 1889. This
mill was sold and a home was purchased in Ripley Village. He
still retained possession of his farm which he owned at the time
of his death, which took place at his Village home Jan. 16, 1912.
His beloved wife preceded him in death a few years. She died
at the same home Sept. 20, 1900.

Mr. and Mrs. Gay were distinguished among all their relatives
and friends as persons of a genial, social and happy nature.
They seemed always to be trying to make all the world around
them to brighten with sunshine and smiles. Their home was a
most delightful place for neighbors and friends to visit. They
contributed much to make life worth living by their joyful and
genial ways.

Mrs. Gay was a member of the Baptist church at Ripley, N. Y.,
later uniting with the M. E. church of the same place. Her
husband supported the church by his contributions but did not
join any church. He firmly believed in the christian religion
and the Bible as its inspired exponent.

There were born to Ira and Diana Mason Gay three children
named Edith, Bertha and Cassius.

I. Edith Mason Gay was born at Ripley, Chautauqua Co.,
N. Y. Dec. 16, 1852. She married Allen Prince Bartlett of Buf-
falo, N. Y., at North East, Pa., Oct. 14, 1874. Mr. Bartlett was
born at Perrysburg, Cattaraugus Co., N. Y., Apr. 8, 1850.
There were born to them three children named Gay, Allen and
Fanny Edith.

1. Gay Bartlett was born at Buffalo, N. Y., Apr. 25, 1876.
He died at Buffalo Jan. 25, 1878, being at his death one year and
nine months old.

> "See Israel's gentle Shepherd stand,
>   With all engaging charms;
> Hark, how He calls the tender lambs,
>   And folds them in His arms."

> "Permit them to approach" He cries,
>   "Nor scorn their humble name;
> For 'twas to bless such souls as these,
>   The Lord of angels came."
>   Selected.

2. Allen Prince Bartlett, second son, was born at Buffalo, March 17, 1879. He married Lena Rowley at Gowanda, Erie

IRA GAY
Born May 5, 1830   Died January 16, 1912
Husband of Diana Mason

Co., N. Y. March 16, 1901. Miss Rowley was born at Ashtabula, Ohio, March 18, 1880. There were born to them at Buffalo, on Apr. 10, 1902, a son.

3. FANNY EDITH BARTLETT was born at Buffalo, N. Y. March 19, 1881. She married Dr. Fred Conley Rice at North East, Pa. May 4, 1904. Mr. Rice was born at Ripley, Dec. 24, 1877. There were born to them three children named Laura, Allen and Edith, all born at Ripley, N. Y.

1. LAURA MAY RICE was born May 20, 1906.

2. ALLEN BARTLETT RICE was born May 12, 1910.

3. EDITH GAY RICE was born Sept. 26, 1911.

Mr. Bartlett, the father of the above named children, died and his widow married as her second husband Henry Sylvester Nash at North East, Pa., Jan. 19, 1901. Mr. Nash was born at Girard, Erie Co., Pa., Nov. 9, 1844. By this marriage there are no children. Mr. and Mrs. Nash have a fine farm and a beautiful home located east of the Village of North East, Pa., on the Main road between Buffalo and Erie. Mr. Nash died at his home Aug. 30th, 1915.

II. BERTHA ROSINA GAY, 2nd daughter of Ira and Diana Mason Gay was born at Ripley, N. Y. Oct. 8, 1856. She married Moses H. Smith at North East, Pa., Dec. 31, 1873. Mr. Smith was born at North East, Pa., Aug. 1852. There were born to Mr. and Mrs. Smith three sons, named Jay, Ira and Guy.

1. JAY GAY SMITH was born at Northville, Chautauqua Co., N. Y., Jan. 23, 1875. He married Miss Maud Whitman at Buffalo, N. Y. Nov. 14, 1893. She was born in Virginia in 1876. They have three children named Byron, Leslie and Naomi.

1. BYRON MOSES SMITH was born at Bradford, Pa., Dec. 23, 1898.

2. LESLIE MILTON SMITH was born at Bradford, Pa., Jan. 13, 1901.

3. NAOMI SMITH was born at Bradford, Pa., July 15, 1903.

2. IRA R. SMITH was born at Northville, Chautauqua County, N. Y., June 10, 1877. He married Miss Flossie Hall at Blackwell, Oklahoma, Dec. 26, 1901. There were born to them six children named as follows: Edgar, Ira, Raleigh, Bertha, Grace and Mildred.

1. EDGAR RUSSELL SMITH was born at Alleghany, Pa., Feb. 6, 1903 and died at the same place Feb. 15, 1903.

2. IRA RALPH SMITH was born at Latrobe, Pa., June 26, 1904.

3. RALEIGH EUGENE SMITH was born at Sprangler, Pa., Aug. 17, 1906, and died at the same place Feb. 9, 1907.

4. BERTHA ELIZA SMITH was born at Sprangler, Pa., Aug. 17, 1906 and died at the same place Dec. 9, 1906.   Raleigh and Bertha were twins.

5. GRACE LILLIAN SMITH was born at Los Angeles, Cal., Jan. 26, 1909.

6. MILDRED HAZEL SMITH was born at Los Angeles, Cal., Feb. 14, 1911.

3. GUY MOSES SMITH, third son of Moses H. and Bertha Gay Smith, was born at Northville, N. Y. Aug. 1, 1880.   He married Mabel Ross, who was born in Ripley, N. Y. Sept. 30, 1880.

There were born to them two children, Ruth and Irma.

1. RUTH SMITH was born at Buffalo, N. Y. in May, 1902.

2. IRMA SMITH was born in Albany, N. Y. March 1, 1910.

3. CASSIUS MASON GAY, Refrigerating Engineer and Inventor, Los Angeles, California, was born at North East, Pennsylvania, November 17, 1862, the son of Ira R. Gay and Diana (Mason) Gay.   He married Julia I. Fessenden (born August 12th, 1860) at Chicago, Illinois, September 20, 1885 and to them there have been born six children.

1. BYRON S., born August 20, 1886.

2. NORMAN H., born March 10, 1888.

3. IRA F., born April 5, 1890.

4. EDITH A., born February 22, 1892.

5. BERTHA A., born December 24, 1893.

6. CASSIUS MASON, JR., born December 19, 1898.

Mr. Gay received a public school education, graduating from the Westfield, New York, High School in 1880, and followed this with a year's study at Bryant and Stratton's Commercial College, Buffalo, N. Y., and later took a post-graduate course in mathematics and physics under a private tutor.

His father being engaged in the flour milling business, Mr. Gay's first work was in that line.   After learning the milling business thoroughly, he left his father to become secretary to the General Manager of the Flint and Pere Marquette Railroad. He remained in that capacity until 1884, when he resigned to take a position with the Consolidated Ice Machine Company of Chicago.   He was with this concern about six years and then, in 1890, organized the Carthage Ice & Cold Storage Company, at Carthage, Mo.   Mr. Gay held the controlling interest in the Company and also served as General Manager.   In 1893 he sold his interest and went to Winfield, Kansas, where he organized the Winfield Ice & Cold Storage Company.

This Company he conducted until 1895 and then sold out to J. P. Baden, at the same time being appointed manager of the Baden interests.   The capital of the Company being steadily increased, its operations were similarly broadened until, in 1900, the produce business it handled was the largest of any plant in the West. While managing the Winfield business Mr. Gay had, in 1896, designed and erected the Southern Ice & Cold Storage Company's plant at Fort Worth, Texas.

In 1897, Mr. Gay went abroad and investigated the development and practice of Refrigeration in foreign countries.

In 1900 Mr. Gay severed his connection with the Baden interests to become Manager of the Pittsburg office of The Vilter Manufacturing Company, of Milwaukee, Wisconsin. He also acted as consulting engineer and refrigerating expert for the Company, maintaining his headquarters in Pittsburg until the year 1905, when he transferred to Los Angeles as General Coast Representative for his Company. There he has taken a leading position among professional men.

In 1907, Mr. Gay was sought out by the Santa Fe Railroad Company to solve the problem of precooling fruits directly in cars so that they could be transported great distances. He conducted a series of experiments and other investigations into the conditions of railroad refrigerator service and the result was the designing and patenting by him of a system of pre-cooling in cars which upon trial proved so entirely successful that the Santa Fe Railroad adopted his designs and patents and built a great pre-cooling and icing station at San Bernardino, California. This plant was designed and constructed by Mr. Gay. It has an ice-making capacity of 80,000 tons of ice per annum, ice storage capacity of 30,000 tons, a pre-cooling capacity of 150 cars per day, and a car icing capacity of 240 cars per day.

Experts acknowledge this to be the largest and most efficient plant of its kind in the world, and the pre-cooling of fruits by the trainload prior to their being shipped to distant markets marked an epoch in the history of transportation. Mr. Gay, with his system of balanced air circulation in cars, not only shortened the time of handling and transportation of perishable fruits, but also made certain the preservation of their fresh qualities.

For many years a contributor to leading engineering journals and a recognized authority in Refrigeration, his inventions in the new field of Railroad pre-cooling work has placed him in the front rank as a successful Pioneer and Inventor in this field.

Mr. Gay is a member of the International and American Associations of Refrigerating Engineers, the Los Angeles Chamber of Commerce and a 32nd Degree Mason. His clubs are the Los Angeles Athletic and the Athenian, of Oakland, California.

The author is indebted to Mr. Gay himself for this well written sketch of his life and business career. It shows not only good business ability but also a measure of inventive genius. His residence, at this date, 1913, is at Los Angeles, Cal.

III. FRANCIS HENRY GAY, third child and second son of Henry and Clarissa Tennant Gay, was born at Ripley, N. Y., Aug. 28, 1837. His first marriage was to Martha L. Clark at Ripley, N. Y. Dec. 24, 1860. By her he had two children named Claribel and Henry Frank.

.1. CLARIBEL GAY was born at Ripley, Chautauqua Co., N. Y. Nov. 28, 1863. She married George Sprague Bright at Corry, Erie Co., Pa., on the 8th of March, 1882. Mr. Bright was born at Fabius, N. Y. Sept. 14, 1858. There was born to them at Corry, Pa., a son whom they named John Gay Bright. This son died Dec. 24, 1889.

Mrs. Bright was graduated from the High School of Corry, Pa. in May, 1880. Her husband at the present time, 1912, is engaged in the Life and Accident Insurance business with headquarters at Jamestown, N. Y. He is an intelligent, wide-awake and successful business man who wins by honesty and industry and wise business methods.

2. HENRY FRANK GAY, second child and only son of Francis Henry and Martha L. (Clark) Gay, was born at Ripley, N. Y. July 11, 1862. He married Mary Agnes Crocker at Corry, Pa. Sept. 23, 1886. Miss Crocker was born at Fredonia, N. Y. Jan. 18, 1864. There were born to them three sons named Carleton, Frank and Robert, all born at Corry, Erie Co., Pa.

.1. CARLETON ONEIDA GAY was born Sept. 14, 1890.

2. RALPH FRANK GAY was born April 13, 1895.

3. ROBERT MANLEY GAY was born Nov. 6, 1901.

Mr. Gay has been engaged in the meat market business for the past thirty years. He is at this date, 1912, located at Warren, Pa. His son, Carleton is a student at the Bellefont Academy, Bellefont, Pa. and his son, Robert Manley attends the grammar school of his home city. The above children are great-grand-children of Henry Gay and his wife, Clarissa Tennant Gay.

IV. ALONZO WASHINGTON GAY, fourth child and youngest son of Henry and Clarissa Tennant Gay, was born at Ripley, Chautauqua Co., N. Y., Feb. 8, 1842. His first marriage was to Emma Boswell of Ripley, N. Y. This marriage was annulled by mutual consent. There were no children born. Mr. Gay married subsequently Miss Maria Josephine Sheller at Bradford, Warren Co., Pa., March 16, 1879. Miss Sheller was born at Buffalo, N. Y., Dec. 26, 1859.

Mr. Gay died June 5, 1899 and was buried at Ripley, N. Y., in the Village Cemetery on the 7th of the same month.

After the death of her first husband, Mrs. Gay married Mr. Harry Nelson at Chicago, Ill., Feb. 12, 1903. Mr. Nelson was born in North Carolina about 1845. At the age of two years he went with the family to Cincinnati, Ohio. At the beginning of the war of 1861 and 1865 he enlisted as a drummer boy, being then about sixteen years of age. He died at Chicago, Nov. 23, 1908. By her second husband, Mr. Nelson, she had no children. There were born to her by her first husband, Alonzo Gay, four sons, Clarence, Earl, Gilbert and Ira.

1. CLARENCE EUGENE GAY, the first son was born at Warsaw, N. Y. Jan. 25, 1879. He married Ethel Mowby at Chicago, Ill. Mar. 3, 1903. Their home is at Springfield, Mass. They have no children at this date, 1912.

2. EARL ALONZO GAY, second son, was born at Parsons, Kan., July 9, 1880. He married Miss Carrie Pepper of Rockford, Ill. at Chicago, Ill. in 1902. There were born to them one child, a daughter, named Romona Lillian Gay, at Rockford, Jan. 10, 1903. Mr. Gay died at Rockford, Ill. Feb. 15, 1904. Mrs. Gay and her daughter since her husband's death have lived with her parents, Mr. and Mrs. Asa Pepper at Rockford, Ill.

3. GILBERT HENRY GAY, third son, was born at Parsons, Kan. Nov. 15, 1881. He married Miss Hattie Constance Johnson at Denver, Colo., June 17, 1907. Miss Johnson was born at Brooklyn, N. Y., May 7, 1876. They are now living, Jan. 1913, at Terra Haute, Ind. They have no children.

4. IRA ALBERT GAY, the youngest son, was born at Chicago, Ill., June 9, 1892. He lives with his mother at No. 3658 Western Ave., Chicago, Ill.

The above records number the descendants of Clarissa Tennant and Henry Gay as follows:

Children 4
Grand-children 14
Great-grand-children 35
Great-great-grand-children 27
                                            ——
    Total 80

These comprise six generations with parents and grand parents.

PART I.

CHAPTER VIII.

SARAH TENNANT.

MISS SARAH TENNANT was the daughter of John Tennant and his second wife whose name is unknown to the author of this work. She was a half-sister of Delinda Tennant, and of course, of her two brothers and four sisters.

———

THE story of SARAH TENNANT's birth and life was related to the writer by his sister, Fannie, Mrs. George Mason, later Mrs. Hough. The story was written out and preserved immediately after it was told, while fresh in memory. Our mother was its original author.

Grandfather Tennant, our mother's father, immediately after the death of his first son, Alfred, became very gloomy and sad. Neighbors thought his mind had become very seriously effected. His son's death, caused by an accident, was very sudden and unexpected. (See Part I, Chapter 5th). After this death he lost his wife by death, the beloved Elizabeth Loomis. Although he had other children left to him, a dark cloud of sorrow and bereavement over-shadowed his heart. Added to this, he signed a large note with a friend to help him in financial distress. This friend finally failed in business, and the note Grandfather had signed with him became due, and he was responsible for its payment. Although he had property enough to pay the note, he would have nothing left after it was paid. At that time, in New York State, the law legalized imprisonment if he could not pay the note, and the anticipation of losing all the property he had, drove him to leave home and friends and seek a retreat from human society. So he fled from Otsego County, N. Y., into the wilds of Michigan, then heavily wooded and thinly settled. For many years he was lost to his children and friends, no trace of him could be found. How he lived can only be conjectured.

After a few years a family of white settlers came into his neighborhood, purchased land and built a log cabin. This family took pity on the lonely man and admitted him to their humble home and employed him on their farm. Time went on, how long is not known, when the husband of the family died. His widow now had charge of the farm and Grandfather continued in her employment. After a suitable time had elapsed, Grandfather married the widow with whom he lived. This marriage was the prelude to the birth of Sarah Tennant, whom we children, in subsequent years, well knew as Aunt Sarah.

At her home in Michigan she grew into young woman-hood. Now, another death took place at her home, this was the death of her mother. It seems from the subsequent movements after this mother's death, that either the property went back to the original owner or to other unknown relatives of Mrs. Tennant. This, however, is known, the daughter, Sarah went to Chicago to learn dressmaking, and her father returned to New York State to make his home with his daughters at Ripley, Chautauqua County, N. Y.

Aunt Sarah, having learned her trade at Chicago, now came to Buffalo, N. Y., to follow her trade, which she did for a number of years. Either while at Chicago, or at Buffalo, she adopted a daughter. This daughter's family name was never known to any of her adopted relatives. During Aunt Sarah's residence in Buffalo, she visited her half-sisters in Ripley. The last time the writer remembers seeing her was in the winter of 1854 when sister Fannie was very sick with typhoid fever. Cousin Dr. Galusha Phillips, then a resident physician at Sherman, N. Y., came over by an urgent call to see and treat our sister. He and Aunt Sarah sat up all night and administered to her care and treatment. The very following morning the fever broke, the fearful muscular crampings she had endured ceased, and her mind became once more clear and rational.

An old school friend of the author was on a visit to Buffalo. There she chanced to meet our Aunt Sarah. She introduced to this friend a gentleman by the name of Reynolds. He was our aunt's fiance and they were then soon to be married, and afterwards did marry and moved to New Jersey. He is said to have been a man of some fortune. His death took place sometime before that of his wife.

Before this event, the adopted daughter had married and settled in New Jersey. After the death of Mr. Reynolds, Aunt Sarah went to the home of her adopted daughter, and there lived and died. The exact place and date of her death and the place of her burial has never been known to her half-sisters and their families.

This sketch of the life of SARAH TENNANT REYNOLDS, has been written by the author without any personal knowledge of its truthfulness, but on what he believes to be perfectly reliable testimony. The most important statements are certainly true. The whole story reveals to the writer the secrets of a life wholly unknown to him till in the few years previous to his com-

mencing his work on this genealogy in September, 1911.   But
the life record of a half-sister of his mother could not be left
out of a family history.   In some way the future may disclose
all the facts of her life and correct any errors that may occur in
this memorial article.

PART SECOND.

GENEALOGY OF
MOSES TENNANT, SR.,
AND HIS DESCENDANTS

By His First Marriage.

Selden Tennant, Betsey Tennant, Polly Tennant
and David Tennant, and Their
Descendants.

PART II.

CHAPTER I.

Containing a sketch of the life of MOSES TENNANT, SR., his birth; his first and second marriage; his church relations; his family; his occupation; his death and burial.

MOSES TENNANT, SR.

So comparatively little is known by his descendants of this distinguished head of a numerous branch of the Tennant Family that the writer may well hesitate to declare anything concerning him, when facts and truths are beclouded in such obscurity. There need not have been such obscurity had family records been made and preserved. The place and date of his birth can only be approximately determined by the places and dates of the births of his children and some other events of his life. The place and date of his first marriage and even the maiden name of his first wife are involved in some obscurity. (For information concerning MOSES TENNANT'S ancestors, see a letter from Willis H. Tennant, Part V, Article First).

As young people married quite young in the early history of this Country, it is probable that MR. TENNANT was married when he was near twenty-one years of age. His birth must have been somewhere between twenty and twenty-two years before the birth of his son, Selden, that is about 1765, and his marriage one or two years before his oldest child's birth, about 1785. All this is only a conjectural computation.

Again there is an equal obscurity concerning the maiden name of his first wife, the mother of his four children, Selden, Betsey, Polly and David. There is a tradition among some of her descendants that her maiden name was Welch, and again that it was Betsey Tennant, and that her oldest daughter, Betsey was named after her mother. Amidst such uncertainties it is unsafe to make any positive assertions; the facts may be revealed to the descendants in some future time. However we have the testimony of one of the oldest members of the Baptist Church of Springfield, who died in January, 1913, then ninety-three years old, and who was well acquainted with MOSES TENNANT and all the Tennant families, that Moses Tennant's first wife's maiden name was Betsey Tennant, and that her oldest daughter was given the name of her mother, Betsey. This information came to the author by correspondence with Mr. Bennett's son, Mr. T. R.

Bennett of Springfield Center, N. Y.   On this testimony the author ventures to believe that her name was Betsey Tennant before her marriage to MOSES TENNANT.

That Mr. and Mrs. Tennant were married in Connecticut may be inferred from the fact that their oldest child, Selden, was born there, September 7th, 1787.

When Selden was a young child, Mr. and Mrs. Tennant moved to the State of New York, and finally settled at Springfield, Otsego County, N. Y.   Here all the children younger than Selden were born.   The first child born at Springfield was the oldest daughter Betsey, born June 30th, 1789.   Sometime between the dates of the births of Selden and Betsey the family moved from Connecticut to New York State, that is, between September 22nd, 1787, and June 30th, 1789.

Mr. Tennant and his wife resided at Springfield, N. Y., during the time of the births of their three children Betsey, Polly and David.   David was born at Springfield, January 4th, 1792, so their residence there was certainly five years before a great change took place in the loss by death of the wife and mother of his four children.

MRS. MOSES TENNANT must have died some time during the year 1792, probably soon after the birth of her son, David.   The writer would be glad to give a description of her character and life if he could get a truthful representation at this late day. Her husband was a Christian man and a member of the Baptist Church of Springfield, and an honored deacon of the Church, elected to this office in 1796.   We can scarcely doubt but his wife was also a member of the same church and lived a worthy Christian life, performing her duties in her family and in the church and society with conscientious fidelity and loyalty.   Mrs. Tennant died and was buried at Springfield but the exact date is lost.

Her husband, now left with four young children, who much needed a mother's care and love, was compelled to look for a housekeeper, a nurse and guardian.   This friend was found in the person of Mrs. Isaac Shaw, then a widow, whose maiden name was Sarah Selden Jewett.   She had been twice married and she had a child then living by each of her husbands, Nathaniel Baker and Isaac Shaw, named Sarah Baker and Deborah Shaw.

The story of the life of Mrs. Shaw will be told in Part III, Chapter II, of this Book.   It is sufficient to say in this connection that the coming of Mrs. Shaw into the home of Mr. Tennant with her two children, resulted in their marriage.   The Tennant family Bible record fixed the date of this marriage in 1791.   This date cannot be correct.   David, the youngest child by Mr. Tennant's first marriage, was born at Springfield, N. Y.

Jan. 4th, 1792. His marriage to Mrs. Shaw could not have taken place before the birth of David. The oldest child by the second marriage. Lucy, who married John Champion, was born June 7th, 1794. Hence, the second marriage of Mr. Tennant to Mrs. Shaw could not have been earlier than the last months of 1792 or the first months of 1793.

Mrs. Shaw, now MRS. MOSES TENNANT, told to her youngest daughter, Esther, (Mrs. David Hollenbeck) in subsequent years, that she could not endure the cries of Mr. Tennant's four children after the loss of their own mother. She went into the family from a deep sympathy for four motherless children. This fact was related by Mrs. Esther Tennant Hollenbeck to her daughter, Miss Ellen Hollenbeck, from whom the author received this interesting story.

The family life of Mr. Tennant, after his second marriage, will be more fully related in Chapter I of Part III of this work.

Before giving the family record of MOSES TENNANT and his four children, Selden, Betsey, Polly and David, we speak more fully of him as a Christian man and his relations and standing in the Baptist Church of Springfield, N. Y., and the community where he lived.

In a report of a Centennial Celebration of the Springfield Baptist Church, published in the Freeman's Journal of June 24th, 1887, MOSES TENNANT is mentioned as having been appointed a Deacon of the Church in 1796.

To show still further the standing of the Tennant and Way families in the Baptist Church and community at Springfield, the writer quotes further facts from the Freeman's Journal. "Martin Way, the son of Sterlin Way, was chosen Deacon of the Baptist Church in 1789; the father was chosen Deacon in 1794. Another Sterlin Way was chosen Deacon in 1814. He was the husband of Betsey Tennant. Their son, Martin Way, was appointed Deacon of the Baptist Church in 1869."

We relate these facts as showing that Moses Tennant, Sr., the great-grandfather of all the descendants of Selden, Betsey, Polly and David Tennant, children of his first marriage, and Lucy, Olivia, Moses, Asel, and Esther Tennant, children of his second marriage. was a good man, a worthy citizen, an active and loyal Church member, and a man of great influence in the community where he lived so many years.

MR. TENNANT passed the last days of his life at Springfield. The date of his death has never been reported in family records, and hence is lost to his descendants. There is no data that the writer has been able to find by which to fix approximately this date. His youngest child, Esther, by his second marriage, was born July 29th, 1804. By the estimates made in this Article, he

was born in 1765, or near that year.   At the birth of his youngest daughter, Esther, he was about thirty-nine years of age.
How long he lived after her birth is unknown to the writer.   His
devoted Christian life leads us to believe that he died in the tri-
umphants of a Christian faith and hope.   So far as we know of
his life, we, his living descendants, can feel safe in resting in the
same faith and in following his footsteps so far as he walked in
the King's Highway of Holiness.

Deacon Tennant was buried in the Village Cemetery at Springfield.   The writer's oldest brother, Alvin Tennant, visited
Springfield a few years before his death.   He went to the cemetery to see if he could find any of the graves of the Tennant or
Way family who were buried there.   It is sad to relate, that he
could not find a board or headstone that marked the burial place
of his grandfather or grandmother, or of his mother's sister,
Olive Eilzabeth, the wife of his uncle, Rev. David Tennant; all
was obliterated by time and nature's elements.

The life of Moses Tennant's second wife, Sarah Selden
(Jewett) Tennant will be related in Part III, Chapter I of this
Book.

PART II.

CHAPTER II.

This Chapter contains a record of the birth, marriage, death and burial of SELDEN TENNANT, the oldest child of Moses Tennant, Sr., and his wife, Betsey Tennant; a sketch of his life; his change of residence from Sweden, Monroe County, N. Y., to Camden, Lorain County, Ohio; and his descendants by family names: Williamson, Kingsbury, Smith, Marsh, Humphrey, Kennedy, Howe, Lance, Cashner, Eggleston, Bronson, Holcomb, Breckenridge, Johnston, Brown, Bartles.

SELDEN TENNANT, the oldest child of Moses Tennant, Sr., and his wife, whose maiden name was Betsey Tennant, was born at Millington, East Haddam Township, Middlesex County, Connecticut, September 22nd, 1787. This date was taken by the writer from the grave-stone set at his uncle's grave in the cemetery at Camden Center, Lorain County, Ohio, upon his visit there, and is supposed to be correct. SELDEN was the oldest of four children, Selden, Betsey, Polly and David. When but a young child he came with his parents to Otsego County, N. Y. The family settled at Springfield. No account of his early life has been given to the writer. His father was a farmer, and he was taught to work as farmers' boys usually are. He was given a good common school education, such as was available for children and young people at that time. The change of the residence of the family from Connecticut to New York, must have taken place between the birth of Selden in 1787 and the birth of Betsey, the next younger child, born at Springfield, Otsego County, N. Y., June 30th, 1789. No account of his life has been given to the author from the time of the settlement of the family at Springfield up to the time of his marriage to Miss Lydia Allen at Sweden, Monroe County, N. Y. The date of this marriage has never been given to the author. It certainly was a year or more before the birth of their oldest child, Moses, born May 22nd, 1812. Miss Lydia Allen was a native of Sweden, born May 8th, 1794.

The life of Mrs. Tennant was continued at Sweden till there came to bless their home, seven children. It is sad to record the separation of a mother from seven children, whatever their ages may be at the time the separation takes place. Mrs. Tennant died in 1832 when her youngest child, Hannah, born May 12th,

1831, was but a babe in her mother's arms. She was buried at Sweden, N. Y. The loss to the family of this wife and mother must have been very great, bringing sorrow and mourning to bereaved hearts, and desolation to a happy home.

From the subsequent lives of her children and grandchildren, we can believe that she was a woman of a bright intellect, and a warm genial heart; that she was a Christian in the truest sense, and taught her children to respect the ordinances of religion and to honor God in their faith and in their lives. There can be no doubt but that she died in the triumphs of a christian hope, and is now receiving the rewards of the righteous in the home of redeemed spirits.

Mr. Tennant was left with seven young children with no mother to look after their wants, to sympathize with them in their sorrows, nor to guide them in their training and education. With this large family to look after and to provide for, he never saw fit to marry the second time. He was a farmer, industrious and frugal, a thoroughly wide awake business man.

There were born to Selden and Lydia Allen Tennant, seven children named in the order of their ages: Moses, Ruben, Betsey, Allen, Lydia, David and Hannah, all were born in Sweden, Monroe County, N. Y.

After the death of their mother in 1832, the family continued to reside at Sweden for about fifteen years up to the Spring of 1847. About this time, emigration to the near west had set in and many families were moving from New York State to Pennsylvania, Ohio, Michigan and Wisconsin. Mr. Tennant now determined to change his place of residence. Accordingly he went to Lorain County, Ohio, and purchased land in Camden Township. After making this purchase he returned to Sweden to dispose of his property and to make arrangements to move his family. Meantime his son, Allen Russell, had married Miss Nancy Cook, and they immediately went to Ohio and settled on fifty acres of the land his father had previously purchased. This farm his father subsequently gave to his son Russell.

In the Spring of 1847 Mr. Tennant and part of his family started for Ohio from Sweden, Monroe County, N. Y., with teams and covered wagons. The group that composed this first movement consisted, as the writer has been informed, of nine members of the family, as follows: Selden Tennant, the head of the family; his son-in-law, David Morgan Tennant and his wife, Lydia Tennant, and their little daughter Mary Ann, then past two years of age; his son, David Russell Tennant and his wife Melita (Burpee) Tennant; his daughter Betsey and her husband, Mr. Charles Kingsbury; and Hannah, the youngest daughter, who was sixteen years old the 12th of May, 1847, the year this movement took place.

They reached their destiny the 31st of March, 1847. All the above is taken by the writer to be in the main true, as communicated to him by members of the family now living.

The writer is informed that the family put up over nights at hotels, getting thereby good rest for themselves and their teams.

The group of the family that went to Ohio at this time did not include the entire family of seven children. Others of the members moved west later into other parts of Ohio and into Michigan.

When Uncle Selden moved to Ohio, the writer remembers well what an excitement there was among the children of Moses Asel Tennant, when they looked out toward the road and saw a big covered wagon coming through the gate. Father said to me "Albert, we must kill a sheep, Uncle Selden has come and all his family and we must have meat for them to eat." I was then past twelve years old, and stood by while the fat sheep was killed and its body hung on a limb of a tree to cool. That visit of Uncle Selden and family I shall always remember. Some of our family had married and gone from home, but there were enough of us left to have a jolly good time with our Uncle and cousins. We lived at this time two and one-half miles south of Ripley Village, Chautauqua County, N. Y., in the hill country, in a log house with two rooms and a framed lean-to with two rooms. No matter, our house was an omnibus where there was always room for a few more.

Selden Tennant was a prosperous farmer. He was able to add more land to his first purchase, till he had a large property in land, farming tools and stock. As old age approached, he saw fit to divide his land between his children. He spent the last years of his life with his son, David Russell and his family. For many years he had been an active member of the Baptist Church of Camden Center, supporting the organization with liberal contributions. On the 22nd of November, 1871, having served his day and generation, he died at the home of his son, being at his death eighty-four years, and two months old, leaving a large family of children and grand-children to perpetuate his name and to mourn their loss.

In the Summer of 1912 the writer visited a granddaughter of Mr. Tennant, Mrs. Herbert Howe, at the old home of Rev. David Tennant at Camden, Ohio. While there he visited the two graves of his Uncles, Selden and David Tennant. The cemetery is located at Camden Centre. It is a plot of ground elevated

above the surrounding country.   There he stood by their graves
under the shadow of a beautiful grove of evergreen trees.

AT THE GRAVES OF MY UNCLES.

Rest: fathers, brothers and uncles,
   Your life work is finished in time:
At a good old age you passed on before,
   Leaving friends and kindred behind.

'Twas the triumph of faith that made you so calm,
   In the hour when death drew so nigh:
You had long put your trust in a Savior Divine,
   And now He draws near as you die.

He watches your tombs by day and by night,
   He is waiting His Father's command;
To bring back your bodies to life once again
   By the strength of His Almighty Hand.

These graves shall be opened at some future day;
   The dead shall come forth, and you'll see
The Evergreen Tree of Life that will cast
   Its fruits and its shadow for thee.

We now pass to record the births, marriages and deaths of the
descendants of Selden Tennant and his wife, Miss Lydia Allen.

THEIR DESCENDANTS.

I.   Moses Selden Tennant, the oldest child, was born at
Sweden, Monroe County, N. Y., May 22nd, 1812.   He married
Mary Jane Billings at Sweden, N. Y.,—date not been given to the
writer.   Miss Billings was a native of New York State, born
July 20th, 1820.

They moved to Camden, Lorain County, Ohio.   The date of
their moving has not been reported to the writer.   It was doubtless after the settlement of his father in Ohio.   He was a successful farmer and owned land in Camden.   He died at Camden
in the month of April, 1890, aged seventy-seven years and
about ten months.   His remains were buried in the beautiful
rural cemetery at Camden Center.   His widow survived him for
about seventeen years.   She moved to Oberlin after the death
of her husband and lived there till her death, which took place
in the year 1907.   She was eighty-seven years and a few
months old at her death.   She was buried in the cemetery at
Camden Center, O.

There were born to Mr. and Mrs. Moses Selden Tennant,
two children named William and Celeste.

HON. WM. SELDEN TENNANT
Born February 7, 1842   Died February 13, 1897

MRS. JOSEPHINE SUTTEN TENNANT
Born August 15, 1865

I. WILLIAM SELDEN TENNANT was born in Camden, Lorain County, Ohio, February 7th, 1842. He married Miss Mary Josephine Sutton at Flint, Genesee County, Michigan, August 15th, 1865. Miss Sutton was born at Flint, August 5th, 1845. She is, at this date, 1912, living at Saginaw, Michigan. Mr. Tennant died at Pontiac, Michigan, February 13th, 1897.

Among the memorial Tributes in Part IV, Division 2nd, further mention is made of the life and public service of Mr. Tennant.

There were born to Mr. and Mrs. Tennant five children, three of whom are still living. Their names are William, John, Daisy, Frank and Sidney.

1. WILLIAM MOWRY TENNANT was born at Flint, Michigan, in 1866. At this date, 1912, he is unmarried. He is engaged in the practice of law.

2. JOHN SELDEN TENNANT was born at Saginaw, Michigan, October 7th, 1867. He married Sarah Olive Banard at Saginaw, August 30th, 1899. He is connected with the Woodenware Manufacturing Company of Saginaw, Michigan. They have two children named John and Florence.

1. JOHN SELDEN TENNANT, JR., was born at Saginaw, Michigan, February 3rd, 1906.

2. FLORENCE BANARD TENNANT was born at Saginaw, November 29th, 1907.

3. DAISY DURANT TENNANT, oldest daughter, was born at Flint, August 14th, 1871, and died the same year, August 29th, aged fifteen days.

4. FRANK ALMER TENNANT was born in Saginaw, Michigan, January 22nd, 1879. He is engaged in the hardware business as a merchant at Saginaw, Michigan.

5. SIDNEY SUTTON TENNANT was born at Saginaw, August 23rd, 1882. He died in the month of March, 1885.

II. CELESTIA MINERVA TENNANT, only daughter of Moses Selden and Mary Jane Billings Tennant, was born at Camden, Lorain County, Ohio, July 20th, 1845. She graduated from Oberlin College in the class of 1866. She married John A. Williamson, January 21st, 1869, with whom she lived a happy life to the day of her death, which took place at Norwalk, Ohio, November 5th, 1880, after an illness of only ten days. Her husband was living at this time, and her death was a crushing blow upon him. From an obituary notice the writer gathers the following facts:

Mrs. Williamson joined the Baptist Church at Camden when she was but ten years old. From this Church she received a letter of dismission and recommendation about three years before her death. At the time of her death, although not formally uni-

ted with any other Church, she was actively identified with the
M. E. Church at Norwalk, being President of the Ladies' Society
and foremost in every good endeavor.   She was active and energetic in temperment, loving and gentle toward all, and was beloved and honored by a large circle of friends and acquaintances.
Her funeral services were conducted by Rev. F. M. Searles, a
former College classmate, assisted by Rev. George Mather of the
M. E. Church and F. Clatworthy of the Baptist Church of Norwalk.   Her remains were laid to rest in the Greenlawn Cemetery of Norwalk, there to await the resurrection of the just.

Mr. Williamson was born in the year 1843.   We here quote
from a newspaper obituary notice of Mr. Williamson's death:

"Word has reached this city (Saginaw, Michigan,) of the
death at his home in Norwalk, Ohio, April 19th, 1899, of Hon.
John A. Williamson.   He was fifty-seven years old at his death.
He was a highly esteemed and prominent attorney and business
man.   He resided at Saginaw, Michigan, during the year 1868,
when he was a partner in law with the Hon. William Selden
Tennant.   Mr. Williamson served several terms in the Ohio
Legislature, and was chosen Speaker of the House during his
second term, being recognized as one of the best presiding offi-
cers that Assemblage ever had.   At the time of his death, he was
a heavy stockholder in several Banks and President of one of
them.   By appointment of Governor Bushnell he was a member
of the Board of Trustees of the Ohio Institute for Feeble Mind-
ed Youths."

II.   RUBEN TENNANT, the second child and second son of
Selden and Lydia Allen Tennant, was born at Sweden, Monroe
County, N. Y., June 2nd, 1814.   He died at the place of his
birth October 2nd, 1814, being three months old at his death.

III.   BETSEY TENNANT, third child and first daughter of Selden and Lydia Allen Tennant, was born in Sweden, Monroe
County, N. Y., April 27th, 1818.   She married Charles Kingsbury at Sweden, Monroe County, N. Y.   The date has not been
given to the writer.   By him she had seven children named Selden Bingham, Lydia, Jane, Alice, Evangeline, Charles, James
and Amy.

After the birth of these children, Mr. Kingsbury died at Camden, Lorain County, Ohio in October 1865.   Mrs. Kingsbury,
the widow, married Mr. Albert Bronson at Camden, Ohio.
They had no children.   Mrs. Bronson died in Dec. 1886, at Farrington, Oakland County, Michigan.   Her remains were brought
to Camden, Ohio for burial.

The following is the family record of Charles Kingsbury and
Betsey Tennant, his wife.

1. SELDEN BINGHAM KINGSBURY was born in Camden, Lorain County, Ohio, October 29th, 1840. He married Miss Hulda Corning at Mentor, Lake County, Ohio, August 17th, 1865. Miss Corning was born at Mentor, July 25th, 1844. Her father's name was Nathan Corning, and her mother's maiden name was Phoebe Wilson.

MR. KINGSBURY was married the second time at Winnepeg, Manitoba, Canada, to Miss Katydid J. Jones of Washington, D. C., on September 25th, 1907. She was the daughter of John William Jones of Delaware, Ohio, and Katharine (Berkeley Williams) Jones of Virginia.

MR. KINGSBURY was appointed by the President of the United States, Theodore R. Roosevelt, as Circuit Judge of the Second Circuit of the Territory of Hawaii on the 9th day of March, 1909. He located at Wailuku Mani, T. H., where he now resides, 1914, and conducts the business of his office. He is an able and efficient Judge and lawyer.

There were born to Mr. Kingsbury by his first wife, five children named as follows: Nathan, Elizabeth, Frederick, Helen and Ross.

1. NATHAN CORNING KINGSBURY was born at Mentor, Lake County, Ohio, on July 29th, 1866. He married Miss Lillian Blanche Prescott of Duluth, Minnesota, June 6th, 1893. Miss Prescott was born in Marinette, Wisconsin, September 6th, 1872. She was the daughter of Dwight S. Prescott and his wife, whose maiden name was Sarah Eliza Holgate. Miss Holgate was born in Leeds, England, and came to the United States when she was a little girl.

Mr. and Mrs. Kingsbury had a daughter named Eleanor Kingsbury, born March 27th, 1910, at Chicago, Ill.

Mr. Kingsbury kindly sent to the Author the following sketch of his life, issued by the United Press Syndicate of New York City.

"NATHAN CORNING KINGSBURY was born at Mentor, Ohio, July 29, 1866, the son of Sheldon B. and Huldah (Corning) Kingsbury. He is of English ancestry through both the paternal and maternal lines of descent.

After attending the public schools at Constantine, Michigan, he entered the business world in New York City, his first position being in a housefurnishing store. In 1882 he went to Idaho, where he obtained employment as a Clerk in the Post Office of the Town of Hailey. A little later he was working as a printer's "devil" in a printing establishment at Hailey, in which Town a telephone system had just been installed; and it was here he gained his first knowledge of the telephone—it being a part of his duties to attend the switch-board during the lunch hour. In

1884 he entered the railway mail service, running over the Oregon Short Line and the Union Pacific Railroad. Returning East he became a student in the preparatory schools at Oberlin, Ohio, and then entered Oberlin College. He left College in 1891, when in his Junior year, in order to go to Duluth, Minnesota, with the Marinette Iron Works Company. While connected with this concern he took up the study of law, and, in 1877, went to Columbus, Ohio, where he finished his law course in the University of Ohio. After graduation he became general counsel of the Jeffrey Manufacturing Company, of Columbus, and remained in this capacity until November, 1906, at which time he was made vice-president of the Michigan State Telephone Company, with his office at Detroit, Michigan. He was chosen president of the Company in October, 1907. On January 1, 1910, having become vice-president of the Harris Trust and Savings Bank, of Chicago, he removed to that city, still retaining, however, the presidency of the Michigan State Telephone Company. He was elected vice-president of the American Telephone and Telegraph Company January 1, 1911, and removed to New York to take up the duties of this important office, in which he continues to serve. He is also a director of the Harris Trust and Savings Bank and of the Michigan State Telephone Company."

2.   ELIZABETH ALICE KINGSBURY was born in September, 1868. She died November 24th, 1871, at the age of three years and two months, and was buried at Mentor, Ohio.

3.   FREDERICK CHARLES KINGSBURY, third child and second son of Selden Bingham and Hulda Corning Kingsbury, was born at Constantine, St. Joseph County, Michigan, December 16th, 1875. He married Miss Pasa Cushman Love at Fremont, Dodge County, Nebraska, January 4th, 1905. Miss Love was born in Kansas, June 12th, 1876. She is the daughter of Mr. J. W. Love and Theresa Cushman Love. They have no children.

Mr. Kingsbury has kindly given to the writer the following sketch of his life.

"At the age of five, my parents moved from Michigan to Haley, Idaho, a small mining town. I attended the Public Schools of Haley until the age of twelve, when I went to work in a drug store.

In the fall of 1892, I went to Oberlin, Ohio, and entered the Oberlin Academy. Graduated from Oberlin Academy in 1895, and entered Oberlin College, from which I graduated with the degree of A. B. in 1899.

During the year 1900-1901, I was Bailiff in the Supreme Court of Idaho at Boise, Idaho, during which time I also studied law and was admitted to the Idaho Bar in 1901.

In the Fall of 1901, I went to Washington, D. C., as the Secretary of United States Senator, George L. Shoup, of Idaho, and was later made Clerk on the Senate Committee of Territories. During my work in Washington, I attended the lectures of Columbia University Law School, graduating in 1903 with the degree of L. B.

Returning to Boise, Idaho, I engaged in the practice of Law with my father, under the firm name of Kingsbury and Kingsbury, and continued such practice until I suffered from an illness which made it necessary for me to give up office work, and I went to Northern Nevada and engaged in mining. Later I went to Crown King, Arizona, as Assistant Manager of the Crown King Mines Company, and was later made General Manager.

After my marriage in 1905, I went to Columbus, Ohio, and took the position of Liquidating Agent of the Merchants and Manufacturers National Bank of Columbus, and was later appointed Receiver of said Bank and had control of the currency. I continued as such Receiver, winding up the affairs of the Bank, until 1910, during which time I also engaged in the manufacturing business, and was President of the Ohio Brass and Iron Manufacturing Company.

In 1911 I moved to Los Angeles, California, and engaged in the oil and mining business, until January, 1914, when I went into the Real Estate business, becoming Vice-President of The James R. H. Wagner Company.

At the present time I am President of the Engineers Oil Company; President of Kern-4 Oil Company; President of Zamboanza Plantation Company, Vice-President of the Potrero Mining Company, and Vice-President of The James R. H. Wagner Company."

4. HELEN L. KINGSBURY, the fourth child and second daughter, was born in Constantine, St. Joseph County, Michigan, February 28th, 1879. She married in the City of New York, September 16th, 1903, Captain Charles Fredric Humphrey, a son of Major General Charles Fredric Humphrey and his wife, whose maiden name was Juanita DaCosta Foster.

They have a daughter named Elizabeth Humphrey, born in Honolulu, T. H., August 24th, 1904.

Mrs. Humphrey was educated at the Oberlin College, Ohio. She was a student at Oberlin of the Conservatory of Music.

Mr. Humphrey is an officer in the United States Army. At this date, July, 1914, he is Captain in the 12th United States Infantry. His first station was at Columbus Barracks, Columbus, Ohio. Since then he has been located at the following stations: Honolulu, T. H.; Fort Porter, Buffalo, N. Y.; Portland, Maine; Washington, D. C.; the Presidio Montorey, California, the Presidio. San Francisco, California; where he is now, July 1914, stationed. He has been sent, however, to the Mexican border where he is at the above date in camp.

5. Ross SELDEN KINGSBURY was born in 1892. He married Miss Josephine Ellicott in 1910. There was born to them a daughter named Priscilla Kingsbury.

The writer could obtain no further report concerning the life or family of Mr. Kingsbury.

II. LYDIA JANE KINGSBURY was born at Sweden, N. Y. She married Jerome Culver. She died in the early Spring of 1913. Left two sons, Roy and Guy Culver. Addresses 320 S. Washington St., Saginaw. The writer could get no further report.

III. ALICE KINGSBURY was born at Camden, Ohio. She married a Mr. Huckins. They have one son who resides at Saginaw, Michigan, Seth G. Huckins, 320 S. Washington St., Saginaw, Mich. No further report could be obtained.

IV. EVANGELINE KINGSBURY was born at Camden, Ohio, died about 1890. She married a Mr. Ackins. She died at Salt Lake City. No further report.

V. CHARLES HENRY KINGSBURY, the fifth child and second son of Charles and Betsey Tennant Kingsbury, was born at Camden, Lorain County, Ohio. He married Miss Rena Abbott at St. Louis, Michigan, August 21st, 1859. She was the daughter of Edgar M. Abbott and his wife, Juliett Daily, born in Rome Township, Lenawee County, Michigan, May 28th, 1868. Mr. and Mrs. Kingsbury have a daughter named Helen Kingsbury, born at St. Louis, Gratiot County, Michigan, September 10th, 1898. She is a High School student at this date, 1913.

VI. JAMES DAYTON KINGSBURY, sixth child and third son of Charles Kingsbury and Betsey (Tennant) Kingsbury, was born in Camden, Lorain County, Ohio, October 16th, 1856. He married Mary Alida Abel at Saginaw, Michigan, August 6th, 1879. She was the daughter of Joseph Azel Abel who died January 27th, 1912, and his wife, Anna Louise (Perry) Abel, who died October 9th, 1879. Miss Abel was born at Algonac, St. Clair County, Michigan, May 20th, 1857.

There were born to Mr. and Mrs. Kingsbury, seven children named James, Jr., Ora Louise, Fred, Ralph Abel, Raymond, Selden and Edwin.

I. JAMES DAYTON KINGSBURY, JR., was born at Saginaw, Michigan, July 22nd, 1880. He married Mary Susan Gallup at Pueblo, Colorado, May 20th, 1906. Miss Gallup was born at Pueblo, Colorado, October 1st, 1876. There were born to Mr. and Mrs. Kingsbury, two children, named Dorothy and Marian.

1. DOROTHY ALIDA KINGSBURY was born at Pueblo, Colo., January 4th, 1908.

2. MARIAN JUDITH KINGSBURY was born at Memphis, Tenn., September 15th, 1909.

II. ORA LOUISE KINGSBURY, the second child, was born at Muskegon, Michigan, January 6th, 1883. She married Ezra Durham Smith at Detroit, Michigan, November 5th, 1903. Mr. Smith was born at Oberlin, Ohio, October 16th, 1875. There were born to them two children both at Detroit, Michigan, named June and Beatrice.

1. JUNE ERNESTINE SMITH was born June 17th, 1905.

2. BEATRICE RAE SMITH was born September 15th, 1911.

III. FRED CARLISLE KINGSBURY, the third child and second son, was born at Oshkosh, Wisconsin, August 8th, 1886. He is not married.

IV. RALPH ABEL KINGSBURY, the fourth child and third son of James Dayton and Mary (Abel) Kingsbury, was born at Oshkosh, Wisconsin, June 29th, 1889.

V. RAYMOND LAWRENCE KINGSBURY was born at Saginaw, Michigan, June 23rd, 1891. He died December 25th, 1898, aged seven years, six months, and two days.

VI. SELDEN BINGHAM KINGSBURY, the sixth child and fifth son, was born at Saginaw, Michigan, March 2nd, 1894.

VII. EDWIN BOOTH KINGSBURY was born at Saginaw, Michigan, June 3rd, 1896. He was the youngest child and sixth son of James D. and Mary (Abel) Kingsbury.

VIII. AMY KINGSBURY, the seventh and youngest child of Charles Kingsbury and Betsey (Tennant) Kingsbury, was born at Camden, Lorain Co., Ohio, Jan. 23rd, 1859. She married Edward W. March at Farmington, Oakland Co., Mich. June 25th, 1876. Mr. Marsh was born at Glaston, Somerset Co., England, Nov. 1847. He is the son of William and Jamson Marsh of England.

Mr. and Mrs. Marsh have one child, a daughter, name Alice Ernestine Marsh, born Sept. 8th, 1882. She married Charles Jenner at her home in Pontiac, Mich., July 4th, 1912. Mr. Jenner is the son of Nathan Jenner and his wife, Katherine McGann Jenner of Virginia.

IV. ALLEN RUSSELL TENNANT, fourth child and third son of Selden and Lydia Allen Tennant, was born in Sweden, Monroe County, N. Y., July 10th, 1820. He married Miss Nancy Cook at Sweden, N. Y. Date of marriage could not be obtained.

After his father had purchased land in Camden, Lorain County, Ohio, his son, Allen, after his marriage, moved to Ohio, and settled on a portion of the land his father had purchased. He improved the land, and afterward his father gave him that portion he had improved. He never had any children.

V. LYDIA TENNANT, fifth child and second daughter of Selden and Lydia Allen Tennant was born in Sweden, N. Y., May 22nd, 1822. She married David Morgan Tennant, a son of Rev. David Tennant, her uncle, at Springfield, Otsego County, N. Y., September 10th, 1844. The history and genealogy of Mrs. Tennant may be found in this book under and including that of her husband's parents, Rev. David and Olive Elizabeth Tennant. See Part II, Chapter V.

VI.   DAVID RUSSEL TENNANT was born at Sweden, Monroe County, N. Y., August 20th, 1826, and died June 5th, 1908. He married Miss Melita Burpee at Sweden, N. Y., November 19th, 1846. She was born July 29th, 1827, and died March 5th, 1899, in Camden, Lorain County, Ohio. There were born to David Russel and Melita Burpee Tennant, six children named Franklin Russel, Emily Dorinda, Ellen Arminda, Clara Melita, George William and Mary Almina.

1.   FRANKLIN RUSSEL TENNANT was born at Camden, Ohio, December 3rd, 1847. He married Miss Ella Damon at Hinckley, Ohio, February 28th, 1871. Miss Damon was born at Hinckley, Ohio, July 6th, 1849. There were born of this marriage the following children named Eugene, Roy, Ray, Clayton and Frank.

1.   EUGENE TENNANT, oldest child, was born at Camden, Ohio, January 4th, 1872, and died at Cleveland, Ohio, October 2nd, 1877, being at his death five years, eight months and twenty-eight days old.

There is a mystery that surrounds the death of the young,
    That cannot be solved in this life,
We only can wait till the mists have all passed,
    And we see things by eternity's light.

2.   ROY RUSSEL TENNANT was born at Cleveland, Ohio, October 29th, 1875. He married Mattie Eastman, September 28th, 1904, at Elyria, Ohio. They have one daughter, Alice Amelia Tennant, born at Munger, Michigan, October 6th, 1908.

3.   RAY DAMON TENNANT was born at Munger, Michigan, January 4th, 1881. He married Miss Etta Histed at Munger, Michigan, December 3rd, 1902. Miss Histed was born at Munger, October 14th, 1883. They had three children as follows: Hulda, Gertrude and Gilbert.

1.   HULDA ALBERTA TENNANT was born at Munger, Michigan, March 17th, 1905.

2.   GERTRUDE LOUISE TENNANT was born at Munger, Michigan, May 14th, 1907.

3.   GILBERT LAWRENCE TENNANT, a twin brother to Gertrude, hence born at the same place, May 14th, 1907.

4.   CLAYTON FRANKLIN TENNANT, fourth son of Franklin Russel Tennant, was born at Munger, Michigan, August 19th, 1883. He married Eva Madill at Munger, Michigan, May 27th,

FRANKLIN RUSSELL TENNANT
Born December 3, 1847

MRS. ELLA DAMON TENNANT
Born July 6, 1849

1906. There were born of this marriage two children, named Ellen and Dorothy.

1. ELLEN LOUISE TENNANT was born at Munger, Michigan, March 3rd, 1908.

2. DOROTHY EVELINE TENNANT was born at Bay City, Michigan, June 18th, 1909.

5. FRANK CLYDE TENNANT, fifth son, was born at Munger, Michigan, June 19th, 1892. He married Miss Florence Mae Carvey at Munger, Michigan, June 24th, 1912. Miss Carvey was born at Munger, December 13th, 1891.

II. EMILY DORINDA TENNANT, second child and oldest daughter of David Russel and Melita Burpee Tennant was born at Camden, Ohio, April 22nd, 1850. She married Albert Kennedy at Camden, Ohio, July 19th, 1876. They have had three children as follows: Mabel, Clarence and Alberta.

1. MABEL KENNEDY was born at Springfield, Ohio, May 14th, 1878. This child only lived to August 9th, 1878, when the Angel Reaper came and gathered the young spirit into the Lord's Garner above, with the ripened fruits of His glorious harvest.

2. CLARENCE HAMILTON KENNEDY was born at Brockport, Indiana, June 20th, 1879.

3. ALBERTA MELITA KENNEDY was born at Brockport, Indiana, September 14th, 1881. She married Benjamin Franklin Huffman at Brockport, Indiana, June 28th, 1906.

III. ELLEN ARMINDA TENNANT, third child and second daughter of David Russel and Melita Burpee Tennant, was born at Camden, Ohio, April 7th, 1852. She married Herbert H. Howe at Camden, Ohio, February 12th, 1874. There were born to Mr. and Mrs. Howe four children, named as follows: Myrtle, Lena, Grace and Maud.

I. MYRTLE HOWE was born at Norfolk, Ohio, October 19th, 1875, and died at the same place, November 6th, 1875, being only eighteen days old.

There is a mystery that surrounds the death of the young,

That cannot be solved in this life;
We only can wait till the mists have all passed,
And we see things by eternity's light.

Shall we wish her back to our arms of love,
This darling so blest and so free?
No! rather let us believe she is much better off,
In God's bosom of love to be.

II. LENA LENORA HOWE was born at Bath, Ohio, September 1st, 1878. She married Robert E. Lance at Medina, Ohio, June

29th, 1899.   There were born to them two children, Sidney and Iona.

1.   SIDNEY HERBERT LANCE was born at Lafayette, Medina Co., Ohio, May 12th, 1900.

2.   IONA LENORA LANCE was born at Lafayette, Ohio, November 14th, 1902.

III.   GRACE ELLEN HOWE was born at Herner, Ohio, December 28th, 1881.   She married Abraham Burton Cashner at Buffalo, N. Y., October 4th, 1905.   There was born of this marriage a son named Gerald Burton Cashner, at Lansing, Michigan, June 29th, 1908.   His sad death occurred on July 2nd, 1908, being only three days old at his death.

> Does parental love cease at death,
>   Or does it take its flight,
> And follow loved ones far away
>   To realms of pure delight?
>
> Parental love is love divine,
>   Created to endure;
> Its fountain head is God's own love,
>   Eternal, strong and pure.

A second son was born at Camden, Lorain Co., Ohio, Jan. 8th, 1915, named Ralph Herbert Cashner.

Since the above record was made the sad news came to the author of the death of the wife, mother and grand-mother of this family at her home in Camden, O., on Sept 20th, 1914, at the age 62 years, 5 months and 13 days.   A little over a year before her death, Mrs. Howe had a severe stroke of paralysis caused by apoplexy, which rendered her helpless and dependent.   She had during this time the tenderest care of her family and of an efficient nurse.   Her case was hopeless from the beginning.   But she endured this long trial with patience and trust.   She had long since put her supreme confidence in an unseen but an ever present Savior and Lord.   Her life had been spent in His service in the conscientious performance of her domestic and church duties. At an early age she united with the Baptist church of Camden, Ohio, and remained a loyal and faithful member till she passed from the church militant to the church triumphant in the kingdom of heaven.

Her funeral was held at her home in Camden.   Her remains sleep in the beautiful cemetery at Camden near those of the loved ones who have gone before her.   Two stanzas of a beautiful hymn comes to the mind of the writer:

GEORGE WM. TENNANT
Born September 29, 1856

MRS. MATTIE GIFFORD TENNANT
Born February 22, 1859

"Why should we mourn departing friend,
  Or shake at death's alarms?
Tis but the voice that Jesus sends
  To call them to His arms."

"Why do we tremble to convey
  Their bodies to the tomb?
There the dear flesh of Jesus lay,
  And scattered all its gloom."

And—"Jesus said unto her, I am the resurrection and the life: He that believeth in me though he were dead, yet shall he live; And whosoever liveth and believeth in me shall never die, Believeth thou this?"   *John's Gospel Chapter 11, vv 25 and 26.*

IV.   MAUD LULA HOWE was born at Bath, Ohio, May 22nd, 1887.   She married Roy H. Eggleston at Camden, Ohio, April 11th, 1909.   They have one child, a daughter, named Thelma Ellen Eggleston, born at Elyria, Ohio, September 14th, 1911.

IV.   CLARA MELITA TENNANT, fourth child and third daughter of David Russel and Melita Burpee Tennant, was born at Camden, Ohio, August 27th, 1854.   She married Frilelo Hebert Bronson at Camden, Ohio, March 15th, 1876.   They have one child, a daughter named Rossella Adelia Bronson, born at Camden, Ohio, December 19th, 1884.   This young daughter, having matured into womanhood with all the bright hopes that are enkindled in hearts of young people of her age, on the 15th of August, 1904, at her home, passed from the earthly transitory life to the celestial and eternal life of which it is written in God's Book, Rev. XXII: 3, 4 & 5.

"And there shall be no more curse; but the throne of God and the Lamb shall be in it; and His servants shall serve Him:
And they shall see His face; and his name shall be in their foreheads.
And there shall be no night there; and they need no candle, neither light of the sun; for the Lord God giveth them light; and they shall reign forever and ever."

V.   GEORGE WILLIAM TENNANT, fifth child and second son of David R., and Melita B. Tennant, was born at Camden, Ohio, September 29th, 1856.   He married Mattie Gifford at Camden, Ohio, March 13th, 1879.   There were born to them six children, named as follows: Ernest, Albert, Arthur, George, Ada and Emma.

1.   ERNEST PERRY TENNANT was born at Camden, Ohio, September 10th, 1880.   He married Miss Clara Horton, April 2nd, 1903, at Munger, Michigan.

2.   ALBERT WILLIAM TENNANT was born at Munger, Michigan, June 11th, 1883, and died at the same place February 12th, 1884.

The Prophet Zechariah speaking of the Ancient Jerusalem as the Type of the New Jerusalem, says: "And the streets of the City shall be full of boys and girls playing in the streets thereof."

Zech. 8:5.

3. Arthur Sidney Tennant was born at Munger, Michigan, January 5th, 1885. He married Dora Allison at Munger, Michigan, February 22nd, 1907. There were born to them two children, Albert and Arthur.

1. Albert Lee Tennant was born at Munger, Michigan, April 25th, 1908.

2. Arthur Perry Tennant was born at Munger, Michigan, July 26th, 1911.

4. George Clinton Tennant, fourth son of George William and Mattie Gifford Tennant, was born at Munger, Michigan, March 2nd, 1890. He married Miss Maud E. Beckwith at Munger, September 17th, 1912. Miss Beckwith was born at Munger, December 8th, 1891.

5. Ada Tennant, first daughter and fifth child of George William and Mattie Gifford Tennant, was born at Munger, Michigan, September 25th, 1891.

6. Emma Tennant, second daughter, was born at Munger, August 12th, 1894.

VI. Mary Almina Tennant, sixth child and fourth daughter of David R. and Melita B. Tennant, was born at Camden, Ohio, April 1st, 1859, and died at Cleveland, Ohio, September 8th, 1882, at the age of twenty-three years, five months and seven days.

"There's a land that is fairer than day,
    And by faith we may see it afar;
And the Father waits over the way,
    To prepare us a dwelling place there.

In the sweet bye and bye,
    We shall meet on that beautiful shore,
In the sweet bye and bye,
    We shall meet on that beautiful shore."

Selected.

VII. Hannah Tennant, youngest child and third daughter of Selden and Lydia Allen Tennant, was born in Sweden, Monroe County, N. Y., May 12th, 1831. At the age of sixteen she moved with her father to Camden, Lorain County, Ohio. She married Moses Holcomb at Elyria, Ohio, November 1st, 1848. Mr. Holcomb was born in Ohio, May 12th, 1823. After her marriage she and her husband made their home in Ohio till June 4th, 1881, when they moved to Wiota, Iowa. Mr. Holcomb died at Wiota, Iowa, April 10th, 1895, being at his death seventy-one years, ten months and twenty-eight days old. His beloved wife survived him till 1908, when on the 2nd of September, she passed into the spirit life, at the age of seventy-seven years, three months and twenty days. There were born to them six children, named, Elida, Oliva, Truman, George, William Page and Fred Grant.

I. ELIDA HOLCOMB was born in Camden, Lorain County, Ohio, August 6th, 1849. She married Henry Breckenridge at Camden, July 4th, 1867. There were born to them two children named Mattie and Earl. Mrs. Holcomb died July 25th, 1874.

1. MATTIE BRECHENRIDGE was born in Gratiot County, Michigan. The date of her birth could not be obtained. She married Robert Johnston in 1885. She died in June, 1888. They had a son named Leon Johnston, who was born at Wiota, Cass County, Iowa, December 2nd, 1887.

2. EARL BRECKENRIDGE was born in Gratiot County. The date of his birth was not given. He lived till he was past four years old. The place and date of his death has not been given.

II. OLIVA HOLCOMB, second child and second daughter, was born in Camden, Ohio, January 23rd, 1858. She married Derastus Brown in Camden, June 27th, 1877. There were born to Mr. and Mrs. Brown three children, named Nettie, Charles and Albert.

1. NETTIE BROWN, the oldest child and only daughter, was born in Camden, Ohio, May 9th, 1873. She married Mr. W. F. Sump at Elyria, Ohio, August 22nd, 1895. They have one daughter named Florence Stella Sump, born in Elyria, June 30th, 1897.

2. CHARLES BROWN, oldest son, was born in Camden, Ohio, July 27th, 1877. He is unmarried and lives at this date, 1912, in Nebraska.

3. ALBERT BROWN, the youngest child of Derastus and Oliva Holcomb Brown, was born at Wiota, Cass County, Iowa, January 23rd, 1879. He married Miss
at Elyria, Ohio, September 16th, 1903. Miss
was born   . There were
born to them two children, Kathryon and Charles.

1. KATHRYON BROWN was born at Elyria, Ohio, November 9th, 1905.

2. CHARLES BROWN was born in Lorain, Ohio, September 4th, 1908.

III. TRUMAN HOLCOMB, third child and first son of Moses and Hannah Tennant Holcomb, was born at Camden, Ohio, November 16th, 1855. He married Miss Clara Campbell at Camden, Ohio, February 22nd, 1877. By her he had two children, named Mamie and Frank.

1. MAMIE HOLCOMB was born at Wiota, Iowa, April 25th, 1879. She married Charles Bartles at Greenfield, Iowa, January 18th, 1899. There were born to Mr. and Mrs. Bartles, eight children, named Clara, Ora C., Luluh, Roy, Glenn, Fay, Clifford and Myrtle.

1. CLARA BARTLES was born in Cass County, Iowa. She died May 2nd, 1900.

Ora C., Luluh, Roy, Glenn and Fay were born near Sheridan, Cass County, Iowa.

2. ORA C. BARTLES was born March 26th, 1901.

3. LULUH BARTLES was born September 29th, 1903.

4. ROY BARTLES was born near Sheridan, Worth Co., Missouri in 1905.

5. GLENN BARTLES was born at the same place, Sheridan in 1907.

6. FAY BARTLES was born no date given.

7. CLIFFORD BARTLES was born in Miami County, Kansas, in 1911.

8. MYRTLE BARTLES was born September 13th, 1912, and died when she was about a month old.

2. FRANK M. HOLCOMB was born at Wiota, Cass County, Iowa, October 25th, 1880. He married Miss Lulu Whiston in Greenfield, Iowa, November 18th, 1902. Mr. Holcomb is a machinist. There were born to Mr. and Mrs. Holcomb six children named as follows: Mildred, Welma, Donald, Doris, Dale and Fred.

1. MILDRED L. HOLCOMB was born June 5th, 1903.

2. WELMA L. HOLCOMB was born August 8th, 1904.

3. DONALD F. HOLCOMB was born January 7th, 1907.

4. DORIS J. HOLCOMB was born August 1st, 1907.

5. DALE E. HOLCOMB was born February 9th, 1910.

6. FRED W. HOLCOMB was born January 2nd, 1912.

MRS. CLARA CAMPBELL HOLCOMB, wife of Truman Holcomb, died at Wiota, Cass County, Iowa, in April, 1883. After her death Mr. Holcomb married for a second wife, Mrs. May Whitney, at Camden, Ohio, September 7th, 1898. Mrs. Whitney's maiden name was May Walker, born at Holland, Lucas County, Ohio, November 4th, 1856, and her first husband was Melvin H. Whitney born August 10th, 1856. By his second wife, Mr. Holcomb had one daughter named Leita Louise Holcomb, born at Greenfield, Clair County, Iowa, May 25th, 1900.

IV. GEORGE HOLCOMB, fourth child and second son of Moses and Hannah Tennant Holcomb, was born at Camden, Ohio, May

25th, 1858. He died at the place of his birth, June 6th, 1861, being at his death three years and eleven days old.

. V. WILLIAM PAGE HOLCOMB, fifth child and third son was born at Camden, Ohio, November 16th, 1862. His death took place at Camden, Ohio, August 9th, 1863, being at his death eight months and twenty-three days old.

We can but notice that two sons of this family die in childhood within a little over two years. No one can estimate the sorrow of parents when young children are taken from them. Sad memories of the dear little ones will never be erased from the mind, but will constantly recur to depress the parental heart. Only can a firm reliance in the wisdom and love of God in the giving and taking of young children, will bring comfort and hope to bereaved and sorrowing parents. God creates no human being without an eternal purpose. Whether the immortal soul enters the mortal body before or after birth is a secret with Him who creates. Of this we may be assured, that at the birth of a child, it is possessed of a never-dying and imperishable soul. Then, however, early in life the mortal body returns to dust, the "Spirit, or soul returns to God who gave it." On this great truth rests the promise of our Lord when He said of little children "Of such is the Kingdom of Heaven."

VI. FRED GRANT HOLCOMB, the youngest child and fourth son, was born at Camden, Ohio, March 1st, 1865. He married Miss Emma Stark at Wiota, Iowa, October 17th, 1888. Miss Stark was born near Cruthersville, Jackson County, Indiana, December 29th, 1869. She came with her parents to Atlantic, Iowa, in 1877. After this marriage Mr. Holcomb and his wife moved to Adair County, Iowa, where they have resided for about fourteen years previous to 1913. In an obituary notice sent to the writer is given an account of Mrs. Holcomb's death. She was taken to Cottage Hospital in Grovetown, and after the operation there were fond hopes that she would recover, but the hopes were all blasted, for she died August 28th, 1913, being at her death forty-three years, seven months and twenty-nine days old. She was a faithful and beloved member of the Presbyterian Church. Her body was laid to rest in the Greenfield cemetery.

TIME IMPERSONATED.

Shall we say that Time is cruel,
Taking from us dearly loved ones?
But 'twas Time that gave them to us,
And He only takes His own.
Let us wait Time's coming changes
Ere we judge His firm decrees;
He will only bring us gladness

When His ends we clearly see.
Here on earth there's naught that's finished;
Life itself is just begun:
In the future, now unknown,
We shall see what Time has done.
From that distant point of vision,
Turning back our eyes to see;
We'll behold our earthly treasures,
Full of wealth as they could be.
Let us then look up and onward,
Take this world for what it's worth;
Never thinking that it's blessings
Are the sum of all on earth;
For the future will reveal us
What the fruits of Time will be;
When the clouds that blind our vision,
Are dispelled by Eternity.

The descendants of Selden Tennant and Lydia Allen Tennant number as follows, in the above list.

Children 7
Grand-children 26
Great-grand-children 49
Great-great-grand-children 39
                                            —
    Total 121

The total descendants of Selden Tennant must include the descendants of his son, David Morgan Tennant and his wife, Lidia Tennant, a daughter of Rev. David Tennant and Olive Elizabeth Tennant, his wife, who was a daughter of John Tennant and Elizabeth Loomis, his wife, whose ancsetors are named in Part I, Chapter First of this Genealogy. As will be seen by this reference, the line of ancestry extends back to Dea. John Loomis, born in England in 1662 and died in 1688.

STERLIN WAY
Born in 1775   Died December 8, 1858
Husband of Betsey Tennant. who died August 13, 1842

PART II.

CHAPTER III.

This Chapter contains a record of the birth, marriage
and death of BETSEY TENNANT, second child and oldest
daughter of Moses Tennant, Sr., by his second wife.
Betsey Tennant; and second wife of Sterlin Way; and
her descendants by family names: Way, Doolittle,
Jaqua, Van Horn, Nicholson, Himes, and Burst.

———

MISS BETSEY ELIZABETH TENNANT was born at Springfield,
Otsego Co., N. Y., June 30th, 1789. She was the second
child and first daughter of Moses Tennant, Sen., and his wife,
Betsey Tennant; the daughter was given her mother's name. She
married Sterlin Way, at Springfield, Otsego Co., N. Y., in June,
1813. She was his second wife. The name of Mr. Way's first
wife, and the place and date of her birth is not known by the writer. He had by her a daughter named Delia Way, who married
John Doolittle. All the writer is able to learn of this husband
and wife is that their last residence was on a farm near Wattsburg, Erie County, Pa., where the husband died June 20th, 1856,
in the sixty-third year of his age, and his wife died at the same
place March 26th, 1856, in the fifty-seventh year of her age.

The writer regrets that he cannot record the place and date of
the birth of this husband and wife, nor the place and date of their
marriage, nor the year they settled in Pennsylvania. The author
believes they were New York State people and moved westward a
few years after their marriage.

MR. STERLIN WAY was born at Springfield, N. Y., Apr. 14th,
1772. He and his wife lived all their married life at or near
Springfield, N. Y. Other members of the family moved westward, some to Western New York, and some to Pennsylvania,
Ohio, and Michigan. From a circle of many friends they were
at last separated by death; both died at Springfield, the wife on
the 13th of August, 1842, being at her death fifty-two years, one
month and thirteen days old, and the husband on the 5th of December, 1858, at the age of eighty-six years, 7 months and 21
days. Both had lived devoted Christian lives, being members of
the Baptist Church at Springfield. MR. WAY was an honored
Deacon of the Church, elected in 1794, and performed the duties
of this office with commenable zeal and faithfulness to the time
of his death in 1858.

There were born to Mr. and Mrs. Sterlin Way seven children,

named as follows: Lucy Ann, Maria, David S., Martin, Dulcena, Elizabeth and Eli.

I.   LUCY ANN WAY was born at Springfield, N. Y., April 18th, 1814.   She married Dr. William Way at Springfield, June 14th, 1832.   Dr. Way was a nephew of Sterlin Way, his wife's father.   They had one child, a daughter, named Helen Maria Way, born August 16th, 1840.   Mrs. Way died at Springfield Center, N. Y., in November, 1893.

II.   MARIA WAY, second child and second daughter of Sterlin and Betsey Tennant Way, was born at Springfield, N. Y., May 22nd, 1816, and died at the same place May 16th, 1831.   At the age of fourteen years, eleven months and twenty-four days, this young daughter was taken from her fond parents and a circle of young companions and friends, by the Angel of death, who spares neither old or young in the sweep of his remorseless power.   If there was no promise or hope of immortality and eternal life how dark and dismal our earthly life would be.   But through the blessed revelation which God has been pleased to give us in his Holy Word, we may believe that the life, after physical death, has in store for all God's children a height and depth of peace, happiness, blessedness and glory, such as the human soul can never experience in man's earthly life.   Over eighty-one years from the time that these memorial lines are being penned, this young daughter, cousin and friend, has been basking in the light and glory that fills the whole realm of the Heavenly World, to which God takes His beloved children.   Let us not complain when even the young are taken away from earth, for their future inheritance is made ready for them, and God only knows what He has in reserve for them, when their earthly life is passed, however long or short that life may be.

This daughter was buried at Springfield, N. Y., there to await the resurrection of the dead.

III.   DAVID STERLIN WAY, the third child and oldest son of Sterlin and Betsey Tennant Way, was born in Springfield, N. Y., December 5th, 1818.   He married Miss Margaret Elizabeth Mosher at Springfield, February 2nd, 1841, who was a native of Connecticut, born November 8th, 1818.

MR. WAY was a farmer and pursued his business in the Town of Springfield, up to the time of his moving to Indiana, where he lived for two years.   He went West and then returned to Springfield, N. Y., where he lived for several years.

On the 3rd of July, 1865, the family moved to Lowville, Venango Township, Erie County, Pa.   Here he continued farming up to the time of his death, which took place at the home of his grandson, Orville Way, in Wayne Township, Erie County, Pa., December 6th, 1905, being at the time of his death eighty-seven

MRS. LUCY EMILY DOOLITTLE
Born April 18, 1849

years and one day old. His beloved wife survived him for over five years, when she died at the same home June 10th, 1912, being at her death ninety-three years, seven months and two days old.

There was born to David Sterlin and Margaret Elizabeth (Mosher) Way, three children, named David Watson. Lucy Emily and Eli Sylvester.

1. DAVID WATSON WAY was born at Springfield, N. Y. March 31st, 1844. He was a wagon maker, having learned his trade in the Village of Herkimer, N. Y. He married Miss Maria E. Stanbro, daughter of Orville and Susan Stanbro, at Unadilla Forts, Herkimer County, N. Y., February 14th, 1866.

MR. WAY moved from Springfield, N. Y. to Indiana in about 1863. In 1865 he moved to Pennsylvania and located at Lowville, Erie County, where he died August 5th, 1883, being at his death thirty-nine years, four months and four days old. His mortal remains were buried at Beaverdam, Erie County, Pa.

There was born to Mr. and Mrs. David Watson Way a son, named Orville Way.

1. ORVILLE DAVID WAY was born at Beaderdam, Pa., October 17th, 1867. He married Miss Ida Viola Tompkins at Magnolia, Chautauqua County, N. Y., November 20th, 1890, Rev. Eli S. Way performed the ceremony.

MISS TOMPKINS was the daughter of George Tompkins and his wife Jerusha (Blakeslie) Tompkins. She was born in Wayne Township, Erie County, Pa., July 2nd, 1867. There was born to them a son named Carl Watson Way, in Wayne, Pa., October 20th, 1896.

MR. WAY is a farmer located in Wayne Township. It was at his home that his aged grandmother, Margaret E. Way, died.

2. LUCY EMILY WAY, the second child and only daughter of David S. and Margaret Mosher Way, was born in Springfield, Otsego County, N. Y., April 18th, 1849. She married Martin Julett Doolittle at Wattsburg, Erie County, Pa., October 25th, 1871.

MR. DOOLITTLE was born at Bookfield, Madison County, N. Y., December 22nd, 1843. He came west from New York State and settled in Erie County, Pa. He was a farmer. He died in the Township of North East, December 22nd, 1909, aged sixty-six years. His widow is still living with her son, Marion, on a small farm about five miles south of the Village of North East. In the month of June, 1913, the writer had the pleasure of visiting his cousin and her son. She has given him much information about the descendants of his aunt, Betsey Tennant Way.

There were born to Mr. and Mrs. Doolittle, two sons, Manley and Marion.

1. MANLEY FREEMAN DOOLITTLE was born at Lowville, Erie

County, Pa., August 21st, 1876, and died at the same place August 27th, 1876, being at his death six days old.

2. MARION MARTIN DOOLITTLE was born at Harbor Creek, Erie County, Pa., August 24th, 1883. He is now living (1913) in North East Township, Erie County, Pa., with his mother on a small farm.

MR. DOOLITTLE married Miss Orpha Clarinda Prindle at Ripley, N. Y., December 15th, 1913. Miss Prindle is the daughter of Chauncey M. Prindle, and his wife whose maiden name was Sarah Ella Northrup. She was born in Greenfield Township, Erie County, Pa., at the home of her parents, October 5th, 1894.

MR. DOOLITTLE took his wife to his mother's home on the little farm in North East Township, Erie County, Pa. He has all the elements of character and business ability that give assurance of success in farming or any other business to which he may devote his time and energies. They have a daughter named Beatrice May, born in Greenfield, Pa., May 29, 1915.

3. ELI SYLVESTER WAY, third child and youngest son of David S. and Margaret Mosher Way, was born at Springfield, Otsego County, N. Y., October 21st, 1851. He married Miss Lucy Maria Jacquay at Wattsburg, Erie County, Pa., February 7th, 1872. Miss Jacquay was the daughter of George and Barbara Salton Jacquay. She died at Hartfield, N. Y., April 10th, 1893. There were born to them two children named Adah and Nellie.

1. ADAH VENETT WAY was born in Wayne Township, Erie County, Pa., December 18th, 1872. She married Munson Enoch Himes at Hartfield, Chautauqua County, N. Y., December 15th, 1869. Mr. Himes is the son of William C. Himes and his wife, Oliva Scriven. He was born at Hartfield, N. Y., October 12th, 1867. They have one son, Hobart Himes, born at Hartfield, on August 7th, 1896. Mr. Himes was in the employ of the Buffalo Abstract Company located at Mayville, N. Y., but at this date, 1913, is an employee in the Abstract Department of the County Clerk's office of Chautauqua County, N. Y., at Mayville.

2. NELLIE DE ETTE WAY, the second daughter, was born in Wayne Township, Erie County, Pa., April 21st, 1874. She is unmarried and resides at Akron, Ohio, and is employed as a bookkeeper and clerk .

Mr. Way's first wife died at Hartfield, Chautauqua County, N. Y., April 10th, 1893. Left as he was with two children he married for his second wife, Mrs. Julia Carver Parkhurst, at Hartfield, N. Y., November 21st, 1894. She was a daughter of Cyrus and Amanda (Lattin) Rhodes, born at Springfield, Otsego County, N. Y.

By his second wife, MR. WAY has a son named Altice Morton

REV. ELI S. WAY
Born October 21 1851
Pastor of the Baptist Church, Sweet Valley, Pa.

Way, born at the Rapids, Niagara County, N. Y., January 8th, 1896.

MR. WAY had a common school education at Sugar Grove, Pa. Believing he was called to enter upon the work of the Christian ministry, and being a member of the United Brethren Church, he took the course of reading and study required by the United Brethren Conference of Candidates for their ministry. MR. WAY was licensed to preach by the United Brethren Conference, August 29th, 1889, at Sugar Grove, Warren County, Pa. Subsequently he was ordained at Geneva, Crawford County, Pa., in 1892, by the United Brethren Conference. In connection with this Denomination he served as Pastor at Magnolia Charge, Chautauqua County, six years; at Niagara Charge, Niagara County, N. Y., two years; at Cassadaga, N. Y., one year; at Little Cooly Charge, Crawford County, Pa., four years. All the above mentioned pastoral service of thirteen years was in connection with the United Brethren Church.

In November, 1903, lead by his convictions of duty, he withdrew from the United Brethren Church and accepted a call from the Baptist Church of Clymer, Chautauqua County, N. Y. At this place he was ordained in June, 1904, by a Baptist Council called by the Clymer Church. He served this Church till November, 1904. From Clymer he was called to the Pastorate of the Baptist Church of Kennedy, Chautauqua County, N. Y., where he served till August 21st, 1910, a term of nearly six years. Terminating his labors at Kennedy he accepted a call from the Baptist Church of Great Valley, Cattaraugus County, N. Y., where he is now at this date, June 1913, rendering faithful service in the Master's Cause. Since his consecration to the Christian Ministry, in 1882, he has rendered thirty-one years of service and been pastor, in the two Denominations above mentioned, of eight Churches. We can only mention the outward form of a Pastor's service; the invisible and spiritual effect of such a ministry can only be known and computed by the Great Shepherd of the Church, who knows His sheep and is known of them, and who will gather them all into His Fold in Heaven, for no enemy will ever be able to pluck them out of His Father's Hand.

IV. MARTIN WAY, fourth child and second son of Sterlin and Betsey Tennant Way, was born at Springfield, Otsego County, N. Y., August 21st, 1821. He married Miss Ruth Ely at Springfield Center, June 25th, 1844. It appears that Mr. Way and his wife spent their life after marriage at the place of their marriage; for at this place, Springfield Center, N. Y., Mr. Way died, October 18th, 1901, and his beloved wife died January 21st, 1907. He was elected Deacon of the Baptist Church of Springfield in 1869. There were born to them five children named as follows: Mary, Richard, Heman, Lydia and Will Burt.

1. MARY MARIA WAY, the oldest child of Martin and Ruth (Ely) Way, was born at Springfield, Otsego County, N. Y., May 26th, 1847. She married Harry Van Horn at Springfield, N. Y.

There were born to Mr. and Mrs. Van Horn eleven children, seven of whom at this date (1914) are living, and four are dead. The names of those who are dead have not been given to the writer. The names of the living children and their family records as far as could be obtained are as follows: dates of births, marriages and deaths could not be obtained.

1. LENA VAN HORN was born at Springfield, Otsego Co., N. Y. She married Will Hersey. There was born to Mr. and Mrs. Hersey a daughter named Gladys Hersey.

2. RUTH VAN HORN was born at Springfield, N. Y. She married Ralph Russell. They have no children.

3. LIZZIE VAN HORN was born at Springfield, N. Y. She married George Hecox. There were born to them two sons named Fred and Harold Hecox.

4. GEORGE VAN HORN was born at Springfield, N. Y. He is married and lives in the western part of this county. The maiden name of his wife could not be obtained. They have two children, whose names and birth records could not be obtained.

5. ALLY VAN HORN was born at Springfield, N. Y. He is unmarried.

6. BELVA VAN HORN was born at Springfield, N. Y. She married Jessy Riesdorph. They have four children named Niram, Florence, Anna and an infant child. Florence died.

7. EDNA VAN HORN was born at Springfield, N. Y. She is not married.

2. RICHARD S. WAY, the second child, was born at Springfield, N. Y., February 6th, 1852. He married Miss Gertrude S. Small at Cooperstown, Otsego County, N. Y., June 30th, 1875. She was the daughter of Frederick and Manda (Stocking) Small, born at Hartwick, N. Y., September 11th, 1853. There was born to them a daughter named Edith Way, at Cooperstown, October 24th, 1880. She married Floyd Burst at Springfield, N. Y., November 13th, 1907. Mr. Burst was the son of David and Ida White Burst.

3. ·ELI HERMAN WAY, the third child of Martin and Ruth (Ely) Way, was born in Springfield, N. Y., December 31st, 1859. He married Miss Flora Heckerman at Clinton, Iowa, April 16th, 1891. She was born in White Side County, Illinois, October 8th, 1868. She was the daughter of Gabriel Nelson Heckerman, born in Pennsylvania, and his wife, Lydia Elizabeth Knight, born in White Side County, Illinois.

There were born to Mr. and Mrs. Way, two children, Pearl May, and a son whose name has not been given.

1. PEARL MAY WAY was born at Clinton, Iowa, February 8th, 1892. The son was born at Davenport, Iowa, October 12th, 1894; he died in infancy.

MR. WAY writes the author that he received his education in the Public School at Springfield, Otsego County, N. Y. His wife is a graduate of the High School of Clinton, Iowa, in the Class of 1888. She taught school up to the time of her marriage in 1891. Mr. and Mrs. Way have made their home at Clinton, Iowa, since their marriage, except five years at Davenport, Iowa. He is now engaged at Clinton, in the oil and gasoline trade.

PEARL WAY, the daughter, has supervision of the Bell Telephone Company office.

4. LYDIA WAY, fourth child and second daughter of Martin and Ruth Ely Way, was born at Springfield, N. Y., September 30th, 1861. She died at Springfield, February 22nd, 1889, being at her death twenty-seven years, four months and twenty-two days old. She was never married.

From an Obituary Notice the writer quotes the following:

"Her amiable and cheerful disposition won for her a large circle of friends." "A beautiful floral tribute 'Gates Ajar', arranged by friends and presented by her Sabbath School scholars, was placed at the head of the casket." The following poem was taken from the obituary:

"Sleep on, though we weep for thee,
And sigh the heart away;
We know thy soul reigns pure and free
In Heaven's Eternal day."

"Asleep in thy Redeemer's Love;
Happiness for every woe;
Thy portion's with the Blest above,
'Tis ours to weep below."

5. WILLIE BURT WAY, the youngest child of Martin and Ruth Ely Way, was born at Springfield, N. Y., July 30th, 1865. He married Miss Maude Rathburn at Warren, Herkimer County, N. Y., October 4th, 1893. She was the daughter of George L. Rathburn and his wife, Elsie M. (Jones) Rathburn, born at Warren, N. Y., January 12th, 1873.

V. DULCENA WAY was born at Springfield, N. Y., November 17th, 1823. She married Delos Nicholson at Springfield, N. Y., November 21st, 1839. She was the fifth child and third daughter of Sterlin and Betsey Tennant Way. Years ago they moved west. Mr. Nicholson became blind. Her husband died

several years ago.   They have children but the writer can obtain
no family record.

VI.   ELIZABETH WAY, sixth child and fourth daughter of
Sterlin and Betsey Tennant Way, was born at Springfield, N. Y.,
June 2nd, 1826.   She died at the place of her birth, December
26th, 1846, being at her death twenty-years, six months and
twenty-four days old.

It is sad beyond measure to record the death of persons in the
morning of life.   No doubt the death of this daughter, who had
just entered upon that period of life when the body and mind
have just begun to assert their natural vigor and strength, and the
heart is light and hopes are bright, made a great void in the
hearts and homes of her parents, and cast a wave of sorrow over
the hearts of her young companions and friends.   No matter how
many years may have intervened between the present and the
past in our experience of sorrow and bereavement,sweet memories
will bridge the distance and bring to the heart and thought the
precious treasures of goodness, virtue and beauty that once we
enjoyed and admired in the lives of those whom we loved in the
by-gone years, and whose spirit-presence seem to hover around us
like angel visitors who come to lift the burden of our sorrow and
to cheer and comfort us.

> E—lizabeth, a name most sweet,
> L—ike perfumes of the morning flowers;
> I —n Bible History thou didst reach, the
> Z—enith of woman's saintly powers.
> A—cross the years that intervene
> B—etween the living and the dead.
> E—nchanted memories cast their light
> T—o show the path and upward flight,
> H—eavenward, of loved ones from us fled.

VII.   ELI WAY, the youngest child and third son of Deacon
Sterlin Way and Betsey Tennant Way, was born at Springfield,
N. Y., December 13th, 1830, and died at the same place, Decem-
ber 8th, 1850, being at his death twenty years and five days old.

In the morning of life this young son was stricken down never
to realize his fondest earthly hopes.   We know not what a high
and noble career was ended by his death.   We only can hope
that what actually appears to be the ruin of a useful life has
proved the realization of a greater good, a higher life in the mysterious realm of spirit beings in the great and endless future.

> "The flowers that bloom in earthly soil,
>   When withered in the bud;
> Oft re-appear in ripened fruit,
>   On land beyond the flood.

> Then let us not be quick to judge,
>   That life is lost in death;
> Eternal ages will reveal,
>   Why here we are bereaft
> Of friends we love so dearly now
>   While we on earth are left."
>
> —Selected

The relatives who read the above genealogy of the descendants of BETSEY TENNANT and her husband, Sterlin Way, will doubtless be disappointed in not finding fuller records of some families. The author has made repeated efforts, by correspondence, to obtain full records of their families. But after repeated writing and enclosing stamps for a reply no answer could be obtained. Relatives will not be slow to discern where the blame rests for the incompleteness of the history of such family.

The catalogue of the descendants of this branch of the Tennant family, as herein reported, number as follows:

Children 8
Grandchildren 9
Great-Grandchildren 15
Great-Great-Grandchildren 2
                                              ——
Total 34

These include with the parents and grand parents six generations.

CHAPTER IV.

This Chapter contains a brief sketch of the life of POLLY TENNANT. The writer regrets that after repeated efforts to obtain the names of her children and their residences, he has utterly failed. The given name of her husband, Mr. Howard, cannot be obtained. The writer of the brief sketch has no apology to offer for not securing a full family record, as he has done all he could do to secure such a record.

POLLY TENNANT, the third child and second daughter of Deacon Moses Tennant, and his first wife, Betsey Tennant, was born in New York State, doubtless at Springfield, Otsego Co., N. Y. The date of her birth is lost, but it must have been between the dates of the birth of her next older sister, Betsey Tennant, born June 30th, 1789, and that of her younger brother, Rev. David Tennant, whose birth was on the 4th day of January, 1792. These dates indicate that POLLY TENNANT was born either in 1790 or 1791. Her brother Selden was born, as the writer believes, in Middlesex County, Connecticut, September 22nd, 1787. He was the oldest child and his next younger sister, Betsey, was born in Springfield, N. Y. We conclude from these facts that Moses Tennant, their father, moved from Connecticut to New York State after the birth of the oldest child, Selden, and before the birth of the next child, the daughter Betsey, that is, either in the year 1788 or 1789. As both Betsey and David are known to have been born in Springfield, N. Y., we conclude that their sister Polly was born at the same place, namely, Springfield, N. Y.

POLLY TENNANT married a Mr. Howard. With no direct proof of this from any of her relatives, the writer wrote to a member of the Baptist Church of Springfield, N. Y., and obtained from the records of the Church, that POLLY TENNANT HOWARD was received into the membership of this Church by letter of dismissal from the Baptist Church of Albany, N. Y., bearing date February 27th, 1830. Afterwards she was dismissed by letter bearing date December 26th, 1835, to return to the Albany Church. This record shows that Mrs. Howard had a residence in Albany, N. Y., before 1830, and after 1835. Between these dates she resided at Springfield, N. Y., for about five years. In April, 1913, the writer received a letter from the Clerk of the First Baptist Church of Albany, N. Y., bearing date of the 7th, in response to inquiries concerning MRS. POLLY HOWARD. He writes that the First Church was organized in 1811, that MRS. POLLY HOWARD joined the Church by Baptism the same year (1811), in the month of June; that she was granted a letter to unite with the Springfield Church, May 30th, 1828. When she returned to Albany, she joined the Emanuel Church, January 7th, 1836, and died in the year 1849. The Clerk further writes: "I found the name of Ephraim Howard on the Church book, but I have no idea as to whether he was the husband of POLLY HOWARD."

If the Writer can obtain nothing more concerning his Aunt Polly, all the above are interesting facts worth recording. The intervals between some of the above dates arise doubtless from MRS. HOWARD holding her letter from the First Albany Church for some time before she offered it to the Springfield Church.

There were born to Mr. and Mrs. Howard, three children, a son and two daughters. The name of one daughter only has been given to the author, that of Juliette, who married a Mr. Pifield. The son, when still in his youth, met with tragical death by drowning. The writer has not been able to learn anything concerning the life or place of residence of the second daughter.

This record of POLLY TENNANT and her family is very incomplete and unsatisfactory. No places or dates of the births of the three children have been reported to the author, although he has made a diligent search by correspondence to learn more about the family. He understands that Mr. Howard died many years ago, not long after the tragical death of his son. He has been informed that the death of the son hastened the death of the father, but the place or date of these deaths are unknown to the author.

PART II.

CHAPTER FIFTH.

This Chapter contains a history of the life of REV. DAVID TENNANT, son of Moses Tennant, Sr., and his wife, Betsey Tennant; his marriage to Olive Elizabeth Tennant, daughter of John Tennant and Elizabeth Loomis; his early education; his call to the Christian Ministry; his first and last pastorate as Pastor of the Baptist Church of Springfield, Otsego County, N. Y.; his wonderful power as a preacher; his mental derangement caused by an accident but not hereditary; his forced retirement from the pulpit and pastoral service; and his descendants by family names: Tennant, Champion, Williams, Laycock, Comfort, Differed, Carl, Curtis, Fergerson, Bunnell, Myer, Snow, Raymond and Dunham.

REV. DAVID TENNANT.

I N giving a sketch of the life of this remarkable man, the author obtains all his information from his own parents, Moses Asel and Delinda Tennant, and from Rev. David's and his brother Selden Tennant's grand-children and the family records in their possession.

REV. DAVID TENNANT was born at Springfield, Otsego County, N. Y., January 4th, 1792. He married Miss Olive Elizabeth Tennant, daughter of John Tennant and his wife Elizabeth Loomis Tennant at Springfield, on Dec. 25th, 1813. Olive Elizabeth was a next older sister of Delinda Tennant and sister of all her brothers and sisters whose family records may be found in this book of Genealogies, Part I.

REV. DAVID was the son and youngest child of Moses Tennant, Senior, and his wife, Betsey Tennant. Her maiden name is not positively known by the author of this work. By correspondence with some of the oldest members of the Baptist church of Springfield, N. Y., of which both Moses Tennant and his wife were members, the writer has been well informed that her given name was Betsey, and it is thought, by the same persons, that her family name was Tennant. Notwithstanding the uncertainity concerning her name, the writer ventures to publish it as Betsey Tennant, and that her oldest daughter Betsey, who married Sterlin Way, and whose biography may be found in Part II. 3rd Chapter of this book, was named after her mother.

REV. DAVID TENNANT was a farmer's son, and had to work for a living, so he obtained only a common school education. He was, in early years, under the influence and guidance of Christian parents and teachers, and this lead him to make a public profession of faith in Christianity, and to unite with the Baptist Church of Springfield, N. Y., in early life. Rev. Jacob Knapp, the great preacher and evangelist, was, at one time, the pastor of the Springfield Church. He came to this field from his college course. Rev. Tennant was brought, either before or after his conversion, under the inspiring influence of this great and devout man. How much this influence had to do in moulding Mr. Tennant's life and character is not known by the author. However, while he was yet a young man, he felt called of God to enter the Christian Ministry. The Baptist Church of which he was a member, after listening to his preaching a few times, licensed him to preach. This was only the giving of the approval of the Church to occupy the pulpit, but was also a recommendation to him to improve his talent and prepare himself for a life long work in this holy calling.

The author has frequently heard his father and mother speak of the preaching of his uncle David. His sermons were characterized by a profound and wide knowledge of the scriptures, by clearness and consecutiveness in utterance, and by great zeal and earnestness in delivery. The people liked to hear him. He studied hard to give to his congregation the best his mind and heart could produce.

The writer has had correspondence with one of the older members of the Baptist Church of Springfield, Otsego County, N. Y., Mr. T. P. Bennett, who has been a member of this Church for forty years and a deacon for twenty years. He has examined the records of the Church, and sends the folowing facts taken from the records.

"At a meeting held by this Church on May 6th, 1819, brother DAVID TENNANT appeared before the body for examination as an applicant for a license to preach. By request of the Church Rev. Calvin Hulbert conducted the examination. After this, the minutes of the meeting read: "The Church was called upon to show their fellowship with BROTHER TENNANT as one called of God to preach the Gospel." "The Church voted to give him a letter of fellowship and recommendation." This action granted him a license, under the approval of his brethren, to occupy the pulpit and improve his gifts.

A subsequent action of the Church called him to an examination for ordination. The minutes read, "On the 7th of February, 1823, the Church agreed to set apart and ordain REV. DAVID TENNANT, on the First Wednesday of March, 1823, for the Gospel Ministry, and a committee was appointed to sit in council at that date."

The Church records show that after examination, the council expressed by vote their satisfaction with reference to the candidate's Christian experience, call to the ministry, and his qualifications for this high calling, and proceeded with the ordination services.

This double action of licensing and ordaining REV. TENNANT, proves the confidence his brethren had in him as a suitable person to enter the Christian Ministry.

How long REV. TENNANT served the Church of which he was Pastor, before the sad occurrences which now must be related, the writer is unable to learn with any certainty—it is doubtless more than three years.

Now there came upon the life of this talented and Godly young man a providence so strange and unaccountable that it is beyond human wisdom to understand, why, under such circumstances, this young man's life should be wrecked. The story is best told in the words of a grand-daughter, Mrs. Olando F. Bunnell of Willoughby, Ohio. She writes, "Grandpa Tennant met with an accident while he was riding upon a horse through a piece of timber. He was going home from Church. The wind was blowing very hard, and a limb broke off and fell striking him on the head. He fell from his horse and the horse went home. His brethren got a lot of men, and they searched for him for some time. He was badly hurt, and was delirious when they found him. They took him home, and got medical aid. He was confined to his bed for some time; but finally got around, and when he thought he was well, he went to preaching. The Doctors told him he must not, but he did, and they called him crazy."

From this mental derangement he never recovered. He had intervals in which he seemed perfectly rational. The Baptist Church of Springfield continued his services with them for a time, for, when in the pulpit, he was apparently of sound mind, and prayed and preached with great clearness and earnestness. But the closing of his services had to come at last, for instead of improving, his mental condition grew worse. While he was compelled to cease all pastoral work, he was able in subsequent years to render some light service about the farm and house.

Mention will be made in a separate article of his beloved wife. It is sufficient here to say, that her husband's affliction blighted all her earthly hopes, she died broken hearted many years before the death of her husband. (See Part I Chapter V.)

REV. TENNANT lived at Springfield, N. Y., till after the death of his wife, and till his children had left New York State for Ohio and Michigan. His oldest son, Alfred Augustus went to

DR. DAVID M. TENNANT
Born August 20 1820   Died December 20, 1892

MRS. LYDIA ALLEN TENNANT
Born May 22, 1822

Michigan when a young man. As will be seen in his family record, this son married and settled near Pontiac, Michigan. In 1849 his father visited him remaining only a few months,when he suddenly left and went to Camden, Lorain County, Ohio, to spend the rest of his days with his son, David Morgan. While here, REV. DAVID was accustomed to go into the loft of the barn for secret devotions. His grandson, Selden David, then living at home, relates to the author, that he at times went to the barn to hear his grandfather pray. He says that he never listened to more eloquent and fervent prayers. In prayer, REV. DAVID was perfectly rational. Upon the death of a little grandchild, that he greatly loved, he burst out with this exclamation, "Why could it not have been me; here I am a wreck and a useless mortal." REV. DAVID TENNANT died at the home of his son, David in Camden in 1879, being 87 years old at his death.

There were born to Rev. David and Olive Elizabeth Tennant, four children named Alfred Augustus, Levantia, Harriet Eliza and David Morgan.

I. ALFRED AUGUSTUS TENNANT, oldest child, was born at Starkville, Herkimer County, N. Y., October 2nd, 1814. He married Fanny Louisa Wheeler at Blissfield, Lenawee County, Michigan, May 15th, 1847. Miss Wheeler was born in Huron, Huron County, Ohio, April 13th, 1826. Mr. Tennant died at Delta, Fulton County, Ohio, September 9th, 1891, at the age of seventy-six years, eleven months and seven days. He was buried at Blissfield, Michigan. His wife survived him over twenty-one years and died at Metamora, Fulton County, Ohio, November 26th, 1912, being at her death eighty-six years ,seven months and thirteen days old. The last fourteen years of her life were passed at the home of her daughter Harriet, Mrs. Abram Jewett Champion, where she had the tenderest care till she passed away.

There were born to Mr. and Mrs. Tennant three children, Harriet Stanley, Francis Augustus and Oliva Sarah.

1. HARRIET STANLEY TENNANT, oldest child of Alfred Augustus and his wife, Fanny Louisa Wheeler, was born in Blissfield, Lenawee County, Michigan, June 5th, 1848. She married Abram Jewett Champion at Metamora, Fulton County, Ohio, June 5th, 1873 or 1874. She was his second wife. In this marriage the line of the descendants of John and Lucy Tennant Champion and the line of the descendants of Rev. David and Olive Elizabeth Tennant come together in the children of Abram Jewett Champion and Harriet Stanley Tennant. The records of these children, five in number, will be mentioned in the family record of their father. (See descendants of John and Lucy (Tennant) Champion. (Part III, Chapter 3d.)

II. FRANCIS AUGUSTUS TENNANT, second child and first son

of Alfred and Louisa (Wheeler) Tennant was born in Blissfield,
Michigan, August 7th, 1849. He married Miss Elsa Rosette Corbin at Ogden, Michigan, March 7th, 1874. Miss Corbin was
born October 9th, 1855. She was a daughter of Seneca and Hannah (Young) Corbin.

Mr. Tennant writes the author that he had common school advantages for an education; that he followed mercantile business
till he was forty years old; then on account of ill health, went
into factory work for four years; then into a Railroad office for
one and one-half years; then took up carpenter work in which he
has continued to the present time, 1913. His address is 3035
Monroe Street, Toledo, Ohio.

There were born to Mr. and Mrs. Tennant five chilrden
named Frank, Oliva, Belle, Joseph and Harriet. All their children were born at Blissfield, Lenawee County, Michigan, except
Frank, who was born at Amboy, Ashtabula County, Ohio.

I.   FRANK ADELBERT TENNANT was born at Amboy, Ashtabula County, Ohio, August 15th, 1875. He married Mary Caroline Parry in Van Wert County, Ohio, December 27th, 1904.
There were born to them three children, Edward, Eloa and Esther.

1.   EDWARD AUGUSTUS TENNANT was born at Cleveland,
Ohio, October 5th, 1905.

2.   ELOA BERNICE TENNANT was born at Cleveland, Ohio,
January 15th, 1907.

3.   ESTHER JANE TENNANT was born at Erie, Erie County,
Pa., February 25th, 1912.

II.   OLIVA AILEEA TENNANT was born at Blissfield, Lenawee County, Michigan, April 21st, 1877. She was the oldest
daughter and second child of Francis Augustus and Eloa (Corbin) Tennant. She married Edgar Mauier Williams at Toledo,
Ohio, December 15th, 1898. Mr. Williams was born at Danville, Illinois, January 27th, 1862. The ceremony was by Rev.
Houck of the First Baptist church.

There were born to Mr. and Mrs. Williams three children
named Emily, Anabelle and Charles.

1.   EMILY ELOA WILLIAMS was born at Indianapolis, Ind.,
December 26th, 1899. She died by accidental poisoning September 16th, 1913.

2.   SARAH ANABELLE WILLIAMS was born at Indianapolis,
Ind., February 24th, 1901.

3.   CHARLES AUGUSTUS WILLIAMS was born at Toledo,
Ohio, April 20th, 1906.

III.   BELLE TENNANT, third child and second daughter of
Francis Augustus and Eloa (Corbin) Tennant, was born in
Blissfield, Lenawee County, Michigan, September 3rd, 1881.
She married Thomas Joseph Laycock in Toledo, Ohio, Septem-

ber 17th, 1900.   Mr. Laycock was born in Camden, Kent County, Ontario, Canada, February 17th, 1863.   He was the son of Joseph and Elizabeth (Bador) Laycock.

There were born to Mr. and Mrs. Laycock six children named Doris, Francis, Edgar, Eloa, Frank and Rosemary, all born in Toledo, Ohio, except Eloa Josephine who was born in Sylvania, Ohio.

1.   DORIS ELIZABETH was born November 6th, 1901.

2.   FRANCIS ELLSWORTH was born July 15th, 1903.

3.   EDGAR was born December 10th, 1905, and died December 21st, 1905, aged 12 days.

4.   ELOA JOSEPHINE was born January 15th, 1906.

5.   FRANK MAXWELL was born July 6th, 1907.

6.   ROSEMARY RUTH was born March 30th, 1909.

All the above named children are great-great-grand-children of Rev. David and Olive Elizabeth Tennant.   Rev. David's father's name was Moses Tennant and his wife, Olive Elizabeth, was the daughter of John Tennant and his wife Elizabeth Loomis.

IV.   JOSEPH EDWARD TENNANT, fourth child and second son of Francis Augustus and Eloa (Corbin) Tennant was born at Blissfield, Michigan, October 28th, 1882.

V.   HARRIET TENNANT, fifth child and third daughter was born at Blissfield, Michigan, May 2nd, 1884, and died July 22nd, 1884, being at her death two months and twenty days old.

III.   OLIVA SARAH TENNANT, third child and second daughter of Alfred and Fanny Wheeler Tennant, was born in Blissfield, Mich., August 30th, 1853.   She married Samuel Emlen Comfort son of Ellwood and Elizabeth (Salterwaite) Comfort, at Tecumseh, Michigan, October 12th, 1884.   She was Mr. Comfort's second wife.   His first wife's maiden name was Miss Abihu Gardner.   By her Mr. Comfort had a daughter who lived only about six weeks and died in September 1881.   One month after the death of this daughter, in October 1881, the mother died. Mr. Comfort had been a widower for three years before his second marriage to Miss Tennant.

MR. COMFORT was born at Tecumseh, Lenewee County, Michigan, August 30th, 1853, and died at the same place January 10th, 1895, being at his death 41 years, 4 months and 10 days old.   His wife preceded him in death over six years and died at Rea, Monroe County, Michigan, August 14th, 1888, being at her death 35 years and 1 day old.

There were born to them two daughters named Frances Elizabeth and Olive Sarah.

1.   FRANCES ELIZABETH COMFORT was born at Tecumseh, Michigan, August 9th, 1885.   She is unmarried.   MISS COMFORT writes the author that after the death of her mother in

1888 she lived with her grandfather, Mr. Elwood Comfort, except a period of about one and a half years, during which she
lived with her father and his third wife.

At twelve years of age, after her Grandfather's death, she
lived with a maiden Aunt, Miss Sarah S. Comfort, until she was
about twenty-one years old. Then she and her sister Olive
lived with a cousin of their Father's, Elizabeth S. Mead, for
about a year at Sutton, Michigan, a few miles from Tecumseh.
In the fall of 1907 she went to California. Since then her home
has been with her Grandmother, Mrs. Lemisa L. Comfort at No.
549 Orange Grove Avenue, Pasadena, California.

In the Spring of 1904 she was graduated from the Raisen
Valley Seminary in the County of Lenawee, Michigan. She
taught for three years. After coming to Pasadena, California,
she took a complete commercial course. Having finished the
course, she became one of the Faculty in the Fall of 1910, and
taught there up to September 11th, 1913. On October 8th,
1913, she entered into the service of Messrs. C. G. Brown and
Company, of Pasadena, California, a Real Estate and Insurance
firm. At this date, January 1914, she is still an employee of
this firm.

The writer has had a pleasant correspondence with this cousin and wishes for her much prosperity and happiness.

2. OLIVE SARAH COMFORT was born near Tecumseh, Lenawee County, Michigan, June 25th, 1887. She married Alfred
Ernest Difford at Pueblo, Colorado, March 28th, 1908.

MR. DIFFORD was the son of William B. Difford and his wife
Mary A. (Robbins) Difford, born at Belvidere, Boone County,
Illinois June 18th, 1887.

They had a son named J. William Difford born at Wichita,
Sedgwick County, Kansas, October 16th, 1911. This child died
on the day of his birth. The age of a child at its death does
not change the promise of our Lord who took little children in
his arms and blessed them and said: "Of such is the Kingdom of
Heaven."

Mrs. Difford writes the author a brief sketch of the changes
that took place in her early life up to the time of her marriage.
She writes: "My mother died near Tecumseh, Michigan, in
1888; my father died in 1895. After my Mother's death I went
to live with Aunt Harriett Champion, my Mother's sister. After
two years or so I went to my father and was taken to Leslie,
Michigan. I lived there until I was four or five years old. From
there I went to live with my father and stepmother. After my
father's death I lived with my grandparents until my grandfather's death. My grandfather was Elwood Comfort. Then our
Aunt Harriett took sister Frances and I, and we lived in Tecum-

seh, Michigan, for about three years. Afterwards I lived for four years at different places. Then, from Tecumseh, I went to Colorado by myself and married my husband after an acquaintance of three years."

Mr. Difford's present home is Valley Center, Sedgwick County, Kansas.

To finish a record of Mr. Comfort's family, the writer here states, that he married a third wife, Gertrude Saxon, at Dundee, Monroe County, Michigan, March 15th, 1893. By her he had two children both born at Tecumseh, Michigan, the older was born and died the same day, December 28th, 1893. The younger, Edward Emlen Comfort, was born December 18th, 1894. The mother of these children died October 1st, 1900. Her children were not descendants of the Tennant family and are only mentioned for the reason above stated.

II. LEVANTIA TENNANT, second child and first daughter of Rev. David and Olive Elizabeth Tennant was born at Springfield, Otsego County, New York, August 14th, 1816. She died in childhood and the date of her death is lost.

III. HARRIET ELIZA TENNANT was born at Springfield, New York, March 24th, 1818. She married Sylvester Covill. By him she had a son, Alfred Covill, whose family lived at Albion, New York. Mr. Covill died and his widow married J. P. Curtis in the summer of 1866. Mrs. Curtis died in December 1875.

Alfred Covill's address is Kent, Orleans County, New York.

IV. DAVID MYRON TENNANT, fourth child and youngest son of Rev. David ad Olive Elizabeth Tennant, was born at Springfield, Otsego County, New York, August 20th, 1820. He married Miss Lydia Tennant, daughter of Selden Tennant brother of Rev. David Tennant, at Springfield, New York, September 10th, 1844. Miss Lydia Tennant was born at Springfield, New York, May 22nd, 1822.

We here make a break in the family record to mention the moving of DAVID M. TENNANT and his family to Camden, Lorain County, Ohio. The writer is told that he owned a farm in Kendall, Orleans County, New York. This farm he sold to his brother-in-law, Mr. Sylvester Covill, the husband of his sister, Harriet Eliza. He gathered up all he could carry in a covered wagon and moved West. On his way he stopped over night at hotels to give his family and his team good rest. He reached Camden on the 31st of March, 1847. He and his wife, his little daughter, Mary Ann, two years old in the following October, constituted the small family group that made this journey. The writer is told that MR. TENNANT'S father did not go at this time with his son to Ohio but went a short time afterward. His uncle, Selden Tennant, and other members of his family, went to

Ohio at the same time. A sketch of this movement may be found in the history of Selden Tennant and family in this book. Other members of both families moved from New York State later to Ohio and Michigan. (See Part II Chapter 2nd).

MR. TENNANT was an industrious, well-to-do farmer. He was located in one of the rich farming sections of Ohio, Lorain County. He was a firm believer in the Christian Religion and brought up his family in the same faith, teaching them by precept and example to live virtuous lives, to attend upon public worship, and to be active and useful members of the Church and of Society. He lived on his farm in Camden township until the time of his death, which took place December 20th, 1875, being at his death 55 years and 4 months old. Thus passed from earth a noble and worthy man having run his race and finished his course, and obtained the crown of righteousness. He was buried in the beautiful cemetery of Camden Center where his beloved wife and her father and his father were buried, to await the recurrection of the just.

His beloved wife lived a widow till August 21st, 1881, when she married for her second husband Mr. William S. Furgerson, at Oberlin, Ohio. Mr. Furgerson died at Oberlin before the death of his wife, leaving her a widow for the second time. After her second marriage she lived about eleven years, and died at Oberlin, July 22nd, 1892.

> "Asleep in Jesus: blessed sleep,
> From which none ever wake to weep—
> A calm and undisturbed repose,
> Unbroken by the last of foes."

> "Asleep in Jesus! O how sweet
> To be for such a slumber meet;
> With holy confidence to sing,
> That death has lost his venomed sting."

> "Asleep in Jesus! far from thee
> Thy kindred and their graves may be;
> But thine is still a blessed sleep,
> From which none ever wakes to weep."

There were born to David Morgan and Lydia Tennant five children named Mary Ann, Alfred Myron, Eleanor Lydia, Selden David, and Hiram Adelbert, all grandchildren of Rev. David and Olive Elizabeth Tennant.

I. MARY ANN TENNANT, the oldest daughter was born at Kendall, Orleans County, N. Y., October 30th, 1845. She came with the family from Orleans County, N. Y., to Camden, Lorain County, Ohio, in the Spring of 1847. She married Orlando

MRS. MARY ANN TENNANT BUNNELL
Born October 30, 1845

Francis Bunnell at Camden, February 11th, 1866. He was born at Kirtland, Lake County, Ohio, November 17th, 1844.

After their marriage they located at Wakeman, Huron County, Ohio, where they engaged in farming for four years. From this place they moved to Linn County, Missouri, where they lived for about four years, when they came back to Ohio and settled on a farm in Willoughby, Lake County, Ohio. This was in 1875. At this place they have a farm of one hundred and eighty-three acres, on which is a pear orchard of six acres. They also own a farm of eighty acres in Chester Township, Geauga County, Ohio. They are engaged in general farming.

There were born to them two sons, Eli Granger and Charley Orlando, who are great grandchildren of Rev. David and Olive Elizabeth Tennant.

I. ELI GRANGER BUNNELL was born in Wakeman, Huron County, Ohio, August 17th, 1867. He married Miss Minnie Edna Ernst at Willoughby, Ohio, October 10th, 1888. Miss Ernst was born at Luana, Iowa, December 7th, 1869. There were born to them at Willoughby, Ohio, nine children, whose names, except the two who died in early infancy, follow: 1. Leah May, 2. Orlando Alpheus, 3. Lila May, 4. Luana Julia, 5. Lila Edna, 6. William Eli, 7. Florence Minnie.

1. LEAH MAY BUNNELL was born August 5th, 1889. She lived only one year and four months, when, on the 13th day of December, 1890, He who said "Suffer little children to come unto me and forbid them," claimed His own and took her to be with Him in His heavenly glory.

2. ORLANDO ALPHEUS BUNNELL, the oldest son, was born November 17th, 1897. He married Miss Ida Frances Wright at Willoughby, April 11th, 1912. Miss Wright was born at Perry, Lake County, Ohio, January 10th, 1892. Immediately after their marriage they started for Iowa, expecting to be gone a year before returning. He is a farmer and has talent and ambition to make success in life, in whatever business he engages.

There were born to them three children, Loyd Felix, Harland Stanley and Thomas Marvin.

1. LOYD FELIX BUNNELL was born in Decoria, Iowa, March 25th, 1913, and died at Calman, Iowa, Oct. 5th, 1913, being at his death 7 months and 12 days old.

> The Savior, on earth a sweet promise has given,
>   To parents and friends bereaved;
> When He said of the children He held in His arms,
>   "Of such is the Kingdom of Heaven."

2. HARLAND STANLEY BUNNELL was born at Eyota, Minnesota, May 16th, 1914.

3. THOMAS MARVIN BUNNELL was born at Willoughby, Ohio, June 7th, 1915.

3. LILA MAY BUNNELL was born August 5th, 1893.

4. LUANA JULIA BUNNELL was born May 25th, 1896.

5. LILA EDNA BUNNELL was born August 16th, 1902.

6. WILLIAM ELI BUNNELL was born May 31st, 1906.

7. FLORENCE MINNIE BUNNELL was born June 1st, 1908.

II. CHARLES ORLANDO BUNNELL was born December 21st, 1878. He married Miss Vernie Beatrice Saxton at Painsville Lake County, Ohio, June 15th, 1904. Miss Saxton was born July 16th, 1878.

There have been born to them at Willoughby, three children named Leslie, Howard and Rosetta.

1. LESLIE CHARLES BUNNELL was born May 11th, 1906.

2. HOWARD MELVILLE BUNNELL was born March 24th, 1908.

3. ROSETTA BUNNELL was born August 2nd, 1910.

II. ALFRED MYRON TENNANT, second child and first son of David M. and Lydia Tennant, was born in Camden, Lorain County, Ohio, March 31st, 1848. He married for his first wife Mary Jane Schafer in Camden, Ohio, October 4th, 1871. She was born in Camden, October, 1848. By her he had two children, Eva Josephine and Myron J.

The mother of these two children died at Camden, December 9th, 1878. On September 14th, 1880, at Oberlin, Ohio, Mr. Tennant married for his second wife, Miss Carrie Estella Smith, who was born in Illinois, February 14th, 1858.

There were born of this second marriage four children named Marybelle, Julia, Dorothy and Alfred.

The record of these six children here follows:

Children of the first marriage:

1. EVA JOSEPHINE TENNANT was born in Camden, Ohio, March 12th, 1875. She married Charles W. Myres at Ashland, Ohio, December 20th, 1895.

2. MYRON J. TENNANT was born in Camden, Ohio, December 2nd, 1878. He married Miss Cora Gault at Ashland, Ashland County, Ohio, January 25th, 1903.

Children of the second marriage:

3. MARYBELLE TENNANT was born at Rochester, Lorain County, Ohio, August 28th, 1883. She married Herbert Chandler Snow in Elgin, Lake County, Ohio, November 16th, 1905. Mr. Snow is the son of Chandler Snow and his wife, whose maiden name was Mary Cottrell.

He is a machinist and an automobile engineer. He was graduated from the Case School of Applied Science. Mrs. Snow is a graduate of a High School.

SELDEN DAVID TENNANT
Born October 27, 1857

There were born to Mr. and Mrs. Snow, two children named Winifred and Shirley, both born at Cleveland, Ohio.

 1. WINIFRED BELLE SNOW was born May 13th, 1907.

 2. SHIRLEY ELIZABETH SNOW was born October 13th, 1910.

 (4). ESTELLA JULIA TENNANT was born at Huntington, Ohio, July 4th, 1889. She married Henry Thomas Bostance at Cleveland, Ohio, May 19th, 1911.

 (5). DOROTHY MARGOE TENNANT was born at Ashland, Ashland County, Ohio, March 14th, 1895.

 (6). ALFRED EUGENE TENNANT was born at Ashland, Ohio, November 29th, 1900.

 III. ELEANOR LYDIA TENNANT was born at Camden, Ohio, December 20th, 1851, and died July 7th, 1858, at the age of six years, six months and seventeen days. She was the third child and second daughter of David M. and Lydia Tennant.

The taking away by death is one of the greatest mysteries of human life, and it is ten-fold mysterious when it relates to childhood. The only reasonable explanation of the mystery is, that the God who gives life has for children a higher, purer and happier life in reserve for them in the spirit world, the blessed glorious and eternal home of the soul.

 IV. SELDEN DAVID TENNANT, fourth child and second son of David M. and Lydia Tennant, was born at Camden, Ohio, February 27th, 1857. He married Anna Cudebach of Vermillion, Ohio, June 14th, 1877. She was born near Vermillion, August 9th, 1854. By her he had six children named Jessie, Nellie, Charles, Myrtle, Archie and Ray.

 1. JESSIE ASTELLA TENNANT was born at Camden, Lorain County, Ohio, May 1st, 1878. She died at Camden, Ohio, April 24th, 1879, being one year old, less by six days. She was buried in the beautiful cemetery at Camden Center.

  "And I saw the dead, small and great, stand before
  God; and the books were opened; and another book
  was opened, which is the book of life." Rev. 20:12.

 2. NELLIE ANNA TENNANT was born at Camden, Ohio, May 11th, 1880. She married Charles Orwin Raymond at Lorain, Ohio, August 7th, 1901. He was born near Cleveland, Ohio, June 4th, 1879. Mr. Raymond is foreman in the Bessemer Department of Steel Works. The present home of the family is 3105 Library Ave., Cleveland, Ohio. They have one son named Glenn, born at Lorain, Ohio, February 7th, 1904. Mrs. Raymond graduated from the Lorain, O. High school in 1898.

 3. CHARLES ADELBERT TENNANT, the third child and first son, was born in Camden, Ohio, April 22nd, 1882. He married Miss Josie Pellant of Milwaukee, Wis.

 4. MYRTLE E. TENNANT was born at Camden, Ohio, June

4th, 1886. She married Charles Willis Dunham at her father's home in Pittsburg, Pa., on April 27th, 1910.

Her father writes concerning this daughter:

"She has been my mainstay since the death of her mother. It would have nearly broken my home to let her go. However, she and her husband have been with me for the past year, 1911 or 1912."

MR. DUNHAM was born in Cleveland, Ohio, May 11th, 1883. He is an Electrical Civil Engineer.

Mr. and Mrs. Dunham have two daughters named Adah Elizabeth Dunham, born at Pittsburg, Pa., March 13th, 1911, and Ruth Myrta Dunham, born at Swissvale, Alleghany County, Pa., June 6th, 1913.

5. ARCHIE R. TENNANT was born in Lorain, Ohio, April 30th, 1889 and died Aug. 19th, 1891, being at his death 2 years, 3 months and 19 days old.

6. RAY S. TENNANT was born at Lorain, Ohio, March 31st, 1893. He is a student in the High School at Pittsburg, Pa.

MR. TENNANT'S first wife died at Lorain, Ohio, January 14th, 1899. His second marriage took place at Elyria, Ohio, December 15th, 1904. The bride was Miss Florence H. Eldred, who was born in Elyria, Ohio, August 12th, 1867.

Immediately after their marriage they moved to Pittsburg, Pa., Mr. Tennant's business was located there.

In a few days less than a year and two months, the second wife died, February 21st, 1906, of pneumonia, surviving less than three days after the attack. By her he had no children.

In the year 1913 the author and his wife enjoyed a pleasant visit with this cousin at their home in Silver Creek, N. Y.

Mr. Tennant writes the author his business career as follows:

"In former years I worked at my trade, cabinet work, on the Cleveland, Lorain and Wheeling Railway, now a part of the Baltimore & Ohio System. I left them and followed for sometime the inspecting of new material and equipment, leaving this for the Superintendency of the Pittsburgh Coal Company. For the last two years (1912 and 1913) I have been foreman of the Planing Mill for the Pittsburgh and Lake Erie Railroad Company, which is part of the New York Central System."

IV. HIRAM ADELBERT TENNANT, the youngest child and third son of David M. and Lydia Tennant, was born at Camden, Ohio, May 25th, 1861. He married Mary J. Short of Huntington, Ohio, September 1st, 1886. By her he had four children, Floyd, Adelbert, Jenness Emily, Bernice Wilberta, and Levantia Grace; all born at Elyria, Lake County, Ohio.

1. FLOYD ADELBERT TENNANT was born June 13th, 1887.

He married Miss Mabel Hardy Wilson of Crown Point, Indiana, at Deadwood, South Dakota, July 1st, 1911. He is a civil engineer and draftsman in the employ of C. W. Haux & Co., of Sioux City, Iowa, who are builders and contractors. They have one daughter named Florence May Tennant, born at Sioux City, Iowa, August 28th, 1912.

2. JENNESS EMILY TENNANT was born May 27th, 1890. She died August 6th, 1890, aged two months and nine days.

3. BERNICE WILBERTA TENNANT was born October 13th, . 1894. At this date, 1912, she is attending the High School at Elyria, Ohio, intending to continue her studies till graduated.

4. LEVANTA GRACE TENNANT, the youngest child, was born February 9th, 1897. She also is in attendance at the High School of her native city hoping to be able to be graduated.

The above record of Rev. David and Olive Elizabeth Tennant contains a full statement of all their descendants with a few exceptions of amilies whose childrens' names the writer could not obtain. Ie records their descendants as follows.

Children 4
Grandchildren 9
Great-grandchildren 25
Great-great-grandchildren 30
                                              ——
Total 68

These include four generations, and with the parents and grandparents six generations.

PART THIRD

SARAH SELDEN JEWETT

AND HER

DESCENDANTS

By Her 1st, 2nd and 3rd Marriage.

Sarah Baker, Deborah Shaw, Lucy Tennant,
Olivia Tennant, Moses Asel Tennant,
Esther Tennant.

PART III.

Chapter I.

"There is a divinity that shapes our ends,
Rough-hew them how we may."
                              —Shakespeare.

"The lot is cast into the lap, but the whole disposal thereof is of the Lord." Solomon in Proverbs 16:33.

MISS SARAH SELDEN JEWETT.

Her Ancestry, Birth and Early Marriage—Her Separation from her first husband—Her long journey through forest—Her residence in Springfield, Otsego Co., N. Y.—Her struggle for maintenance—Her second and third Marriage—Her numerous family—Her move to Chautauqua County, N. Y.—Her great Industry—Her personal character—Her sickness, death and burial.

———

IN Part I the first chapter we gave a brief account of John Tennant and his wife Elizabeth Loomis and her ancestors and brothers and sisters. John Tennant, father of Delinda Tennant, was related by birth to Deacon Moses Tennant father of Moses Asel Tennant. This relationship is explained in a letter to the author from Willis H. Tennant of Buffalo, N. Y. This letter may be found in Part V, Article 1st of this book. The letter, as will be seen, reveals Alexander Tennant of Rhode Island as the grandfather of Deacon Moses Tennant and John Tennant. The author has heard his father and mother say that they possibly might be second or third cousins.

We have now to sketch the history of one whose life extends back to the 18th century and whose ancestors are lost in the shadows of the past but whose descendants, living and dead, extend through many branches and several generations till the increase has become very numerous and widespread in different localities in this country.

SARAH SELDEN JEWETT was born in the State of Connecticut April 24, 1763. The place of her birth cannot be fully determined at this late date. This is known, that her early home was near the banks of the Connecticut river. In later years she told of her father swimming with her on his back across this river. It is a strange fact, that the writer is unable to obtain any account of her father or mother save that her father's surname was

Jewett. Her mother's maiden name is lost to the family. It is greatly to be regretted that no family record has preserved the parental names of her who has so many descendants.

Miss Sarah Jewett's early education was limited to the common school of her day. Yet she had, by nature, a bright mind that readily gathered information from the ordinary contact with the world of mankind, from a close observation of current events, and from the open book of nature which was always before her.

At the age of sixteen, in the year 1779, she married Nathaniel Baker. The date of her marriage is taken from the Tennant family Bible. The place of her marriage was probably the place of her birth.

There was born to them a daughter whom they named Sarah. The place and date of her birth is lost. It is only known that she was born in Connecticut. She married a Mr. Whipple whose given name is lost. By him she had one child, a son, named Timothy Whipple. He worked on the Erie Canal and spent his winters when the canal was closed, with his uncle, Moses Asel Tennant, first in Springfield, N. Y., and afterwards in Ripley, Chautauqua Co., N. Y., where he died and was buried in a new cemetery, started in a pasture land on the farm of Mr. Parker in Ripley. The date of his death and the spot where he was buried is lost. The writer remembers this cousin very well. He was a kind-hearted young man, was never married, and lived a quiet, industrious, sober life. He used to take the writer, when he was a small boy, for a ride on his back to the neighbors.

Now we have to relate an event in the life of Mrs. Sarah Jewett Baker that brought a flood of sorrow to her young heart. While her daughter Sarah was a young child, Mrs. Baker caught her husband making counterfeit money. Living as she had during the period of the Revolutionary War, and having her young heart instilled with sentiments of true loyalty to the government under which she lived, her husband's violation of the laws of the land to enrich himself with ill-gotten gain, stirred her to administer to him a severe rebuke. She threatened to expose him if he did not stop the illegal business. At this, her husband took offence and fright, and fled. She saw nothing of him for some time. At last she received a letter from him written in New York State. He wrote her to sell all the household goods and come to him, and they would begin life over again. This she did, reserving a bed and some cooking utensils. She hired a man and team with a lumber wagon, and started through the wilderness, expecting in a few weeks to be reunited to her husband. When she finally reached the place where she expected to meet him, behold, he had fled again, and she never saw him afterwards.

It is easy to relate such a sad story, but what young girl would care to have such an experience? All this occurred in the first years of Mrs. Baker's married life. She probably was under twenty years of age. She was left with a young child, homeless and without money. She gave the man she hired for his services, her feather bed and a few other articles. Left among strangers, what could she do? She must work for her living or beg. To beg she was too proud and independent. Whether, just at this extremity in her life, she learned the weaver's trade, the writer does not know, but he does know, that she became an expert with the loom and the shuttle and wove most beautiful fabrics of woolen and linen goods. Some of the checkered blue and white woolen coverlids of her weaving are now in the possession of her grand-children; also beautiful linen table cloths.

The place to which MRS. BAKER went to be reunited with her husband is not known. This is known, that she came to New York State. After this desertion a few years of her life is shrouded in such obscurity that the writer can only surmise her movements. It would be most natural, she being a young girl, to decide to return to the place of her birth and first marriage in Connecticut. This she could have done, but the man she hired refused to allow her to return with him, possibly because she had no money to reward him. This fact she related long afterwards to her youngest daughter Esther.

MRS. BAKER'S movements are now lost in absolute obscurity. What she did for a livelihood, to what place did she go, can only be inferred by the known events of her future life. We have no right to write history that has no foundation in real facts. But the events which are known to have taken place in Mrs. Baker's life, lead to the conclusion, that soon after her first husband deserted her, by some unknown means she found her way to Springfield, Otsego Co., N. Y. It is known that she married for a second husband Isaac Shaw, a man of good repute, by whom she had one daughter named Deborah Shaw. This daughter married Calvin Gibbs, by whom she had several children. It is not known where or when this marriage took place but the history of the Gibbs family traces their residence to Otsego Co., N. Y., and it is probable that the marriage of Mrs. Baker and Isaac Shaw took place in Otsego Co. and that their daughter Deborah was born and married in this County.

We have now to record the death of Sarah Selden Jewett's second husband, ISAAC SHAW. The time of his death nor the place cannot be learned by the writer. He believes it must have been in Otsego County, N. Y., and not many years after his marriage to Mrs. Baker. At the time of her third marriage to Moses Tennant she was about thirty years of age. She had passed through about fourteen years of her life at the time of this third marriage, since her first marriage to Nathaniel Baker in 1779. The struggles and trials through which she had passed, the sorrows which had overwhelmed her, were sufficient to crush her spirits and render her unable to enter upon her life work with any great pleasure or satisfaction. From early years, she had possessed a firm christian faith, and had learned to lean upon the strong arm of her Divine Guide and Protector. There can be no doubt, that it was this faith in God her Savior, that supported her through these years of disappointment and trial.

We come now to the third period of Sarah Selden Jewett's life. In many respects this was the most remarkable period of her life.

In the year 1793 at Springfield, Otsego Co., N. Y., she married Moses Tennant, then a widower with four children. She was now about thirty years of age. The writer has been reliably informed by a grand-daughter of this third marriage (Miss Ellen Hollenbeck) that Mrs. SHAW, then a widow, went into the family of Mr. Tennant, where four young children, Selden, Betsy, Polly and David had been left motherless by the death of Mrs. Tennant, their mother. There is much obscurity concerning the maiden name of this mother. By correspondence with some of the older members of the Baptist Church of Springfield, N. Y., the writer has been told that her name was Betsey Tennant before her marriage to Mr. Tennant. If this be true, she named her first born daughter after herself, Betsey Tennant. This is so natural and probable, that the writer has assumed it to be true in all future reference to her. But the date of her birth, marriage and death is still left in obscurity. This grandmother to a large number of descendants, through these four children above named has no known record preserved of her ancestors, of her early life and home. Gladly would the writer tell her life history if it could be dug out of the annals of the past. Such obscurity of family records is greatly to be regretted and deplored. From what is known of her descendants, and of the noble and worthy character of her husband, we may justly infer that she was of that noble stock of New England women, for she was doubtless born in Connecticut, which were an honor to their country in that they had high ideals of life, were true to their marriage vows, honored motherhood, stood for the right in the perilous periods of their country's history, and who co-operated in every wise movement for the improvement of society, for the growth of the Christian church, and for the education of their own children and the youth of the land.

The probabilities are that she died and was buried in the cemetery at Springfield, Otsego Co., N. Y. Her husband, Moses Tennant, was an honored member of the Baptist church of Springfield and served as deacon of the church for a number of years to the day of his death.

It was in Mr. Tennant's home life that he made the acquaintance of Mrs. Shaw, as he had engaged her as housekeeper and foster mother to his children, after their own mother's death. This close acquaintance lead to their marriage.

In the Moses Asel Tennant family Bible the date of this marriage is recorded as 1791, the day and the month is not given. The writer is inclined to believe this date is incorrect, that it could not have been earlier than 1793. The youngest child of Moses Tennant by his first wife, Betsey Tenant, was his son, David, born January 4, 1792. This date we must believe is reliable as it is taken from records, the correctness of which cannot be reasonably disputed. It is evident that the father did not marry the second wife before the birth of his son David. We conclude that the date of the marriage of Moses Tennant and Mrs. Shaw cannot well be placed earlier than 1793.

As an aid to determine the date of their marriage the writer has had reported to him by one of the older members of the Baptist church of Springfield, N. Y., that the church record reads that Deacon Moses Tennant and Sarah Selden Tennant were received into the membership of the church Oct. 18th, 1795. She was certainly married to Mr. Tennant before this date, as she now bears the name Tennant. Of this marriage the first child born was Lucy Tennant, born June 7th, 1794, who became the wife of John Champion in subsequent years. All these dates, and the facts associated with them, show conclusively that Lucy Tennant was not born at Lyme, New Bedfordshire Co., Conn,. but at Springfield, Otsego Co., N. Y.

As SARAH SELDEN JEWETT was born April 24, 1763, she was one month and 13 days past 31 years of age at the birth of her daughter Lucy. She was now in the prime of young womanhood. Thirteen years had intervened between her first and third marriage; from 1779 to 1792. Her two daughters, Sarah Baker and Deborah Shaw, were certainly less than thirteen years of age—Deborah much less than thirteen. The writer does not know whether those two children of her first and second marriage were taken into the family with the four step-children Selden, Betsey, Polly and David. It is not improbable they were. The writer has no information that any of these six children, at these early years of their lives, were placed in other homes, and so without the loving care of parents in their tender years. Six children did not make a large family. As both parents were christians and members of the Baptist church of Springfield, N. Y., without positive knowledge it is reasonable to suppose that Mr. and Mrs. Tennant kept their children together under the same roof, to eat at the same table, to attend together the same school, and to attend the same church. Selden, the oldest son, was born as will be seen Sept. 22, 1787, and was less than eight years old at the time of his father's marriage to Mrs. Shaw, so there were six young children, the oldest only about thirteen years of age. But the parents were in the prime of life, and six young children only made them a nice little family to care for and educate. We must believe that these children were brought up in the "nurture and admonition of the Lord." After a time passed Deborah Shaw was taken into a family by the name of Comstock. With this family she had a home till the time of her marriage.

In the natural course of events there came other children by birth to this family. Between the years 1794 and 1804 four children were born to Mr. and Mrs. Moses Tennant, Sr. Their names we give in the order of their ages. Lucy, Olivia, Moses Asel and Esther. Each of these children married and had a large number of descendants. Also the six children above mentioned, of their parents first marriages, married and had a numerous prosterity. All these ten children and their descendants, will furnish a large portion of the interesting facts recorded in this Tennant Genealogy.

When the above mentioned children grew into manhood and womanhood, marriages and separations commenced. Some of the older and first married, took to their homes some of the younger and unmarried members of the family. This would be a very natural occurrence in a family of ten children, especially after the death of their father.

DEACON MOSES TENNANT died at Springfield, N. Y., and was buried in the Village cemetery. The exact date of his death is lost but it probably occurred either in 1807 or 1808 as shown by the records of the Baptist church of Springfield as hereafter quoted. Fixing the date of his marriage to Mrs. Shaw in 1792 and their married life must have continued through eleven years or more. Mrs. Tennant's daughters, Sarah Baker and Deborah Shaw, would have reached a marriageable age somewhere between the ages of 18 and 24 years.

In a centennial history of the Baptist Church of Springfield, N. Y., published in the Freedmen's Journal of Cooperstown, N. Y., in the issue of June 24, 1887, there is found a list of the deacons of the church that served during the 1st century of her history. Among them is found the name of Moses Tennant whose appointment was made in 1796. In subsequent years his son, Moses Asel was elected deacon of the Baptist church of Ripley, Chautauqua Co., N. Y.

The records of the Baptist Church of Springfield state, that at a meeting of the church held on the 12th of Feb. 1807, deacon Moses Tennant was appointed on a committee. This is the last mention of his name in the records. At a meeting of the church held June 25th, 1808, Moses Franklin was chosen deacon to succeed Deacon Tennant. We cannot doubt that Moses Tennant died sometime between these two dates above given. It is exceedingly interesting to be able to determine so nearly the date of the death of this grand-father of the descendants of Selden, Betsey, Polly, David, Lucy, Olivia, Moses Asel and Esther Tennant, whose children and grand-children, and great grand children can only be enumerated by hundreds. Fixing the date of his death in 1808 between January and June, and the youngest daughter, Esther, would be about four years of age at her father's death.

SARAH SELDEN JEWETT's fourth marriage was to Daniel Morse. When and where this marriage took place we are not informed; it was doubtless at Springfield, N. Y. and he died and was buried at the same place. According to the records of the Baptist church his death was in 1831. We are informed that Mr. Morse was a worthy Christian man and held the office of Clerk in the Baptist church of Springfield, elected in 1812. By this marriage there were no children.

It is but truthful for the writer to say that although his grandmother was known and called by the name "Moss," her 4th husband's real name was "Morse" and not "Moss." As evidence of this, the writer wrote to the Clerk of the Baptist Church of Springfield to inquire if the names of Daniel Morse and Sarah Selden Jewett were entered on the church record as husband and wife. The reply was in the affirmitive. Another evidence is that the granite marker set at her grave in Ripley cemetery bears the name "Morse" and not "Moss." This testimony to the name of our grand-mother's 4th and last husband must be accepted by the writer as conclusive and final.

Time passes away and many changes came into the life of our "grandmother Morse." All of her children were married, and she was left a widow without a home of her own or means for her own support save the labor of her own hands. By an arrangement mutually agreed upon between her son, Moses Asel and his sisters, she was to have a home with him and his family. Time went on, and the son thought best to change his place of residence. Just at this time emigration was following the "star of Empire" in its westward movement. Western New York, northern Pennsylvania, Ohio, Indiana, Illinois and Michigan were being rapidly settled by eastern people. In the Spring of 1833 about the first of May, the son Moses, decided to move westward. The family, including the six oldest children, the mother and grandmother Morse came on the Erie Canal as far as Buffalo,

N. Y. The son had gone on before them to make arrangements for their coming. The family came on the Erie Canal to Buffalo. At Buffalo they took a small two-masted schooner called "The Red Rover" for a voyage up Lake Erie to a small lake port called Barcelona, the only landing place in Chautauqua County west of Dunkirk. When the vessel reached a point opposite Dunkirk, the wind had risen into a furious gale. The captain dare not atempt to land at Dunkirk, as the harbor at that time was unprotected by an adequate break-water, and so was Barcelona. So he cast anchor, and the little vessel rocked all night long on the angry waves while the wind howled about her in mad fury. At day-dawn the wind moderated, the captain set sail, and in a few hours they landed at Barcelona. The family was taken in a farmer's lumber wagon with all their household goods to Ripley, Chautauqua County, N. Y.

From the time of the settlement of her son, Moses Asel and his family at Ripley, the mother followed and shared the fortunes of her son. She was known and called by the entire family as "Grandmother Moss," but her true name was Morse. As long as she could work with her loom and shuttle, she helped much in the clothing and support of the family. She was an ambitious worker, and never gave herself a vacation for rest. This activity continued unabating until she was far along in old age. She was small and slight of stature and weight and it was marvelous how much work she could endure. She never cared to talk much about her past experience. Her life record was concealed in her own heart; her trials and sorrows were buried there.

During this period of her life, she took a trip to Michigan to see her daughters. She doubtless enjoyed this visit but she was so restless for work that one of the daughters bought a loom for her that she might be more contented and remain longer on her visit. The writer has been told that she said to her youngest daughter Esther. Mrs. David Hollenbeck, *"It seems to me Esther, that I have shed barrels of tears."* It seems that she suppressed her sorrows by hard work. Yet these words reveal the depths of her heart, as she looked backward over the past, and reviewed the changing scenes and experiences through which she had lived.

That she was not crushed under life's burdens and sorrows, must be credited to her strong and unwavering christian faith. At what time in life she became a christian, and united with the Baptist Church, is unknown to the writer. He only knows that she was a member of the Baptist Church of Springfield and of Ripley, N. Y. She was always a regular attendant upon church service. She had a strong motherly love for her children and grand-children. She was ever especially anxious about her grand-son Timothy Whipple, the son of her daughter Sarah Baker. In her advancing years, she did not forget the daughter of her first marriage and her son. This accounts in part, for Timothy Whipple spending his winters when the Erie Canal was closed, with his uncle Moses and his grand-mother.

From 1833 in the Springtime to 1852 in the summer time, nineteen years intervened, during which grand-mother Morse spent her advancing years with her son Moses Asel and his family. On the 24th of April, 1833, the year the family moved to Ripley, she was seventy years old. Long after she was eighty years old she continued her weaving. But age will bring its final results in every human life. In the Spring of 1852 her son sold his hill farm and bought a farm in East Ripley Village. On to this farm the family moved that same Spring. Grandmother Morse was now feeble in mind and body. The writer remembers how she was carried on a feather bed from Ripley Hill to this new home. Up to this time she had no disease that required a physician's treatment. Old age alone had seized upon her physical and mental powers, till there was but the slightest manifestation of life and intelligence left. For some days just before her death, she called her son, Moses by name almost constantly. At last the end came, and on the 13th of July, 1852, the Angel of Life drew near and transported her spirit to the realms of immortality and eternal life. She was 89 years, 2 months and 19 days old at her death.

Her restful body was buried in the beautiful Ripley Cemetery on the Tennant lot where her son and his sons caused to be erected a monument of Scotch marble, beneath the shadow of which lies the mortal remains of a faithful wife, a loving mother, a patriotic citizen and a true and loyal christian.

A MEMORIAL POEM

By Her Grand-son.

Rest weary soul, life's battle is fought,
  You have done what you could to make it successful;
The fruits you have borne are certainly great;
  On the bosom of Love you repose calm and restful.

Sad disappointments have troubled your heart;
  Holy ties have been broken you could not fortell;
Yet, true to yourself, your God and your country,
  You stood for the right whatever befell.

The weeds of widowhood oft hung on your brow;
  The sorrows of bereavement flooded your heart;
But a Hand Divine has guided you on
  And brought you new joys as the old ones depart.

When childhood and infancy called for your help,
  You offered them then a true mother's care;
You sat by the cradle and rocked them to sleep
  While angels about them your vigilance shared.

A numerous posterity you left here on earth;
  How little they know what your life-work has been;
But your life has given their lives to them,
  In a line of descendants that seems not to end.

When the cycles of time have finished their rounds,
  And the earth and the sea shall give up their dead;
Then in joyful reunion in God's kingdom above,
  With crowns of bright glory adorning their heads,
The mother and grand-mother will sing the New Song,
  And the host of her children will be part of the throng.

PART III.

CHAPTER II.

This chapter in two Sections, contains a record of the birth, marriage and death of SARAH BAKER, the only child of Sarah Selden Jewett by her first husband, Nathaniel Baker, and a sketch of the life of Timothy Whipple, her only son. Also a record of the birth, marriage and death of Deborah Shaw, the only child of Sarah Selden Jewett by her second husband, Isaac Shaw, and her descendants.

SECTION I.
MISS SARAH BAKER.

WE have already given in the preceding Chapter a history of the marriage of MISS SARAH SELDEN JEWETT to Nathaniel Baker and their unhappy separation. The place in the State of Connecticut of this marriage is not given in any family record, but the date of the marriage as given in the Tennant family Bible is 1779. As MISS JEWETT was born April 24th, 1763, she was about sixteen years of age at the time of her first marriage. How soon after her marriage her daughter Sarah was born in unknown, hence her birthday is lost to the family. However, it is known that she was born in Connecticut, and that her birth took place before her father and mother separated. Hence she was with her mother on that long journey to New York State, and subsequently to Otsego County, N. Y. It has already been stated in the previous Chapter, that Sarah was living at the time of her mother's second marriage to Isaac Shaw, and also at the time of her mother's third marriage to Moses Tennant in 1791. Her mother, as before stated, was about thirty years of age at the time of her marriage to Moses Tennant. Her daughter, Sarah, was about thirteen years of age at this time. She was doubtless with her mother till the time of her marriage.

SARAH BAKER married a Mr. Whipple, whose given name is not known by the writer. As she and her mother resided at Springfield, Otsego County, N. Y., her marriage doubtless occurred at that place, but the date of the marriage is lost.

TIMOTHY WHIPPLE.

There was born to Mr. and Mrs. Whipple a son they named TIMOTHY WHIPPLE. The place of his birth was doubtless

Springfield, N. Y., but the date of his birth is not known by the writer.

After her marriage and the birth of her son Timothy, the record of her life and death, and that of her husband, is buried in obscurity—no records having been kept. It is known that both his father and mother were dead when Timothy used to visit his Grandmother and his Uncle Moses at Ripley, N. Y. He was a young man at this time, was unmarried, and was employed on the Erie Canal. The writer well remembers of his cousin Tim taking him on to his shoulder and carried him to one of the neighbors. I was but a small boy about three or four years old. After his parents' death, he never had a home only as he visited his grandmother Morse and his Uncle Moses, and he was always welcomed by this Uncle and the entire family on these winter visits. He was the fourteenth member of the family one winter. There were the parents, nine children, and our father's mother and our mother's father and Timothy. There was a garret in the log house, two rooms below, and two rooms in the framed lean-to. Some way, unknown to the writer, we all had plenty to eat and a place to sleep.

But Cousin Timothy visited us for the last time. He had quick consumption and came to his Uncle Moses' home to live for a short time and to die. Strange to say the date of his death is lost as it was never recorded. He was buried in a new burial ground started on the farm of Gamaiel Parker on East Ripley Hill. This ground was afterwards abandoned as a Cemetery, was ploughed over, and the place of Cousin Timothy's grave was lost. A diligent search was made by his Uncle Moses but it could not be found.

The reader of this story of the life of TIMOTHY WHIPPLE, should remember that he was the son of the first child of Sarah Selden Jewett, whose numerous posterity is recorded in this Genealogy. It gives the writer a feeling of deep regret and sadness that the story is wanting in so many of its parts to make it complete. The history of all families should be recorded with current events, before the facts are lost from the memory of the living.

COUSIN TIMOTHY.

A MEMORIAL TRIBUTE.

Dear Cousin "Tim" you rest all alone,
In a grave long deserted, and now is unknown;
No monument marks the place where you sleep,
But angels above you, their vigilance keep.

Few comforts of home you had in your life;
Alone you wandered, no children, no wife;
Still, your heart was most happy and calm all your days,
For Nature had touched you with her brightest rays.

At some future time happy spirits will meet,
In that far away home, each other to greet;
Then mother and grandmother, long since gone to rest,
Will welcome their son in that land of the blest.

Sweet peace to your soul, is our humble prayer,
While joys most celestial in heaven you share;
The dark nights of earth have all passed away,
And the dawn has arisen of an Eternal day.

SECTION II.
MISS DEBORAH SHAW.

DEBORAH SHAW was the daughter of Sarah Selden Jewett by her second husband, Isaac Shaw. She was born in Springfield, Otsego County, N. Y., in the year 1788, the day and month is not known by the writer.

She married Calvin Gibbs, but the place and date of this marriage is not known with certainty by the writer, but the place was doubtless Springfield, N. Y. Mr. Gibbs was a native of New York State, but the exact place and date of his birth has not been given to the writer.

The early home of MRS. GIBBS was in Otsego County, N. Y. This was the home of her childhood. Either before or soon after the marriage of her mother to Moses Tennant, she was taken into the home of a family by the name of Comstock. She may have remained in this home till her marriage. In the preceding Chapter of this Third Part, will be found a reference to her childhood. She received a common school education, became in early life a member of the Baptist Church of Springfield, and maintained a church relationship during her entire life.

The residence of Mr. and Mrs. Gibbs continued in Springfield for a number of years, a period extending from the time of their marriage to their settlement in Michigan, probably in October 1821. This movement took place soon after the marriage of Esther Tennant, her half-sister, and David Hollenbeck on September 2nd, 1821. The writer understands that Mr. and Mrs. Gibbs and Mr. and Mrs. William Phillips went at the same time to Michigan from New York State. Mr. Gibbs ultimately settled upon a farm in Troy Township, Oakland County, Michigan, located east of Pontiac. Here they lived up to the time of the death of Mr. Gibbs. The date of his death has never been reported to the writer, but it was before 1835.

The David Hollenbeck family, in the year 1830, moved from Otsego County, N. Y., to Michigan, and settled on a rented farm in Troy Township, Oakland County, locating east of Pontiac. Here they were near neighbors to MRS. DEBORAH (SHAW) GIBBS, then a widow. This was between the years 1830 and 1835. The probabilities are that Mr. Gibbs' death took place during this period or at some earlier date.

After Mr. Gibbs' death, misfortune befell the family, till all their property was swept away. As she was a very industrious woman she was able to obtain a fair livelihood by weaving, knitting and sewing. In a few years after the death of her first husband she married the second time. Her second husband's name was Calvin Marvin. Before this event, some of her children were married and had established homes of their own.

Before finishing the story of MRS. MARVIN'S life, we give the record of her family.

Descendants of DEBORAH SHAW by her first marriage.

There were born to Calvin and Deborah Shaw Gibbs the following children named: Orton, Charlotte, Clarissa, Graham, Eliza, Julia, Monroe, and a daughter whose name has not been given. The places and dates of the births of these eight children can only be determined approximately. The fact that Mrs. Shaw was left a widow as early as 1835 shows that all the older children were born in New York State, before the family moved to Michigan. Some of the younger children may have been born in Michigan. Of these children the writer relates only what has been reported to him.

I.   ORTON GIBBS married a daughter of Deacon Henry Jones. At this time, the Hollenbeck family lived on a farm owned by Avery Jones, a brother of Henry. Mrs. Gibbs was a frequent visitor to the Hollenbeck family home during this period.

II.   CHARLOTTE GIBBS married Johnathan Greene, a cabinet maker, and a farmer. They had a son who died in his youth. They also had a daughter whose name was Zipha. She married Mr. Barnes, a grandson of Calvin Barnes, whom her mother, Mrs. Greene, married as her second husband. Thus Charlotte's mother becomes her grandmother by marriage.

III.   There was another daughter of Mrs. Gibbs who lived and died unmarried. Her name is unknown to the writer.

IV.   CLARISSA GIBBS, the fourth child and third daughter, married Austin Jones, son of Avery Jones, a farmer. About 1894 the family resided at Fenton, Michigan. MRS. JONES lived with the Hollenbeck family for a while, during which her first child, Euseba, was born. Eliza Jones, another daughter married a Mr. McIntyre. She lived with her uncle Graham for a few years before marriage. MRS. AUSTIN JONES had a large family of whom but little is known by other relatives.

V. GRAHAM GIBBS, the fifth child and second son of Calvin and Deborah Shaw Gibbs, was born in Herkimer County, N. Y., but the date of his birth has not been reported. His birth in Herkimer County, shows that his father's family may not have lived continuously in Otsego County. It may be that this child was born while the mother was on a temporary visit to Herkimer. He came with his parents to Oakland County, Michigan. He married a daughter of Alvin and Minerva (Phelps) Louis. Her family were of Scotch descent and she was one of seven children.

There were born to Mr. and Mrs. Gibbs, two children, named Charles and Emma.

1. CHARLES GIBBS was born in Avon Township, Oakland County, Michigan, June 6th, 1848. He married Miss Eva L. Davis near Auburn, Oakland County, Michigan, July 4th, 1868. Miss Davis was born at Avon, Michigan, August 29th, 1852. She was the daughter of Harry and Elizabeth (Swan) Davis, who were natives of New York State.

There were born to Charles and Eva (Davis) Gibbs four children named Eddie, Harry, Minerva and Amelia.

1. EDDIE CHARLES GIBBS, son of Charles and Eva (Davis) Gibbs, was born May 23rd, 1869. He married Miss Ann Welch, September 9th, 1903. Miss Welch was the daughter of Frank and Alma (Everitt) Welch, born at Lafyette, Gratiot County, Michigan, January 29th, 1881.

There were born to Mr. and Mrs. Gibbs four children named Robert, Alma, Alice and Charles.

1. ROBERT EVERITT GIBBS was born at Deerfield, Livingston County, Michigan, July 10th, 1904.

2. ALMA AMELIA GIBBS was born at Deerfield, Michigan, January 13th, 1906, and died at Lavfette, Michigan, October 27th, 1908, aged two years, nine months and fourteen days.

3. ALICE AVALINA GIBBS was born at Byron, Shiawassee County, Michigan, November 30th, 1907.

4. CHARLES HENRY GIBBS was born at Pontiac, Oakland County, Michigan, April 4th, 1911.

2. HARRY GIBBS, second child and second son of Charles and Eva (Davis) Gibbs was born June 6th, 1870. He married and there was born to him and his wife a son named Harry J. Gibbs, who was born at Oklahoma. The writer could not obtain Mrs. Gibbs' maiden name.

3. EMMA MINERVA GIBBS, third child and first daughter of Charles and Eva (Davis) Gibbs, was born in Avon, Oakland County, Michigan, March 5th, 1872. She died at Deerfield, Livingston County, Michigan, December 19th, 1891, being at her death aged eighteen years, nine months and fourteen days.

4. Amelia Maria Gibbs, fourth child and second daughter of Charles and Eva (Davis) Gibbs, was born at Avon, Oakland County, Michigan, July 24th, 1873. She married Oscar Julius Lare at Howell, Livingston County, Michigan, August 25th, 1893. Mr. Lare was born in Osceola, Livingston County, Michigan, April 10th, 1870. He was the son of Adam Lare and his wife, Mary Cornelius (Batchelor) Lare.

There were born to them seven children named Alice, Horatio, Paul, Howard, Charles, Gladys and Ruby, all born in Deerfield Township, Livingston County, Michigan.

1. Alice Mae Lare was born May 25th, 1895.
2. Horatio Roy Lare was born August 17th, 1897.
3. Paul Lare was born December, 1898.
4. Howard W. Lare was born November 13th, 1900.
5. Charles Graham Lare was born November 16th, 1903.
6. Gladys Viola Lare was born August 15th, 1905.
7. Ruby Irene Lare was born February 21st, 1908.

This finishes the record of the descendants of Graham Gibbs.

VI. Eliza Gibbs, the sixth child and third daughter of Calvin and Deborah (Shaw) Gibbs, married a Mr. Leonard of Sheewassee County, Michigan. No further report of Mrs. Leonard and her family has been received.

VII. Julia Gibbs, seventh child and fourth daughter of Calvin and Deborah (Shaw) Gibbs, married Johnathan Gould. No further report has been received.

VIII. Monroe Gibbs, the eighth child and third son of Calvin Gibbs and Deborah (Shaw) Gibbs, has been unknown to the family for many years. This is the only report the author has received of this son.

We resume the life story of Miss Shaw, now Mrs. Marvin. We have spoken of her efforts to support herself by such work as she could obtain and was able to do. Finally, as has been already stated, she married a Mr. Marvin, a farmer in Troy, Michigan. Hoping to better their circumstances they moved to what was then known as "The Grand River Country," a wilderness, but the promised land for the poor. There they remained till their extreme poverty compelled a change. Mrs. Marvin came back to Pontiac, Michigan. Later her husband followed till he reached Birmingham, Michigan. Here he was taken ill, sent word to his faithful wife, who immediately answered his call; but when she reached Birmingham, she found her husband had passed away over the Jordon of death into the promised land. After this, Mrs. Marvin twice widowed, was homeless. She lived here and there, supporting herself by weaving, knitting, piecing quilts and such work as she could find to do. She was left with one son by Mr. Marvin, whose name was John Marvin. He died when he was but seven years old in the Grand River Country. She finally went to her son Graham Gibbs, expecting to spend the rest of her life, but this hope was blasted.   Her last visit to the Hollenbeck home was in the year 1871.   Her daughter Charlotte, Mrs. Greene, moved to St. Johns, Michigan.   Here her mother found an asylum during the last years of her life, and here she died in old age after many changes and misfortunes. The date of her death is not known to the writer.

The author regrets that he has been unable to make the history of the descendants of Mrs. DEBORAH SHAW GIBBS complete in all its parts.   Time obliterates so much of history from the memory of the living descendants, that it is no wonder that events cannot be recalled from which a connected family history could be written.   It should not be forgotten, that MISS DEBORAH SHAW was a daughter of Sarah Selden Jewett by her second husband, Isaac Shaw.   These descendants herein mentioned add a considerable list to those who were Miss Jewett's children and grandchildren by her third husband as recorded in the following Chapter of Part III.

The descendants of DEBORAH SHAW and Calvin Gibbs number as follows:

Children 7
Grand-children 6
Great-grand-children 4
Great-great-grand-children 12
By second husband, Mr. Marvin 1
                                               ——
    Total 30

TIME'S RECORDS.

The records of Time may all fade away,
Like the mists of the morning at the break of the day;
But eternal realities will surely abide,
They sternly resist Time's devastating tide.
How wise then to lay up our treasures above,
Where they can't be destroyed by fire or flood;
Where rust corrupts not and thieves cannot steal,
And rob us of life's most precious weal.
Friends come and go, they pass like the wind,
That blows fair and soft, congenial and kind;
But no sooner do they come than they pass us away,
Leaving hearts sad and broken, on earth still to stay.
Can we hope for reunions on the heavenly shore,
Where the changes of Time can reach us no more?
Will families unbroken be there gathered in,

Free from all sorrow and trouble and sin?
Yes! the promise of God is sealed by the blood
Of our Gracious Redeemer, who is now gone above;
He rose from the dead and ascended on high,
To give us the pledge that we never shall die,
But rise with Him to the life He gave,
A victory complete over death and the grave.
Let us then journey on to the end of the race,
Till we meet one another, face to face;
With fathers, mothers, dear sisters and brothers
To join in that chorus with thousands of others,
In ascribing to Jesus dominion and power,
Who saves us from death in death's trying hour.

JOHN CHAMPION
Born July 12, 1788.   Died at Los Angeles, Cal., January 4, 1853.

MRS. LUCY TENNANT CHAMPION

Born June 7, 1794   Died November 8, 1822

PART III.

CHAPTER THREE.

This Chapter contains a record of the birth, marriage, death and burial of Lucy Selden Tennant, oldest child of Moses Tennant, Sr., and his second wife, Sarah Selden Jewett, and wife of John Champion; her family emigrated from New York state to Michigan; Mr. Champion's journey to California and his death and burial at San Francisco, together with the genealogy of their descendants by family names: Champion, Beals, Clark, Holden, McKay, Pratt, Loomis, Morean, Shultz, Hewes, Harding, Wilcox, Graves, Potter, Tiffany, VanEvera, Wallace, Carlton, Stephens, Welch, Cooper, Champion, Stanley, Colvin, Clark, Kahle, Loar, Crockett, Petee, Vrooman, Rogers, Frisbee, Hopkins, Smith, Rice, Clough, Wilcox, Kimball and Scott.

Lucy Selden Tennant, the oldest child of Moses Tennant, Sr., and Sarah Selden Jewett (her maiden name), his second wife; was born at Springfield, Otsego County, N. Y., June 7th, 1794.

In the "Champion Genealogy" the birthplace of Lucy Selden Tennant is said to be Lyme, Conn. The writer of this book questions the correctness of this statement, and believes for many reasons, that her birthplace was Springfield, Otsego County, N. Y., where she was married and where her brother Moses Asel and her sisters Olivia and Esther were born. Her half-brother, Selden Tennant, was born in Connecticut, but her half-brother, Rev. David Tennant and her half-sisters, Betsey and Polly were all born in Springfield, N. Y.

The mother of Lucy Tennant never returned to Connecticut after she came to New York State to be re-united with her first husband, Nathaniel Baker, who had forsaken her and then sent for her to come to him and they would begin life over again. The story of this separation is related in Chapter 1, Part III, of this book. The only child born to Sarah Selden Jewett in Connecticut, was Sarah Baker, a daughter by her first husband.

Lucy Tennant married John Marvin Champion at Springfield, Otsego County, N. Y., January 14th, 1810. Mr. Champion was born in Chatham, Columbia County, N. Y., July 12th, 1788.

Before her marriage Mrs. Champion lived for a time with a

half-sister, daughter of her father by his first wife, named Betsey Tennant, who married Sterlin Way, a deacon of the Baptist Church of Springfield, N. Y. Here the writer quotes from the Champion Genealogy, pages 137 and 138, edited by Francis B. Trowgridge and published in 1891.

"JOHN MARVIN CHAMPION, named after his maternal grandmother's family, studied surgery in his youth, and was drafted for the war of 1812, but on account of his young family he accepted a volunteer substitute and in a few days returned to his home in Starksville, Herkimer County, N. Y. He then learned the trade of millwright which he followed until 1848. From the time of his marriage until the summer of 1830 he resided in Starksville, N. Y., with the exception of a few months in 1824, which he passed in Paines Hollow, N. Y. In 1830 he removed to Litchfield, Herkimer County, N. Y., where he resided until 1832 when he removed to Winfield, Herkimer County, N. Y., and in 1837 to Columbia, Herkimer County, the same State, where he resided eleven years. In 1848 he emigrated with his family to Ohio and settled in the Township of Amboy, Ashtabula County. In the Spring of 1852 he set out with a party of pioneers for California. All the horses died on the way except one which was given to him to ride. His strength however was not equal to the hardships of the journey and he died a few months after his arrival in San Francisco, and was buried by the Masonic Fraternity in that City."

His death took place January 4th, 1853. His widow survived him until November 8th, 1882, when her death occurred at Metamora, Fulton County, Ohio. The writer of this genealogy wishes here to express his great pleasure and gratitude in being able to find so reliable an account of the last days of his Uncle John and Aunt Lucy Tennant Champion.

The writer has met only four of this large family, John Harris, Esther, Caroline second, and Ruth. If we can judge of parents by the children, these parents were persons of good moral and mental qualities, who carefully and wisely governed and guided their children, training them to industry and frugality in order to make them good citizens and to fit them for duties and responsibilities of home-life and an influential and honorable position in society. He will speak more particularly of the children and grandchildren of these worthy parents in some of the following pages of this book, all of which will reveal the excellent and high qualities of mind and heart which this large family inherited from their worthy and noble parentage.

There were born to John and Lucy Tennant Champion, ten children named as follows: Eliza Ann, Moses Tennant, John Harris, Lucyette, Abram Jewett, Caroline 1st, Esther, Dan Nelson, Caroline 2nd, and Ruth.

JOHN HARRIS CHAMPION

Born December 13, 1814   Died August 13, 1895

ABRAM JEWETT CHAMPION
Born March 26, 1819   Died ————

1. ELIZA ANN CHAMPION was born in Starkville, Herkimer County, N. Y., March 18th, 1811. She married Horatio Beals at Starkville, N. Y., August 27th, 1829. Mr. Beals was born March 17th, 1808, at Litchfield, N. Y. Mrs. Beals died at Fulton, Oswego County, N. Y.,October 27th, 1898, being at her death eighty-seven years, seven months and nine days old. She was buried at Fulton.

There were born to Mr. and Mrs. Beals five children named as follows: Mary, Lucinda, Horatio, Avoline and Caroline.

1st. MARY ELIZA BEALS, the oldest child, was born at Cedarville, Herkimer County, N. Y., March 5th, 1831. She married Henry T. Clark at Cedarville, N. Y., August 16th, 1846.

MR. CLARK was born at Sauquoit, Oneida County, N. Y., April 15th, 1828. He enlisted in the Union Army of the Civil War and served to the end of the war in 1865. He is still living, December, 1913, at the age of eighty-six years. Mr. and Mrs. Clark's married life extended through a period of twenty-one years and four months, when she died at Whitesboro, Oneida County, N. Y., December 16th, 1867, at the age of thirty-six years, nine months and eleven days. She was buried at Fulton, N. Y.

There were born to them five children named Zachariah, Ella, Clayton, Emma and Henry Worthington.

1. ZACHARIAH CLARK was born at Cedarville, Herkimer County, N. Y., February 26th, 1848. He was never married. He enlisted in the Union Army of the United States and served from 1860 to 1865. At the close of the war, he was honorably discharged. He died in a Southern Hospital August 22nd, 1869, and was buried in Virginia near the Hospital.

2. ELLA ANN CLARK, second child and first daughter of Henry and Mary (Beals) Clark, was born in Fulton, N. Y., June 16th, 1849. She married Charles C. Holden in Mexico, Oswego County, N. Y., November 27th, 1865. Mrs. Holden died at Fulton, N. Y., May 19th, 1891, aged forty-one years, eleven months and three days. Two months after the death of his wife, Mr. Holden died at the same place, July, 1891, aged forty-two years.

There were born to them three children named Anna, Addie and James.

1. ANNA HOLDEN, the oldest child, was born at Whiteboro, Oneida County, N. Y., July 4th, 1867. She married Robert McKay in New York City, January 14th, 1890. Mr. McKay was born in New York City, May 10th, 1867.

There were born to Mr. and Mrs. McKay, five children named Elaine C., Sarah H., Louise A., Charlott E., and John Angus. All were born in Brooklyn, N. Y., except John Angus, who was born in Syracuse, N. Y.

1. ELAINE C. McKAY was born July 6th, 1891.

2. SARAH H. McKAY was born June 12th, 1893.

3. LOUISE A. McKAY was born August 10th, 1895. She died in October, 1912, being seventeen years of age.

4. CHARLOTTE E. McKAY was born January 17th, 1898.

5. JOHN ANGUS McKAY was born February 22nd, 1900.

MRS. McKAY died of quick consumption September 19th, 1901, aged thirty-four years, two months and fourteen days. Her children were all young at the time of their mother's death. The death of the daughter Louise, was the second in the family. She survived her mother a few days over eleven years. How blessed and comforting is the promise and hope of Eternal life!

2. ADDIE HOLDEN, the second child, was born at Lamson, Onondaga County, N. Y., May 23rd, 1870. She married Charles E. Pratt at Oswego, N. Y., August 23rd, 1886. Mr. Pratt was born at Phoenix, Oswego County, N. Y., March 31st, 1865. There were born to Mr. and Mrs. Pratt three children named Margaret, Robert and Mabel.

1. MARGARET M. PRATT was born at Granby, N. Y., June 2nd, 1907.

2. ROBERT E. PRATT was born at Fulton, Otsego County, N. Y., September 13th, 1908.

3. MABEL E. PRATT was born in Syracuse, N. Y., May 4th, 1911.

3. JAMES HOLDEN, third child and only son of Charles and Ella Ann (Clark) Holden, was born at Fulton, N. Y., June 27th, 1872. He married Minnie Marline of Canada, at Minetto, Oswego County, N. Y., August 3rd, 1890. There were born to them a daughter named Ethel May Holden, at Syracuse, N. Y., January 7th, 1892. She died March 30th, 1893, being at her death one year, two months and twenty-three days old.

1. IDA MAY CLARK, the oldest child, was born at Sandy Creek, Oswego County, N. Y., January 28th, 1881. She married Eugene Benway at Harrisville, Lewis County, N. Y., May 18th, 1896. There were born to Mr. and Mrs. Benway three children, named Blanch, Isadore and Hattie.

1. BLANCH EDNA BENWAY was born at Jayville, St. Lawrence County, N. Y., May 30th, 1897.

2. HATTIE MAY BENWAY was born at Jayville, January 14th, 1900. She died at Newton Falls, St. Lawrence County, N. Y., October 7th, 1900, being at her death eight months and twenty-three days old.

3. ISADORE MERLIN BENWAY was born at Benson Mines, St. Lawrence County, N. Y., September 6th, 1901.

2. JOHN HENRY CLARK, the second child, was born at Redfield, Oswego County, N. Y., August 20th, 1882. He married

Edith Madelin at Ogdensburg, N. Y., October 25th, 1911. Miss Madelin was born at Ogdensburg, N. Y., July 5th, 1893. They have one child, named Helen Margaret Clark, born at Carthage, Jefferson County, N. Y., November 24th, 1912.

3. MAUD EDNA CLARK, the third child and second daughter, was born at Oswego, N. Y., June 9th, 1884. She married Ross H. Smith at Hannibal, Wayne County, N. Y., August 4th, 1911. They have no children. Their residence at this date, July 1914, is 429 South Avenue, Rochester, N. Y.

4. FRANK WORTHINGTON CLARK was born in Redfield, N. Y., April 19th, 1886. He died at the place of his birth when but eleven months old, and was buried at Green Burrow, Oswego County, N. Y.

5. CLAYTON JAMES CLARK, the fifth child, was born at Redfield, N. Y., May 16th, 1887, and died at Ryeutes, St. Lawrence County, N. Y., February 26th, 1907, at the age of nineteen years, nine months and ten days. He was buried at Harrisville, N. Y. He never married.

6. ZONA ANN CLARK, the sixth child, was born at Redfield, N. Y., November 18th, 1891. She married Daniel S. Smith at Plainville, N. Y., in 1908. They had one child, born at Jayville, N. Y., February 13th, 1909, named Florence Gertrude Smith. She died at Herring, N. Y., July 21st, 1909, being five months and eight days old. She was buried at Harrisville, N. Y.

All the above named are children and grandchildren of Henry Worthington Clark by his first wife, Josephine Elizabeth Pelow. Mrs. Clark died, as has been stated, at Jayville, N. Y., August 11th, 1896.

Mr. Clark married for his second wife, Nellie Allan of Sandy Creek, Oswego County, N. Y. No children by second marriage.

II. LUCINDA ROXANA BEALS, second child and second daughter of Horatio and Eliza Champion Beals, was born in Cedarville, Herkimer County, N. Y., October 30th, 1832. She married James W. K. Loomis at Cedarville, N. Y., January 3rd, 1854. He was a farmer. He died at Palermo, N. Y., July 3rd, 1911. His beloved wife survived him about ten months and died at Palermo, March 26th, 1912, being at her death seventy-nine years, three months and twenty-six days old. Both were buried at Fulton, N. Y.

There were born to them six children named as follows: Carlton, Arthur, Earl, Victor, Albertus C., and Charles.

1. CARLTON JEWETT LOOMIS was born at Palermo, N. Y., March 21st, 1855. He married Miss Carrie Kuney at Kilburn, Wisconsin, June 27th, 1878. There were born to Mr. and Mrs. Loomis four children: Lotta, Rodney, Emily and Gerald.

1.   LOTTA LUCINDA LOOMIS was born at Kilburn, Wisconsin, March 31st, 1879.   She married Frank Edward Moran, May 31st, 1897.   Mr. Moran was born August 26th, 1877.   There were born to Mr. and Mrs. Moran three children, named Mignon, Charlotte and Carlton.

1.   MIGNON BESSIE MORAN was born March 31st, 1898.
2.   CHARLOTTE FRANCES MORAN was born June 20th, 1901.
3.   CARLTON EDWARDS MORAN was born August 24th, 1903.
2.   RODNEY CARLTON LOOMIS, the second child of Carlton and Carrie (Kuney) Loomis, was born in Portage, Wisconsin, January 28th, 1882.   He married Miss Pearl Itine, January 23rd, 1907.

MISS ITINE was born in Lincoln, Nebraska, July 22nd, 1884. At this date, 1913, they have no children.

3.   EMILY JESSIE LOOMIS was born at Portage, Wisconsin, February 22nd, 1887.   She married Frederick Louis Shultz, May 18th, 1909.   Mr. Shultz was born April 4th, 1887.   They have one son named Frederick Louis Shultz, born January 3rd, 1910.

4.   GERALD PATTERSON LOOMIS, fourth child of Carlton and Carrie (Kuney) Loomis, was born February 5th, 1899.
II.   ARTHUR HERBERT LOOMIS, the second child and second son of James and Lucinda (Beals) Loomis, was born at Palermo, N. Y., March 21st, 1855.   He married Miss Ida Cornelia Jennings at Palermo, N. Y., November 7th, 1878.   There were born to them two children, Lee C. and Inez Irene.

1.   LEE CARLETON LOOMIS was born at Palermo, N. Y., March 21st, 1886.   He married Miss Sara Fidelia Burnhams at New Haven, N. Y., September 19th, 1906.   Miss Burnhams was born at LeRoy, Jefferson County, N. Y., July 6th, 1886. They had one child, a son named Charles Donald Loomis, born at Sunrise, Wycming County, N. Y., December 9th, 1908.   After the birth of her son she lived only from December 9th to April of the next year.   She died at New Haven, N. Y., April 30th, 1909, and was buried in the Cemetery of that City.   After the death of his first wife, Mr. Loomis married Elizabeth Collins at Palmero, N. Y., October 20th, 1912.   She was born at Palermo, May 13th, 1891.   By his second wife he has a son named Horace Arthur Loomis born at Palermo, N. Y., Sept. 24th, 1914.

2.   INEZ IRENE LOOMIS, second child, was born at Palermo, N. Y., November 1st, 1887.   She married Mr. Fred James Trimble at Palmero, N. Y., June 16th, 1909.   No children.   Address is Fulton, N. Y.

III.   EARL DAN LOOMIS, third child of James and Roxanna Beals Loomis, was born at Palermo, N. Y., October 13th, 1863. He married Miss Lina Pritchard at Central Square, Oswego

County, N. Y., February 9th, 1881. Miss Pritchard was born at Gilberts Mills, N. Y., October 22nd, 1867. They had three children named Glenn, Letta Belle and Carlton. Mr. Loomis died at Volney, N. Y., July 5th, 1911, and was buried at Fulton, N. Y. He was forty-seven years, eight months and twenty-two days old at the time of his death.

1. GLENN LOOMIS was born at Palermo, N. Y., July 1882. He died in infancy but the place and date has not been given.

2. LETTA BELLE LOOMIS, the second child of Earl Dan and Lina Pritchard Loomis, was born at Palermo, N. Y., December 2nd, 1886. She married Irving J. Hewes at Buffalo, N. Y., October 3rd, 1903. There have been born to them four children named Vida, Clarence, Lula and Dorothy.

1. VIDA PEARL HEWES was born at Fulton, N. Y., May 13th, 1905.

2. CLARENCE EARL HEWES was born at Fulton, N. Y., September 27th, 1906.

3. LULU MARIE HEWES was born in East Syracuse, N. Y., June 17th, 1908, and died October 5th, 1908, at the age of three months and eighteen days.

4. DOROTHY BELLE HEWES was born at East Syracuse, N. Y., October 1st, 1909.

III. CARLTON LOOMIS, the third child of Earl Dan and Lina Pritchard Loomis was born at Palermo, N. Y., March 27th, 1897.

IV. VICTOR JAMES LOOMIS, fourth child and fourth son of James and Lucinda (Beals) Loomis, was born at Palermo, N. Y., January 23rd, 1867. He married Miss Mary Louise King at Fulton, N. Y., January 23rd, 1889. Miss King was born at Granby Center, N. Y., June 20th, 1866. Mr. Loomis was Treasurer of the Oneida Steel Pulley Company. Mrs. Loomis was a teacher before her marriage. There were born to them four sons named Harold, Cameron, Donald and Kenneth.

1. HAROLD VICTOR LOOMIS was born at Palermo, N. Y., November 22nd, 1890. He was graduated from the Syracuse University.

2. CAMERON PLATT LOOMIS was born in Fulton, N. Y., November 20th, 1893.

3. DONALD KING LOOMIS was born in Fulton, N. Y., August 18th, 1900.

4. KENNETH MOORE LOOMIS was born in Oneida, N. Y., September 6th, 1906.

V. ALBERTUS CHESTER LOOMIS, the fifth son of James and Lucinda (Beals) Loomis, was born at Palermo, N. Y., September 3rd, 1868. He married Miss Cora R. Wilcox, August 29th, 1894. Miss Wilcox was born at Fremont, Minnesota, October

27th, 1868. She died at Minnesota City, May 5th, 1901, and was buried at Winona, Minn. There were born of this marriage two children named Eleanor May and Myron Albertus, both born at Minnesota City.

    1. ELEANOR MAY LOOMIS was born August 11th, 1896.

    2. MYRON ALBERTUS LOOMIS was born April 17th, 1899.

After the death of Mrs. Loomis at Minnesota City, May 5th, 1901, Mr. Loomis married his second wife, Miss Mary Walsh at Winona, Minn., June 19th, 1903. Miss Walsh was born at Winona, Minn., December 6th, 1868.

VI. CHARLES RODNEY LOOMIS, youngest child, was born at Palermo, N. Y., September 28th, 1871. He was unmarried. After an operaiton at a hospital in New York City he died December 9th, 1904. His remains were buried in Woodlawn Cemetery, N. Y.

III. HORATIO CHAMPION BEALS, the third child and first son of Horatio and Eliza Champion Beals, was born at Litchfield, Herkimer County, N. Y., February 18th, 1838. His first marriage was to Josephine Oterlin at Cedarville, N. Y., November, 1852. She died soon after her marriage. His second marriage was to Adalina Jewett Mustizer of Palermo, N. Y., February 28th, 1861. His third marriage was to Eva Estelle Flint, September 3rd, 1877, who died in Mexico, N. Y., October 26th, 1878. His fourth marriage was to Endora Olive Flint, October 27th, 1879. She was a sister of his third wife. She is still living, 1913. The author of the "Champion Genealogy" says "He served three years in the Union Army, nearly ten months of which was passed in Andersonville prison. He was an artist and resided at one time in Fulton, N. Y." He left no children. His second wife left him and married a Confederate officer by whom she has two sons, who entered the United States service in the Phillpines.

IV. AVOLINE CORNELIA BEALS, fourth child and third daughter, was born at Cedarville, Herkimer County, N. Y., August 26th, 1840. She married Henry Harding of Fulton, N. Y., September 26th, 1861, at Palermo, N. Y. Mr. Harding was born Jan. 1st, 1836, and died at Palermo, N. Y., March 13th, 1910, being at his death aged 74 years, 2 months and 13 days. He was buried at Volney Center, N. Y. His beloved wife died at Palermo, March 17th, 1910, aged sixty-nine years, six months and twenty one days. She was buried at Volney Center, N. Y. There were born to Mr. and Mrs. Harding five children named Carrie, Frederick, John, Helen and Carlton.

    1. CARRIE JEANETTE HARDING, the oldest child, was born June 29th, 1863. She married Seward A. Green, May 13th, 1882. Mr. Green was born June 16th, 1861.

There were born to Mr. and Mrs. Green six children named as follows: Eudora Eliza, Mable Louise, Frances Cornelia, Clarence Floyd, Mary Avoline and Ruth Hazel.

1. EUDORA ELIZA GREEN was born March 25th, 1883. She married Charles Jensen June 10th, 1901.

There were born to Mr. and Mrs. Jensen three children named Richard, Essel and Seward.

1. RICHARD JENSEN was born March 11th, 1902.
2. ESSEL JENSEN was born April 25th, 1904.
3. SEWARD JENSEN (The writer has no report of his birth. He died in May 1910.)

After the birth of these children Mr. Jensen died, and his widow married Mr. William Rolfe in July 1910.

2. MABLE LOUISE GREEN, the second daughter, was born October 28th, 1884. She died November 13th, 1890, at the early age of six years and fifteen days.

3. FRANCES CORNELIA GREEN, the third daughter, was born February 21st, 1888. She died August 13th, 1888, at the age of five months and twenty-two days.

THE GOOD SHEPHERD.

Dear Shepherd of Israel, thou lovest thine own,
The lambs of thy flock thou wilt never disown;
To thy bosom of love thou dost gather them in,
Safe from all sorrow, trouble and sin.
Why then should we weep for the children that die,
Seeing they only pass up to their home on high?
Secure in the arms of the Saviour Divine,
They live in the glow of the Heavenly sunshine.

4. CLARENCE FLOYD GREEN, the fourth child, was born January 22nd, 1891. He married Miss Nyda Caroline Douglas July 12th, 1910.

5. MARY AVOLINE GREEN, was born March 14th, 1901.

6. RUTH HAZEL GREEN, the youngest child, was born February 12th, 1904.

II. FREDERICK RILEY HARDING, the second child and first son of Henry Harding and his wife Avoline Cornelia Beals was born at Palermo, Oswego County, N. Y., November 14th, 1865.

He is unmarried at the date of this record. He lives at Fulton, Fulton County, N. Y.

III. JOHN CHAMPION HARDING was born at Palermo, N. Y. March 7th, 1870. He is unmarried at the date of this record. He now lives in Cleveland, Ohio.

IV. HELEN MAY HARDING, the fourth child and second daughter of Mr. and Mrs. Henry Harding, was born at Volney, Oswego County, N. Y., April 8th, 1880. She married Alonzo

Chester Pettengill at Vermillion, Oswego County, N. Y., May 25th, 1898.   He was born April 19th, 1875.

Mr. and Mrs. Pettengill have a son born in the township of New Haven, Oswego County, N. Y., October 14th, 1907, named Glenn Millard Pettengill.

V.   CARLTON BEALS HARDING was born at Volney, Oswego County, N. Y., November 15th, 1883.

V.   CAROLINE CORDELIA BEALS was a twin sister of Avoline, born at Cedarville, Litchfield Township, Herkimer County, N. Y., August 26th, 1840.   She was the fifth child and fourth daughter of her parents.   She married Mr. Harvey Frederick Wilcox at Bristol Hill, N. Y., June 19th, 1854.   Mr. Wilcox was born in Palermo, N. Y., April 21st, 1832.   Immediately after their marriage they moved to Fremont, Minn., where they lived for thirty-three years.   In 1897 they sold their farm and moved to Stockton, Winona County, Minn., where they remained until May, 1903, when they moved back to Palermo, N. Y., and there lived up to the time of Mrs. Wilcox's death which took place at Palermo, January 21st, 1912.   She was seventy-one years, four months and twenty-five days old at her death.   Mr. Wilcox is living at Palermo at this date, December 1913.   Mr. and Mrs. Wilcox had three children named Ida May, Elmina Avoline and Eunice Ann.

1.   IDA MAY WILCOX was born at Palermo, N. Y., April 4th, 1862.   She married Oliver McPhail in Fremont, Winona County, Minn., January 1st, 1896.   Mr. McPhail was born in Ontario, Canada, January 6th, 1856.   There were born to them a daughter at Fremont, Minn., named Ethel May McPhail, on December 19th, 1896.

2.   ELMINA AVOLINE WILCOX, second child, was born in Winona County, Minn., September 13th, 1864.   She married at Fremont, Winona County, Minn., Mr. Charles Harrison Nettleton on April 17th, 1884.   Mr. Nettleton was born at Utica, Minn., January 6th, 1856.   There were born to them three children named Minnie, Gertrude and Earl, all born at Utica, Minn.

1.   MINNIE MAY BELL NETTLETON was born April 24th, 1885.   She died at the place of her birth, August 20th, 1886, being at her death aged one year, three months and twenty-six days.

2.   GERTRUDE EUNICE NETTLETON was born November 12th, 1886.   She is unmarried and lives at the home of the family at Stockton, Minn.

3.   DR. EARL HOWARD NETTLETON was born September 17th, 1889.   He is a Dentist at Yankton, South Dakota.

3.   EUNICE ANN WILCOX, third child of Harvey and Caroline (Beals) Wilcox, was born in Fremont, Winona County, Minn.,

November 8th, 1869. She married Sanford Aseph Graves in Stockton, Minn., December 7th, 1898. Mr. Graves was born at Clifford, Oswego County, N. Y., November 4th, 1860. There were born to Mr. and Mrs. Graves three children named Vernice, Harvey and Richard.

1. VERNICE EUNICE GRAVES was born in Stockton, Minn., September 22nd, 1899.

2. HARVEY ASEPH GRAVES was born in Palermo, N. Y., November 10th, 1901.

3. RICHARD SANFORD GRAVES was born in Palermo, N. Y., January 1st, 1904.

II. MOSES TENNANT CHAMPION, second child and first son of John and Lucy Tennant Champion, was born at Starkville, Herkimer County, N. Y., December 7th, 1812. He had a common school education at Starkville, and a short preparation for College at Fairfield Academy, Fairfield, N. Y. He finally abandoned this course of training and learned the carpenter's trade; emigrated to Tecumseh, Michigan, in 1837; studied law and was admitted to the bar in 1841. After all this preparation for a noble and successful life work, he died of consumption at Tecumseh, Mich., January 23rd, 1842, being at his death twenty-nine years, one month and sixteen days old.

II. JOHN HARRIS CHAMPION was born December 13th, 1814, at Starkville, Herkimer County, N. Y. He married Caroline Cornelia Fowler at Oriskany Falls, N. Y., May 25th, 1842. Miss Fowler was born in Augusta, N. Y., January 12th, 1820. They had no children. Mr. Champion, after teaching school in his native village, entered the medical department of Hobart College, New York, and was graduated in 1841. After practicing in his profession for thirteen years, he went West in 1854. He then entered upon the work of journalism. At Adrian, Michigan, for a number of years he was Editor and Proprietor of the Adrian Watch Tower. Subsequently he was Editor and Proprietor of the Owasso Weekly Press at Owasso, Mich.

The writer visited this cousin at Adrian in October, 1855, while on his way to Niles. Mich., in search of a location as teacher. He was just past twenty-one years old and was at the time a student in the Grand River Institute, Austinburg, Ashtabula County, Ohio. Again he visited him in the Summer of 1871 at Owasso. Upon each of these visits he was most cordially greeted. At the time of this second visit he was returning to his work in the Rochester Theological Seminary, having spent the summer months of his first vacation supplying the pulpit of the Baptist Church of Portage, Iona County, Mich. All these events call to mind many pleasant remembrances of this talented cousin. 'A more extended account of Mr. Champion and his life work will be found in a Memorial Tribute in Part IV, 2nd Division of this book. His death took place at Owasso, Shiwassee County, Mich., August 13th, 1895, at the age of eighty-one years and seven months.

IV. LUCYETTE CHAMPION, the fourth child and second daughter of John and Lucy Tennant Champion, was born at Starkville, Herkimer County, N. Y., January 6th, 1817. She married Asa Ames Potter at Sepatchet, East Winfield, Herkimer County, N. Y., September 24th, 1835. Mr. Potter was born at Foster, R. I., April 1st, 1802, and died at Oneida, N. Y., June 4th, 1888, being at his death eighty-six years, two months and three days old. His beloved wife survived him for over four years, and died at Passaic, N. J., December 9th, 1892, being at her death seventy-five years, eleven months and three days old. She was buried at Oneida, N. Y. There were born to Mr. and Mrs. Potter six children named as follows: Juliet, Helen, Abbie, Abraham, Mary and Annie.

1. JULIET POTTER, the first child, was born at Sepatchet, East Winfield, Herkimer County, N. Y., July 17th, 1836. She married William Henry Tiffany at East Winfield, April 12th, 1860. By this marriage she had two children, Emmett and Mann. Mr. Tiffany died in 1872. Mrs. Tiffany, after the death of her first husband, married Mr. Ryman Van Evera in New York City, June 16th, 1875. By this second marriage she had a son named Potter Van Evera.

In the above sketch we have only given an outline of the changes that took place in the life of MISS JULIET POTTER. Between her first and second marriage, she studied to become a physician. She entered the Homeopathic College of New York City and was graduated with the degree of M. D. She was afterwards elected to the chair of "Diseases of Women and Children." In this position she lectured for fourteen years. She was also appointed as an Examiner on the New York State "Board of Lunacy." The education she received, the extensive practice in her profession she secured, and the high honors conferred upon her by State authorities, reveal her remarkable talents and true worth of character, and the high social position she occupied.

Her first husband, Mr. Tiffany, was a talented lawyer of Metamora, Fulton County, Ohio. Her second husband was a well-to-do merchant of New York City of good standing in the business life of that great City.

We will give the record of her three sons, the first two by her first marriage, and the last by her second marriage.

1. EMMETT TIFFANY was born at Metamora, Fulton County, Ohio, February 2nd, 1861.

We take the following account of his early life from the "Champion Genealogy."

"EMMETT TIFFANY was admitted upon recommendation to the West Point Military School. While there, he was vaccinated with smallpox virus. This produced weakness of the eyes which compelled him to make a change, as he was unfitted for miliatry duty. He went to Kansas, studied law, was admitted to the Bar and practiced his profession for many years. He also became an editor."

MR. TIFFANY married Miss Evelyn Brown July 15th, 1891. There was born to them a daughter named Harriet Tiffany. Mr. Tiffany after many changes and much labor died at the home of the American Counsul at Madeiro, Old Mexico, December 19th, 1897, at the age of thirty-six years, ten months and seventeen days.

2. MANN TIFFANY was born at Oneida, N. Y., June 8th, 1863. Before he was five years old, on April 17th, 1868, he was drowned in Oneida Creek, during a spring freshet.

3. POTTER VAN EVERA, the son of the second marriage, was born in New York City. He married Miss Theresa Tahrenschone at Sherrill, N. Y., December 28th, 1910. They have no children at this date, 1912.

II. HELEN L. POTTER was born at Cedarville, Herkimer County, N. Y., December 6th, 1837. She never married. Her life has been connected with educational matters as pupil, teacher and lecturer. For five years she taught in private and public schools; ten years as special teacher of voice and physical expression connected with colleges. After this she entered upon Lyceum work as lecturer and entertainer, in which she achieved great success both artistically and financially. She gave over eighteen hundred dramatic recitals before Lyceum audiences. Ambitious to excel, she spared neither body or brain to that end. Her reputation for many years was national, as she had addressed and thrilled many audiences in all parts of the United States. She spent money lavishly not only as necessary to succeed in her life work, but for benevolent objects as well. She opened her hand to assist in cases that appealed to her sympathies and to her judgment as worthy of aid.

The author of this Genealogy has asked MISS POTTER to write her auto-biography for this work. It will appear in separate Chapter, in Part IV of this book.

III. ABBIE MAHALA POTTER, the third child and third daughter of Asa and Lucyette (Champion) Potter, was born near Cedarville, N. Y., February 9th, 1842. She married Adrian Emmett Wallace in Winfield, Herkimer County, N. Y., December 19th, 1860. Mr. Wallace was born in New Lisbon, Otsego

County, N. Y., November 28, 1834. Mr. Wallace died in Passaic, N. J., August 9th, 1896, aged seventy-one years, eight months and eleven days. His beloved wife survived him till April 2nd, 1909, and died in Passaic, at the age of sixty-seven years, one month and twenty-three days. Both were buired in Oneida Castle Cemetery, N. Y. They had three children named William, Charles and Victor Moreau.

1. WILLIAM ADRIAN WALLACE was born in East Winfield, October 2nd, 1861. He married Anna A. Bernard in Oneida, N. Y., December 3rd, 1885. Miss Bernard was born at Worchester, Mass., March 20th, 1868. They had nine children named Adrian, Carlton, Louis, Raynard, Milton, Milford, Bernard, Juliet and Anna.

1. ADRIAN CHARLES WALLACE was born at Oneida, N. Y., September 8th, 1886.

2. CARLTON FRANCIS WALLACE was born at Guthrie, Oklahoma, July 24th, 1889.

3. LOUIS NATHANIEL WALLACE was born at Passaic, N. J., November 23rd, 1890. Died at Passiac, N. J., April 11th, 1894, aged three years, four months and eighteen days. He was buried at Cedar Lawn Cemetery, Passaic, N. J.

4. RAYNARD ABRAM WALLACE was born at Oneida, N. Y., January 13th, 1892.

5. MILTON GRATTON WALLACE was born at Passaic, N. J., September 7th, 1893. Died at Passaic, N. J., April 11th, 1894, aged one year. He was buried at Cedar Lawn Cemetery, Passaic, N. J.

6. MILFORD COOPER WALLACE was born at Passaic, N. J., September 16th, 1895.

7. BERNARD CLINTON WALLACE was born at Passaic, N. J., January 28th, 1897.

8. JULIET MARIA WALLACE was born at Brooklyn, N. Y., December 20th, 1898.

9. ANNA DOROTHY WALLACE was born at Brooklyn, N. Y., March 12th, 1902.

II. CHARLES S. WALLACE, second child, was born at East Winfield, N. Y., June 7th, 1863.

III. VICTOR MOREAU WALLACE, the third son of Adrian and Abbie (Potter) Wallace, was born at Winfield, N. Y., August 12th, 1865. He married Miss Edna Adelle Rudy at Oneida, N. Y., July 17th, 1884. Miss Rudy was born at Glenmore, N. Y., June 1st, 1866. There were born to them eight children named Edith, Mabel, Helen, Victor, Frank, Chester, Edna and Donald. The first four of these children were born at Oneida, N. Y.

1. EDITH WALLACE was born April 24th, 1885. She died in Memphis, Tenn., November 17th, 1912, buried in Evergreen Cemetery.

2. MABEL WALLACE was born September 17th, 1887.

3. HELEN WALLACE was born October 12th, 1891.

4. VICTOR MOREAU WALLACE was born February 10th, 1894, and died in New York City, February 7th, 1897, being two years, eleven months and twenty-seven days old.

5. FRANK HOBART WALLACE was born at Passaic, N. J., June 30th, 1896.

6. CHESTER EARL WALLACE was born in New York City September 27th, 1899.

7. EDNA ADELLE WALLACE was born at Richmond Hill, N. Y., February 2nd, 1902.

8. DONALD MEREDITH WALLACE was born in New York City July 27th, 1905. He died November 27th, 1907, at the age of two years and five months.

IV. ABRAM CHARLES POTTER, fourth child and first son of Asa and Lucyette (Champion) Potter, was born at Cedarville, N. Y., May 13th, 1844. He married Miss J. Louise Meisinger at Oneida, N. Y., July 9th, 1891. Miss Meisinger was born at New Britain, Conn., July 9th, 1856. There was born to them a son named Carleton Ames Potter, in New York City, July 6th, 1894.

MR. A. C. POTTER enlisted at Fort Schuyler, Herkimer County, N. Y., July 23rd, 1862, in Company B. 121st Regiment, New York Volunteers, and was mustered out July 23rd, 1865, in Washington, D. C., as Sergeant in Company B. 20th Regiment of Veteran Reserve Corps, by reason of expiration of his term of service, having served three years. While in Washington he saw President Lincoln and took him by the hand.

MR. POTTER has taken all degrees of Masonry up to Knights Templars, and then took the degree of "Nobles of the Mystic Shrine." This is not a regular Masonic degree, yet none but Knights Templars and 32nd degree Masons are eligible to that order. He was "Excellent High Priest" of Englewood Chapter, No. 176, Royal Arch Masons, during the year 1882, in Illinois. He was Deputy Sheriff of Chicago, Cook County, Ill., for fourteen years and served on the Staff of Governor Oglesburg. He attended officially General Grant's fuenral and other public ceremonies.

His wife was a descendant of a noble German family, the Meisinger family, founded in 1575 by Hans Mossinger, an officer at the Court of Bishop of Banbury, Germany. After the war, MR. POTTER engaged in business in Chicago, Ill. From Chicago he came to New York City and was appointed Assistant Superintendent of the public schools of the city.

V.   MARY EMMA POTTER, the fifth child and fourth daughter of Asa and Lucyette (Champion) Potter, was born at Sepatchet, Winfield Township, Herkimer County, N. Y., October 28th, 1852.   She married Edmund Carlton, M. D., at Oneida, N. Y., January 1st, 1873.   Mr. Carlton was born in Littleton, New Hampshire, December 11th, 1839, and died in Oneida, N. Y., June 15th, 1912.

Concerning the Carleton family, Miss Helen Potter, a niece of Mrs. Carleton writes the following interesting facts: We quote her words, "Dr. Edward Carleton was the son of Judge Edward Carleton of Littleton, New Hampshire.   They were prominent in the "underground railroad" during anti slavery days, their home being the meeting place of Wendell Phillips, William Lloyd Garrison, and other abolitionists.   At the breaking out of the Civil War Dr. Carleton enlisted in the Union army and served as despatch bearer.   He participated in thirteen battles, and was correspondent for the Boston Transcript during the war.   After the war he practiced medicine in New York for forty-one years, and was instrumental in the founding of the Homeopathic Hospital in that City.   He was a member of many hospital staffs of medical societies and Professor of Surgery at the Medical College for Women and   Emeritus Professor of Homeopathic Philosophy at the New York Medical College and Flower Hospital.   His last work was the writing of a unique book "Homeopathy in Medicine and Surgery," now in press."

The above quotation from the pen of Miss Potter shows Dr. Carleton as a man of unusual and superior ability in his chosen profession, and at the same time a conspicuous character in the moral and political struggles of his day.

There were born to Dr. Edward and Mary Emma (Potter) Carleton, four children named Spencer, Mary, Mabel and Bertha.

1.   SPENCER CARLETON was born in New York City October 14th, 1873.   He was a college bred man and had conferred upon him the degrees of A. B. and M. D.   He was a chemist and inventor and after fifteen years, a successful practitioner.   He kept on hand medicines for scientific research.   He has at this date, 1913, an extensive practice.   DR. CARLTON married Miss Ernesta Stephens in New Jersey, August 22nd, 1903.   Miss Stephens was born in New York City October 14th, 1879.   She died in New York City, May 30th, 1910.   There were born to them two children named Baldwin and Ernest, both born in New York City.

   1.   BALDWIN CARLTON was born October 10th, 1904.
   2.   ERNEST CARLTON was born September 1st, 1906.
   2.   MARY CARLETON, daughter of Edward Carleton, was born

in New York City, July 10th, 1875, and died at the same place January 21st, 1876, at the age of six months and eleven days.

3. MABEL CARLETON, the third child of Edward Carleton, was born in New York City, October 31st, 1876, and died at the same place, March 19th, 1878, being at her death one year, four months and nineteen days old.

4. BERTHA CARLETON, A. B., daughter of Edward Carleton, was born April 11th, 1880. She married Wilbur Abbott Welch, A. B., in New York City, June 28th, 1904. Mr. Welch was born in New York City, June 7th, 1873. There were born to Mr. and Mrs. Welch five children named Oliver, David, Barbara, Madeline and Herbert.

1. OLIVER LOOVELAND WELCH was born in New York City, April 26th, 1905, and died October 8th, 1905, at the age of five months and twelve days.

2. DAVID WELCH was born in New York City, January 7th, 1907.

3. BARBARA WELCH was born in Nyack, N. Y., June 4th, 1910.

4. MADELINE CARLETON WELCH was born in Pasadena, California, August 29th, 1911.

5. HERBERT WELCH was born in Monrovia, California, April 5th, 1913.

VI. ANNIE LOUISE POTTER, sixth child and youngest daughter of Asa and Lucyette (Champion) Potter, was born in Chapatchet, Herkimer Co., N. Y., Feb. 3d, 1855. She married Charles Mulford Cooper in New York City Dec. 30th, 1874. Mr. Cooper was born in Freehold, Monmouth County, N. J., September 8th, 1851. He is an artist, engraver and inventor, is a descendant of one of the old Dutch Barons, dating their ancestry back to 1600. Mr. Cooper is a musician with a very superior voice. Their home and business at this date, 1913, is in New York City. They have no children.

V. ABRAM JEWETT CHAMPION, the fifth child and third son of John and Lucy Tennant Champion, was born at Starkville, Herkimer County, N. Y., March 26th, 1819. He married Miss Lanah Maria Miller at Columbia, Herkimer County, N. Y., April 12th, 1840. She was the daughter of William and Betsey (Smith) Miller of Breenbush, N. Y. She was born in Columbia, August 5th, 1823. By this marriage there were seven children born named Francena, Adelia, Lavinia, William, Kendrick, LeClaire, and Maxwell. The first four were born in Columbia, N. Y. After the birth of the fourth child, William John, the family moved to Metamora, Fulton County, Ohio, in 1848, where the three younger children were born. The birth of Maxwell, the youngest child, was on October 1st, 1864, and he died at Metamora, Ohio, August 17th, 1865, being at his death ten months and sixteen days old. On the 2nd day of September, 1865, Mrs. Champion died at Metamora at the age of forty-two years and twenty-seven days. She lived after the death of her son, Maxwell only sixteen days. These two were the first and only deaths that had occurred in the family for many years.

MR. CHAMPION was a farmer. Now bereft of his wife and with six young children to support and educate, it was no light burden he had to carry on heart and hands. He had, with all, several township offices, and these increased his cares, duties and responsibilities. On June 5th, 1873, he married Miss Harriet Stanley Tennant, duaghter of Alfred A. and Fanny Louisa (Wheeler) Tennant, who was born in Blissfield, Lenawee County, Michigan, June 5th, 1848. There were born to them five children named Llewellyn, Jewett, Ralph, Arthur and Merrill. We now give the record of this family of twelve children.

CHILDREN OF THE FIRST MARRIAGE.

1. FRANCENA LOUISE CHAMPION was born in Herkimer County, N. Y., March 22nd, 1841. She married Bradley Gilman Stanley at Metamora, Fulton County, Ohio, November 1st, 1860. Mr. Stanley was born in Chautauqua County, N. Y., March 29th, 1837. His father's name was Abner Stanley, and his mother's maiden name was Abigail Cotton. MRS. BRADLEY G. STANLEY died at Ossawatomie, Miami County, Kansas, April 13th, 1908. There were born to them two children named Earl and Alcesta.

1. EARL STANLEY was born at Tipton, Lenawee County, Michigan, June 29th, 1867. He married Miss Estella Hunt at Ossawatomie, December 29th, 1878. Her father's name was Asail Hunt and her mother's maiden name was Mary Jane Sherar. There were born to them at Ossawatomie, Kansas, two children named Helen and Mary.

1. HELEN MARGARET STANLEY was born December 21st, 1905.

2. MARY FRANCENA STANLEY was born January 18th, 1913.

2. LIZZIE ALCESTA STANLEY, daughter of Bradley and Francena (Champion) Stanley, was born at Adrian, Michigan, November 6th, 1871. She married Walter Scott Colvin at Ossawatomie, Kansas, April 24th, 1909. Mr. Colvin was born at Scotia, Illinois, November 28th, 1877. He is the son of Garland Thomas Colvin, who was born in Boone County, Missouri, October 25th, 1842, and his wife Katy Moxley Guthrie, born at Shelbyville, Kentucky, May 6th, 1853. There was born to Mr. and Mrs. Colvin a son named John Nigel Colvin, at Osawatomie, Kansas, September 16th, 1910. Mr. Colvin was graduated from the High School at Osawatomie in the Class of 1895. He has

been actively employed in Railroad work since 1898. Since their marriage Mr. and Mrs. Colvin have resided at Osawatomie to the present date, December, 1913.

II.   ADELIA JEWETT CHAMPION, second child and second daughter of Abram Jewett and Lanah Maria (Miller) Champion, was born at Columbia, Herkimer County, N. Y., June 20th, 1843. She married Dr. Sanford Monroe Clarke of Adrian, Michigan, at Metamora, Fulton County, Ohio, in 1860. Mr. Clarke was born at Clarkson, Monroe County, N. Y., May 12th, 1836. He was appointed Assistant Surgeon in the United States Navy in 1856 and re-appointed in 1861 ; and promoted to be surgeon; he was wounded on the gunboat James A. Adgar in 1862; was treated for his wounds on shipboard, and was finally honorably discharged from the Navy at the Brooklyn Navy Yards, N. Y., December 15th, 1864.

During his connection with the United States Navy, he served at the following stations: The European, the China, the East Indian, the Pacific and the North Atlantic.   After retirement from the navy, he was chosen surgeon of the Wellington Blaine G. A. R. Post.   He is at this date, May, 1913, making his home at Metamora, Fulton County, Ohio.

DR. SANFORD CLARKE was the son of Dr. Dorman Clarke and his wife, Sophronia (Morris) Clarke.   The father was born at Cherry Valley, Otsego County, N. Y., October 21st, 1813, and died at Burr Oak, Michigan, March 12th, 1858.   The mother was born at Cazenovia, N. Y., in 1815, and died at Adrian, Michigan, April 7th, 1847.   There were born to Dr. Sanford and Adelia (Champion) Clarke, three children, Lanah, Jay and Dorman.

1.   LANAH AUGUSTA CLARKE was born at Metamora, Fulton County, Ohio, February 16th, 1862.   She married Miles A. Kahle.

MR. KAHLE was born in Butler County, Pennsylvania, February 4th, 1851.   He was a son of James and Mary (Gates) Kahle, the former born in Alsace-Loraine, France, and the latter in Clarion County, Pa.   The Author has received from MRS. MILES A. KAHLE, the following interesting sketch of the Kahle family, taken from a family history.   This sketch is re-written by the author for brevity.   He begins with the history of James Kahle, the father of Miles A. Kahle, who married Lanah Augusta Clarke, a daughter of Dr. Sanford Clarke and his wife, Adelia Jewett (Champion) Clarke, who was a daughter of Abram Jewett Champion, who was a son of John Champion and his wife Lucy Tennant Champion, a daughter of Moses Tennant, Sr., and his second wife, whose maiden name was Sarah Selden Jewett.   This traces back the descendants of Miles

A. Kahle to their Tennant origin through his wife, Lanah Augusta Clarke.

JAMES KAHLE was of French extraction, born in Alsace-Loraine, France. He was a Mason by trade and emigrated to America when a young man in 1828, and located in Clarion County, Pa. Here he made the acquaitance of Miss Mary Gates, whom he married in Clarion County. There were born to Mr. and Mrs. James Kahle nine children, one of whom, a son, was named Miles A. Kahle. Mr. Kahle and his family lived in Clarion County up to 1849, when they moved to Butler County, Pa., where he continued his trade till 1864, when they moved to Fulton County, Ohio, and settled in Dover Township. Here he purchased one hundred and eighty-five acres of land and a saw mill. He lived on this farm for four years, then moved to Lucas County, Ohio, and purchased one hundred and fifty acres of land and later eighty acres near Metamora, Ohio. About the same time he purchased ninety-seven acres on which he resided for about seven years. On this last purchase his son Miles A. now resides. As age advanced, he broke up housekeeping and resided among his children. His death took place in Fulton County, Ohio, March 28th, 1889, at the venerable age of eighty years. His farms, except one, were inherited by his children. His beloved wife passed away in 1888, at the age of sixty-eight years. Both husband and wife were faithful and loyal members of the Lutheran Church.

MILES A. KAHLE, the son, was thirteen years of age when his parents moved to Fulton County, Ohio. His early education was had in Pennsylvania, his native State. Having reached manhood he engaged in the stave and lumber business in Blissfield, Michigan. Here he purchased a farm of eighty-eight and one-half acres. By purchase he increased this farm to one hundred and sixty-eight acres. On this farm he now lives, 1913. By well directed effort he has made the farm one of the most valuable estates in Lenawee County, Michigan. Mr. Kahle was one of the founders of the Farmers & Merchants Banking Company of Metamora, and Vice President since its organization in 1899. In politics he is a Democrat. He has served several terms as Trustee of Amboy Township, and has held minor township offices.

Mr. Kahle married Miss Lanah Augusta Clarke. There were born to Mr. and Mrs. Kahle five children named Lulu, Rose, Clarke James, William Henry, and Nelson.

1. LULU ADELIA KAHLE was born in Metamora, Ohio, December 24th, 1881. She married Mr. Asbury Loar at Metamora, Ohio, June 6th, 1899. Mr. Loar was born at Loartown, Alleghany County, August 8th, 1876. His parents names are Na-

than Loar and Ellen Morgan Loar. There were born to Mr. and Mrs. Loar, two children, Ronald and Marie.

1. RONALD LOAR was born near Metamora, Ohio, May 19th, 1900.

2. MARIE LOAR was born at the same place, February 29th, 1904.

2. ROSE ZELLAH KAHLE was born at Metamora, Ohio, April 23rd, 1883. She married Russell B. Crockett at Metamora, November 30th, 1905. Mr. Crockett was the son of Willard Crockett and Hannah (Rice) Crockett. He was born on a farm in Ogden Township, Lenawee County, Michigan, November 23rd, 1879. There were born to Mr. and Mrs. Crockett two children named Ruth and Willard, both born at the same place as their father.

1. RUTH ADELIA CROCKETT was born October 31st, 1909.

2. MILES WILLARD CROCKETT was born November 8th, 1912.

3. CLARK E. JAMES KAHLE, third child and first son of Miles and Lanah (Clarke) Kahle, was born at Metamora, Ohio, January 7th, 1885. He married Miss Wilhelmina Shepard Cogwin at Wilmington, Delaware, January 15th, 1908. Miss Cogwin is the daughter of Hamden A. Cogwin and Ellen Delight (Shephard) Cogwin. She was born near New London, Oneida County, N. Y., May 3rd, 1884.

Mr. and Mrs. Kahle have one child named Charles Miles Kahle, born at Metamora, Ohio, February 16th, 1909.

4. WILLIAM HENRY KAHLE was born in Metamora, Ohio, September 2nd, 1886. He is at this date, May, 1913, unmarried.

5. NELSON ALEXANDER KAHLE was born in Metamora, Ohio, August 7th, 1892. He is at this date, May, 1913, unmarried.

II. JOHN JAY CLARKE, second child and first son of Dr. Sanford and Adelia (Champion) Clarke, was born in Franklin, Lenawee County, Michigan, September 12th, 1866. He married Alta Crockett at Metamora, Ohio, October 28th, 1888. She was the daughter of David Crockett. Mr. and Mrs. Clarke have three children named Sanford, Mabel and Pearl.

1. SANFORD MONROE CLARKE was born at Metamora, Ohio, October 14th, 1890. He married (Name not reported) in Oklahoma. They have one child, Kenneth Sanford Clarke, born (not reported).

2. MABEL CLAIR CLARKE, daughter of John Jay and Adelia (Crockett) Clarke, was born in Ogden, Lenawee County, Michigan, March 22nd, 1892. She married Fred Petee at Blissfield, Michigan, April 10th, 1909. Mr. Petee is the son of Paul Petee and his wife Rose (Pernney) Petee. He was born in Blissfield, Michigan, May 16th, 1889. There were born to Mr. and Mrs. Petee, two children, a son and a daughter, named Howard and Wanda, both born at Blissfield.

1.   HOWARD PETEE was born January 10th, 1911.

2.   WANDA PETEE was born July 22nd, 1912.

3.   PEARL CLARKE, third child, was born at Blissfield, Michigan, May 16th, 1895, and died when four months old.

III.   DR. DORMAN JEWETT CLARKE, the third child and second son of Sanford and Adelia (Champion) Clarke, was born at Tipton, Lenawee County, Michigan, February 15th, 1869. He married Miss Sarah Emeline Robinson at Angola, Steuben County, Indiana, June 4th, 1902.   She is the daughter of Mr. Nathan Dixon Robinson and his wife, Sarah Malissa Townsend, and was born at Angola, Indiana, February 12, 1878.   At this date, 1913, her parents reside at Angola, Ind.   Mr. Clarke is a physician now practicing in Toledo, Ohio, and resides at 1729 Superior Street.   No children reported.

III.   LAVINA ALCESTA CHAMPION, third child and third daughter of Abram Jewett Champion and Lanah Maria Miller, was born at Starkville, Herkimer County, N. Y., November 9th, 1845.   She married Lewis Henry Vrooman at Adrian, Michigan, November 9th, 1871.   Mr. Vrooman was born at Fundy, N. Y., May 28th, 1840.   Mrs. Vrooman died in Ripley, N. Y., October 13th, 1903.   Her husband died in Metamora, Ohio, January 1st, 1895.   Both were buried at Metamora.   They had two children, Edward and Adelia.

1.   EDWARD ERNEST VROOMAN was born at Danville, Vermillion County, Illinois, January 15th, 1873.   He married Miss Sarah Alzma White, a daughter of Albert W. White and his wife, Seelinda White, at Ogden, Michigan, November 2nd, 1898. Miss White was born at Fairfield, Lenawee County, Michigan, November 15th, 1873.

2.   ADELIA JANET VROOMAN was born at Metamora, Ohio, October 10th, 1880.   She married Walter S. Colwin at Oswatomie, Kansas, January 20th, 1901.   They separated and Mrs. Colwin married William J. Sumner.   No children reported.

IV.   WILLIAM JOHN CHAMPION, fourth child and oldest son of Abram and Maria Miller Champion, was born at Starkville, N. Y., September 14th, 1848.   He married for his first wife at Metamora, Ohio, January 2nd, 1869, Miss Emily Pigott, daughter of Charles and Sophia Pigott.   Miss Pigott was born in Loy, England, August 8th, 1850, and died at Adrian, Michigan, March 3rd, 1882.

MR. CHAMPION married for his second wife Miss Susan Barber at Joliet, Illinois, February 6th, 1883.   She was the daughter of Richard and Sarah (Town) Barber, born at Low, Ontario County, Canada, June 3rd, 1852, and died at Battle Creek, Michigan, March 29th, 1904, being at her death fifty-one years, nine months and twenty-six days old.

Mr. Champion married as a third wife Mrs. Susie Bristol Biddle at Battle Creek, Michigan, November 3rd, 1907. There were no children by this marriage.

There were born to William John and Emily (Pigott) Champion, three children named Maud, Frances and William.

1. Maud Champion was born September 11th, 1869, and died March 6th, 1871, being at her death one year, three months and twenty-seven days old.

2. Frances Amy Champion, second child and second daughter of William John and Emily (Pigott) Champion, was born at Adrian, Michigan, September 20th, 1873. She was married to Walter A. Rogers, October 14th, 1891. By him she had no children. Her second marriage took place on the 20th of October, 1900, when she became the wife of William Eli Frisbie. Mr. Frisbie was born in Chelsea, Michigan, October 2nd, 1867. He was the son of Joseph Frisbie and his wife Delphia Jane Glover. They were New York State people. Both parents are dead. There was born to Mr. and Mrs. Frisbie a daughter, Frances Lillian Frisbie, at Battle Creek, Michigan, April 14th, 1902. Mr. Frisbie is at this date, 1913, working in Oakland, California. Their home is at Watsonville, Santa Cruz County, California.

3. William Champion, youngest son, was born in Adrian, Michigan, June 10th, 1880, and died September 22nd, 1880, at the age of three months and twelve days. The children of his second marriage to Susan Barber, were four, named Charles, George, Bessie and John Wesley.

1. Charles Richard Champion was born in Joliet, Illinois, March 9th, 1885. His present residence is at 1420 Ludeand Avenue, Poplar Grove, Salt Lake City, Utah.

2. George Abraham Champion was born in Detroit, Michigan, April 20th, 1886. At this date, 1913, he is unmarried and resides at Valparaiso, Indiana.

3. Bessie Olive Champion was born in Detroit, Michigan, November 25th, 1888. She married Herbert Fred Hopkins at Battle Creek, Michigan, November 22nd, 1907. Mr. Hopkins was born in South Haven, Michigan, October 30th, 1886. He is Accountant for the Postum Cereal Company of Battle Creek, Michigan. There was born to Mr. and Mrs. Hopkins a son named Stainton Hopkins, born at Battle Creek, October 27th, 1908.

4. John Wesley Champion was born in Detroit, Michigan, May 3rd, 1892. He married Miss Marguerite Abbey at Battle Creek, Michigan, August 14th, 1911. Miss Abbey was born in Charlotte, Michigan, July 6th, 1892. His present address is 57 Wood Street, Battle Creek, Michigan. They have no children at this date, March, 1913.

V. KENDRICK ABRAM CHAMPION, fifth child and second son of Abram Jewett and Maria (Miller) Champion, was born in Metamora, Fulton County, Ohio, April 1st, 1855. He married at Metamora, Ohio, Miss Anna Eleanora McIntyre, July 4th, 1879. Miss McIntyre was born at Monroe Centre, Ohio, December 17th, 1858. There were born to them six children named Amelia, Grace, Earl, Catherine, Pearl and LaClaire, all at Metamora, Ohio.

1. LAMAH AMELIA CHAMPION was born January 5th, 1882. She died at Metamora, February 5th, 1889, at the age of seven years and one month.

2. GRACE MILDRED CHAMPION was born September 21st, 1890, and died on the 28th of the same month and year.

3. EARL STANLEY CHAMPION was born May 28th, 1893. He married at Toledo, Ohio, Blanch Rosetta Cecelia LaLoud, October 19th, 1910. She was born at Toledo, Ohio, February 3rd, 1891. They have one child, born January 22nd, 1911, and died on the 25th of the same month and year.

4. CATHERINE JANETTE CHAMPION, the fourth child and third daughter, was born February 23rd, 1895.

5. PEARL IRENE CHAMPION was born December 24th, 1897.

6. LaCLAIRE SMITH CHAMPION was born June 9th, 1901. He was the sixth, and youngest child of Kendrick Abram and Anna Eleanora McIntyre Champion.

VI. LaCLAIR SMITH CHAMPION, the sixth child and third son of Abram Jewett and Maria (Miller) Champion, was born at Metamora, Ohio, March 3rd, 1861. He married in Adrian, Michigan, December 25th, 1881. Miss Julia Etta Conklin, daughter of Robert and Emeline (Taylor) Conklin of Syracuse, N. Y. There were born to them four children named Florence, Laura, Cesta and John, all born at Metamora, Ohio.

1. FLORENCE CHAMPION was born October 22nd, 1883. She married Ray Card Smith at her home in Metamora, Ohio, December 25th, 1907. Mr. Smith was born at Chagrin Falls, Ohio, June 24th, 1884. He was the son of Albert W. Smith and his wife Amelia A. (Perkins) Smith, both of Chagrin Falls, Ohio. There was born to them a daughter, Vivien Smith, at Lyons, Ohio, May 16th, 1911. Mr. and Mrs. Smith, after their marriage, lived the first six weeks on a farm near Blissfield, Michigan. On the 10th of February, 1908, they moved to Lyons, Ohio, and started a lumber and grain trade with a partner. The Company name was The Lyons Grain and Coal Company, of which Mr. Smith was manager. On January 12th, 1912, he gave up the grain and coal trade, moved to Toledo, Ohio, and in partnership with his brother, Vernon W. Smith, started in the Real Estate and Insurance business under the firm name of

Smith & Smith. His residence at this date, March, 1913, is at No. 720 Woodland Avenue, Toledo, Ohio.

2. LAURA CHAMPION was born October 20th, 1885. She married Samuel L. Rice at Metamora, Ohio, December 25th, 1907. Mr. Rice is a native of Ohio, born at Metamora, Fulton County, August 31st, 1877. Mr. and Mrs. Rice have a son named Vergwin Rice, born September 13th, 1913, at Metamora.

3. CESTA CHAMPION was born May 23rd, 1891.

4. JOHN CHAMPION, the fourth child and only son of La Clair and Julia Etta Conklin Champion was born August 8th, 1897.

VII. MAXWELL CHAMPION, the seventh and youngest child and fourth son of Abram Jewett and Maria (Miller) Champion, was born at Metamora, Ohio, October 1st, 1864, and died at the same place, August 17th, 1865, being at his death ten months and sixteen days old.

The above ends the record of the descendants of Abram Jewett Champion by his first wife, Maria (Miller) Champion.

The following is the record of his descendants by his second wife, Harriet S. (Tennant) Champion. We give again the names of these children, Llewellyn, Harris, Ralph Waldo, Arthur and Fullman Merrill Monroe, all born at Metamora, Ohio.

CHILDREN OF THE SECOND MARRIAGE.

I. LLEWELLYN EARL CHAMPION was born at Metamora, Ohio, September 23rd, 1875. He married Miss Martha Miser at Siney, Ohio, in May, 1894. By her he had a son named Lloyd Earl Champion, born at Siney, Ohio, March 17th, 1896. Mr. Champion married the second time, Miss Mildred Stanley Richardson at Toledo, Ohio, May 29th, 1899. Miss Richardson was born at Yarmouth, Nova Scotia, December 26th, 1878. She is the daughter of Mr. and Mrs. Charles Schreor Richardson and his wife, whose maiden name was Catherine Elizabeth Nickerson, born at Birchtown, N. S., October 23rd, 1852. Mr. Richardson was born at Yarmouth, Novia Scotia, August 8th, 1854. No children have been reported of the second marriage.

II. HARRIS JEWETT CHAMPION was born July 14th, 1876, and died February 9th, 1877, being at his death six months and twenty-five days old.

III. RALPH WALDO CHAMPION, the third child of Abram Jewett and Harriet S. Tennant Champion, was born at Metamora, Fulton County, Ohio, June 20th, 1879. He married Miss Mabel Alice DeMuth at Monroe, Michigan, April 9th, 1907. Miss DeMuth was born in Monroeville, Ohio, March 14th, 1883. She was of French-German extraction. Her father's name was Joseph DeMuth, born in the State of Maryland, March 14th, 1836, and her mother's name was Mary Freize, born in Maryland in 1840, of French-German parents, but her husband was French; both were American born citizens.

MR. CHAMPION lived at Metamora, Ohio, for twenty-seven years, working as a farm hand during eight months of the year and attending school the winter months. His father died when he was thirteen years old. From this time on the mother had heavy burdens to carry in the support of her family and the care of her children. At his death her husband left her a home and some money that was only sufficient to pay off present indebtedness.

At the end of twenty-seven years MR. CHAMPION went to Toledo, Ohio, and learned the trade of a machinist. After his marriage, his wife became ill which increased largely his family expenses and the burden of life. With courage and strength he labored on and made for himself and family a comfortable home in Toledo, Ohio, where he now resides, January, 1913, at 1326 Detroit Avenue. Mr. and Mrs. Champion have no children.

IV. ARTHUR CHAMPION was born June 26th, 1881, and died on September 8th, 1882, being at his death one year, two months and twelve days old.

V. FULLMAN MERRILL MONROE CHAMPION was born May 16th, 1883. He married Miss Olive Emma Scott at Monroe, Michigan, November 6th, 1911. She is the daughter of Edwin P. Scott and his wife, Olive Fancuff Scott of Toledo, Ohio, and was born at Walbridge, Wood County, Ohio, May 17th, 1894. Mr. and Mrs. Champion have a daughter named Constance Ydoemie Champion, born at Toledo, Ohio, November 10th, 1912.

VI. CAROLINE CHAMPION, sixth child and third daughter of John and Lucy Champion, was born at Starkville, N. Y., February 3rd, 1821, and died July 13th, 1822, being at her death one year, five months and ten days old.

VII. ESTHER CHAMPION, seventh child and fourth daughter of John and Lucy Tennant Champion, was born at Starkville, N. Y., October 4th, 1823. She married Rev. James Sims in Columbia, N. Y., January 4th, 1846. He died in 1851. For a second husband she married Frederick Leonardson at Amboy, Ohio, April 2nd, 1856. By her second husband she had a son named Frederick Leonardson, born in Sylvania, Ohio, April 14th, 1858. He was at one time a telegraph dispatcher located at Mahoning, Pennsylvania. Mr. Leonardson died in 1861. His widow married the third time. Her third husband was Reuben Rockwood.

VIII. DAN NELSON CHAMPION was born at Starkville, Herkimer County, N. Y., November 26th, 1825, and died April 25th, 1833, being at his death seven years, four months and twentynine days old.

IX. CAROLINE MARVIN CHAMPION, the ninth child and fifth

daughter of John and Lucy (Tennant) Champion, was born at
Starkville, Herkimer County, N. Y., October 27th, 1827. (She
had a sister by the same name who died in infancy.) She married Ephraim Clough at Amboy, Ohio, June 15th, 1850. Mr.
Clough was born in New York City, August 23rd, 1823, a son
of Salmon and Lucy (Wightman) Clough. He died in Ogden,
Michigan, November 8th, 1866. His business was farming, but
he early enlisted in the Civil War and served till the close. Mrs.
Clough married as her second husband, Robert Randall of Ripley,
Chautauqua County, N. Y., in Ripley, May 8th, 1870. Mr. Randall was born at Danby, Vermont, May 8th, 1811. He was a
son of Caleb and Lydia (Conger) Randall, was a farmer near
Lansing, Michigan. He died at Ripley, N. Y.

For many years after the death of Mr. Randall she lived in
her home at Ripley Village. As years advanced her physical
powers weakened and at last she became very feeble but not entirely helpless. Most of the time she lived alone, except a short
period when her niece, Miss Helen Potter, came to her assistance
and to be company for her. Gradually failing in her strength,
at last the end came and death took her from her sufferings into
the spirit life of immortality. She died on the 15th of April,
1914. By her request her remains were taken to Buffalo, N. Y.,
and cremated, and her ashes returned to the Ripley Cemetery
to be buried by the side of her husband.

MRS. RANDALL was a person of intelligence and excellent moral qualities. She was liberal in her religious views, and for the
last few years of her life adhered to what is known as Christian
Science. A reader of that Cult officiated at her funeral.

MRS. RANDALL lived to a good old age, being at her death
eighty-six years, five months and eighteen days old. She was
the last living member of a family of ten children. She survived her next younger sister, Ruth, for a number of years.
She left no children to mourn their loss or perpetuate her
memory.

X. RUTH ANN CHAMPION, the youngest of the family of
John and Lucy Tennant Champion, was born at Litchfield, Herkimer County, N. Y., November 10th, 1830. She married in
Amboy, Ohio, Johnathan Wight Clough, April 21st, 1850. Mr.
Clough was born in New York City, July 17th, 1825. He was
a brother of Ephraim Clough. He enlisted in the Civil War
and did great service in hospitals as assistant Surgeon for three
years. He was a volunteer in the 47th Ohio Regiment. After
the War he retired to his farm in Ogden, Michigan. He has
served two terms as Justice of the Peace. In his younger days
he was a lay-preacher and brought up his large family under the
best of religious influences and culture. Mr. Clough died at

Perrysburg, Ohio, August 23rd, 1900. His beloved wife survived him for a few months over eight years, and died at the same place, February 13th, 1909. Her daughter Ruth, (Mrs. Scott) writes the author concerning her mother. "She lived a devoted christian life. She was talented, a genius by nature, very gifted, and could have made a successful public speaker. But she lived a quiet, graceful Christian life, giving her life to her family in an unselfish devotion."

The writer met this cousin in Ripley Village upon a visit with her sister Caroline to their Uncle Moses Tennant and his family, in the year 1847 or 1848. He remembers her as a beautiful young woman seventeen or eighteen years of age. How little do we know of the changes that future years will make in our lives. If time produces such marvelous changes, what wonderful vicissitudes will come over us in the eternal ages.

There were born to Mr. and Mrs. Clough ten children named as follows: John, Joseph, Ephraim, Carrie, Clara, Solon, Henry, Almong, Lucyette and Ruth.

1. JOHN MORTON CLOUGH, oldest child of Ruth Ann Champion and Johnathan W. Clough, was born in Amboy Township, Fulton County, Ohio, June 8th, 1851. He married Miss Letetia Alice Smith in Palmyra Township, Lenawee County, Michigan, June 15th, 1880. Miss Smith was born in Harvyville, Luzerne County, Pennsylvania, July 22nd, 1849. There were born to Mr. and Mrs. Clough, six children named Solon, Samuel, John, Amos, Nelson and Sherman. The four oldest were born near Ogden, Lenawee County, Michigan; the two youngest near Palmyra, Michigan.

1. SOLON D. CLOUGH was born March 6th, 1881. He married Miss Flossie Russell in Hillsdale, Hillsdale County, Michigan, February 7th, 1912. Miss Russell was born in Ogden Township, Lenawee County, Michigan, August 3rd, 1880. They have a daughter named Louise M. Clough, born in Palmyra, Lenawee County, Michigan, October 11th, 1912.

2. SAMUEL H. CLOUGH, the second child, was born January 26th, 1882. He married Miss Vera C. Bailey, at Adrian, Lenawee County, Michigan, March 24th, 1908. Miss Bailey was born at Ogden, Michigan, June 16th, 1891. There were born to Mr. and Mrs. Clough, two children named Hellen E. and John B.

1. HELLEN E. CLOUGH was born in Ogden, Michigan, June 29th, 1909.

2. JOHN B. CLOUGH was born in Raisen, Michigan, January 2nd, 1913. He died at the same place January 11th, 1914, a few days less than a year old. At the date of the recording of this death, May 21st, 1914, this dear little son has been one year and

five months in the spirit life. The Good Shephard carrieth the lambs in His bosom. None will be lost in the wilderness of an earthly life.

3. JOHN B. CLOUGH, the third child and third son of John Merton and Letetia Alice Smith Clough, was born in Ogden, Michigan, January 20th, 1883. He married Miss Mabel Stone at Blissfield, Michigan, February 19th, 1913. Miss Stone was born in Detroit, Wayne County, Michigan, January 14th, 1893.

4. AMOS M. CLOUGH was born at Ogden, Michigan, January 21st, 1884. He married Miss Grace M. Dickerson at Ogden, September 25th, 1912. Miss Dickerson was born at Ogden, April 12th, 1891. They have a son named Lawrence D. Clough, born May 8th, 1914.

5. NELSON MAR CLOUGH, was born at Palmyra, Michigan, February 25th, 1885. He married Miss Mabel Kaffer at Adrian, Michigan, January 20th, 1909. Miss Kaffer was born in Portland, Oregon, January 17th, 1891. There were born to Mr. and Mrs. Clough two daughters named Esther and Marjorie, at Ogden Center, Michigan.

1. ESTHER L. CLOUGH was born June 12th, 1909.

2. MARJORIE F. CLOUGH was born December 22nd, 1912.

6. SHERMAN OBED CLOUGH was born in Palmyra, Michigan, February 8th, 1893. He is the youngest child of John Morton and Letetia Alice Clough.

II. JOSEPH HAMILTON CLOUGH, second child and second son of Johnathan and Ruth (Champion) Clough was born at Amboy, Fulton County, Ohio, February 18th, 1854. He married Miss Rachel Priscilla Frier, who was born in Preston County, West Virginia, June 20th, 1854. They were married on the 8th of June, 1879, at Palmyra, Lenawee County, Michigan. There were born to them eleven children named Rose, Frederick, Jennie, Johnathan, Amelia, Matilda, Myra, Ephraim, Emma, Florence and Earl. The seven first named were all born in Ogden, Lenawee County, Michigan. The four last named were born at Metamora, Fulton County, Ohio.

1. ROSE MARY CLOUGH was born July 13th, 1880, and died August 3rd, of the same year, in Lenawee County, Michigan, being at her death twenty-one days old.

2. FREDERICK BARTON CLOUGH was born June 28th, 1881. He died February 15th, 1892, aged ten years, seven months and seventeen days.

3. JENNIE ELIZABETH CLOUGH was born April 9th, 1883. She was the third child and second daughter.

4. JONATHAN BRADLEY CLOUGH was born June 11th, 1885, and died in Lenawee County, Michigan, February 5th, 1892, aged six years, seven months and twenty-four days.

5.   AMELIA VICTORIA CLOUGH was born the 19th day of August, 1887.   She died January 25th, 1892, aged four years, five months and six days, in Lenawee County, Michigan.

6.   MATILDA ALICE CLOUGH was born August 4th, 1889, and died February 4th, 1892, aged two years and six months.   She died in Lenawee County, Michigan.

7.   MYRA ADELIA CLOUGH was born the 9th day of August, 1891.   She died in Lenawee County, Michigan, February 15th, 1892, aged six months and six days.

8.   EPHRAIM RICHARDSON CLOUGH, the eighth child, was born November 26th, 1892.

9.   EMMA LENA CLOUGH was born December 12th, 1893. She was the ninth child and sixth daughter.   She died June 14th, 1894, aged six months and two days.

10.   FLORENCE LADELIA CLOUGH was born March 30th, 1896. She was the tenth child and seventh daughter.

11.   OTIS EARL CLOUGH was born September 9th, 1900, the eleventh child and fourth son.

The author can but notice the inroads that death made upon this family of eleven children.   The first born, Rose May, died in infancy.   Frederick the second born, was over ten years old at his death.   It will be seen that the first born, the second born, the fourth, the fifth, the sixth and the seventh and ninth child born, died in young and tender years.   Of eleven children seven died, and four only were left.   It is impossible to realize what depth of sorrow must have overwhelmed the hearts of the parents when these sad deaths occurred.   Four of these dear children died in 1892.   In all, five daughters and two sons were taken away.   Only the strongest faith in the Divine Goodness can enable anyone to say under the burden of such bereavements, "The Lord gave, the Lord hath taken away; Blessed be the name of the Lord."

MY PRAYER AND VOW.

Father, I would not doubt thy infinite love;
    Though tears over-shadow my feeble sight;
I'll trust to thy grace in every event,
    Believing what is, must surely be right.

What was mine was first Thine. I do not deny,
    Thou hast taken away only what was Thine own;
The treasures Thou gavest I hand back to Thee,
    However sadly and lonely hereafter I roam.

Up the hills of life's journey I press my way on;
    Bright visions of glory appear long before;
I'll follow my Shepherd wherever He leads,
    Till the lambs He has taken, to me He restores."

III. EPHRAIM THEODORE CLOUGH was born in Ogden, Michigan, March 10th, 1856. He married Esther Viola Wilber, October 12th, 1879, who was born at Foisfield, Michigan, May 30th, 1860. He was a farmer at Amboy, Michigan. They had three children, William, David and Royann, born in Fulton County, Ohio. Mrs. Clough died Dec. 25th, 1907, being 47 years, 6 months and 25 days old.

1. WILLIAM JAMES CLOUGH was born November 12th, 1880. He married Miss Sarah Stewart. They have three children, whose names have not been reported.

2. DAVID THEODORE CLOUGH was born January 30th, 1885. He lived only three months.

3. ROYANN CLOUGH was born (no further report.)

IV. CARRIE MARIAH CLOUGH was born at Ogden, Michigan, June 1st, 1860. She married William Horace Wilcox, October 20th, 1880. He was born July 17th, 1861. MRS. WILCOX died April 2nd, 1908. Mr. Wilcox was employed by the Lake Shore Railroad at Newport, Michigan, as an operator and express agent. Mrs. Wilcox was a school teacher. There were born to them three children named Ella, Oliver and Florence, all born in Ogden, Michigan.

1. ELLA WILCOX was born January 27th, 1883. She married a Mr. Sanford. They have three children, whose names have not been reported.

2. OLIVER WILCOX was born May 28th, 1885.

3. FLORENCE WILCOX was born December 5th, 1887.

V. CLARA EUGENIA CLOUGH was born at Ogden, Michigan, September 10th, 1862.

VI. SOLON GRANT CLOUGH, sixth child and fourth son of Johnathan and Ruth Champion Clough, was born at Ogden, Michigan, September 19th, 1867. MR. CLOUGH is unmarried His address is Hotel Frederick, Huntington, West Virginia.

VII. HENRY JEWETT CLOUGH, the seventh child and fifth son, was born in Ogden, Michigan, October 11th, 1869. He married Miss Martha Guernsey, September 7th, 1888. They have one child named Fulton Clough, born September 1st, 1899.

VIII. ALMOND JAY CLOUGH, eighth child and sixth son, was born in Ogden, Michigan, March 22nd, 1870. He studied to be a physician at Advent College, Battle Creek, Michigan.

IX. LUCY ETTE CLOUGH, the ninth child and third daughter of Johnathan and Ruth Ann Champion Clough, was born in the Town of Ogden, Lenawee County, Michigan, February 12th, 1871. She married William Ambrose Clough, a son of Ambrose and Harriet M. Clough of Chardon, Ohio. The son was a native of Chardon, born December 14th, 1860. The marriage took place at Chardon, Ohio, July 6th, 1896. They have no children of their own, but they adopted a daughter named Hazel

Ruth Clough, born in Denver, Colorado, November 2nd, 1900. Mr. Clough belongs in another branch of the Clough family who were distant relatives of his wife's parents. He is employed by A. T. Lewis and Son, dry goods merchants of Denver, Colorado.

X. MISS RUTH ANN CLOUGH, the tenth child and fourth daughter of Johnathan and Ruth Champion Clough, was born in Ogden, Lenawee County, Michigan, April 24th, 1872. She married William Kimball in Toledo, Ohio, February 23rd, 1896. Mr. Kimball was born in Pennsylvania, September 1st, 1863. There was born to them a daughter named Helen Juliette Kimball, at Perrysburg, Ohio, December 12th, 1896. Mrs. Kimball married the second time. Her second husband was William Franklin Scott of Kentucky. They were married at Bedford, Kentucky, November 26th, 1898. Mr. Scott died in Kentucky, December 13th, 1911. There were born of this second marriage at Perrysburg, Ohio, two children named Jessie Kirby and Wade Hamilton.

1. JESSIE KIRBY SCOTT was born December 12th, 1899.
2. WADE HAMPTON SCOTT was born February 13th, 1902.

MR. SCOTT, the second husband, died in Kentucky, December 13th, 1911. He was the son of James B. Scott, whose wife was a daughter of William Morgan, who was closely related to General Wade Hampton Morgan of the War of 1863 and 1865. Mr. Scott was a cousin of General Morgan.

This closes the record of the descendants of John Champion and Lucy Selden Tennant. The descendants number as follows:

```
Children .................................10
Grand-children ...........................34
Great-Grand-children .....................82
Great-Great-Grand-children ...............72
Great-Great-Great-Grand-children .........27
                                         ——
    Total descendants ....................225
```

These include seven generations.

WILLIAM PHILLIPS

Born in 1796   Died March 13, 1873

MRS. OLIVIA TENNANT PHILLIPS

Born June 1, 1799   Died October 2, 1869

PART III.

CHAPTER IV.

Contains a record of the birth of MISS OLIVIA TEN-
NANT, and her marriage to William Phillips, and of
their descendants by family names. Phillips, Auton,
Hastings, Crowther, Otting, Leadbetter, Wenthworth,
Covert, Farwell, Beottelyon, Burleson, DeHart, Perry,
Bradley, Simmons, Plumsted, Potter, Baisley, Van Ku-
ren, Wait and Jinkins.

MISS OLIVIA TENNANT was born in Springfield, Otsego County, N. Y., in 1796. She was the second child of Sarah Selden Jewett by her third husband, Moses Tennant. Before her marriage she made her home with her half sister, Betsey Elizabeth
Tennant, whose husband was Sterlin Way. She married William
Phillips at Springfield a short time before 1821, the year of the
marriage of her youngest sister Esther. Soon after their marriage in the Fall of 1821, they moved to Oakland County, Michigan, and purchased land near Pontiac. On this farm they
lived till 1845 or 1846, when they sold out and bought eighty
acres of land in Richfield Township, Genesee County, Michigan.
Mr. Phillips owned several plots of land in the vicinity of his
first purchase. He was in every sense a successful farmer.

MRS. OLIVIA (TENNANT) PHILLIPS' married life extended
through a period of at least forty-five years. Her only brother,
Moses Asel Tennant, visited this sister near the year 1852.
When he returned home he told his family a little of a conversation he had with his sister Olivia. It seems that Olivia had an
offer of marriage from a young man of excellent character and
who possessed a handsome fortune. But Olivia rejected his offer. Her brother asked her, "Olivia, don't you wish you had
married that young man of fortune in Otsego County? he thought
all the world of you?" "No" was the quick reply, "I rather
have William Phillips' old boots." The writer can testify to this
story by his Father. After many years of willing, loving toil
with her husband, she died at their home in Genesee County,
Michigan, in 1886, being at her death seventy-seven years of age.

Sometime after her death, her husband married a Mrs. Car-
man, a widow of excellent character and of good reputation, with
whom he lived a few years up to the time of her death. Mr.
Phillips lived to the year 1873 and died at the old home in Richfield, Genesee County, Michigan, being past seventy-seven years
of age.

"Blessed are the dead that die in the Lord, from hence forth: Yea, saith the Spirit, that they may rest from their labors; and their works do follow them." Rev. 14:13.

There were born to Mr. and Mrs. Phillips eight children, named as follows: William Jewett, Esther, John Galusha, Andrew Jackson, Sarah, Cleantha, James Francis and Mariah.

I. WILLIAM JEWETT PHILLIPS was the oldest son, born at Springfield, Otsego County, N. Y., March 15th, 1820. He married Nancy Maria Holden at Pontiac, Oakland County, Michigan, May 4th, 1843. Miss Holden was born at (place and date could not be obtained) and died in Richfield, Michigan, August 17th, 1905. MR. PHILLIPS was a farmer and lived on a farm in Genesee County, Michigan. He died at Pontiac, Oakland County, Michigan, September 29th, 1887, being at his death sixty-seven years, six months and fourteen days old.

There were born to Mr. and Mrs. Phillips, four children named, Otto Francis, Louisa, George and William Holden. All were born in Richfield Township, Genesee County, Michigan.

1. OTTO FRANCIS PHILLIPS was born January 17th, 1844, and died the next day after his birth.

2. LOUISA PHILLIPS was born August 14th, 1847, and died April 10th, 1851. She was three years, seven months and twenty-six days old at her death.

3. GEORGE PHILLIPS was born in Richfield. The writer could not obtain any further record save that he died a number of years ago.

4. WILLIAM HOLDEN PHILLIPS was born in Richfield, Genesee County, Michigan, January 18th, 1854. He married Ida Almira Conger in Burton, Genesee County, Michigan, September 14th, 1881. Miss Conger was born in Burton, Michigan, April 14th, 1857. MR. PHILLIPS inherited from his father a splendid farm of two hundred and thirty acres in Richfield, Genesee County, Michigan. He is a successful farmer getting good returns each year for the labor bestowed. In August of 1911 the writer visited this cousin and his family. At his home was the first reunion of the descendants of William and Olivia Tennant Phillips joined by some of the descendants of other branches of the Tennant family. Between thirty-five and forty guests were present. A reunion was at this meeting organized with Mr. Holden Phillips elected President and Mrs. Cora DeHart, wife of William DeHart, of Bridgeport Village, Secretary. The day was most happily spent in visiting and amusements. They resolved to meet annually. They adjourned to meet in 1912 at the home of Mr. and Mrs. Ellis Perry of Bridgeport, Michigan.

There were born to Mr. and Mrs. Holden Phillips three children named, Bessie, Elvira and Jewett.

JANE LOUISE GIDLEY
Born August 1, 1913
Daughter of John and Elvina Phillips Gidley

1. BESSIE PHILLIPS was born in Richfield Township, Genesee County, Michigan, on the same farm where her father was born, November 12th, 1882. She was graduated from Mae College, Michigan, in the Spring of 1905. She married Claude Isaac Auten at her home in Richfield, Michigan, August 25th, 1905. Mr. Auten was born at Highland, Oakland County, Michigan, April 7th, 1882. He was graduated as Civil Engineer from Mae College, Michigan, in June, 1905.

There were born to Mr. and Mrs. Auten two children, named Dorothy and Phillips George.

1. DOROTHY AUTEN was born at Flint, Michigan, December 12th, 1909.

2. PHILLIPS GEORGE AUTEN was born in Detroit, Michigan, September 16th, 1911.

2. ELVIRA PHILLIPS, the second daughter of Holden and Ida Phillips, was born in Richfield Township, Michigan, January 7th, 1886. She married at her home in Richfield where she was born, Dr. John Burton Gidley, on June 12th, 1912. Dr. Gidley is an osteopathist physician, and at the time of his marriage was practicing at Hamilton, Ontario County, Canada, to which place he took his wife immediately after thier marriage, and they commenced housekeeping. In a few months, he returned to Michigan and settled at Hastings, Weschester County. He was born at Davison, Genesee County, Michigan, November 4th, 1886. In 1913 he moved to Flint, Michigan, and went into the office of Dr. Harlem. Later, in 1913, he opened an office and went into practice by himself. There was born to Mr. and Mrs. Gidley a daughter named Jane Louise Gidley, on August 1st, 1913, at Flint, Michigan.

3. JEWETT PHILLIPS was born in Richfield, Michigan, July 4th, 1888. At this date, 1913, he is at home with his parents, working on the farm.

II. ESTHER OLIVA PHILLIPS, second child and oldest daughter of William and Olivia Tennant Phillips, was born in Pontiac, Genesee County, Michigan, December 19th, 1826. She married Henry Hastings in Richfield, Genesee County, Michigan, in 1843.

MR. HASTINGS was born in Connecticut, August 7th, 1816, and died at Cincinnati, Ohio, May 28th, 1900, aged eighty-three years, nine months and twenty-one days. His beloved wife preceded him in death about six years; she died at Cincinnati, Ohio, March 9th, 1894, being at her death sixty-seven years, two months and twenty days old.

There was born to Mr. and Mrs. Hastings four sons named George, Frank, William Jewett, and John Fulker.

1. GEORGE PHILLIPS HASTINGS, the oldest son of Henry and Esther Olivia Phillips Hastings, was born at Hart, Oceana Co.,

Mich., Aug. 15th, 1845.   He was graduated from the University
of Cincinnati, Ohio.   He studied medicine and became a practicing physician at Friendsville, Susquehanna Co., Pa.   He married Miss Sophia Glidden at Friendsville, Pa., Aug. 18th, 1873.

MISS GLIDDEN was the seventh child of Benjamin and Emma
(Stephens) Glidden, born at Friendsville, Apr. 28th, 1853.

After pursuing his profession for a number of years, Mr.
Hastings was taken ill and died at Friendsville, Pa., Feb. 10th,
1883, being at his death 37 years, 5 months and 23 days old.
His death was followed by other misfortunes which taken together, cast a burden of care and labor upon the devoted wife
that he left, which was too great for her to bear.   After a few
years she was taken with an incurable disease that blighted all her
fondest earthly hopes and unfitted her for the duties of life.   The
family thought best to have her go to an asylum for treatment,
but her illness was not cured after a thorough trial.   She is still
living at this date, September, 1913.   Concerning her parents,
their daughter Alice, writes the author the following appreciative
words "Both my father and mother were people of excellent mental and moral qualities, and if they could have been spared to us
children, how proud we should be of them.   As it is, we have
their memory and their lives before us as they trained us while
little children, and these have been our guide all our lives."

There were born to Mr. and Mrs. George Hastings four children named Alice, Jessie, George and Wilmot.

1.   ALICE OLIVIA HASTINGS, the oldest child, was born at Cincinnati, Ohio, July 31, 1874.   She prepared herself for teaching
and was graduated from the High School at Montrose, Susquehanna Co., Pa., in the summer of 1893.   She attended for one
term at Wyoming Seminary, Kingston, Pa.   She was engaged
in teaching thirteen years.   It is impossible to estimate the good
that was accomplished during these years of teaching.   The
fruits of training and guiding the minds of children and young
people are always accumulative in after years, not only in their
personal development of character, mind and heart, but also in
their usefulness in the spheres of life in which they perform their
duties and exert thir influence.

MISS ALICE was never married.   After years of toil at home
and in the school room, she was taken ill, and all that kind friends
and medical skill could do to save her precious life did not avail.
She fell asleep and passed into the realm of the spirit life at Montrose. Pa., Sept. 28th, 1906.

The writer here quotes a few verses of a beautiful poem by
John Greenleaf Whittier, entitled "The Eternal Goodness,"
which are so well suited to lift weak human spirits above the
clouds of disappointment, bereavement and sorrows:

"I long for household voices gone,
　For vanished smiles I long,
But God hath led my dear ones on,
　And He can do no wrong.

I know not what the future hath
　Of marvel or surprise,
Assured alone that life and death
　His mercy underlies.

And if my heart and flesh are weak
　To bear an untried pain;
The bruised reed He will not break,
　But strengthen and sustain.

And so beside the silent sea
　I wait the muffled oar;
No harm from Him can come to me
　On ocean or on shore.

I know not where His islands lift
　Their fronded palms in air;
I only know I cannot drift
　Beyond His love and care.

And Thou, O Lord, by whom are seen
　Thy creatures as they be,
Forgive me if too close I lean
　My human heart on Thee."

　　2.　JESSIE MAY HASTINGS, the second child and second daughter, was born at Little Meadows, Susquehanna Co., Pa., Aug. 6th, 1876.　She married Alexander John McDonald at Portland, Oregon, June 10, 1913.　Mr. McDonald was born at Lock Garry, Glengarry, Ontario, Canada Dec. 16, 1865.　He was the son of John Isaac McDonald and his wife Isabella O'Brian.　The father was born in Inverness, Scotland, and the mother at Alexandria, Ontario, Canada.　They now reside in Portland, Oregon. The son is a construction engineer.

　　MRS. McDONALD has been a teacher in a graded school in Pa. for seventeen years.　She was graduated from the High School at Montrose, Susquehanna Co., Pa., in 1895.　She took a short course in Domestic Science and Art.

　　It is only just to say that these two sisters, Alice and Jessie Hastings, have proved their ability and strength of character in obtaining an education and fitting themselves for honorable positions and useful lives notwithstanding the great obstacles they had to overcome in the afflictions that were brought upon the family in the death of their father and the incurable illness of their mother.　It is enough to imagine what their cares, labors and deprivations were, without any attempt to portray them in words which must be inadequate to convey the whole truth. There are occasions when silence is more comforting and befitting than words. Shakespeare says "There is a divinity that shapes our ends, rough hew them how we may." In that Divinity we can safely trust our lives and unseen destiny for all time and eternity.

3. GEORGE HENRY HASTINGS, the third child and first son of George and Sophia (Glidden) Hastings, was born at Culver, Ottawa Co., Kansas, Oct. 7, 1878. His business is plumbing, gas-fitting and farming. He is located at Dixion, Ill.

4. WILMOT GLIDDEN HASTINGS, the youngest child, was born at Culver, Ottawa Co., Kansas, Feb. 11, 1880. He was educated at the Clark University of Worcester, Mass., and the University of Michigan at Ann Arbor. He is employed by the United States in the Bureau of Forestry with headquarters at Portland, Oregon. He married Miss Marion Kathreen McVey at Portland, Oregon, Nov. 3d, 1913. Miss McVey was born at Geneva, N. Y., Jan. 25th, 1884. She is the daughter of Mathew McVey, born in Scotland, and his wife Mary Lucy (Moss) McVey of South Bridge, Mass.

MRS. HASTINGS is a Dietician receiving her Degree from Limmouse College, Burton, Mass. Their residence at this date, Jan. 1914, is 701 Everet St., Portland, Oregon.

FRANK TENNANT HASTINGS was born in Genesee, Genesee Co., Mich., December 20th, 1849. He was the second son of Henry and Esther Phillips Hastings. He married Jessie Weston at Cincinnati, Ohio, Sept. 27th, 1876. He was a carpenter by trade. For a while Mr. Hastings lived in Utah, then went to Canada, Province of Alberta. About the year 1903 or 4 he took up a government claim near Redwillow. This land he still owns. (1912.)

Mr. and Mrs. Hastings have two children named Julianna and Frank.

1. JULIANNA MARIE HASTINGS was born in Cincinnati, Ohio, Feb. 22nd, 1878. She married Arthur Clemens Crowther. Mr. Crowther was born at Salina, Salina Co., Kansas, Nov. 25th, 1870. There were born to them eight children named as follows: Artha, Julianna, Ellison, Enid, Ada, Joseph, May and Bryce.

1. ARTHA CLEMENS CROWTHER was born at Salina, Salina Co., Kansas, April 16th, 1900.

2. JULIAN FRANK CROWTHER was born at Salina, Salina Co., Kansas, July 14th, 1901.

The following children were born at Redwillow, Alberta Province, Canada.

3. ELLISON ANDREW CROWTHER was born June 13th, 1905.
4. ENID OLIVE CROWTHER, a twin sister to Ellison was born at the same time and place.
5. ADA JESSIE CROWTHER was born Dec. 13th, 1906.
6. JOSEPH ARTHUR CROWTHER was born June 29th, 1908.
7. MAY DeVERNE CROWTHER was born Nov. 10, 1910.
8. BRYCE CARROL CROTHER was born June 17th, 1912.

Mr. and Mrs. Crowther lived in Salina, Kansas for four years where he was station engineer and subsequently fireman on the Union Pacific R. R. In the Spring of 1903 the family moved to Canada locating at Red Willow, Alberta province or district.Here he located on a government claim and has pursued farming to this date, 1912.

2. FRANK WESTON HASTINGS was born in Salina Co., Kan., Jan. 20th, 1880. He married Miss Margueretta Florence Maymill Sellick at Edmonton, Alberta, Canada, Sept. 9th, 1905. Miss Sellick was born at Prince Edward Island Oct. 3rd, 1887. They have one son named Henry James Weston Hastings, born at Red Willow, Albert, Canada, October 30th, 1911.

MR. HASTINGS is an industrious farmer now located on a farm near or at Red Willow, Alberta, Canada which was taken up by his father as government land in the years 1903 or 4. Property in that region has increased in value as the country's population has increased by immigration. This increase has made the family comfortably well off, and gives them an encouraging prospect for a good fortune in the future.

3. WILLIAM JEWETT HASTINGS, third child and third son of Henry and Esther Phillips Hastings was born in Genesee Township, Genesee Co., Mich., Dec. 11th, 1852. He married Miss Alice Margaret Allen, Feb. 10th, 1886. Miss Allen was born at Lewiston, Pa., July 14th, 1865. After their marriage they began housekeeping on a farm near Trescott, Kansas.

There were born to them three children named, Anson, Charles and William.

1. ANSON JEWETT HASTINGS was born near Trescott, Kan., December 9th, 1886.
2. CHARLES EMMERSON HASTINGS was born Dec. 12th, 1890 near Grasslake, Mich.
3. WILLIAM VERNON HASTINGS was born at Ossawatomie, Kansas, August 30th, 1897.

MR. HASTINGS, the father died at Kansas City, Feb. 22nd, 1912. Mrs. Hastings still occupies their home at that place No. 230 South Eleventh St., Kansas City, Kan. Further mention will be made of him in a memorial Tribute found in Part IV, 2nd Division.

4. JOHN FULLER HASTINGS fourth son of Henry and Esther

Hastings was born at or near Flint, Mich., Aug. 7th, 1855. He married Elizabeth Davison on March 17th, 1876 at Cincinnati, O. Miss Davison was born at Cleveland, O., Dec. 8th, 1855. Mr. Hastings died at Cincinnati Feb. 18th, 1901.

There were born to them five children Esther, Carolyn, Fuller, Leslie and Bessie, all were born at Cincinnati, O.

1.   ESTHER PHILLIPS HASTINGS was born Mar. 2nd, 1877. She died at Cincinnati Jan. 13th, 1880 being at her death 2 years, 10 months and 11 days old.

2.   CAROLYN MAY HASTINGS was born May 29th, 1880. Miss Carolyn at this date is a teacher in a ward school in Cincinnati, O.

3.   FULLER HUTCHINSON HASTINGS was born Mar. 20th, 1886.   He died at Cincinnati, July 24th, 1887 being at his death one year, four months, and four days old.

4.   LESLIE DAVISON HASTINGS was born on the 21st of July, 1887.   He died at Cincinnati on Mar. 5th, 1888, being at his death seven months and fourteen days old.

5.   BESSIE J. HASTINGS was born on the 13th of Feb. 1891. She was employed for a few years as a stenographer in the office of the publishers of a magazine in her home city.   She was graduated from a business college before entering upon this work and is well prepared for a useful life in any sphere in which she may be employed.   On Sept. 18th, 1912, she married Mr. William Beinshagen Otting of Cincinnatti, O.   Mr. Otting was born in Cincinnatti, O., Aug. 23, 1887.   He is assistant Editor of an advertising magazine devoted to homes and their equipments, named "The Harness World," his home has always been in Cincinnatti, O.

III.   JOHN GALUSHA PHILLIPS was the third child and second son of William and Olivia Tennant Phillips, born in Mich., August 24th, 1823.   He married in Mich. Lydia Morrison by whom he had one son named Austin Phillips who enlisted in the civil war.   After the close of his services he returned to Mich. married and settled in the Northern part of the state where he died leaving children.   The writer can obtain no further information concerning this son or his family.

GULUSHA was a physician.   After the death of his first wife, he came to Chautauqua Co., N. Y., in 1848 or 49, and located at the village of Sherman where he pursued his profession.   Here he married Miss Amanda Darrow.   By her he had three children named Delaski, Hortens and Elizabeth.   Hortens married at Ripley, Chautauqua Co., N. Y., John Allen, a man much older than herself.   The writer has also been informed that Elizabeth also married and lived near Rochester, N. Y.   He has never heard of the marriage of Delaski.

In later years DR. PHILLIPS returned to Mich. where he spent the last years of his life. His second wife went to him during his last sickness, and was with him at the time of his death, which took place on the 21st of Feb. 1870. He was buried in the cemetery of Richfield Township, Genesee Co., Mich.

The writer regrets that his information concerning the life of this cousin and his family is so limited. He was well acquainted with him and his wife when they lived at Sherman. She belonged to a respectable family and was well esteemed by all who knew her. Cousin Gulusha had his faults as many others, but he was a warm hearted, jovial, and companionable man, fond of good company and always loyal to his friends. While at Sherman he had a good paying practice as a physician, and so far as the writer knows sustained a good reputation among the collegues of his profession and in the community. He suffered much from the asthma, and was compelled to resort to breathing the fumes of burning saltpetre to relieve his hard breathing. We can well cast a mantle of charity over all his failings and judge him as we ourselves would be judged by the righteous Judge of all.

IV. ANDREW JACKSON PHILLIPS, third son and fourth child, of William and Olivia Phillips was born at Pontiac, Mich., May 4th, 1828. He married Emily Blackmer. They had two children Elvira and Edison.

1. ELVIRA OLIVIA PHILLIPS was born in Richfield Township, Genesee Co., Mich., June 16th, 1850. She married Roscoe Leadbetter, at Bridgeport, Saginaw Co., Mich., in June 1869.

There were born to them three children named Helen, Charles, Edison and Charles Curtis.

1. HELEN LEADBETTER was born in Bridgeport Township. She died in infancy.

2. CHARLES EDISON LEADBETTER was born at Saginaw, Mich. He died in infancy.

3. CHARLES CURTIS LEADBETTER was born at Saginaw, March 13th, 1876. He married for his first wife (Name not reported). She died leaving no children. He married for his second wife (Name not reported). By her he had two children named Charles and Catharine, both born in Saginaw, Mich.

1. CHARLES AUSTIN LEADBETTER was born Oct. 29th, 1910.

2. CATHARINE GRACE LEADBETTER was born August 6th, 1912.

2. HORACE EDISON PHILLIPS, son of Andrew Jackson Phillips and his wife Emily (Blackmer) Phillips was born at Geneseeville, Genesee Co., Mich., Feb. 23rd, 1855. He married Miss Rosa Tuttle in 1880. Miss Tuttle was born at Saginaw, Mich., Dec. 4th, 1861. MR. PHILLIPS was connected with the Grand

Union Tea Co., for many years at Calmut, Mich.   He had an attack of Brights disease and died April 24th, 1909, being at his death 54 years, 1 month, and 1 day old.

There were born to Mr. and Mrs. Phillips three children named Jay, Gertrude and Ora.

1.   EDISON JAY PHILLIPS was born at Saginaw, Mich., July 26th, 1881.   He married Miss Gertrude May Retullie at Calmut, Mich., who was born at Calmut, Oct. 28th, 1880.

2.   GERTRUDE PHILLIPS was born at Calmut, Mich., Sept. 22nd, 1897.

3.   ORA PHILLIPS was born at Calmut, Mich., July 14th, 1899.

We take the following facts from newspaper of Saginaw, Mich.

MRS. EMILY PHILLIPS died at Detroit on Wednesday, at midnight.   She was one of the pioneers of Saginaw County.   She was the widow of Andrew Jackson Phillips, and was born in Genesee County, N. Y., May 24th, 1829.   She moved with her parents to Richfield, Genesee County, Mich., in 1840 and married Andrew Jackson Phillips, Oct. 27th, 1848.   They moved to Saginaw in 1851 where Mr. Phillips engaged in the grocery business for several years.   In 1861, they settled on a farm in Bridgeport Township where they lived till 1911.   After the death of Mr. Phillips, she made her home with her grandson, Mr. Charles C. Leadbetter of Detroit, Mich.   She is survived by many friends and relatives among whom are a sister, Mrs. George Bridgman, a brother, Horace Blackmer, and six grandchildren.

The author of this genealogy had the plaesure of meeting this cousin at her home in Saginaw and at the second annual meeting of the Phillips reunion.   Mrs. Phillips was in many respects a very interesting character.   She held her youthful spirits and vigor in advanced years, and impressed her cousin, the writer, as a person of a well balanced mental powers of a high order of moral and spiritual development.   She performed her life work in her home, in society and the church with consciencious fidelity and loyalty to the highest ideals of true womanhood. Among the many beautiful poems Mrs. Hemans has written we quote the following lines from a poem entitled "A. Dirge."

"For there is hushed on earth
A voice of gladness—there is veiled a face
Where parting leaves a dark and silent place.
        By the once-joyous hearth.
A smile hath passed, which filled its home with light

A soul, whose beauty, made that smile so bright,
"But the glory from the dust,
And praise to Him, the merciful, for those
On whose bright memory love may still repose,
    With an immortal trust!
Praise for the dead, who leave us when they part,
Such hope as she hath left—the poor in heart."

V. SARAH PHILLIPS, fifth child and second daughter of Wm. and Olivia Phillips was born at Pontiac, Mich., Jan. 15th, 1833. She married Gibbins Wensworth at Richfield, Mich., Oct. 29th, 1848. He was born July 25th, 1821. He was a farmer and lived near Geneseeville, Genesee Co., Mich. He died of a cancer. His wife also died. They had four children named as follows: Emma, Amanda, Mary and Elvira.

1. EMMA JANE WENTWORTH was born in Genesee Township, Genesee Co., Mich., Aug. 22nd, 1852. She married Joseph R. Burt in April 1877. Mr. Burt was born April 17th, 1854 and died in October 1880. On Aug. 21, 1894, Mrs. Burt married Mr. William Smith. At this date 1912, he owns and furnishes a fine art store at No. 123 North Franklin St., Saginaw, Mich. The writer called at this store in the summer of 1911, the month of August and in August 1912, he visited them at their home.

Mr. Smith and family moved to Detroit, Mich.

2. AMANDA C. WENTWORTH, second child was born in Genesee Township, Genesee Co., Mich., June 21, 1855. She married Mr. Walter Eugene Covert at Genesee, Mich., May 3rd, 1881. Mr. Covert was born in Burten Township, Genesee Co., Mich., July 26th, 1856. He is a contractor and has spent much of his life in Saginaw and Flint, Mich. His great sorrow came to him in the loss of his beloved wife, who died at Flint, Mich., May 18th, 1908, being at her death aged 52 years, 10 months and 27 days old.

'Tis blessed to know when our friends pass away,
    That Infinite Love has determined the hour;
Faith, hope and love then follows them upward,
    As they are set free by deaths merciful power.

There was born to Mr. and Mrs. Covert, a son named Harry Wentworth Covert. His birth was at Saginaw, Mich., Nov. 22nd, 1882. He married Miss Frances May Osborne at Rochester, Mich., Feb. 13th, 1911. Miss Osborne was born in Detroit, Mich., April 7th, 1887.

MR. COVERT was educated in the high school at Flint, Mich. For three years up to 1912, he has been employed by the National Refining Company of Cleveland, O., as a traveling salesman, for the company in the state of Mich. His employment in this company is abundant proof of his business ability, and of his upright moral character. His present home is in Rochester, Mich., (1912).

3.   MARY WENTWORTH, 3d child was born in Genesee Township, Genesee Co., Mich., June 5th, 1864.   She married Seth Farwell, at the same place June 28th, 1883.   Mr. Farwell was born Feb. 23rd, 1863.   He was a business man much interested in church and public affairs.   He accumulated a handsome fortune, built a church edifice, and left his family in independent circumstances.   He died at Flint, Mich.

Mr. and Mrs. Farwell had five children named, Edith, Ethel, Austin, Marguerite and Gertrude.

1.   ELIZABETH MAUDE FARWELL was born in Genesee Township, Genesee Co., Mich., July 4th, 1885.   She died at Flint, Mich., Jan. 31, 1907, being at her death 21 years, 6 months and 27 days old.   She never married.   The writer had a conversation with the mother at her home in Flint in the summer of 1911. Time cannot quench the love of a mother for her children nor can it remove the sorrow that fills her heart when her loved ones are taken from her.   Edith had grown into full womanhood with an education and accomplishments which enriched and beautified her life, and attached her relatives and friends to her, with the strongest bounds of human affection.

> Shall we say she is dead? no let us say that she lives,
>   The body alone is the victim of death;
> The spirit, the soul, that immortal part,
>   Of it's presence and love we can't be bereft.
>
> Shall we meet her again in the life she now lives?
>   Shall we know her and love her as now?
> Will the veil that conceals her from our weeping eyes,
>   Be removed from her glory-crowned brow?
>
> Yes!   the love that first gave will surely restore;
>   God's promises never will fail;
> Reunions will come in that heavenly land,
>   Where love, peace and glory prevail.

2.   ETHEL CLARA FARWELL was born at Flint, Mich., April 14th, 1887.   This dear little daughter lived only four months and six days.   She died Aug. 20th, 1887 at Flint, Mich.

> (My birdling has flown to her heavenly nest,
>   On wings of the spirit she soared above;
> By angels escorted, she passes from earth,
>   To nestle so sweetly in God's bosom of love.)

3.   AUSTIN BURLINGTON FARWELL was born at Flint, Mich., June 5th, 1888.   He is an upright and industrious young man. employed in the automobile works at this date, 1912.   As far as

SETH FARWELL

Born February 23, 1863   Died July 17, 1910

MRS. MARY WENTWORTH FARWELL
Born June 5, 1864

the son can take the place of a father in a family, this son fills his father's place now vacated by death. The writer met him at his home with his mother on his visit in August 1911. Later, the writer has learned that this son died at Flint. Mich., Aug. 24th, 1914.

4. MARGUERITE FARWELL was born at Flint, Mich., May 20th, 1890. She married at Flint, Mich., Oct. 21st, 1909 Edwin J. Beottelyon who was born Oct. 28th, 1881. Their home is now with the wife's mother at Flint. He is an employee in the auto works of that city. Their son, Henry Wentworth was born March 9th, 1914.

5. GERTRUDE PHILA FARWELL was born at Flint, Oct. 4th, 1897. She is attending school and is seeking to fit herself for a useful and happy life. She married Donald· Timmerman at Flint, Mich., March 12th, 1915. Mrs. Farwell married for her second husband Mr. Ernest Kelsey at Flint, Mich., March 12th, 1915.

4. ELVIRA WENTWORTH, fourth daughter and last child of Mr. and Mrs. Gibbins Wentworth was born in Genesee Township, Genesee Co., Mich., May 28th, 1863. She married Mr. Frank Alfred Burleson at Genesee, Mich., Jan. 16th, 1887. Mr. Burleson was born in Saginaw, Saginaw Co., Mich., July 29th, 1868.

There was born to them a son named Fred Wentworth Burleson. He was born at Saginaw, Mich., July 14th, 1888. At this date, 1912, he resides at Detroit, Mich.

Mr. and Mrs. Burleson after their marriage lived from Jan. 1887 to Oct. 1891 at Saginaw. Their next residence was in Detroit. Mich., from Oct. 1891 to July 1905. His occupation has been for many years a Locomotive Engineer on the M. C. R. R. Since 1905 the family home has been at Stonington, Delta Co., Mich. He has retired on a farm at this place, which he owns.

VI. CLEANTHA PHILLIPS, sixth child and third daughter of William and Olivia Phillips was born in Oakland Co., Mich., May 5th, 1835. She married Gilbert DeHart in Genesee Co., Mich. in 1855, and lived in that region 'till 1863, when they moved to Johnson's Corners, Ohio. Here they lived till 1865, when they returned to Mich., and settled in Saginaw Co., about the year 1871. From Saginaw they moved to Loomis, Isabella Co., Mich., where Mr. Phillips engaged in the lumber trade. After engaging in this business for about three years he died there, on the 4th of Sept. 1874. Mrs. DeHart now returned to Saginaw. When the estate was settled she had but a small income to support her family. It was a long and hard struggle to make a living, but by courage and continuous effort, and by trust in God, she succeeded in supporting and educating her children.

Many times she has been known to say, "I wish only to live, so I may be ready to meet my Savior." The performance of life's duty with reliance on God, was the adequate preparation she sought, and which she certainly gained.

In 1853, Mrs. DeHart, at the age of eighteen, visited her uncle, Moses Tennant and his family at Ripley, Chautauqua Co., N. Y. In the Spring of the preceeding year, the family moved from the hill country to the village. The author was at home that summer, and had the pleasure of making the acquaintance of his cousin. They visited together her brother, Dr. Gulusha Phillips at Sherman, N. Y. He can testify to the beautiful and lovely character of his cousin, and to the great pleasure he had in visiting her children and grand children at the family reunion in the summer of 1911.

Thomas K. Henry writes the following beautiful lines:

"I know thou hast gone to the house of thy rest,
    Then why should my soul be so sad?
I know thou hast gone where the weary are blest,
    And the mourner looks up and is glad;

Where love has put off; in the land of its birth,
    The stain it had gathered in this;
And hope the sweet singer that has gladdening the earth,
    Lies asleep in the bosom of death."

Children and Grand Children of Gilbert and Cleantha (Phillips) DeHart.

Their children were named as follows, Elsie, Olivia, Lewis, William, Herbert, Gilbert Edison, and Juliette.

1. Elsie Olivia DeHart was born at Geneseeville, Genesee Co., Mich., Aug. 23, 1857. She married Adoniram Perry Sept. 8th, 1874. By him she had two children, Clyde and Lynn, both born at Loomis, Isabella Co., Mich.

1. Clyde Perry was born March 23, 1875. He married Miss Anna Louise Brastal at Wheeler, Mich., June 16th, 1897. There were born to them, three children at Wheeler, Gratiot Co., Mich., named as follows: Dana Perry born Jan. 25th, 1899, Bertha Edna Perry born Sept. 30, 1905, Anna Cora Perry born Feb. 23, 1907.

2. Lynn Perry was born June 28, 1877. He married Jennie Wilson at Wheeler, Mich., May 15th, 1901. There were born to them two children, a son and a daughter, named Kenneth Lynn and Madaline Beatrice.

1. Kenneth Lynn Perry was born at South Sharon, Pa., July 27th, 1903.

2. Madaline Beatrice Perry was born at Bridgeport, Mich., July 16th, 1905.

The above is the record of the children and grand children of Elsie Olivia DeHart by marriage to Adoniram Perry.

MR. PERRY died in Sept. of 1877. In the year 1880, on the 15th of December. Mrs. Perry married Charles Wesley Bradley at Bridgeport, Mich. By Mr. Bradley she had four children named Ethel Elizabeth, an infant Edna Clemantha, and Lewis Gilbert, all born at Wheeler, Gratiot Co., Mich.

1. ETHEL ELIZABETH BRADLEY was born March 18th, 1885.

2. BABY BRADLEY was born March 5th, and died on the 15th of the same month in 1887.

3. EDNA CLEANTHA BRADLEY was born April 14th, 1891.

4. LEWIS GILBERT BRADLEY was born June 30th, 1895.

MR. BRADLEY is a carpenter by trade. He is at this date, April 1912, erecting a harness shop at a place called Birch Run, Mich., and expects soon to move his family to this place.

2. LEWIS JAMES DEHART was born in Genesee Co., Mich., on the 12th of June 1863. He never married. His death took place on Oct. 19th, 1888.

3. WILLIAM JEWETT DEHART was born in Bridgeport, Saginaw Co., Mich., Feb. 23, 1867. He married Miss Cora Lee Smith. Miss Smith was born at Elleston, Frederick Co., Maryland, Jan. 16th, 1867. There were born to them four children named Ellis, Elbert, Vera and William.

1. ELLIS JEWETT DEHART was born at Cuyahoga Falls, O., July 20th, 1898.

2. ELBERT WILLIAM DEHART was born at South Sharon, Pa., Dec. 3rd, 1902.

3. VERA SUSAN DEHART was born at Midland, Mich., Oct. 15, 1905.

4. WILLIAM WALLIS DEHART born at Ambridge, Pa., Jan. 26th, 1909.

MR. DEHART, the brother, is a progressive business man who does not let opportunities pass without making a good use of them. The author met him and his family in August of 1911 at his home in the village of Bridgeport, Mich. He was conducting a grocery business with fairly good success. He has a lovely family of children, and they will no doubt be educated to make good citizens and to live honorable and useful lives.

4. HERBERT CORNELIUS DEHART was born at Bridgeport, Saginaw Co., Mich., May 1, 1870. He married Miss Frances Edith Dorr at Midland, Midland Co., Mich., April 25th, 1894. Miss Dorr was born at Midland Nov. 8th, 1874. MR. DEHART moved to Ambridge Pa., in July 1906 and entered into the employment of the American Steel Bridge Co. of that city and is at this date, 1912, still in this employment, as foreman of the establishment. There were born to Mr. and Mrs. DeHart six

children named Florence, Gilbert, Willis, Cleantha, Dorothy and Ruth.

1. FLORENCE NELLIE DeHART was born at Bridgeport, Mich., March 6th, 1895. She was graduated from the high school of Ambridge, Pa., May 28th, 1912.

2. GILBERT EDISON DeHART was born at Midland, Mich., Sept. 1st, 1897.

3. WILLIS DeHART was born at Bridgeport, Mich., Aug. 22, 1900.

4. CLEANTHA BERNICE DeHART was born at Bridgeport, Mich., July 25, 1902.

5. DOROTHY FRANCIS DeHART was born at Ambridge, Pa., Sept. 16, 1907.

6. RUTH EDITH DeHART was born at Ambridge, Beaver Co., Pa., Sept. 28th, 1910. The above named children are the great grandchildren of William and Olivia Tennant Phillips, their grandmother was Cleantha Phillips DeHart on their father's side of the family.

5. GILBERT EDISON DeHART fourth son was born at Loomis, Isabella Co., Mich., July 6, 1873. He never married. He died Jan. 19th, 1894.

6. JULIETTA DeHART was born at Richfield, Genesee Co., Mich., Oct. 20th, 1859. She married Ellis Perry Oct. 27, 1878. He is a prosperous farmer in the Township of Bridgeport, in Saginaw Co., Mich. His farm of 80 acres is located about three miles from the village of Bridgeport near the trolley line toward Flint. Mr. Perry purchased this land when it was covered with pine stumps. In about 23 years the farm was cleared of stumps, a new house and a large barn has been built and the buildings for housing farm tools erected.

They have four children named Lela, Lola, Arthur and George.

LELA and LOLA were twin sisters born at Bridgeoprt, Mich., June 21, 1882.

1. LOLA CLEANTHA PERRY married George P. Simmons at Bridgeport, Mich., June 11, 1906. There was born to them a son named Selvin E. Simmons, born May 29th, 1909.

We have now to record the sad and painful separation of this beloved daughter, wife and mother from all her earthly relations. Thirteen days after the birth of her child, with but a short warning to her loved ones, she was taken away by the angel of death. This occurred on June 11, 1909. A few years before her death in 1899, she made a public profession of her christian faith and united with the First Congregational church of Saginaw, Mich. Later she became a devoted Christian Scientist.

MISS FLORENCE DeHART
Born March 6, 1895
This picture was taken when dressed for her graduating exercises at
the High School of Ambridge, Pa., May 28, 1912.

MISS LELA A. PERRY
Daughter of Ellis and Georgette DeHart Perry
Born June 21, 1882

"Thou art not dead beloved, nor yet sleeping;
But free from earthly strife,
Art living in thy Father's holy keeping,
The pure and holy life.

We sadly miss thy loss and sweet communion,
Yet would we not repine;
But wait with chastened hearts complete reunion,
In God's own time."

(Poem selected by her Mother)

2. LELA ANNA PERRY is unmarried and is engaged in teaching (1912) at the Village of Bridgeport. She is an accomplished young woman, and has commenced a career of usefulness that will certainly have a great influence in uplifting and inspiring other lives.

3. ARTHUR PERRY the oldest son was born at Bridgeport, Mich., Nov. 11, 1885. He lived and worked on the farm until 1911 when he passed a civil service examination and obtained an appointment by the Post Office Department of the Government as a mail carrier at a salary of $600.00 a year.

4. GEORGE ROSCOE PERRY was born at Bridgeport the 8th of June 1888. He is at home and works on the farm. He married Louise Maria Korndahle Nov. 27th, 1913. They have a son, George Roscoe, born Aug. 13th, 1914.

The above is a full record of the children and grand children of Gilbert and Cleantha Phillips DeHart down to the year 1912.

VII. JAMES FRANCIS PHILLIPS the seventh child and fourth son of William and Olivia Phillips was born at Pontiac, Oakland Co., Mich., July 28, 1843. He married Miss Frances Lucy A. Miller in the township of Burton, Genesee Co., Mich., March 18, 1862. In this town they lived for 18 years. From Burton they moved to Owasso, Shiawassee Co., Mich., and lived there for 6 years; from Owasso they moved to Bancroft, Mich., and lived there for 3 years; afterward moved to Saginaw, Mich., and lived ther for 6 months when they moved to Bay City, Mich. Here they lived up to the time of Mr. Phillips death, Aug. 8, 1888. At his death he was 55 years and ten days old. Mr. Phillips was a farmer most of his life. His beloved wife was a New York State girl born in St. Lawrence Co., May 13th, 1847. When she was six years old her people moved to Mich. Their happy married life continued for thirty six years. Mrs. Phillips is still living at this date, 1912, with her daughter, Mrs. Baisley at Flint, Mich.

There were born to them six children named as follows: James B., Selden Tenannt, Susie Olivia, Floy Esther and Bessie V., and a child who died in infancy.

1.   JAMES B. PHILLIPS, oldest son of James Francis Phillips was born at Burton, Genesee Co., Mich., May 21, 1865. He lived only 22 months and died March 5th, 1867.

2.   SELDEN TENNANT PHILLIPS, second son was born at Burton, Genesee Co., Mich., July 25th, 1871. He married Anna Agnes Duling at Bay City, Mich., June 3, 1891. Miss Duling was born at Cayuga, Ont., Oct. 8th, 1863. For a number of years their home was at Bay City, where their three children were born. Their children are as follows:

1.   BESSIE THERESA PHILLIPS was born April 19, 1892.
2.   JAMES JOSEPH PHILLIPS was born Feb. 7, 1894.
3.   MARIAH LAUREI PHILLIPS was born Aug. 4, 1895.

From Bay City the family moved to Saginaw, Mich., where their home now is. Mr. Phillips has been for a number of years an employee of the Pere Marquette R. R. His faithful services earned him a promotion to the position of engineer. In this capacity he has served for several years. He writes to the author that the winter of 1911 and 12 has been the severest and most trying of any year since he entered the service. The reader may imagine what sturdy elements of character is required in a man who will stand by the throttle of an engine rushing through snow drifts and storms, never baffled by hardships nor shirking responsibility for fear of disasters and dangers to life and limb.

At the time of this writing, 1912, Mr. Phillips children are all unmarried.

3.   SUSIE OLIVIA PHILLIPS, third child and first daughter, was born in the Township of Burton, Genesee Co., Mich., on July 25th, 1872. When just past 21 years old she married William P. Plumsteel Oct. 4th, 1893, at Bay City, Mich. There was born to them one daughter, Susie Irene, Oct. 2, 1894. Mr. and Mrs. Plumsteel lived at Bay City all their married life. She died at that place Oct. 5, 1902 at the age of thirty years.

4.   FLOY ESTHER PHILLIPS, 4th child and 3rd daughter was born March 5th, 1875, at Burton, Genesee Co., Mich. She married Archie Potter at Bay City, Mich. in 1892. By this marriage she had two children, Fannie L. and Leola D. Potter. Fannie was born May 24, 1893 and Leola was born Sept. 11, 1895, both were born at Bay City, and both are now living.

MRS. POTTER separated from her first husband. On Oct. 4, 1897, at Saginaw, she married John Schell. By this marriage she had two sons, John Phillips born Sept. 29, 1902, and Floyd Selden born May 10th, 1904. Both children were born at Saginaw, Mich. The mother died at Saginaw, March 3, 1907, being at her death 31 years, 11 months, and 28 days old. The author of this sketch of the life of his cousin, can only imagine what trials and sorrows she may have passed through.

MISS FLOY ALPHA BAISLEY
Born April 10, 1908

Sunshine and shadows encompass our lives,
We know not what changes may come,
We only know this, that where ever we drift,
On life's stormy sea, Thy will, O Father, is done.

5. BESSIE V. PHILLIPS, 5th child and 3rd daughter, was born at Flint, Mich., Oct. 31, 1877. She married Henry J. Baisley at Flint, June 22, 1907. They have a daughter named Floy Alpha Baisley born at Flint, April 10, 1908. Mr. Baisley was born March 16th, 1868. Since their marriage their family home has been at Flint. He has been employed in the automobile works of that city for a number of years. Their home is at 830 Pastland Ave., at this date, 1912. The writer had the pleasure of visiting them in the summer of 1911 and in 1912.

VIII. MARIAH PHILLIPS, eighth child and fourth daughter of William and Olivia Tennant Phillips, was born in Waterford Township, Oakland Co., Mich., July 22, 1839. She married John Vankuren in Nov. or Dec. of 1854. Mr. Vankuren was born in the town of Porter, Niagara Co., N. Y., Feb. 11, 1828. In the year 1834, he went with his parents to Mich. After his marriage he and his wife settled on a farm in the town of Burton, Genesee Co., Mich., where they lived for 22 years. From Burton the family moved to Brandon Township, Oakland Co., Mich., where they resided for thirty years. At their home in Brandon on the 11th of Nov. 1904, Mrs. Vankuren passed into the spirit life, being at her death 65 years, 3 months and 11 days old. After the death of his beloved wife, Mr. Vankuren made his residence with his son, Andrew, who with his family in Dec. 1906, moved to Evart, Osceola Co., Mich. In the spring of 1912 the Father went to the home of his daughter Olivia, Mrs. Horatio Wait, who resides at Evart, Mich., to live. At this date, 1912, the son writes the author, that his father is old and feeble in mind and body. Being past 84 years of age it is not strange that the body and mind both should begin to fail. In the early years of life we are beginning to live; in the later years we are preparing for physical death. But the death of the body does not involve the death of the soul; rather it is a glorious liberation of the soul from the bondage of death into the freedom of a higher spirit life. As the setting of the sun at the close of day is but the harbinger of the morning, so is the old age but the forerunner of eternal youth, wherein the powers of the soul are renewed from age to age with immortal vigor. Old age should be the happiest period of our lives, especially so, if we have lived for some high and noble purpose and made the best possible use of our time, of our gifts and opportunities.

"Only waiting until the shadows are a little longer grown,
Only waitng till the glimmer of the days last beam has flown,
Till the night of earth is faded from the heart once full of day,
  And the stars of heaven are breaking through the twilight soft
    and grey."   —Selected

There were born to Mr. and Mrs. Vankuren nine children named, as follows: Rosezella, an infant who died in infancy, Emma, Ircha, Mary, Olivia, Andrew, Edward and James M.

1. ROSEZELLA VANKUREN, the oldest child was born at She married Ransom Emerson Rogers. Mr. Rogers was born in N. Y. state, June 6th, 1850. They have a son named David L. Rogers who was born at Davison, Genesee Co., Mich., Sept. 6th, 1875. He married Miss Maud Hartwick at Chapin, Saginaw Co., Mich., Nov. 30th, 1899. Miss Hartwick was born in Chapin, May 9th, 1876.

There were born to Mr. and Mrs. Rogers in Chapin, Mich., five children as follows:

1. MARY JANE ROGERS was born Mar. 1st, 1901.
2. ZELLA MAY ROGERS was born Mar. 26, 1903.
3. CHARLES DAVID ROGERS was born Mar. 13, 1905.
4. ASA RANSOM ROGERS was born Sept. 14th, 1906.
5. RALPH EDWARD ROGERS was born Jan. 12th, 1911,

MRS. ROSELLA VANKUREN ROGERS married for her second husband at Kansas City, Missouri, Mr. Fred E. Burroughs, by whom she had three children, all of whom died in infancy. Mrs. Burroughs married a third husband whose name has not been given to the writer.

2. EMMA VANKUREN, 2nd child and 2nd daughter of John Vankuren and Mariah Phillips, was born in the town of Burton, Genesee Co., Mich., July 28, 1859. She married Albert Erastus Wait at Davison, Mich., July 5, 1874. Mr. Wait was born at Reach, Ontario Co., Ontario, Dec. 16, 1847. On the 14th of Jan. 1864 he enlisted in Co. F of the N. G. H. Artillery. He was in the army till the close of the war in the spring of 1865, and was honorably discharged June 5th, 1865. He has pursued farming since the war, and is now located at Evart, Osceola Co., Mich. Mrs. Wait writes the author these loving words concerning her grandmother, Olivia Tennant Phillips: "When you speak of my grandmother, you speak of some one I loved very dearly. I lived with her the most of my life from the time I was five years old till she died."

There were born to Mr. and Mrs. Wait two children named Della and John.

1. DELLA WAIT was born in the town of Brandon, Oakland Co., Mich., March 30, 1878.

She married Byron Jinkins at Hersey, Osceola Co., Mich., July 4, 1904. There were born to them at Evart, Mich., two children named Neil and Lee.

1. NEIL JINKINS was born Feb. 2, 1906.

2. LEE JINKINS was born July 4, 1907.

JOHN ALBERT WAIT, an only son, was born in the town of Osceola, Osceola Co., Mich., April 18, 1883. He married Mary Laura Faulk Oct. 14, 1903. Miss Faulk was born in the town of Osceola, Mich., July 15, 1879.

They have two children named Albert and Katie both born in Osceola, Mich.

1. ALBERT ANDREW WAIT was born Feb. 5th, 1905.

2. KATIE E. WAIT was born May 16, 1908.

4. IRCHA J. VANKUREN, the fourth child and first son of John and Mariah Phillips Vankuren, was born at Burton, Genesee Co., Mich., Feb. 20, 1865. He married Miss Myrtle Bell Sherman at Brandon, Oakland Co., Mich., June 12, 1892. Miss Sherman was born in Lapeer Township, Lapeer Co., Mich., Oct. 6th, 1875.

Mr. and Mrs. Vankuren after their marriage lived at Hadley, Lapeer Co., Mich., for two years. They then moved to Oak Hill, Brandon Township, Oakland Co., Mich., where they lived for four years. Mr. Vankuren was a blacksmith by trade. He then changed his business to farming which he followed up to the present date, 1913.

There were born to Mr. and Mrs. Vankuren six children named as follows: Vilbert, Nina, Ernest, George, Alice and Andrew.

1. VILBERT JOHN VANKUREN, eldest son, was born at Hadley, Lapeer Co., Mich., Jan. 8th, 1894.

The following children were born at Independence, Oakland Co., Mich.:

2. NINA ESTHER VANKUREN was born Nov. 5, 1896. She died Nov. 10th, having lived but five days.

> To the bosom of love she was taken,
>   From the sorrows of earth she has flown;
> She lives in the eternal presence,
>   Mid the radiance of the great white throne.

3. EARNEST ALLEN VANKUREN was born May 18th, 1902.

4. GEORGE HENRY VANKUREN was born July 15th, 1905.

5. ALICE GRACE VANKUREN was born July 28th, 1908.

6. ANDREW IRCHA VANKUREN was born Aug. 24th, 1912.

5. MARY VANKUREN, fifth child and third daughter of John Vankuren, was born in Brandon Township, Oakland Co., Mich. She died in infancy.

6. OLIVIA NANCY VANKUREN, sixth child and fourth daughter was born in Burton Township, Genesee Co., Mich., April 20, 1866. She married Horatio Bidwell Wait April 25th, 1882. Mr. Wait was born at Wilson, Niagara Co., N. Y., Sept. 29, 1854. He went to Mich. in Nov. 1855 and settled in Hadley Township, Lapeer Co., Mich. He had a good school education and is a carpenter by trade.

MRS. WAIT when a young girl about ten years of age went with her parents to Oakland Co., Mich., in the spring of 1876. She was but a few days past sixteen years of age when married. After their marriage, Mr. and Mrs. Wait went to Hadley, Lapeer Co., Mich., where they lived till March, 1906, when they moved to Evart, Osceola Co., Mich.

There were born to Mr. and Mrs. Wait four children Ethel, Ruby, Mary and Esther at Hadley, Lapeer Co., Mich.

1. ETHEL MARIA WAIT was born Nov. 24th, 1884 and died early in infancy.

2. RUBY LOUISA WAIT was born May 26th, 1887, at Hadley, Lapeer Co., Mich. She moved to Evart, Mich., in March 1906. She married James Henry Allen Dec. 25th, 1906. They have no children.

3. MARY BELL WAIT was born June 29th, 1893. She went with the family from Hadley to Evart, Mich., in March 1906. She finished her school education at a grammer school in Evart. She married at Evart, Mich., Nov. 3rd, 1909, Jasper C. Hillis. Their happy married life was soon ended by death, for Mr. Hillis passed away from earth to the spirit life March 20th, 1911, being at his death 22 years, 7 months, and 16 days old. Mr. Hillis was born at Evart, Osceola Co., Mich., Aug. 4, 1888. How strange is the providence that takes away so early, a life of hope and promise. Just as he was beginning to live in the highest and truest sense,his career is terminated and his fondest earthly hopes wither and perish in death. Let us all hope that youth has a chance for a better and happier life in the unseen world toward which human life on earth is ever drifting.

4. ESTHER EMMA WAIT was born Dec. 17th, 1896. She went with the family when they moved from Hadley to Evart, Mich. She is now atending the high school at the latter place, (1913).

Since writing the above, the author has received notice of the death of Mrs. Olive Wait and her daughter, Mary Bell, Mrs. Hillis. The former died at her home in Evart, Mich., on Saturday, May 24th, 1913, and the daughter died at the same place on May 29th, 1913. Mrs. Wait left to mourn her loss, the husband, Horatio B. Wait, and three children, Mrs. Ruby Hillis, Mrs. Mary Bell Hillis and the unmarried daughter Esther. Her illness was the result of nervous exhaustion and diminished strength. The daughter did not have to mourn the loss of her mother but a few days when she followed her into the realm of the higher spirit life.

A writer for a local paper speaks of the daughter in the following words "She was positive and impulsive in temperament, full or life, and a picture of health until within seven months of her death. A severe cold developed into tuberculosis. Faithful care and the best medical attendance were unavailing. A profusion of flowers about her casket were fit setting to her youth and beauty. A large circle of sympathizing friends and relatives were in attendance at the funeral."

The mother was 47 years, 1 month and 4 days old at her death and the daughter 19 years and four months.

VII.   ANDREW JACKSON VANKUREN, 7th child and 2nd son of John and Mariah Phillips Vankuren, was born in the town of Burton, Genesee Co., Mich., June 28th, 1869.   He married Miss Martha Ellen Copince at Burton, Osceola Co., Mich., Jan. 14th, 1896.

MR. VANKUREN is a prosperous farmer located at Evart, Osceola Co., Mich.

There were born to Mr. and Mrs. Vankuren eight children named as follows: William, Oliver and Eunice born in the town of Brandon, Oakland Co., Mich.   Delos, Beatrice and Hattie born in the town of Independence, Oakland Co., Mich.   Andrew and Harry born in the town of Osceola, Osceola Co., Mich.

1.   WILLIAM EARL VANKUREN was born April 14, 1897.

2.   OLIVER J. VANKUREN was born Sept. 15th, 1898.

3.   EUNICE ROSELLA VANKUREN was born April 2nd, 1900.

4.   DELOS VANKUREN was born May 28, 1902.

5.   BEATRICE CLEMANTHA VANKUREN was born Feb. 18th, 1904.

6.   HATTIE OLIVIA VANKUREN was born Feb. 24, 1906.

7.   ANDREW JAMES VANKUREN was born March 12, 1908.

8.   HARRY LESTER VANKUREN was born Oct. 10th, 1912.

VIII.   EDWARD VANKUREN, 8th child and 3d son of John Vankuren, was born in Burton Township, Genesee Co., Mich., the 2nd day of July, 1876.   He married Miss Tryphena Tulet.

MISS TULET was born in Nevesta Township, Tusceola Co., Mich., March 27th, 1877.

There were born to them two sons named Roy and Adison.

1.   ROY VANKUREN was born in Nevesta Township, Tusceola Co., Mich., Jan. 5th, 1896.

2.   ADISON VANKUREN was born in Independence Township, Oakland Co., Mich., Aug. 12, 1899.

IX.   JAMES M. VANKUREN, youngest child of John Vankuren

was born June 20th, 1879.   He died Oct. 25th, 1897, aged 18
years, 4 months and 5 days.   His remains were buried at Sey-
more Lake, Mich.

This closes the history of the descendants of OLIVIA
TENNANT and her husband, William Phillips.   Of this long line
of descendants the youngest born as herein recorded, is a grand-
daughter of Holden and Ida (Conger) Phillips, a child of their
daughter, Elvira who married Dr. John Burton Gidley.   This
child was born at Flint, Mich., Aug. 1st, 1913, about 117 years
from the birth of her great-great-grand mother, Olivia Tennant
Phillips.   Her name is Jane Louise Gidley.   May her life be
spared to the age of her oldest ancestor.   Her great-great-great-
grand-mother, Sarah Selden Jewett, was born April 24th, 1763,
about 150 years before the birth of this great-great-great-grand-
child, on August 1st, 1913.

The descendants of William and Olivia Tennant Phillips as
herein recorded, number as follows:

Children 8
Grand-children 39
Great-Grand-children 83
Great-Great-Grand-children 28
                                          ——
Total descendants 158

These descendants, including their parents and grandparents,
extend through six generations.   By a careful reading of this family history it will be seen that this is not a full and complete
record.   This is especially true of the family of Galusha Phillips, of the family of Rosezella Vankuren and some others.   No
effort has been wanting on the part of the author to make family records complete.

The descendants herein named, for the most part, have pursued farming.   But the learned professions are well represented
as the reader will readily see.   Surely the ancestors of this numerous progeny have not lived in vain.   A host will rise up and
pronounce them blessed for giving them an existence.

ALVIN JEWETT TENNANT

Born September 18, 1821   Died January 16, 1897

MRS. EMORETTE WATTLES TENNANT
Born January 23, 1827

PART III.

CHAPTER V. IN THREE DIVISIONS.

Descendants of MOSES ASEL and DELINDA TENNANT
—Alvin Jewett, Delos Gibson, Moses Selden, Olive
Eliza, Julia Emma, Wealthy Ann, Albert Milton, Ellen Delinda, Fannie Oliva, John Asel, and their children
and grand-children.

DIVISION I.

MOSES ASEL TENNANT.

MOSES ASEL TENNANT, only son of Sarah Selden Jewett by her
third husband, Moses Tennant, Sr., was born in Springfield, Otsego Co., N. Y., Dec. 23, 1801. He married Delinda Tennant Dec. 19, 1820. Delinda Tennant, daughter of John and Elizabeth Loomis Tenant, was born in the same town and county
April 18, 1802. Both husband and wife were under 19 years of
age at the time of their marriage. MR. TENNANT was a farmer.
His father died when his son was only a boy. His early surroundings were such that in his early years he was quite a wild
boy, fond of the sports that were common at that time. After
his marriage he rapidly passed out of boyhood into manhood.
He was converted to the christian faith, joined the Baptist church
of his native village, and from henceforth sought to live a conscientious christian life. His life and characteristics as well as
those of his beloved wife will be further mentioned in the Chapter composed of Memorial Tributes.

There were born to Moses Asel and Delinda Tennant ten children named Alvin, Delos, Selden, Eliza, Julia, Wealthy, Albert,
Ellen, Fannie and John.

I. ALVIN JEWETT TENNANT, the oldest child, was born at
Springfield, Otsego Co., N. Y., Sept. 18, 1821. He was from
boyhood a gentle, kindly spirit, active and industrious, always
willing to do a full days work, yet economized his strength so
that he could be ready for the next days labor. He was of great assistance in the training and support of his younger brothers and
sisters. He came with the family in the Spring of 1833 to Chautauqua Co. His life will be further mentioned in Part IV, Division 2nd.

ALVIN TENNANT married Miss Emorett Wattles, daughter of
Gurdon H. and Lucretia (Phelps) Wattles, in Wattlesburg, Ripley Township, Chautauqua Co., N. Y., on the 27th day of Sept.
1847. He died at Ripley, Jan. 16, 1897. His widow is still living. She was born Jan. 23, 1827.

There was born to them a son whom they named Jewett Gurdon Tennant.

JEWETT GURDON TENNANT was born at Ripley, N. Y., Nov. 4, 1852. He married Miss Carrie Brown at Buffalo, N. Y., Dec. 15, 1875. Miss Brown was born at Buffalo, N. Y., Dec. 19, 1853.

There were born to Jewett and Carrie Brown Tennant four children named Emma, Leah, Mable and Alvin.

1. EMMA LUCRETIA TENNANT was born at Buffalo, Erie Co., N. Y., Oct. 20, 1876. She is unmarried at this date, 1913, and has always lived with her parents. She has been a great help in the family. Being the oldest daughter, she could aid in the care and education of the younger children and help in household work.

2. LEAH OLIVIA TENNANT was born at Buffalo, N. Y., Jan. 6, 1880. She married William Elmer Stout at Fort Wayne, Ind., Dec. 21st, 1904. They have one child named Margaret Tennant Stout, born at Fort Wayne July 17, 1908.

MR. STOUT was born at Hollandsburg, Ind., Oct. 2, 1868. He was a graduate of the State Normal School of Indiana, attended the University of that State in 1897 and the University of Chicago in 1898 and 99. From 1895 to 1897 he was Principal of one of the schools in Huntington, Ind. He afterwards held the same position in the Hoagland school at Fort Wayne from 1898 to 1905. He then became traveling agent for the D. Appleton Book Co. At the end of two years he entered the service of the Publishing House of Longman, Green & Co., with which he is still connected as western manager with office at 323 E. 23rd St., Chicago, Ill. His wife was graduated from the High School at Fort Wayne in 1898; entered the City Normal School and was graduated in 1899 and taught in the 5th grade of the city schools of Fort Wayne from 1900 to June 1904.

3. MABLE CATHARINE TENNANT was born at Ripley, N. Y., Jan. 13, 1883. She married Ray Duane Adams at Cleveland, Ohio, Jan. 16, 1908. They have two children as follows:

1. DAVID TENNANT ADAMS born in New York City May 28, 1909.

2. KATHARINE TENNANT ADAMS born in New York City Dec. 24, 1910.

MR. ADAMS was the son of Duane and Mary (Wells) Adams and the grandson of James Wells and his wife, Laura (Burchard) Wells. He was born in Sherman, Chautauqua Co., N. Y., June 25, 1881. He was graduated from the Sherman High School in the summer of 1898. After graduation he entered the law office of Mr. Thomas W. Schiller at Sherman, N. Y., and studied law for three years. He was examined for admittance to the bar Jan. 13, 1904 and was admitted by the Appellate Division sitting for the Fourth Judicial Department at Rochester, N. Y., on March 8, 1904, the Hon. Peter B. McLennon Justice presiding.

MR. ADAMS entered at once upon the practice of law at Sherman. This continued till Sept. 15, 1904 when he moved to New York City and became a member of the Law Department of the Title Guarantee and Trust Co., where he is employed at this date, June, 1913.

MRS. ADAMS was graduated from the High School of Fort Wayne, Indiana in 1901 and from the Normal Department in 1903. She then commenced teaching, first at Fort Wayne for three years and then at Cleveland, Ohio, for two years. After this five years of teaching her marriage took place as above recorded. She is a grandchild of Alvin and Emorett (Wattles) Tennant and a great-grandchild of Moses Asel and Delinda Tennant, and her children are their great-great-grand children. The present residence of Mr. and Mrs. Adams is 176 Broadway, New York City.

4. ALVIN JEWETT TENNANT was born at Ripley, N. Y., April 5, 1885. He is the youngest child and only son of Jewett and Carrie Brown Tenant. At this date, 1913, he is engaged in business and promises well for the future.

MR. TENNANT, the father, learned telegraphy under the instruction of H. W. Taylor at Ripley, N. Y., in the winter of 1869 and 1870. He commenced work as operator at Ripley, Sept. 10, 1870. As operator he was located at Harbor Creek, Pa., from Oct. 1, 1870 until the following Spring when he returned to Ripley April 1, 1871 and was there located for one year and a half. Then he went on to the Lake Shore road as brakeman for six months, then took up telegraph operating again. From the Spring of 1875 to the Fall of 1879 he served the city of Buffalo as doorman at the City Hall. In Oct. 1883 he took the office at Silver Creek, N. Y., until March 20, 1885. He then took station agency on Nickel Plate road at Ripley until April 1, 1888. From this time on his business was changed to Traveling Freight Agent. In the Spring of 1888 he was appointed traveling agent for live-stock freight for the western division of the Nickel Plate R. R. from Rocky Road, O., to Hammond, Ind., with headquarters at Fort Wayne, Ind. On March 20, 1905, he was transferred from Fort Wayne to Cleveland, Ohio, to have charge of the entire road from Buffalo to Chicago which position he was given for two years. Again his territory was changed and he had the eastern division from Buffalo to Bellevue, Ohio. On this division he still remains, having served from the Spring of 1907 to the present year, 1913.

He and his son Alvin are members of the Masonic order.

At Fort Wayne, MR. TENNANT's entire family united with the Presbyterian church. He has been from the earliest part of his business career an energetic, live, progressive business man, of high moral ideas and of conscientious integrity. At this date, June, 1913, his family home is at 2025 93rd St., Cleveland, Ohio.

II. DELOS GIBSON TENNANT, the second child and son of Moses Asel and Delinda Tennant, was born in Springfield, Otsego Co., N. Y., July 2, 1823. He came with the family to Chautauqua Co., N. Y., in the Spring of 1833, being past nine years old at this time. He married Miss Sally Eliza Sawin at Ripley, N. Y., March 1, 1843. Miss Sawin was born at Danube, Herkimer Co., N. Y., Feb. 22, 1822. She was the oldest daughter of Col. Ethan Sawin and came with the family to Chautauqua County in 1832. Her father was a brother of Rev. George and Rev. John Sawin. He was called by the Tennant children "Uncle Ethan." He was born, as the writer has been informed, in Herkimer Co., N. Y., on Jan. 15, 1790, and died in Ripley, Chautauqua Co., N. Y., July 7, 1884, being at his death 94 years, 6 months and 22 days old. Mr. Sawin was a self-educated man of excellent natural gifts and was greatly interested in the education of the young. He was chosen town superintendent of schools and the writer remembers how "Uncle Ethan" used to interest the scholars in his addresses upon his visit to the schools. He would say to the boys "How do I know but some boy I am addressing will become President of the United States." Every boy hoped he would be the one.

There were born to Delos G. and Sally Eliza Sawin Tennant three children named Caroline Ellen, Moses Delos and a child that died in infancy. Mr. Tennant was a farmer of great ambition and unusual physical strength. After a life of unremitting toil and a short sickness, he died at Ripley, N. Y., Nov. 9, 1905, being at his death 82 years, 4 months and 7 days old. His beloved wife survived him for a few years and died at the same home in Ripley village on the 23rd day of March, 1908, being at her death 85 years, 1 month and 1 day old.

A Memorial Tribute will be paid to their memory which may be found in Part IV, division 2nd.

1. CAROLINE ELLEN TENNANT was born at Ripley, N. Y., Dec. 15, 1843. She married Ahira Jay Crandall of Ward, Alleghany Co., N. Y., Jan. 1, 1869. Mr. Crandall was born in 1835. He was well educated and made teaching his profession. He was chosen Superintendent of the City Schools of Corry, Pa., and served for a few years. Had his life been spared he would have risen to a high position of honor and usefulness.

DELOS GIBSON TENNANT

Born July 2, 1823   Died November 9, 1905

MRS. SALLY ELIZA SAWIN TENNANT

Born February 23, 1823   Died March 23 1908

THREE GENERATIONS OF TENNANTS
Grandfather, Son and Grandson
Moses Delos, Arthur Smith and Arthur Skinner Tennant

His health failed and after much suffering he died at Ripley, N. Y., in 1889. His widow survived him for many years, and after much physical suffering which continued through all the latter part of her life she died at the same home where her parents died in Ripley, N. Y., Sept. 7, 1911.

They had but one child, a son, Jay, who lived with his mother all his life, until her death.

JAY CRANDALL, only child of Ahira and Caroline Crandall, was born at Ripley, N. Y., May 3, 1879. He married Miss Carrie Ludlow of Ripley, N. Y., in 1901. There were born to them three children, at Ripley, named Darwin, Edna and Harold.

MR. CRANDALL has made his home in Ripley all his life time. After his grandfather Tennant's death he ministered to the comfort of his aged grandmother and his enfeebled mother with a thoughtful devotion quite rarely found in a young man. Environed by circumstances that were difficult to overcome, he tried as best he could to discharge his duties toward all who were dependent upon him for support and comfort.

There were born to them at Ripley, N. Y., three children as follows:

DARWIN CRANDALL was born Dec. 7, 1901.

EDNA CRANDALL was born May 20, 1903.

HAROLD CRANDALL was born Dec. 13, 1909.

2. MOSES DELOS TENNANT was born at Ripley, N. Y., Dec. 3, 1849. He married Miss Helen Smith, daughter of Hon. Austin Smith, at Westfield, N. Y., Sept. 27, 1878. He attended the Westfield Academy, then entered Alfred University at Alfred, Alleghany Co., N. Y., in the Fall of 1867. He took the scientific course for five terms. In 1872 he entered the Law office of Austin Smith at Westfield, N. Y., studied law for three years, and was admitted to the Bar in June, 1875 and practiced law in partnership with Mr. Smith under the firm name of Smith and Tennant until the death of Mr. Smith. Mr. Tennant was elected Justice of the Peace in Nov. 1881 and took the oath of office Jan. 1, 1882. As each term of office was about to expire he was re-elected and so has been continued in the office to the present year, 1913. Having studied surveying, he practiced this profession from 1872 to 1907. This made him familiar with highway and farm lines, and greatly aided him in giving descriptions of farm lands in contracts, deeds and mortgages of which he had hundreds to draw during his long business career. He was also made executor of many estates upon which he had to administer, invariably with great satisfaction to the heirs.

Being a member of the Town Board by virtue of his office as Justice of the Peace, and having many and varied relations with the citizens of his town and county, all gave him a decided influence in determining many public questions, in settling and deciding suits at law, and in his moral influence on the community. His life has been filled with unceasing toil and business cares, the fruits of which have fallen as benedictions upon many lives and families.

MRS. HELEN SMITH TENNANT was born at "The Maples," the old home of the Smith family for many years, in Westfield, N. Y. The day of her marriage to Mr. Tennant was the Golden Wedding Anniversary of her father and mother, Hon. Austin and Sarah A. Smith. She was educated at the Westfield Academy and at Livingston Park Seminary of Rochester, N. Y. Her father died at Westfield, Oct. 1904, at the age of 100 years and 7 months. Her mother died in 1886, being 78 years old.

ARTHUR SMITH TENNANT, only child of Moses and Helen Tennant, was born at Westfield, N. Y., Nov. 3, 1882, and at the old home built by his grand-father Smith in 1830. He married Grace Rachel Skinner, daughter of Arthur and Jeannie York Skinner, at Westfield, Oct. 2, 1906. Miss Skinner was born at Westfield Jan. 13, 1882. Her education was attained at the Westfield High School, the Rye Seminary at Rye, N. Y., and the Pratt Institute at Brooklyn, N. Y., from which she was graduated in 1902. She has served as chief clerk in the office of the Supreme Treasurer of the Royal Arcanum, Edward A. Skinner, her uncle, from the time of her graduation to that of her marriage.

ARTHUR TENNANT was graduated from the High School at Westfield in June, 1900, entered the Cornell University Law School the next Fall, before 18 years of age, from which he was graduated in 1903, receiving the degree of L. L. B. His examination for admittance to the Bar was at Rochester, N. Y., before the N. Y. State Bar examiners in Jan. 1904. He was admitted to the Bar April 14, 1904 by the Appellate Division of the Supreme Court at Rochester, N. Y. He commenced the practice of law in partnership with his father under the firm name of Tennant and Tennant, soon after his admittance to the Bar. In March, 1910, he was appointed Manager of the U. S. Life Insurance Co. with office at Buffalo, N. Y., which position he held until Jan. 1, 1912, when he returned to the practice of law in the office with his father at Westfield, N. Y. Arthur and Grace Skinner Tennant have a son named Arthur Skinner Tennant, born at "The Maples" in Westfield Dec. 30, 1907. This boy's maternal grand-father, J. Arthur Skinner, was Vice President of the First National Bank of Westfield, N. Y., for many years up to the time of his death, Jan. 1903, in California, to which State he had gone for improvement of his health.

HENRY SHAVER

Born April 8, 1822   Died November 7, 1889

MRS. OLIVE ELIZA TENNANT SHAVER

Born August 5, 1827   Died February 26, 1906

III.   MOSES SELDEN TENNANT, third child and third son of
Moses Asel and Delinda Tennant, was born at Springfield, Otsego Co., N. Y., Aug. 2, 1824. He came with the family to Chautauqua Co., in 1833. At the age of six years he was attacked with
epilepsy from which he never recovered.   This was a great affliction on his parents and the entire family. He was a constant care
up to the day of his death which took place at the home on Ripley Hill Aug. 19, 1847, being at his death 23 years and 17 days
old.   For 17 years the home of the family was never left without the presence of someone of its members.   His mental state
was that of partial idiocy rather than insanity.   He could not
be taught any kind of work.   At six years of age, he was as
bright as any one of the children, had commenced to learn the
rudiments of spelling and reading.   The cause of the epilepsy
was the pressure of the brain in its growth upon the skull which
did not have a corresponding growth.   They now operate on the
skull to correct such abnormal conditions.

DIVISION II.

ELIZA, JULIA AND WEALTHY.

IV.   OLIVE ELIZA TENNANT, the oldest daughter, was born at
Springfield, Otsego Co., N. Y., Aug. 5th, 1827.   She came with
the family to Chautauqua Co., in the spring of 1833.   She married Henry Shaver at Ripley, N. Y., Sept. 24th, 1844, Rev. Father Orton of the Presbyterian church officiating.   At this time
the family occupied the Shaver Hotel at the village.   The wedding was in the ball-room.   The family remained in this hotel
only a short time, moving back to the farm on Ripley Hill.   As
her sister Julia was married at the same time and place to her
husband's brother, the two sisters and their husbands continued
the hotel business.

Time produced its changes in the Shaver family.   The father
of the husbands of these two sisters died at his old home in Ripley village in 1846.   His farm property consisting of 80 acres
was deeded by him before his death, jointly to his two sons David
and Henry.   Subsequently the sons divided the property and
Henry come into possession of the farm lying west of the road
leading from Ripley village to the side hill road.   On this land
the old homestead was located, and here Eliza and her husband
lived all her life time, except a few months before her death
during which she was at her daughter's home, Mrs. Kitty Stanton, where she died Feb. 26th, 1906.

HENRY SHAVER was born at Westmoreland, Oneida Co., July
6, 1822.   He came with the family to Chautauqua Co. in 1835.
He was a prosperous farmer, of good business ability, naturally
kind and generous hearted.   He was strongly attached to his

family and labored hard to give them ample support.   He died at
his old home, where his father died before him, in the village of
Ripley, Nov. 7th, 1889.   His brother in law, the author, officiated at his funeral.   He and his beloved wife are buried side
by side in the beautiful Ripley cemetery.

> "Jesus said unto her, I am the resurrection and the
> life; he that believeth in Me, though he were dead, yet
> shall he live."   John 11:25.

MRS. SHAVER will be mentioned in the Memorial tributes.

CHILDREN OF HENRY AND ELIZA (TENNANT) SHAVER.

There were born to them four children as follows: Harriet,
Charles, Kittie and DeEtte.

1.   HARRIET ELIZA SHAVER was born at Ripley, N. Y., June
8, 1846, and died at the same place Dec. 10th, 1900.   Being the
oldest of the family and having a business turn of mind, she was
a great help to her parents and the younger members of the family.   Her death was a sad bereavement to all the family and to
a large circle of warm friends.   She passed away in a full faith
and hope in her heavenly Father and Savior.

> "I go to life and not to death;
>   From darkness to life's native sky;
> I go from sickness and from pain
>   To health and immortality.
>
> Let our farewell then be tearless,
>   Since I bid farewell to tears;
> Write this day of my departure
>   Festive in your coming years."
>
> —Bonar.

2.   CHARLES HENRY SHAVER was born at Ripley, N. Y., Feb.
6, 1853.   He married Priscilla Elliot at Ripley, Dec. 9, 1879.
She was born Dec. 1, 1856.

MR. SHAVER was a farmer, a carpenter and painter.   The
three occupations have taxed his utmost energies.   He inherited
a part of his father's farm, built himself and family a home on
the front part of the land, and there his family enjoy a pleasant
home life.

There were born to them three children, Sara Eliza, Ada De
Ette, and Harold Elliott.

THEIR CHILDREN.

1.   SARA ELIZA SHAVER was born at Ripley, N. Y. Jan. 23rd,
1882.   She learned type-writing and stenography.   For a num-

DAVID SHAVER

Born May 26 1816   Died July 8, 1883

MRS. JULIA E. TENNANT SHAVER
Born January 25, 1829   Died November 25, 1905

ber of years she has worked for the Otis Elevator Co., at Chicago, Ill., but was later transferred at her request to Buffalo, N. Y., to work for the same firm. In her profession she has made excellent success and commands a good salary. She is unmarried.

2.   ADA DEETTE SHAVER was born at Ripley Sept. 8th, 1888. She has received a good education and finds a happy home life with her parents. She is unmarried.

3.   HAROLD ELLIOTT SHAVER was born at Ripley, Dec. 27th, 1898. He was graduated from the Ripley High School. He is at this date, 1912, a student in the Medical College of Buffalo, N. Y., where he is making excellent progress in his studies.

3.   KITTIE BELLE SHAVER, second daughter of Henry and Eliza Tennant Shaver, was born at Ripley, June 22nd, 1856. She married William Lyman Stanton Dec. 9th, 1874. Mr. Stanton was born at Ripley, April 7th, 1852. He is a successful farmer and a competent business man, of high ideals on all moral questions in business dealings. His beloved wife, for a few years, has suffered much from rheumatism but still is the light and comfort of her home. She has always done what she could. Her patience and trust has been a benediction to her family and friends.

4.   CLARA DEETTE SHAVER was born at Ripley, N. Y., Dec. 25th, 1858. She is the youngest of the family, is unmarried and has been all her life one of the strong helpers in her home life. At the present time, 1912, she has a home with her sister, Mrs. Stanton, where she is much needed since the sister has become so dependent.

The number of descendants of Henry and Olive Eliza Tennant are as follows:

Children 4
Grand children 3
                                           —
Total 7

With parents and grand parents they include four generations.

V.   JULIA EMMA TENNANT was born at Springfield, Otsego Co., N. Y., Jan. 25th, 1829. She came with the family to Chautauqua Co., N. Y., in the Spring of 1833. She commenced teaching school when very young, but taught only a few summers. She married David Shaver at Ripley, Sept. 24th, 1844 at the same time and place of the marriage of her older sister Eliza. These sisters husbands were brothers. Their housekeeping commenced, as has been told, in the Shaver hotel at Ripley. Subsequently upon the division of the Shaver property, David owned land north of the village. This was sold and he purchased a farm west of Ripley village in what was known as the Cochrane District. Here the family lived for many years, here nearly all

the children were born. A desire for a change led to the
purchase of a farm near the coast of the Atlantic in
North Hampton Co., Va.   This move did not prove
fortunate.   Dissatisfied and disappointed, the Virginia farm was
sold and the family moved back to Chautauqua Co., purchased a
home in Westfield on the corner of Union and Wood streets,
where they lived till the death of the husband which occurred at
Buffalo, N. Y., July 8th, 1883.   Mr. Shaver was a man of more
than ordinary ability.   His mind inclined to a literary more than
a business life.   He taught school and was elected town superintendent of schools, was well posted in extant literature especially poetical works.   Many years before his death, he made public profession of his faith in the christian religion, united with
the Baptist church of Ripley, N. Y.   In this faith he passed into
the spirit life.   Mrs. Shaver continued her residence in Westfield
for many years.   Finally she sold the property on Washington
St. in Westfield and bought a home in Dunkirk, city, N. Y., where
she lived for a number of years.   Her health failing she went to
the home of her son, Dwight in Angola, N. Y., where she died of
a cancer Nov. 25th, 1905.   She will be mentioned in the Memorial Tributes.

Children of David and Julia Tennant Shaver: Alice, Ella,
Frank, Frederic, Emmerson and Dwight.

1.   ALICE SHAVER, oldest child was born at Ripley, Chautauqua Co., N. Y., the 2nd of July, 1847.   She died August 27th,
1849 at Ripley village.

2.   ELLA MAY SHAVER was born at Ripley, N. Y., Dec. 11,
1851.   She married Elbert C. Goodwin at Caperville, Va., April
27th, 1873.   She went to live with her husband's parents and
lived with the family a few years.   After this she and her husband moved to Atchison, Kan., where he died.   Mrs. Goodwin
came to Westfield, N. Y., after her husband's death, and lived
with her mother for a number of years; and then returned to
Atchison where she now resides at this date, 1912.

3.   FRANK DAVID SHAVER was born at Ripley, N. Y., July
10th, 1853.   He prepared himself for college at Fredonia Normal and entered the University of Michigan at Ann Arbor, in
the fall term of 1872.   He took a classical course and was graduated in the spring of 1876, at the age of 23 years.   After graduation he commenced the profession of teaching at the Normal
school at Holly Springs, Miss., in 1876 where he continued for
two and one half years.   His next work was in the Leland University at New Orleans, from 1878 to 1881.   Then he went to
Bishop College, Marshall, Texas, for eight years, from 1881
to 1889.   Having resigned his position at this institute he came
back to N. Y. State and took the Principalship of the High

MISS BERTHA MAY SHAVER

Was born at Marshall, Texas., February 25, 1882.
She was the daughter of Prof. Frank Shaver and his
first wife, Mrs. Floretta Lewis Shaver, and grand-
daughter of David and Julia Tennant Shaver. She
died a tragical death at the home of her grandmother in the city of Dunkirk, N. Y., in January,
1903. Her remains were buried on the family lot of
the Lewis family in the beautiful cemetery at Fredonia, N. Y.

"NOT CHANGED, BUT GLORIFIED"

"Not changed, but glorified!" O beauteous thought
      For those who weep,
Mourning the loss of some dear face departed
      Fallen asleep!
Hushed into silence, never more to comfort
      The heart of men.
Gone like the sunshine of another country
      Beyond our ken.

How will it look, the face that we have cherished
      When next we meet?
Will it be changed—so glorified and saintly
      That we shall know it not?
Will there be nothing that shall say, "I love thee"
      And I have not forgot?
O faithful heart! the same loved face transfigured
      Shall meet thee there—
Less sad, less wistful, in immortal beauty
      Divinely fair.

Let us be patient, we who mourn with weeping
      Some vanished face;
The Lord has taken but to add more beauty
      And a diviner grace
When through the storm and tempest safely anchored
      Just on the other side,
We shall find that dear face through death's deep shadows
      "Not changed, but glorified."
                      —Selected.

School at Watertown, Jefferson Co., where he labored for two years from 1889 to 1891. This closed the period of his teaching making in all fifteen and a half years. He now entered upon business career which he has pursued to the present time, 1913. On the 25th of Aug. 1880, he married Miss Florette Lewis, daughter of Geo. W. Lewis of Fredonia, N. Y., at Fredonia Aug. 25th, 1880. To them were born three children, two of whom died in early childhood. Their names are as follows: Bertha, Mabel Estella and Edward Tennant.

1. BERTHA MAY SHAVER was born at Marshall, Texas, Feb. 25th, 1882. This daughter was a very promising young woman. She received an excellent education under the guidance of her father and teachers. She studied the Latin and Greek languages and hoped to prepare herself for the profession of teaching. The author was well acquainted with her and regarded her as a young woman of fine culture, of high ideals, of a pure and gentle character, and an ambition to make the best use possible of her gifts and opportunities. Bertha died at the home of her grand-mother, her father's mother in the city of Dunkirk, N. Y., in Jan. 1903. She was buried in the cemetery at Fredonia, N. Y.

Sometime perhaps we shall know,
    Why this loved one was taken away;
A providence accomplished her death
    Which may be revealed some day.

We should not distrust God's love,
    Who permits such bereavements to come;
We should only say with submissive hearts
    Thy will, O, Father be done.

We mourn but not without hope,
    For the Savior in whom she believed,
Has taken his own to his heavenly home,
    From her burdens and cares to relieve.

2. MABLE ESTELLE SHAVER was born at Fredonia, N. Y., June 1883. She died in September of the same year.

3. EDWARD TENNANT SHAVER was born at Fredonia, N. Y., in July 1884 and died the same month and year.

MRS. FLORETTE LEWIS SHAVER died at Fredonia, N. Y., in Nov. 1884. She was in all respects a beautiful character uniting in a pleasing personality, the best elements of an ideal womanly nature. Her departure was a great grief to both her own and her husband's families. She was buried in the cemetery at Fredonia, N. Y.

MR. SHAVER married as the second wife Miss Myrtie Antoinette Culver at Walworth, Wayne Co., N. Y., Sept. 22, 1886. By her he had two children named Dora Winifred and Henry Carlton.

1. DORA WINIFRED SHAVER was born at Marshal, Texas, June 25th, 1887. She married William Clark at Buffalo, N. Y., July 29th, 1909. Rev. J. J. Patterson of Buffalo performed the ceremony. MRS. CLARK, before her marriage took a business course in Bryant and Strattons business college, and before she had completely finished the course she took a position as bookkeeper in the office of James N. Byers, a contractor and builder located at Buffalo, N. Y., beginning Nov. 20th, 1905. She was promoted to a full secretary-ship, having at times sole charge of the office in the absence of the employer. Besides her office work she has been an active worker in the church and Sabbath school, and has been promoted to the superintendency of the Infant Deparmtent. Her marriage to Mr. Clark was a very happy event of her life. Both were members of the same Baptist church, and deeply interested in church work. Mr. Clark was born in Buffalo, N. Y., July 23, 1884. He secured a position as an electrical station operator for the Cataract Power and Conduit Co. His station is in Buffalo.

2. HENRY CARLTON SHAVER was born at Buffalo, N. Y., Oct. 14, 1898. He is at this date a student in a high school in Buffalo, N. Y. Withall he is obtaining an excellent musical education under the efficient instruction of his mother.

PROFESSOR FRANK SHAVER whose family record is sketched in the foregoing pages, received a call to the Principal-ship of the Benedict College located in North Carolina. He entered upon his work there in September 1913. By this change he dropped his agency business and entered again upon the work of teaching in which he had formerly been engaged in Texas and in N. Y. state for fifteen (15) years. This was a happy change for him. He is so well qualified for this work and teaching is so agreeable to him, that the change was like beginning life over again. His family and friends are much pleased that he is again taking up the work, to which his talents and life were at first consecrated. He closed his work at the end of one year.

4. GEORGE FREDERICK SHAVER was born at Ripley, N. Y., Nov. 4th, 1855. He was the 4th child and 2nd son of David and Julia Tennant Shaver. He married Miss Ida Estelle Griswold, Feb. 20, 1855. By his first marriage there were no children. MR. SHAVER married for his second wife Miss Amy Robsart Reis, who was born at Cedar Keys, Fla., in 1858 and died at Riverside, Cal., about 1900.

MR. SHAVER by his second wife had the following children:

Maybelle, Maude, Gladys, Grace, Dorthea, Phillip, David and George.

1. MAYBELLE F. SHAVER was born in Jersey City, N. J., Nov. 4, 1886. She married Jean Celeste, a man of French ancestry.

2. MAUDE SHAVER was a twin child with Maybelle and died when she was only eleven months old.

3. GLADYS AMY SHAVER was born at Yonkers, N. Y., Dec. 6th, 1890.

4. GRACE SHAVER a twin sister of Gladys died at the age of six months.

5 and 6. DAVID and GEORGE SHAVER were twins born at Yonkers, N. Y., 1892. David lived but five months and George lived but six months after birth.

7. DORTHEA MURIEL SHAVER was born at Yonkers, N. Y., Jan. 10, 1894.

8. PHILLIP DAVID SHAVER was born at Brooklyn, N. Y., April 13, 1899. All the above named children, except Maybelle and her husband of New York City, live at Riverside, Cal.

MR. SHAVER married for his third wife Mrs. Lillian Sophia Smith, Oct. 23, 1901. Their home at this date, 1912, is at Sayville, L. I., New York City. He is retired from business.

V. ALVIN EMMERSON SHAVER was born at Ripley, N. Y., Feb. 19, 1858. He married Cora Bennett, daughter of David and Charlott Bennett at Ripley, N. Y., Sept. 20, 1875. Miss Cora was born in Ripley Township July 31, 1858. There were born to them two children named Belle and Roy.

1. HELEN BELLE SHAVER was born at Ripley, N. Y., March 20, 1877. She had an excellent education in academical branches and was well fitted for a useful and successful life. She married William Edward Ferrell at Camden, N. Y., March 19, 1898 who was born in Macon, Ga., Oct. 28, 1866. By him she had one daughter named Dorothy Maybelle Ferrell born in Baltimore, Md., Sept. 5th, 1900.

Her second marriage was to Herman Todd Gilbertson at Baltimore, Md., Jan. 4, 1906, who was born at Lansing, Iowa, Aug. 3, 1877.

By this marriage she has a son named John Randolph Gilbertson born in New York City Sept. 21, 1906. Their home at this date, 1912, is at No. 120 East North Ave., Pittsburg, Pa.

2. ROY BENNETT SHAVER, only son of Emerson Shaver by his first wife, Cora Bennett Shaver was born at Ripley, N. Y., March 14, 1881. He married Miss Jessie Medford at Washington, D. C., in the Trinity Church, June 4th, 1902. Miss Medford was born at Washington, D. C., July 3, 1879.

There was born to them one child, a son, named Homer Medford Shaver who was born at Washington, D. C., April 6, 1904.

MR. SHAVER is an appointee in the Division of Carriers' Accounts Inter State Commerce Commission at Washington, D. C. His work is the examination of Accounts and Records of Rail Roads and other common carriers as provided in the Act of the Congress to Regulate Commerce between the States. It consists in a thorough analysis of the Revenues and Expenses of all common carriers. The examiners work in parties, differing in number according to the extent of the Rail Road to be examined and the work to be done. MR. SHAVER is the third descendant of the Tennant family who have had responsible positions in government employment.

MRS. EMERSON SHAVER died at Ripley, N. Y., while on a visit to her old home, on the 2nd of July, 1904. She was in all respects a noble woman who was highly esteemed and loved by her friends and relatives. Her domestic duties were her first care, and these she performed with fidelity and constancy, giving her children a motherly watch care, a wise and prudent guidance. Her home was her queendom, and she presided over all its various affairs with patience, dignity, industry and economy. The writer was personally acquainted with his niece, and knows that any words he may choose can only do partial justice to the excellency and nobility of her life and character. She was taken away in the prime of her womanhood, when to all human appearance her life work was only in its first important stages of fruit-bearing and harvesting.

Bonar has written these beautiful words:

"I go to life and not to death;
    From darkness to life's native sky;
I go from sickness and from pain
    To health and immortality.

Let our farewell then be tearless,
    Since I bid farewell to tears;
Write this day of my departure
    Festive in your coming years."

MR. SHAVER at fifteen years of age had an ambition to become a sailor. During the summer of 1873 he sailed on the schooner Mammouth, an Atlantic Coaster, returning home in the Fall. In 1874 he took another trip on the Lakes. Left sailing and came home, and worked land on shares from 1874 to 1879. In Nov. of 1879, he went to Mooreheadville to learn telegraphy of his brother Dwight. In May, 1880, commenced work for the Penn. R. R. as operator and clerk. He worked for this company at Erie, Sharon and Wheatland, Pa. In 1883 was appointed agent and operator on the Nickle Plate R. R., at Westfield, N. Y., and commenced work in the spring of 1884. In 1887 he was promoted to the position of train dispatcher with office at Conneaut, O. In April, 1888 was agent on the N. Y. and Northern N. Y. R. R. with location at Yonkers, N. Y. In 1892 served as life insurance agent for a Philadelphia, Pa. Co. In 1893 served as secretary of the Shaver Corporation. In 1894 was Baggage master on the Baltimore and Annapolis, R. R. and was promoted to become conductor, and then as train master with office at Annapolis, Md. In 1898 was train master on the A. M. & B. R. R. In 1903 was appointed General Superintendent of the Annapolis, Washington and Baltimore R. R. This closed his R. R. employment and he went to St. Louis, Mo., to engage in the life insurance business in which he continued up to the time of his last sickness. Mr Shaver's second marriiage was to Miss Katharine Dorothy Brandt, who was born near Hamburg, N. Y., July 2, 1874. They have no children.

Mr. Shaver died in St. Louis, Mo., Jan. 7, 1913, after an illness of a few months. He was genial, kind hearted and social in his nature, and has left a record of a busy upright and honorable life.

VI. Carol Dwight Shaver, the youngest of the family was born at Ripley, N. Y., Sept. 4, 1860. He married Miss Jennie Moorehead at Mooreheadville, Pa., Sept. 20, 1883. Miss Moorehead was born at Mooreheadville, Erie Co., Pa., Jan. 23, 1860.

There were born to them two children named Carol Moorehead and Rolla Emmerson.

1. Carol Moorehead Shaver was born at Northville, Chau. Co., N. Y., June 27, 1884. He died at the same place Sept. 19, 1884, being at his death two months and twenty eight days old.

"But Jesus said, Suffer little children and forbid them not to come unto me; for of such is the kingdom of heaven." Math. 19:14.

2. Rolla Emerson Shaver was born at State Line, N. Y., March 11, 1886. He is at this date, 1912, at a medical college in Buffalo, N. Y.

Mr. Shaver at fifteen years of age was made night watch man on the Lake Shore R. R. at Mooreheadville, Pa., in 1875 and 76. During this period he learned telegraphy, and was appointed station agent and operator, and located at Irvin, Chau. Co., N. Y., in 1877. From Irvin he was transferred to Mooreheadville, in 1877, again to State Line, in May 1882. Here he served till Sept. when he was transferred to Angola, N. Y., where he served in the same position, on the Lake Shore Road, for about 20 years up to about Aug. 14, 1907. Closing his work at Angola, he took an agency in the Prudential Life Insurance Co., and located at Angola for 2 years. He was then appointed Asst. Superintendent with headquarters at Dunkirk, N. Y. To this city he moved his family, Oct. 15, 1909 where now they reside. Financially the change of business was a substantial improvement. MR. SHAVER and his wife have been steady workers in the church-life of the community where they lived. He was of much assistance in maintaining choir singing, and rendering financial aid, while located at Angola.

In the Fall of 1913 he changed his headquarters to Buffalo, N. Y., and moved his family to No. 631 Prospect Avenue.

The descendants of David and Julia Tennant Shaver number as follows:

Children 6
Grand-children 17
Great-grand-children 3

Total descendants 26

With parents and grand-parents they include five generations.

III. WEALTHY ANN TENNANT was born in Springfield, Otsego Co., N. Y., Aug. 24th, 1830. She came witih the family to Chautauqua Co., N. Y., in the Spring of 1833. She gained a common school education, taught school when very young, and yet she learned the art and science of good house keeping. She married Erbin Cone Wattles at Ripley, Oct. 22nd, 1845. He was a second son of Gurdon Huntington and Lucretia Phelps Wattles. He was born at Ripley, N. Y., Feb. 21st, 1825. Mrs. Wattles was taken into the home of her husband's parents, then located on Ripley Hill. Here she lived with the family for a number of years. Finally Mr. Wattles purchased a farm west of Ripley village in the Cochrane district. Onto this farm they moved in 1859. Here they lived for a few years, sold the farm and purchased another nearer the village where they lived until the family moved to Buffalo, N. Y., which has been their home city down to the present time. While living in Ripley the parents of Mr. Wattles died, the father, Nov .1880, the mother in the fall of 1886.

ERBIN WATTLES lived for many years in Buffalo, until old age and disease enfeebled both body and mind, and he became as helpless as an infant. Many years before this while yet a young man, he publicly professed his faith in the Christian religion, joined the Baptist church of Ripley, and never gave up this early faith and hope. He died at his home, 709 Prospect Ave., Buffalo, N. Y., April 17th, 1909, at the advanced age of 84 years, 1

ERBIN CONE WATTLES

Born February 21, 1825 · Died April 17, 1909

MRS. WEALTHY TENNANT WATTLES
Born August 24, 1830

month and 26 days. Mrs. Wattles is now living at this date, 1915, with her youngest son, Jay B., and his family at No. 56 Colonial Circle, Buffalo. There were born to Mr. and Mrs. Wattles three sons and a daughter as follows, Gurdon, Sarah, Bert and Jay B.

1. GURDON MOSES WATTLES was born at Ripley, N. Y., Dec. 26th, 1846. He married Louise Grader at Buffalo, Feb. 28th, 1873. She was his first wife and the mother of all his children. She was born at Buffalo, April 25th, 1847, and died in the same city, April 27th, 1897. She was in every respect a noble woman, possessing unusual business ability, of a kind sympathetic nature, and of great force of character. The loss to her family by her death cannot be estimated. She was a devoted wife, an affectionate mother, and a wise home builder looking after the education of her children and tenderly caring for the wants and comfort of her family. In christian faith and hope she passed away.

After her death a few years intervening, Mr. Wattles married his wife's sister, Mrs. Mary Kemptke. She had two sons by her first husband, named Charles and Harris Kemptke. By her second husband she has no children. Mr. Wattles has been practically all his life in the commission business in Buffalo. By his diligence in business and careful management he has made a good fortune, started his sons in the same business, and at this date, 1912, has no active part in the business except the investments he still holds.

There were born to Gurdon M. and Louise Grader Wattles at Buffalo, N. Y., eight children named, Frank, Maud, Fred, May, Eddie, Jay H., Raymond W. and Florence L.

1. FRANK ERBIN WATTLES was born Mar. 15th, 1876. He married Miss Alice Weller of Buffalo June 27th, 1899. Miss Weller was born at Buffalo May 3rd, 1877.

MR. FRANK WATTLES was initiated early in life in the Commission Mercantile business as an assistant in his father's office. Later he was made a partner in the business under the firm name of Wattles and Wattles. The firm were successful dealers in butter and eggs. They purchased large quantities of these goods in small lots and car lots, usually making a good paying profit. They have also invested large sums of money in real estate in Buffalo, and through this have accumulated a fine fortune, at the same time gaining for themselves a reputation for honesty and integrity, and a wise use of successful business methods.

CHILDREN OF FRANK AND ALICE WELLER WATTLES.

There were born to these parents four children, Elizabeth, Gurdon, Frank, Jr., and Alice. All were born in Buffalo, N. Y.

1. ELIZABETH WATTLES was born Dec. 11th, 1900.
2. GURDON WELLER WATTLES was born Oct. 14th, 1902.

3.   FRANK ERBIN WATTLES, JR., was born Sept. 19th, 1904.
4.   ALICE CATHERINE WATTLES was born June 14th, 1911.

II.   MAUD LENA WATTLES was born May 4th, 1877.   She is
the second child and oldest daughter of Gurdon M. and Louise
Grader Wattles.   She married Benjamin Leslie Hawkins at
Buffalo, N. Y., Oct. 22nd, 1907.

MR. HAWKINS was born Dec. 2nd, 1872.   His father's name
was Richard Watson Hawkins and his mother's maiden name
was Laura Herman Smith.

There were born to Mr. and Mrs. Hawkins three children
named Richard, Louise and Martha; all born in Buffalo, N. Y.

1.   RICHARD WATTLES HAWKINS was born Sept. 20th, 1902.
2.   LOUISE FLORENCE HAWKINS was born Nov. 14th, 1906.
3.   MARTHA HAWKINS was born Sept. 23rd, 1912.

These children are great-grand children of Erbin Cone and
Wealthy Tennant Wattles.

III.   FRED GURDON WATTLES, the 3rd child and second son of
Gurdon M. and Louise Grader Wattles was born July 24th,
1878.   While at the lake he fell from the pier into the water and
was drowned.   His parents were with him but did not happen
to see him when he fell.   He was soon taken from the water,
and every effort possible was made to save his life, but all in
vain.   This sad accident took place at Buffalo, June 26th, 1885.
He was 7 years, 1 month, and 2 days old at his death.

'Twas only the body the floods overwhelmed,
    The spirit that animates cannot be drowned;
The waters may free the soul from the flesh,
    Then upward it soars, when its freedom is found.

So let us not choose the way we would die,
    Nor the time nor the place when we pass away;
'Tis enough that we know in youth or old age,
    God fixes the way, the place and the day.

IV.   MAY LUCRETIA WATTLES the 4th child and 2nd daughter
of Gurdon M. and Louise Grader Wattles was born at Buffalo,
Nov. 8th, 1880.   She married Richard Rawlings at Buffalo, Oct.
17th, 1911.   Mr. Rawlins was born in Washington, D. C., Aug.
1st, 1878.   There were born to them two children, Mary and
Frank.

1.   MARY LOUISE RAWLINGS was born at Seattle, Washington, Nov. 10th, 1908.
2.   FRANK TRUMAN RAWLINGS was born at Washington, D.
C., Jan. 12th, 1912.

V.   EDWIN CLARK WATTLES was born in Buffalo, N. Y.,
April 14th, 1882.   He was the fifth child and third son of Gurdon M. and Louise Grader Wattles.

GORDON MOSES WATTLES
Born December 26, 1846   Died September 15, 1914

MRS. GRACE LOUISE WATTLES
Born April 29 1847   Died July 28, 1899

VI.   JAY HARRY WATTLES, 6th child and 4th son was born at Buffalo, N. Y., Sept. 26th, 1886.

After completing his school work, he entered the office of his father and brother Frank.   He was soon made a partner in the business, and has so continued to this date, 1913.   Some time afterward he went into partnership with his brother Frank in the commission business.

VII.   RAYMOND WILLIAM WATTLES, 7th child and 5th son of Gurdon and Louise Wattles was born at Buffalo, April 20th, 1888.   He married Miss Lucilla Dunbar at Buffalo, Oct. 14th, 1911.   Miss Dunbar was born in Buffalo May 2nd, 1890.   She is the daughter of Harris Thomas Dunbar and his wife Minnie (Hardison) Dunbar.

There was born to Raymond and Lucilla Dunbar Wattles a son named Harris Dunbar Wattles.   He was born at Buffalo, Sept. 13th, 1912, and died at the same place, April 15th, 1913. Another son named Erbin Dunbar Wattles was born Dec. 1st, 1914.

Having learned the Commission Mercantile business in partnership with his father and brother, he started in the same business by himself, in Buffalo, where he is having excellent success.

VIII.   FLORENCE LOUISE WATTLES, 8th child and 3d daughter, was born at Buffalo, Nov. 13th, 1892.   She is now seeking a college education, to fit herself for some high and useful sphere in life.   She is the youngest of a family of eight children.

The above is a complete record of the family of Gurdon M. and Louise Grader Wattles.   Mr. Wattles had no children by his second marriage.   The family have a beautiful home, richly furnished, at 393 Richmond Ave., Buffalo, N. Y.   His son, Frank's residence is at 385 on the same avenue.   The descendents number eight children, five sons and three daughters and eight grand-children.

After preparing the family record of GURDON M. WATTLES for publication, news came to the author of his death at his home on Richmond Ave., No. 393, Buffalo, N. Y., on the morning of September 15, 1914, at the age of 67 years, 8 months and 19 days.   His death was very sudden and unexpected, overwhelming his mother, still living, and his wife and children and grandchildren in a deluge of deep sorrow.

MR. WATTLES had been ailing for a number of months with a disease of the heart and arteries.   About a week before his death he was abl to take a ride out in an automobile.   He visited his mother at his brother Jay's home the day before his death. The following night he was taken with a severe pain in the region of his heart, and while his wife and youngest daughter were seeking means to relieve his suffering, suddenly without the least warning he passed away.   All the members of his own family except two little boys whose deaths have been recorded, are living.   His mother and two brothers, Burt and Jay, survive him.

MR. WATTLES was very successful in business as has already been stated, and leaves a large inheritance to his family.   He died in a full and comforting belief in the christian faith.   Rev. E. H. Dickinson, pastor of the North Presbyterian church of Buffalo, officiated at his funeral which was largely attended. His remains were buried in the Buffalo cemetery on the family lot upon which had been previously erected a gray marble monument of large size and beautiful proportions.

Thus passed into the spirit life a man who as a son, husband, father and brother, was loving, kind and true, and as a citizen loyal, noble and highly esteemed.

2.   SARAH ELLEN WATTLES was born at Ripley, N. Y., July 23rd, 1853.   She was the second child, and first and only daughter of Erbin and Wealthy Tennant Wattles.   She lived just long enough to get her beautiful life nestled down deeply into the love of her parents, when the angel of death came and plucked the blossom from the parent-stem and bore it away to the realm where the sun is ever shining and the flowers never fade.   SARAH died at Ripley, May 20th, 1861, at the age of 7 years, 9 months and 27 days.

MEMORIAL POEM.

Beautiful bud of sweet promise,
    You had just begun to bloom;
    When the Heavenly Gardener came along,
    And plucked the fair bud too soon.

Gladly would we have kept you,
    Had it been our Fathers will;
But now we have only to say
    To our bleeding hearts, "Be still."

There is a Garden above we are told,
    Where celestial flowers grow;
There the river of life refreshes the land,
    And the sun sheds its heavenly glow.

We are waiting and hoping, dear Sara,
    That the gates of that Garden will open;
When we are ripe for the harvest,
    And the call of our God is the token.

3.   BURT HARRY WATTLES was born at Ripley, N. Y., Sept. 2nd, 1862.   He married Miss Johanna Hall at Ripley, Nov. 27th 1883.   She was born at Wallingford, Vermont, June 24th, 1864. They have no children.

MR. WATTLES had an ambition to obtain a college education. At that time he did not know but what it might be his duty at some future date to enter the Christian ministry. But the conditions were as they are in many other cases—no money to pay for a college course. For a few years, he has been located in Buffalo in the office of real estate agency. In 19 he was a foreign agent of the same company and was sent to the Isle of Pines where, at this date, 1914, he is now located with his family.

4. JAY B. WATTLES, youngest son of Erbin and Wealthy Wattles, was born at Ripley, N. Y., Sept. 25, 1867. He married Mrs. Grace Sawin Ellis at Evansville, Green Co., Wis., Jan. 29, 1896. She was the daughter of Lorenzo Sawin and his wife Helen Webster Sawin, and was born at Evansville, Wis.

After their marriage they made their home with Mr. Wattles' parents at 709 Prospect Ave., Buffalo, N. Y. Now we have again to relate a sad ending of a short but happy married life. After enjoying for a few years their pleasant home, Mrs. Wattles was taken ill with an incurable disease and died at her home Mrs. Wattles was a grand-daughter of Rev. John Sawin and his wife, Orel Tennant Sawin, who was the oldest sister of the author's mother, Delinda Tennant.

> "Life is a brittle thread,
> Though made of golden strands;
> They break and then away we go,
> To other scenes and lands."

MR. WATTLES second marriage was to Miss Blanche Fisher, which took place at Buffalo, N. Y., June 26th, 1902. She was born at Evans, Erie Co., N. Y., Sept. 7, 1872. They have one child, a daughter named Janet Blanche Wattles, born at Buffalo, June 18th, 1904.

MR. WATTLES a number of years ago started in the Commission business at Buffalo as assistant and clerk in the office of his oldest brother Gurdon. Having served there for a few years he then set up for himself in the same business, which has been continued with excellent success to the present date. He has been enabled to build a beautiful and costly home at No. 56 Colonial Circle, Buffalo, N. Y. He has been a hard worker, making his business a matter of close and careful study. By this close attention to the trade, his losses have been comparatively small and his gains a slow and safe accumulation.

The descendants of Erbin C. Wattles and Wealthy Tennant Wattles number as follows:

Children 4
Grandchildren 11
Great-grandchildren 10
                                        ——
Total descendants 25

Including parents and grand-parents there are five generations.

Division III.

Albert, Ellen, Fannie and John.

1.   Albert Milton Tennant was born at Ripley, Chautauqua Co., N. Y., Aug. 7th, 1834.   He was the first child born after the settlement of the family in Chau. Co.   His coming into this world took place in a log house on Ripley Hill, one eighth of a mile south of what was known as Palmers Gulf on the west side of the road leading to what was then known as Wattlesberg. At birth, the boy weighed three pounds avoirdupois. A Mrs. Tupper, a neighbor, called in a few days after the birth to see the mother and her child. As she saw the small dimensions of the newcomer she exclaimed, "Well Mrs. Tennant! if that was my child I should hope he would die, for he will never know anything nor be anybody." This was the first compliment the author of this book ever had. As he purposes to write a sketch of his life in a separate article, no more will be written in this connection. (See First Division of Part IV.)

2.   Ellen Delinda Tennant was born in Ripley, in a log house located north of what was known as Palmers Gulf, and west of the road leading from Ripley village to Wattlesburg, on the 26th of Oct. 1836.   She died in infancy from a severe attack of whooping cough. The date of her death was not recorded in the family bible, so is lost.

Thus in early life this little daughter and sister was taken in the arms of the blessed Savior and carried away into the kingdom concerning which He said, "Of such is the kingdom of heaven."

> Can it be we'll never meet you
>   In that land of pure delight?
> Where the saints and angels mingle
>   In their robes of silvery white?
>
> Must we think when you were taken
>   From our loving parents arms,
> That we ne'er again would see you
>   In your lovely infant charms?

GEORGE MASON
Born February 22, 1840   Died May 23 1887

MRS. FANNIE OLIVA TENNANT (MASON) HOUGH
Born February 18, 1838   Died January 11, 1913

Dismiss the thought! it shall not be
  That we must part at death forever;
For there are bonds of love so strong
  That time nor distance cannot sever.

Drawn by these ties in spirit life,
  Loving hearts will find each other;
And reunions there shall come,
  Of brothers, sisters, father, mother,

So we'll wait for that glad day,
  Patiently watching for the vision;
Till the mists of earth are faded,
  And heaven's full glory has arisen.

3. FANNIE OLIVIA TENNANT was born at Ripley, N. Y.,
Feb. 18, 1838. She was the ninth child and fifth daughter of
her parents. She married George Mason, son of George Mason
and Jane Gardner Mason of Ripley at Clymer, N. Y., June 24
1863. The author was the officiating clergyman. By Mr. Mason she had three children, two sons, Charles and Eugene, and a
daughter that died in infancy. Mr. Mason was a farmer who inherited from his father some property. He purchased a farm on
the Lake Shore road in Ripley, where he lived for a few years.
This was sold and he purchased a farm west of Ripley village
in the Cochrane district on the main road. This was sold and
he purchased a smaller farm on the Lake Shore road, north and
west of the village. Here his family lived till his death which
took place May 23, 1887.

A few years after her husband's death, MRS. MASON married
Eugene Hough at Ripley, Nov. 26, 1889. By this marriage there
were no children. Mr. Hough was a skillful photographer, and
a man of excellent qualities of mind and a pure and noble character. His marriage to Mrs. Mason was his second marriage,
his first wife was a sister of his second wife's first husband. Her
maiden name was Frances Mason. Mr. Hough had practiced
his art in New York City, in Barbadoes, one of the West India
Islands, also in Trinidad Island. He returned to America and
opened a gallery at Fredonia, N. Y., where he purchased a home,
at which he died Jan. 2, 1902. He left a beautiful monument to
the memory of his first wife and now to his own memory, in a
remarkably well written "Memorial Tribute to Frances Mason
Hough."

The author has not space to write of these brothers-in-law
as they each deserve to be mentioned. Each had the true elements of nature and character that constitute the highest and
noblest manhood.

CHILDREN OF GEORGE AND FANNIE TENNANT MASON.

1. CHARLES O. MASON was born at Ripley, N. Y., Oct. 22, 1867. He married Minnie Sackett at Fredonia, N. Y., Aug. 16, 1893. She was born in Arkwright, Chau. Co., N. Y., Oct. 23, 1869. Mr. Mason learned the photographical art from his step-father, and the practice of this art has always been his life work. His studio was first established at Fredonia, and remains there at this date, 1915. Mr. Mason and wife have been members of the Baptist church of Fredonia for many years. He was the superintendent of the Sabbath school for a long time, and then secretary and treasurer. They have one child, a son, named George Sackett Mason, born at Fredonia, N. Y., Aug. 4, 1896. He is at this date (1913) attending the State Normal School at his home village. He is becoming quite an expert in wireless telegraphy.

2. EUGENE GEORGE MASON was born at Ripley, N. Y., July 27, 1871. He married Matie Sackett, sister of Minnie Sackett, at Fredonia, Sept. 2, 1895. Matie Sackett was born at Fredonia, N. Y., Feb. 6th, 1871. The two brothers married sisters, both of whom were graduates of the Normal School. MR. MASON graduated at the Westfield Academy, then went to Cornell University at Ithaca, N. Y., where he was graduated. Soon after graduation he received an appointment in the Patent Office Department in Washington, D. C., at a salary of $1200 a year. As clerk he served a few years after which he was re-appointed with an increased salary. During the last years of his service he studied Patent Law till he was admitted to the bar and commenced the practice of law as a Patent law attorney. He located in an office in partnership with Mr. Sylvester at Washington, D. C., where at this date the firm of Sylvester and Mason have all they can do, often taking long business trips over the country.

Eugene and Matie Sackett have one son named Lawrence Sackett Mason who was born in Washington, D. C., Dec. 21, 1898. He is now attending the High school in Washington, D. C., and gives promise of making a noble and useful man.

4. JOHN ASEL TENNANT was born at Ripley, N. Y., in the old log house on the hill, May 30, 1839. He was the only child born in the old home and was the last and youngest of the family. He married Julia Ann Adams at her home in Ripley, Oct. 26, 1862. She was the second daughter and fourth child of Harry and Lawrence (Pride) Adams, and was born in Ripley Township.

Mr. and Mrs. Tennant have but one child, a son, named Frederick Adams Tennant. As the author purposes to write a Memorial Tribute to the memory of his brother, John, no further account will be made of his life in this connection, except to

JOHN ASEL TENNANT
Born May 30, 1839.   Died August 13, 1906.

MRS. JULIA ADAMS TENNANT
Born April 19, 1838.

announce that he died at the Hamot Hospital in Erie City, Pa., Aug. 13th, 1906.

FREDERICK ADAMS TENNANT was born at Ripley, N. Y., May 18, 1871. He married Miss Evalena Mason at Ripley, Dec. 30, 1896. Miss Mason was born at Ripley, Jan. 10, 1871. She was the daughter of Oscar and Flora Bell Mason. This marriage was the consummation of mutual early love, that was endeared by a sweet congenialty of spirits, and by a perfect harmony of purposes in life. Whenever such true hearts and worthy lives flow together, they form in their unity a river of peace and happiness. It is always sad even to anticipate an early separation, and much more painful to realize that it has already taken place. Mrs. Tennant was in every element of her nature and character a noble and lovely personality. To know her was to love her, and to love her conferred a rich benediction upon all her warm mutual friendships. But the dread monster, consumption seized upon her young life. All was done that could be done for her, a few months were spent in a warm southern climate, but all the means used to save her precious life were unavailing. She was brought home to her parents at Ripley, Mr. and Mrs. Oscar Mason. While sitting on her father's lap for a rest and a little change, her beautiful spirit passed out of the weak frail body, and entered into its eternal rest.

The following lines were chanted at the funeral of Eva's cousin, Nellie Goodrich; they are very appropriate to Eva.

"She passed in beauty like the rose
    Blown from its parent stem;
She passed in beauty like a pearl
    Dropped from a diadem.

"She passed in beauty like the snow
    On flowers dissolved away;
She passed in beauty like a star
    Lost on the brow of day.

"She lives in glory, like the stars—
    Bright jewels of the night;
She lives in glory like the sun
    When at meridian height."

We must not enter into the sad silence of a husband's heart. So sacred a shrine must not be desecrated by unholy hands.

MRS. TENNANT'S funeral took place at the home of her parents. Many relatives and friends were present to take the last look upon her beautiful face, and shed their tears over their loss. Her body was buried in the Ripley cemetery there to wait the summons that will call forth the dead from sea and land.

So young and so pure, why should she be taken
  From friends who loved her with hearts warm and true?
One answer alone can surely be given,
  To explain this deep mystery to me and to you.

The Saviour who bought her with his own precious blood,
  First loved her, first sought her and claimed her his own;
A place up in Heaven for her He prepared;
  On wings of the spirit to that home she has flown.

                    (Johns Gospel 4th Chapt. 2 and 3 v.

After this sad experience MR. TENNANT returned to his duties in the patent office at Washington, D. C. For eight and a
half years his work contiued after the loss of his first wife,
when he married Miss Ann H. White, daughter of William Parker and Amanda Rogers White at Washington, D. C., on Feb.
22, Washington's birthday, 1908. She was born at New Egypt.
N. Y., Dec. 13, 1867.

MR. TENNANT'S early preparation for his life work consisted
of a course of instruction in the Ripley school, till 1886; then
went to the Westfield, N.Y. Academy from which he was graduated in 1888, taking one year of graduate work. He entered Cornell University at Ithaca, N.Y., in the fall of 1889 and was graduated in June of 1893 taking the degree of electrical engineer. He
returned to his home in Ripley and worked on his father's farm
for two years waiting for an opening in the government service.
This came to him on the 18th of August, 1895, when he entered
the United States Patent Office as fourth assistant Examiner.
While thus engaged he studied law at the National University
Law School from 1899 till 1902, 3 years, receiving the degree of
L. L. B. in 1901 and L. L. M. in 1902. This examining of patents and their records was to determine whether a patent was
new and patentable under the law. In this service MR. TEN-
NANT continued for 7 years.

He was soon assigned to the Classification Division. Millions
of patents were being classified on a scientific basis. He worked
at this for two years dealing mostly with metal works. After
this he was assigned to the interference division to determine the
priority of invention between two or more claimants for a patent
on the same invention. The proceedings were much like trials
in the U. S. Equity Courts. From the Interference Division MR.
TENNANT was sent temporarily to the Trade Mark Division to
assist in interpreting and applying a new law of 1905. After
eight months, he was returned to the Interference Division. In
Jan. 1907 he was transferred to the Concessionaries Office to prepare cases which came before him on appeal.

In June, 1907, he was promoted to the position of law clerk
in which he had to appear before the court of appeals as Coun-

FREDERIC ADAMS TENNANT
Born May 18, 1871.

MRS. EVA MASON TENNANT

Born January 10, 1876   Died August 13, 1899

seller for the Commissioner in cases of appeal to that court from his decisions; and also acted for the Commissioner in Mandamus cases brought against him.

After serving as law clerk or law examiner for two years he was nominated by the commissioner as assistant Commissioner. The appointment to this position was made by President Taft and confirmed by the Senate May 8th, 1909. He writes the author that he did not have to ask for this position, nor was it obtained through political influence, but in opposition to strong political influence that was supporting other applicants for the place.

The duties of Assistant Commissioner are various and may be divided into judicial and executive; Executive in that the Assistant has in part charge of the office, directing the examiners work; and judicial in that he has to decide the appeals and petitions that come before the Commissioner each week. To show the responsibility and importance of his position, he cites a case in which he was called upon to decide that involved the sum of $650,000.

MRS. TENNANT at the time of her marriage was filling an important, responsible position in the Patent Office at Washington, D. C. After finishing her school education at Washington she entered the Patent Office as a clerk to aid her father in the maintenance of his large family. Her appointment was made Mar. 27, 1887. In course of time she rose to the highest rank among the clerks. She was an expert typewriter and learned stenography which she also used in her work. One of the duties in her division was the registering of trade-marks. In 1905 a trade-mark law was passed which pertained to inter-state commerce which greatly increased registration, so that in one year, 1905, there were 20,000 to be registered. MRS. TENNANT finally had charge of a large number of clerks, greatly increasing her responsibility and labor. Added to the care of a large force of clerks, she was burdened with the incompetent and ill-tempered, who are always jealous of their superiors in important work.

MRS. TENNANT entered the Patent Office when only 20 years old and remained in constant employment till the time of her marriage in 1908, about twenty one years.

Since writing the above the author has received notice that his nephew has resigned his position as Commissioner of Patents and has entered into partnership with a law firm at Boston, Mass., doing business as patent lawyers. The firm name is Heard, Smith and Tennant. MR. TENNANT's work commenced the 16th of June, 1913, just a day after he closed his work in Washington, D. C.

This closes the records of the descendants of Moses Asel Tennant and his wife, Delinda Tennant. They number as follows:

Children 10
Grand-children 21
Great-grand-children 35
Great-great-grand-children 20

Grand Total 86

With the parents and grand-parents, they comprise six generations.

DAVID HOLLENBECK

Born December 1, 1797   Died December 7, 1886

MRS. ESTHER TENNANT HOLLENBECK
Born July 29, 1804   Died November 6, 1871

PART III.

CHAPTER SIXTH.

MISS ESTHER TENNANT.

This Chapter contains a record of the birth, marriage, death and burial of ESTHER TENNANT, the daughter of Moses Tennant, Sr., and his wife Sarah Selden Jewett; and the wife of David Hollenbeck; and their descendants by family names: Hollenbeck, Robertson, Mackey, Mitchell, Wright, Harvey, Rice, Plumb, Miller, Hills, Frost, McColl, Fellows, Miller, Brown, McLeod, Russell and Kent.

ESTHER TENNANT, the youngest child of Moses Tennant, Sr., and his wife Sarah Selden Jewett Tennant, was born at Springfield, Otsego County, N. Y., July 29th, 1804. She married David Hollenbeck of Danube, N. Y., at Springfield, September 2nd, 1821. Rev. George Sawin officiated at the wedding. He was pastor of the Baptist church of that place. David was the son of Isaac Hollenbeck and his wife, Dolly (Smith) Hollenbeck. Isaac Hollenbeck was born in New Jersey, October 15th, 1777, and died at Starkville, Herkimer County, N. Y., August 8th, 1857, being at his death aged seventy-nine years, nine months and twenty-three days. MRS. HOLLENBECK, his beloved wife, was born March 21st, 1778, and died at Starkville, N. Y., January 16th, 1851, being at her death aged seventy-three years, nine months and twenty-five days.

DAVID HOLLENBECK, their oldest son, was born at Minden, Montgomery County, N. Y., December 1st, 1797. In early life he had an ambition to become a physician, and studied medicine. He changed his purposes, taught school, learned the trade of cloth-making. A few years after his marriage, in company with John Champion, his brother-in-law he built a saw mill. This mill was not well located, and the enterprise proved a financial failure. He never owned real estate in New York. His wife owned thirty acres of the old Tennant farm in Springfield, N. Y.

In the year 1830, MR. HOLLENBECK moved with his family to Michigan. He arrived at Detroit, Mich. May 1st, settled at Pontiac, Oakland Co. At first he worked at the Clothier's trade in a factory owned by Judge Paddock of Pontiac; he also engaged in school teaching. His residence in Oakland County continued for about twenty years, during which he purchased several tracts of land in the vicinity of Pontiac.

On the 20th of June, 1850, he moved to Genesee County, Michigan, and located on a farm in Davison Township. It was the west half of the northwest quarter section. The land was a wilderness, but he hewed out a farm and a home for himself and family, where he spent the remainder of his life.

MR. HOLLENBECK was in all respects an honorable, upright citizen of good reputation, industrious and frugal. His wife faithfully co-operated with him in all his plans and labors. She was intelligent, of a kindly sympathetic nature, attended diligently to the affairs of her household and to the education of her children.

However true and faithful we may be, in this earthly life, we are compelled to look forward and anticipate the end. A cousin writes the author these touching words: "On December 6th or 7th, 1886, DAVID HOLLENBECK reached upward the right hand of his spiritual strength, crying in spirit to the Infinite Friend, "My Father," and to the Loving Son crying "My Brother," and passed into the realm that lieth eternally somewhere beyond the shining stars." His beloved wife, Esther Tennant, passed upward before her husband about fifteen years, having died November 6th, 1871. Both died at Davison, Genesee County, Michigan, and were buried in the Richfield Cemetery.

Our cousin, Ernest Hollenbeck, sent to the author the following beautiful and appropriate lines:

"They sat in the sun together, when the day was almost closed;
And just at the close, an angel stepped over the threshold stone;
He folded their hands, he touched their eyelids with balm,
And their last breath floated upward, like the close of a solemn
     psalm."
"Blessed are the dead who die in the Lord."

Their children and grandchildren:

There were born to David Holenbeck and his wife, Esther (Tennant) Hollenbeck, five children, named as follows: Sarah, Ellen, Dolly Jane, William and Harriet Georgiana.

I.   SARAH OLIVIA HOLLENBECK, first child of David and Esther Tennant Hollenbeck, was born at Danube, Herkimer County, N. Y., March 18th, 1824, and died at Waterford, Oakland County, Michigan, March 18th, 1899, at the age of seventy-five years. She married George Robertson at Pontiac, Michigan, July 3rd, 1843. There were born to them four children named as follows: Maria, Lewis, David and Ovid.

1.   MARIA ROBERTSON was born at Whitelake, Oakland County, N. Y., September 4th, 1844. She married for her first husband Willard Mackey. They had a son named George Mackey.

MRS. MACKEY married for her second husband Henry Mitchell. Mr. Mitchell was born in the Township of Pelham, District of Niagara, West Canada, September 3rd, 1841, and died at Fenton, Michigan, January 10th, 1910, at the age of sixty-eight years, four months and seven days. There were born to Mr. and Mrs. Mitchell, six children named Alfred, William, Ernest, Mary, Edward and Charles.

1. ALFRED MAZEPPA MITCHELL was born at Waterford, Oakland County, Michigan, January 4th, 1868. He is not married, he is a farmer.

2. WILLIAM H. MITCHELL was born in Waterford, Michigan, December 21st, 1869.

3. ERNEST E. MITCHELL was born at Waterford, Michigan, March 6th, 1871. He is in the grocery business in Flint, Mich.

4. MARY MARIA MITCHELL was born at Waterford, Michigan, April 6th, 1874. She died at Hart, Mason County, Michigan, Jan. 4th, 1903, at the age of twenty-nine years, one month and twenty-eight days.

5. EDWARD MITCHELL was born at Holly, Oakland County, Michigan, November 24th, 1880. He is on the police force at Flint.

6. CHARLES MITCHELL was born at Holly, Oakland County, Michigan. He is an agent of the D. & W. R. railroad in an office at Detroit.

II. LEWIS ROBERTSON, second child and first son of George and Sarah Olivia Hollenbeck Robertson. He died when about seven years old.

III. DAVID AND OVID ROBERTSON, twin sons of George and Sarah O. Hollenbeck Robertson. They died in infancy.

IV. ELLEN NORMINA HOLLENBECK, second child and second daughter of David and Esther Tennant Hollenbeck, was born at Danube, Herkimer County, N. Y., May 26th, 1826. She is living at this date, 1913, near Davison, Michigan. In August, 1911, the writer visited her at her home. She was feeble in body, but her mind was clear and active. She has a very retentive memory, which holds all that it receives.

V. DOLLY JANE ELIZA HOLLENBECK, third child and third daughter of David and Esther Hollenbeck, was born at Littlefield County, N. Y., January 10th, 1826. She married John Wright at Davison, Mich., January 15th, 1854, and died at the same place November 3rd, 1896, being at her death seventy years, ten months and twenty-three days old. There were born to Mr. and Mrs. Wright, three children named, Esther, George and Emma.

1. ESTHER WRIGHT was born at Davison, Michigan, August 27th, 1857. She married Elbert C. Harvey at Davison, September 11th, 1878. Mr. Harvey was born in the Town of Enfield, Tompkins County, N. Y., August 9th, 1856. There was born to them a daughter named Emma.

1. EMMA L. HARVEY was born at Davison, Michigan, December 11th, 1879. She marrieid Dr. Ernest Emerson Rice at Durand, Michigan, July 17th, 1901.

DR. RICE was born at Woodstock, Ontario, Jan. 11th, 1877. His father's name was James Rice and his mother's maiden name was Mary Ann Whitesides. There were born to Mr. and Mrs. Rice two children named Esther and Pauline.

1. ESTHER MAE RICE was born at Flint, Mich., Aug. 27, 1904.

2. MARY PAULINE RICE was born at Flint, Aug. 1st, 1906.

2. GEORGE DAVID WRIGHT was born at Davison, Michigan, March 20th, 1860. He married Nellie Wright at Davison, August 21st, 1881.

NELLIE WRIGHT was born at Randolph, Cattaraugus Co., N. Y., March 11th, 1863. Her husband is the son of Wm. Manley Wright whose wife's maiden name was Marrilla Patterson.

There was born to Mr. and Mrs. George Wright a daughter named Florence.

FLORENCE GEORGIA WRIGHT was born at Davison, Genesee Co., Mich., June 18th, 1882. She married William Benjamin Plumb, a son of Wm. Murrell Plumb and his wife, Mary Page Osborne, March 23rd, 1909. They have a son, named Billy Plumb, born at Bakersfield, California, Jan. 12th, 1913.

3. EMMA WRIGHT, third child of John Wright, was born at Davison, Mich., Oct. 13, 1861. She died at Davison, April 18th, 1867. Aged 5 years, 6 months and 5 days.

IV. WILLIAM WARREN HOLLENBECK, the fourth child and first son of David and Esther Tennant Hollenbeck, was born at Pontiac, Michigan, February 22nd, 1835. He married Amarilla Theresa Hewett at Pontiac, October, 1858. He died at Goodrich, Michigan, March 31st, 1897. There were born to them seven children named Jetora, Jenora, David, Tennant, Lila, T. D. and Bertha.

1. JETORA HOLLENBECK was born at Davison, Michigan, March 4th, 1859. She married Noel C. Miller at Davison, December 11th, 1877. There were born to them in Davison Township, Genesee County, Michigan, five children named Lillie, Dennis, Perry, Harold and Noel.

1. LILLIE B. MILLER was born July 1st, 1878.
2. DENNIS MILLER was born March 18th, 1880.
3. PERRY MILLER was born August 28th, 1882.
4. HAROLD MILLER was born July 25th, 1895.
5. NOEL MILLER was born December 15th, 1900.

2. MISS JENORA HOLLENBECK, the second child and second daughter of William Warren Hollenbeck and his wife, was born at Davison, Michigan, March 18th, 1860. She married Charles

Hills, January 8th, 1877. By him she had no children. Her second marriage was to Lyman Frost at Goodrich, Michigan, January 1st, 1882. By him she had no children. Mr. Frost died November 13th, 1912. Mrs. Frost's residence at this date, 1913, is at Grand Blanco Township, Genesee County, Michigan.

3. DAVID G. HOLLENRECK, the third child and first son of Mr. and Mrs. William Warren Hollenbeck, was born at Davison, Mich., Dec. 7th, 1861. He died at Davison, April 27, 1867 at the age of 5 years, 4 months and 20 days.

4. WILLIAM TENNANT HOLLENBECK, the fourth child and second son was born at Davison, Dec. 4th, 1863. He died at Davison, May 28, 1866, at the age of two years, 5 months and 24 days.

5. LELA S. HOLLENBECK, the fifth child and third daughter of Mr. and Mrs. William Warren Hollenbeck was born at Davison, Michigan, June 3d, 1875. She died at Davison, Sept. 2nd, 1876, aged 1 year, 2 months and 25 days.

T. D. HOLLENBECK was born at Davison, Genesee County, Michigan, March 3rd, 1869. He was the sixth child and third son of William Warren and Amarilla Theresa (Hewitt) Hollenbeck. At this date, 1913, he is the only son now living. He married Miss Ellen Wakefield at Millington, Michigan, November 24th, 1899. She was the daughter of Colvin Wakefield and his wife Susan (Wolcott) Wakefield. Mr. and Mrs. Hollenbeck have no children. He is a prosperous farmer residing at this date, 1913, in the Township of Grand Blanco, Genesee County, Michigan.

7. BERTHA MAE HOLLENBECK, the youngest child of William Warren Hollenbeck and his wife, was born at Davison, Genesee County, Michigan, September 11th, 1876. She married D. J. Lorne McColl at Grand Blanco, Genesee County, Michigan, July 19th, 1899. Mr. McColl was born at Danube, Oxford County, Ontario, February 11th, 1880. There were born to Mr. and Mrs. McColl, three children named Ilah Mae, Rena Charlotte and James Lorne.

1. ILAH MAE MCCOLL was born in Flint, Michigan, March 5th, 1900.

2. RENA CHARLOTTE MCCOLL was born at Detroit, Michigan, January 25th, 1904.

3. JAMES LORNE MCCOLL, JR., was born in Detroit, Michigan, May 28th, 1913.

MR. MCCOLL is engaged in the manufacture of automobile bodies, and is also a contractor in this class of work. He has resided in Detroit eleven years at this date, October, 1913.

V. HARRIET GEORGIANNIE HOLLENBECK, the youngest child of David and Esther Tennant Hollenbeck was born at Pontiac, Michigan, February 22nd, 1840. She married Edward Ellen

Fellows at Davison, Michigan, November 10th, 1859. There were born to them eleven children, as follows: Newell, Rhoda. Edna, Clara, David, Cora, Edwin, Hattie, Nellie, Jessie and Bessie. All these named are grandchildren of David and Esther Tennant Hollenbeck.

1. NEWELL H. FELLOWS, oldest child, was born at Davison, Michigan, July 10th, 1861. He married Nellie Godfrey at Saginaw, Michigan, August 26th, 1882. They have one child, a daughter, Celia May. Mr. Fellows died at Saginaw, October 28th, 1899.

2. CELIA MAY FELLOWS was born at Saginaw, Michigan, June 30th, 1883. She married William H. Miller at Saginaw, November 4th, 1900. They have two children named Althea and Ruth.

(a) ALTHEA LUCILE MILLER was born at Saginaw, January 4th, 1907.

(b) RUTH ELLEN MILLER was born at Saginaw, July 18th, 1911.

2. RHODA ANN FELLOWS, second child and first daughter, was born at Davison, Michigan, February 26th, 1863. She married William A. Brown at Saginaw, Michigan, November 1st, 1885. There were born to them at Saginaw, Michigan, four children, named Hebert, Harriet, Esther and Willie.

(a) HEBERT BROWN was born April 25th, 1886. He married Edith Haufe, at Saginaw, November 23rd, 1901. They have one child, Sidney Brown, born at Saginaw, Michigan, December 23rd, 1908.

(b) HARRIET BROWN was born October 24th, 1890.

(c) ESTHER BROWN was born November 25th, 1894.

(d) WILLIE BROWN was born January 2nd, 1902.

3. EDNA ESTHER FELLOWS, third child and second daughter, was born at Saginaw, February 11th, 1865. She died at Saginaw, March 12th, 1866, being at her death thirteen months old.

A reader of Robert Burns' poems might judge that he never had a sad feeling or serious thought. In 1795 he lost by death a beloved daughter in her childhood, and the following short poem expresses his sorrow and his hope.

> "Here lies a rose, a budding rose,
>   Blasted before its bloom;
> Whose innocence did sweets disclose,
>   Beyond that flower's perfume."

> "To those who for her loss are grieved,
>   This consolation's given—
> She's from a world of woe relieved,
>   And blooms a rose in heaven."

MRS. HARRIET GEORGIANNA HOLLENBECK
Wife of Edward Fellows
Born February 22, 1840

4. CLARA ESTELLA FELLOWS, the fourth child and third daughter, was born at Saginaw, December 26th, 1866. She died at Saginaw, July 10th, 1871, being at her death four years, six months and fourteen days old.

5. DAVID TENNANT FELLOWS, fifth child and second son, was born at Saginaw, May 27th, 1869. He died at Saginaw, July 5th, 1871, only five days before the death of his older sister, Clara. He was, at his death, two years, one month and eight days old.

In these deaths occurring so near to each other, a deep wave of affliction and sorrow swept over this beloved family. Well may we pause in our record of events and wonder why Providence should pour out so large measure of trouble and heart-pain in so short time. It brings to the writer's memory a verse of an old hymn of hope and comfort. The third and fourth verses read:

"Judge not the Lord by feeble sense,
    But trust Him for His grace;
Behind a frowning providence,
    He hides a smiling face.

His purposes will ripen fast,
    Unfolding every hour,
The bud may have a bitter taste,
    But sweet will be the flower."

6. CORA ETTE FELLOWS, sixth child and fourth daughter, was born at Saginaw, Michigan, November 21st, 1873. She married at Saginaw, January 29th, 1894, William Duncan Mc-Leod. They have one child named Edna Evelyn McLeod, born at Saginaw, February 17th, 1895. This daughter is at this date, 1912, a senior in the High School of her native City, and hopes to be graduated with honors at the close of another year's work. MRS. MCLEOD has rendered the author of this book efficient aid in gathering records of families for which he wishes to acknowledge his obligations and return his hearty thanks.

7. EDWIN WARREN FELLOWS, seventh child and third son, was born at Saginaw, June 4th, 1875. He married Rose May Jones at Saginaw, July 20th, 1902. They have two children, Harriet and Newell.

(a) HARRIET EDWINA FELLOWS was born at Saginaw, Michigan, February 11th, 1903.

(b) NEWELL EDWIN FELLOWS was born at Saginaw, Michigan, July 5th, 1908.

8. HATTIE ELVIRA FELLOWS, eighth child and fifth daughter, was born at Saginaw, February 8th, 1877. She never married. She died at Saginaw, October 20th, 1898, being at her death twenty-one years, eight months and twelve days old.

This was the fourth death in this family from 1866 to 1898. The son Newell died one year later, 1899, making five deaths in thirty-three years in a family of eleven children.

The writer of this Book, years ago, was in attendance at a religious meeting in the City of Erie, Pa. Phillip Phillips, the "Singing Pilgrim" was present. He sang his favorite composition of music set to a poem by Mrs. Ellen H. Gates, entitled "Home of the Soul."

"I will sing you a song of that beautiful home,
    The far away home of the soul;
Where no storm ever beats on that glittering strand,
    While the years of eternity roll.

Oh, that home of the soul, in my visions and dreams,
    Its bright jasper walls I can see!
Till I fancy but thinly the vale intervenes,
    Between that fair city and me.

There the great tree of life in its beauty doth grow,
    And the river of life floweth by;
For no death ever enters that city, you know,
    And nothing that maketh a lie.

That unchangeable home is for you and for me,
    Where Jesus of Nazareth stands;
The King of all Kingdoms forever is He,
    And he holdeth our crowns in His hand.

Oh, how sweet it will be in that beautiful land,
    So free from all sorrow and pain;
With songs on our lips, and with harp in our hands,
    To meet one another again.

"There remaineth therefore a rest to the people of God."

"Let us labor therefore to enter into that rest, lest any man fall after the same example of unbelief." Hebrews 4th Chapter, 9th and 11th verses.

9. NELLIE MAY FELLOWS, ninth child and sixth daughter, was born at Saginaw, Michigan, May 1st, 1880. She is not married and lives with her parents at their home in Saginaw City, at this date, 1912.

10. JESSIE KETCHUM FELLOWS, tenth child and seventh daughter, was born at Saginaw, February 9th, 1882. She married at Saginaw, May 20th, 1906, Everett M. Russell. They have a son named Warren E. Russell, born May 25th, 1907.

11. BESSIE KETCHUM FELLOWS, eleventh child and eighth daughter, was born at Saginaw, February 9th, 1882. She is a twin sister of Jessie. She married at Saginaw, June 25th, 1903,

A. Earl Kent. They have one child, Junier Lewis Kent, born at Saginaw, February 18th, 1908.

Of this large family of eleven children nine grand-children and four great-grand-children, twenty-four in all, at this date, 1912, there has occurred only five deaths. All are descendants of David and Esther Tennant Hollenbeck, who were married at Springfield, N. Y., September 7th, 1821.

At this date, 1912, Mr. and Mrs. Fellows are living at their home in Saginaw, Michigan, at No. 712 North Bond street. The writer visited the family in August, 1911. Mrs. Fellows welcomed me very cordially and exclaimed "I nexer expected to see a son of my uncle Moses." It appears to be the way of the world that families become separated, their children become strangers to each other, and yet, when in later years they chance to meet, the kinship is warmly acknowledged, and they become friends in loving family bonds. Such renewals of family relationship should be highly esteemed, and made at however great the sacrifice, if for no other reason, than to acknowledge a common parentage and to perpetuate a known union between ancestors and descendants.

Since writing the above, the author has received the sad news of the death of the father of this large family of eleven children. MR. EDWARD ELON FELLOWS died at his home at 712 North Bond street, Saginaw, Mich., June 29th, 1914. The cause of his death was a valvular heart disease. MR. FELLOWS was the son of Hiram Fellows and his wife whose maiden name was Clarinda Castle. He was born at Farma, Herkimer Co., N. Y., July 1st, 1838. He was 75 years, 11 months and 28 days old at the time of his death. He moved to Saginaw in 1861 and went into the lumber business and was foreman in a mill that manufactured lath, located on the Saginaw river. He served in this business for over 30 years up to the time of his illness that eventually ended in his death. At his death, only five of his eleven children survived him, with their mother.

"Many are the afflictions of the righteous but the Lord delievereth them out of them all."

This closes the record of the descendants of MOSES TENNANT, SR., and his wife, Sarah Selden Jewett Tennant, by their children, Lucy, Olivia, Moses Asel and Esther. The record extends to the sixth generation and includes many branches of the family. The fathers and sons among these descendants for the largest number were farmers. But not all were farmers, for we find among them judges, lawyers. professors, ministers, carpenters, civil engineers, railroad engineers, many high school and college graduates, editors, merchants, writers, and men who have held responsible positions in the communities where they have been located. Not one of all these descendants has ever been convicted of any criminal offense against the laws of the State or the Nation. None have been thrown upon charity either public or private for support. For the most part the families have been self supporting and able to contribute their share of labor or money for the maintenance of civil government and public institutions. For the greater part the families belonged to the worthy hard-working middle class, who were neither distressingly poor or immoderately rich. Industry, frugality and economy have been their characteristic virtues.

These descendants have been religious in their proclivities. The heads of the families, with few exceptions, have been members of Christian Churches of Protestant faith. A few have adhered to the Roman Catholic Church.

During the period of the war of the Rebellion, these descendants, then living, although divided politically, were strong supporters of the government and were anti-slavery in their beliefs. A few elisted in the war on the Union side of that great conflict.

All things considered, morality, religion, patriotism, social standing and influence, these descendants have reason to be proud of each other and not ashamed to own their relationship and their family origin.

The descendants of Esther Tennant and David Hollenbeck number as follows:

Children 5
Grandchildren 25
Great grandchildren 27
Great-great-grandchildren 6
                                                                    —
Total 63

With parents and grand-parents, they include six generations.

PART FOURTH

FIRST DIVISION

AUTO-BIOGRAPHIES
MISS ELLEN POTTER
ALBERT M. TENNANT

SECOND DIVISION

MEMORIAL TRIBUTES
—— TO ——
DEPARTED RELATIVES

MISS HELEN L. POTTER
Born December 6, 1837
A Distinguished Elocutionist

PART IV.

DIVISION FIRST.

A LIFE SKETCH OF HELEN POTTER

By Herself.

HELEN L. POTTER was raised on a farm in Central New York and grew in health and vigor by out-of-door life helpnig her father in various kinds of farm work. At this period only lim--ited advantages for education were available in rural districts. The schools were not graded; there were no High Schools, no examinations, no promotions. The solitary teacher of a country school taught all grades, (now called Primary and Grammer grades), in one and the same room, from the alphabet to Algebra, Physiology, etc., if called for, and the teacher competent.

At the age of four years Helen learned the alphabet by looking on while her older sister was being taught. At five she and her sister were sent to school a mile from home. At sixteen she began teaching at a weekly stipend of one dollar and a half, and "board 'round," ie; become a progressive guest of the pupil's parents one week for each pupil attending school. By alternately teaching summer schools and attending a "Seminary of Learning" winters, she soon qualified herself for better schools at better pay.

At twenty-one she went south to start a select or pay school in the Mountains of Kentucky. After two years experience in building a school from five pupils in a log cabin to sixty in a large room (Town Hall), she was obliged to return north on account of political excitement. Lincoln was elected President of the U. S. over Bell of Kentucky and Everett of Massachusetts and his inauguration challenged by the southern hostile element, hence most Northerners felt it safer to return to their native homes.

On her return home she began what ended in a national reputation as a speaker and entertainer. Up to this time, (twenty three), she had never heard a good reader or a great orator, nor had she been inside a theatre. Undaunted by many obstacles, limited means, no introduction, indeed without social or financial backing of any kind, she plunged, alone, into the metropolis of our country to study elocution with the Vanderhoffs.

George Vanderhoff was the son of a distinguished English actor. He was an international lawyer and a scholar of mark, having received five prize medals for scholarship in English Universities. His wife was an accomplished, educated American of fine appearance. Finding this young woman had come to New York knowing no one in the City, they kindly offered her a home with them during her stay for lessons. From them she acquired critically correct pronunciation of English, which was a very valuable acquisition ever after.

Next we find her a teacher of Elocution in Falley Seminary, Fulton, Oswego Co., N. Y. This engagement lasted four years. Her vacations were spent studying in Boston. Prof. T. F. Leonard, a graduate of Harvard, developed her naturally fine voice and trained her in physical expression, gesture, etc. She was also employed as a teacher of teachers by the State Supt. of Public Instruction at the County Institutes which were held annually for the benefit of the teachers of the counties of the State of New York. She was the first woman thus employed at the State's expense. In 1866 she was elected to the chair of Elocution and Physical Culture at Packer Collegiate Institute, Brooklyn, then the most exclusive college for women in the country.

After two years at this Institute she resigned to complete a book for teachers which occupied about two years of her time. This book, "Manual of Reading," was published by Harper Brothers in 1871 and was considered a standard exposition of the English language and its correct use. In 1873 she was one of four teachers and lecturers engaged for teacher's Institute work by the State of Vermont. This tour lasted three months, visiting every county but two in the State for a week's session in each.

Following this tour she was called to Boston by James R. Osgood, publisher, and engaged to lecture on "Industrial Art Education" in the large cities of this country, to impress upon educators and the public the wisdom of using our extensive Public School System for the development of home talent in our industries. After entering the Boston Normal Art School for a term and making special preparations for this new field of work, she began her speaking tour in September of the same year. Her first appearance in the new work was before the National Teachers Association at Indianapolis where she gave an illustrated lecture with free use of blackboard and crayon. This was followed by engagements for 20 to 40 illustrated lectures to the Public School teachers of many large cities in the East and on the Pacific coast.

These engagements lasted two years. In 1875 she left all other work for the Lyceum Platform which was then well under way through the Redpath Lyceum Bureau of Boston. Prior to the Lyceum engagement she had appeared in public as a reader, over five hundred evenings, with more artistic than financial success. Now the long term of preparation and experience gave

REV. ALBERT MILTON TENNANT
Born August 7, 1834.

MRS. MARY C. MORSE (COOK) TENNANT
Born October 20, 1842

ample returns, being one of the few on the Lyceum list whose time was well taken and who received the largest fees. She gave costumed representations of famous living people, and of classical characters. In her public career she gave in all over 1800 recitals.

Retiring from the Lyceum field she prepared a book called "Helen Potter's Impersonations," published by Edgar S. Werner of New York, seeking to perpetuate, by diacritical marks and descriptions, what is now (in 1914) so marvelously and perfectly done by the phonograph. In 1895 she was sent to the Worlds W. C. T. U. Convention in London as a delegate from Massachusetts, and spoke at a mass meeting in Queen's Hall, London. Now she lives quietly with family friends at the advanced age of 76 years.

REV. ALBERT MILTON TENNANT.

A Life Sketch By Himself.

CHILDHOOD DAYS.

In this sketch of my life I shall use the personal pronoun, I trust without being judged an egotist. I have already mentioned the time and place of my birth in the chronological order of the family history.

That humble log house on Ripley Hill, which first sheltered my infant life, has long since been taken down. If the season of the year in which our births take place has omens of the future of our lives, a birthday in the beautiful sunny August, when the world is warmed and lighted by the golden rays of a beneficent Sun, and Earth is laden with the fruits of her products, certainly I should have had a future radiant with happiness, and abounding in the fruits of good works. My parents were poor, and had to make a great effort to exist. As I grew into maturity, I saw the necessity of contributing all I could to help the family. In my boyhood days, this help was surely very small, but I cannot remember the time when I was unwilling to work.

After my father had purchased 100 acres of land on Ripley Hill to make a permanent home for the family, there was then plenty of work for all willing hands. My older brothers and sisters did work and worked hard. Before the axes of father, Alvin and Delos, the big hemlocks, beeches, maples and other trees fell as if swept by a tornado. The big log heaps were piled and burned and the ashes used to make black salts, which were then the only farm product that could be sold for money to pay interest and taxes. Mother, Grandmother Morse, and the older sisters spun wool and flax for cloth to clothe the family.

Someone may ask "Were you a happy family?"   We certainly
were.   We children never quarreled.   We were never punished.
Our home life was never embittered by too severe discipline.
We had the freedom of nature under the restraint and guidance
of wise and wholesome parental instruction.   We were all anxious to get an education, and were sent to the winter and summer district school.

Nature had given every member of the family a voice and a
taste for music.   The old log house echoed and re-echoed with
the music of parent's and children's voices.   I give the first
lines of a few of the home songs we sang.

> "The hills of Chautauqua how proudly they rise,
> And seem in their grandeur to blend with the skies."

Another

> "How dear to my heart are the scenes of my childhood
> When fond recollection present them to view;
> The orchard, the meadow, the deep tangled wildwood,
> And every loved spot which my infancy knew."

Another that parents, uncles and aunts used to sing at their ev-
ening gatherings:
"Should old acquaintance be forgot when we sit down to dine?
Should old acquaintance be forgot and days of auld lang sine?"

Brother Alvin learned to play the clarinet.   He would sit on the
steps of the south door, and discourse sweet music for the whole
neighborhood.   Were we a happy family?   ·Yes.   No kings
and queens in their gilded palaces were happier than we.

One winter, brother Delos and I slept in the garret.   The roof
of the old house was neither snow nor water tight.   One night
the wind blew and it snowed all night long.   We slept good and
warm.   In the morning when we awoke, we found the bed covered two or three inches deep with snow, and a deep snow drift
in front.   There was no other way, so we jumped out of the
bed into the snow drift, laughing because of the fun there was
in it.   We were as hardy as white bears.   We boys wore linen
shirts and the girls were beautifully dressed in calico.   So we
lived and worked, a blest and happy family.

Everything about that early home gave me great delight in my
boyhood, and their memory is sweet today.   The old cat, the old
yellow dog that Delos shot, the blue rats that used to trip across
my face while I was in the trundle bed; the bee-hives at the east
end of the house; the barn with its big swing-beam; the old brin-
dle cow; mother's fried cakes and cookies that Delos and I used
to steal between meals; the big dutch fireplace in the chimney of
which the swallows built their nests in the summertime; the

OLD HOME AT RIPLEY

flocks of swallows that built their adobe homes under the eaves
of the barn; the little brook that played on its silver flutes as it
rambled through the pasture; the many black and red squirrels
that played in the trees or scampered along the fence rails; the
owls that hooted their solemn notes in the evening time; the
great flocks of pigeons that passed eastward; all, all these and
much more than I have space to write about, were ministering angels paying my young spirits daily visitations, making home and
life happy and blest.

The clearing up of the old farm was a source of constant excitement. To see the oxen draw the big logs together; to witness the burning of the great logheaps; to see the wild forest
giving way to the strokes of the civilizing ax; then to see beautiful crops of wheat spring up out of the mold and ashes of
trees; such scenes were enough to make young and patriotic American boys and girls wild with exuberant joy.

I stood by and saw father roll the logs off the walls of the old
house as it was being taken down. The home of my childhood
was disappearing like the visions of a summer dream. It was
needed no more, as our good friend and neighbor, Alexander
Sawin, had built us a new frame house in front of the old one.
In this new home, after the marriage of brother Delos and the
three older sisters, the rest of the family lived for a few years.

Dear home of my childhood, I bid you adieu,

Your memory is sweet to me yet;

Every log in your wall visions early delights,

And reminds me of pleasures I cannot forget.

Back o'er the years that have now intervened,

My thoughts take their swift homeward flight;
Fain would I sit by thy bright fireside,
As often I sat in those cold winter nights.
That dear family circle in memory I see,
When parents and children all gathered around,
Lift their glad voices in harmony sweet,
Singing "Home sweet Home" in rapturous sound.
"Home, home, can I forget thee,
Dear, dear, dearly loved home?
No, no, still I regret thee
Tho' I may far from thee roam.

Home, home, home, home,
Dearest and happiest Home."

Early Education.

My early education was limited to the branches taught in the common district school. Much importance was made of mental arithmetic. Colburn's arithmetic was used in all the schools. The old English Reader was also used and Kirkham's Grammer. Not till I was twelve years of age, was I awakened to the necessity of a good education. Before this, my studies were forced. After this time, they became a pleasant task. I could do but little studying after school hours except evenings as my help was needed on the farm. I can just remember the old log school house on Ripley Hill before it gave place to a frame building. Of the teachers of the summer school I can only remember my cousin, Miss Laura Ann Gay. Of the winter school teachers, I remember Marvin Osborn, David Shaver and Erbin Wattles. Mr. Osborn literally pounded arithmetic and grammer into my head, for I had to have my lessons or take the consequences. I revere his name for what he did for me.

At sixteen years of age I had made sufficient proficiency in my studies as to venture to commence school teaching.

Early Conversion.

During the winter of 1850 and '51 a series of evangelical meetings were held in the old school house on Ripley Hill. The Baptist Church then had no house of worship. Rev. Ira Stoddard was pastor of the church. It was during these meetings that I became deeply convinced that I ought to be a christian. My sins disturbed my conscience, especially the sin of ingratitude that I had received so many blessings from God, and had never even returned thanks for his favors, much less the love of my heart and the service of my life. I was the subject of many prayers; had been taught in the family and the Sabbath school the obligations and duties of a Christian life, but my heart rebelled against everything that was called christian. I did all I could to suppress all religious convictions, till at last I was simply over powered by the Holy Spirit and sweetly compelled to yield to the call of God. When I surrendered and gave my heart to the Lord Jesus, the change that took place in my feelings, my tastes, my purposes, was most decided and radical. I was certain that God for Christ's sake had forgiven my sins, and made me a new creature in him.

In the month of May, 1851, I was baptized and received into the fellowship of the Baptist Church of Ripley.

School Teaching.

In the winter of 1851 and 1852 I taught school in the Tripp district west of Gage's Gulf. I was just past seventeen. My wages were twelve dollars and fifty cents a month. The following Spring, the family moved from the hill country to the Village of Ripley. In the winter of 1852 and 53 I taught the side-hill school. During the next winter commenced a school at Northville, N. Y., but after teaching for a few weeks was taken with typhoid fever and that ended my teaching for that winter.

During the winter of 1854 and 55 I taught at Ripley Village, N. Y. In August, 1855, I was 21 years of age. Dissatisfied with farming, I determined to get a better education. In September following my 21st birthday I went to Grand River Institute, Austinberg, Ashtabula Co., Ohio. There I took up the study of the Greek and Latin languages with advanced Algebra, Chemistry and moral philosophy. I was at this Institute only part of the Fall term when I went to Niles, Michigan to seek a position as school teacher. I soon located in a district on Portage prairie, eight miles southwesterly from Niles, at $25.00 a month for five months. This was a most delightful experience; I had such diligent and dutiful scholars.

Returning home the last week of March, 1856, I went to Grand River Institute where I remained for the Spring and Fall terms. Here I received a higher inspiration and nobler purter from our family physician, Dr. Hopkins of Ripley, N. Y., called my attention to the christian ministry. This letter, unexpectedly received, had a powerful influence upon my mind, and really decided me not to become a lawyer.

The winter of 1856 and '57 I taught the school in the district next east of Ripley Village on the Main road, and the following winter in what was known as the Rogers' District, the 2nd district west of Westfield. This was the winter of 1857 and 58. This closed all my school teaching.

Now came the greatest mental and moral conflict of my life. I did not want to spend my life on a farm. Such a life did not hold out to me the promise of usefulness such as I wished my life to be. I had attended the Westfield and Fredonia Academies, a few terms in each. I was nearly ready to enter college, an advantage for further education which I very much desired, and which was the goal of my highest ambition. One more term in Latin and two in Greek and my preparation would have been adequate. But there stood before me that great mountain of difficulty, lack of money. I saw no way that this mountain could be removed. My father, however willing, was not able to send me to college. Finally, after a long and painful heart struggle, the college course was wholly abandoned, and I settled down to farming for life.

Before my school teaching had ended, there had come into my life an affection for a young woman whom I had known from boyhood. We became betrothed to each other.

My First Marriage.

On the 24th of March, 1859, Miss Ellen Mason, third daughter of George and Gardener Mason, at her home in Ripley, N. Y., and myself were united in marriage by her brother-in-law, the Rev. Wm. R. Connelly. We were happy in each other's love, but there hung over my heart the shadow of disappointed hopes and ambition. I had wanted to go to college. I did not want to spend my life on a farm.

While a student at Fredonia, N. Y., I had tried to preach a few times. My heart still turned from the farm, and the christian ministry was ever before me, a tantalizing vision. Time went on and I worked hard on the farm. Finally my wife was taken with an incurable curvature of the spine, which, after a year or more rendered her practically helpless. This affliction was meant for me. God was subduing my rebellious heart and making me yield to his call. "Go preach the Gospel." My rebellion was too fearful to relate. At last in the Spring of 1862 I yielded to the call. told my convictions to my wife, and a few members of the Baptist Church at Ripley, N. Y., of which I was a member. An appointment was made for me to preach in the Baptist Church on Ripley Hill. The second Sunday following this surrender of myself, I entered upon my life work as a minister of Jesus Christ.

Commenced My Life Work.

On the 23rd of March, 1862, at the old Church on Ripley Hill, I preached from Ps. 46, verse 5, "God is in the midst of her she shall not be moved; God will help her and that right early." Subject—*God the Security of the Church.* My sermon was written in full. Then I could preach in no other way. It was my first discourse of a consecrated life.

During the year 1862 for the first eight months I preached for the Baptist Church. After that time, until Spring opened. I preached for the Presbyterian and Methodists as I had an invitation. My chief work was daily reading and studying in preparation for my lifework. I had no library at the commencement. After a while I purchased John Dick's Theology, Olshausen's Commentary, Edward's History of Redemption, Baxter's Saints' Rest and Bunyan's Pilgrim's Progress. These, with the Bible, constituted my library. Did I study much? Yes, I was constantly at it.

A Donation.

In the Spring of 1863. my brethren and friends at Ripley thought best to aid me in my finances. For all my preaching up to this time I had received nothing. An arrangement was

OLD BAPTIST CHURCH, RIPLEY

made to give us a donation. The place of meeting was at my wife's old home. The house was literally filled with people. One hundred and forty dollars in cash was realized at this gathering. Again the friends on Ripley Hill gave us a donation that stuffed our pockets with $35.00 more. This greatly increased my faith in God that if I do my duty he will provide for my temporal wants.

In the Spring of 1863, having received a call from the Baptist Church of Clymer, Chautauqua Co., I settled there.

Pastorate at Clymer.

My labors commenced the first of May, 1863. A few weeks before moving my goods, my wife went with a sister of hers to Dr. Trall's Institute of New York for treatment. She was there for eleven weeks, at the end of which I went to New York to bring her home. The treatment did her no visible good whatever.

Now came the severest trial of my faith in God and in prayer that I ever experienced. I had prayed many times every day for her recovery. Would God hear my prayer? I firmly believed He would. But He did not, so far as her restoration was concerned. I could not pray any more for her restoration. I could pray only that we both might be submissive to our Heavenly Father's will and have strength to do and endure His will, and to perform our work.

My Ordination.

According to a long established custom in the Baptist denomination, the Church at Clymer called upon the Baptist Churches of Harmony Association to appoint delegates to a council to consider the question of ordaining their Pastor Licentiate to the work of the gospel ministry. Nearly two years before this movement, I was licensed to preach by the Baptist Church of Ripley, N. Y. The delegates appointed under this call met with the Church of Clymer on the 22nd of October, 1863. The Council heard me relate my Christian experience, my call to the ministry, and my views on Christian theology, on ecclesiastical policy and the gospel ordinances.

For this examination, I spent many weeks in preparing a paper to be read, covering all that such an examination required. When I finished reading my paper, not a question was asked. The Council retired and immediately resolved to proceed to ordain the candidate. The ordaining service consisted as follows:

Sermon by Rev. Orson Mallory.

Laying on of hands of Rev. Palmer Cross and others.

Ordaining prayer by Rev. Levant Rathburn.

Charge to the candidate by Rev. Charles Sanderson.

Charge to the Church by Rev. Levant Rathburn,
Right hand of Fellowship by Rev. I. Merriman.

This entire service had a deep meaning to me.   It was a most
solemn renewal of my consecration to the work of the christian
ministry.   Now I laid all upon the altar of self-sacrifice, henceforth I was not to be my own but Christ's.   I had had such a
wicked rebellion against my call to the ministry, but now my
rebellion was all taken away.   The Holy Spirit filled my soul
with peace and joy for I had been made willing in the day of
His power, to use my time, my talents, my all in the service of
the Divine Master.   The surrender was complete.   I could
truly say "For me to live is Christ.   I live, but not I, for Christ
liveth in me."

At the time of this writing when my life work is done,
whether I have kept or broken these Ordination Vows, only God
knows, and He must be my judge.

WAR OF REBELLION.

I was located at Clymer during the two last years of the war
between the South and the North.   The minds of the people
were all absorbed in the great struggle for the preservation of
the Union of the States.   The bodies of two soldier boys were
sent home to be buried, sons of two sisters of my Church.   All
a pastor could do was to keep the doors of the house of worship open for regular church service.   Funerals were heartrend-
ing scenes.   Patriotic songs were sung, the coffins were wrap-
ped in the folds of the Stars and Stripes and decorated with
crowns and crosses, and mottoes in flowers.   The present generation, born since that war, cannot even imagine the great excitement, intensity of feeling, and fearful forebodings that
racked the minds and filled the hearts of the masses of the people both of the North and the South.

LINCOLN'S ASSASSINATION.

I was on the street going to hear the news read when I met
a near neighbor, Mr. Beecher, who told me of the assasination
of President Lincoln.   I turned at once homeward, told my wife
the awful news, and for awhile I walked the floor in agony of
mind.   It seemed to me the whole country was going to chaos
and destruction.

Amid such scenes and experiences the two first years of my
life as a pastor were spent.   In the Spring of 1863 I resigned
my charge at Clymer, N. Y., and accepted a call of the Baptist
Church of Union City, Erie Co., Pa.

COMMENCED WORK AT UNION CITY, PA.

My pastoral work commenced in this city on the first Sabbath of May, 1865 and continued five years and five months. I was the second pastor of the Church, Rev. A. D. Bush being my predecessor. He assisted in the organization of the church, only about two years previous to my settlement, and in building a new house of worship. There were less than thirty-five members composed chiefly of farmers and their families. I had the promise of a $1000.00 salary, but the church could scarcely raise one-half of that amount. They had no parsonage. Supplies for a family were very high; flour $18.00 per barrel and potatoes $1.50 to $2.00 a bushel, and sugar and eggs in the same ratio. It was impossible to rent a house, so I purchased a home located on the same street the church was situated on, running heavily in debt. The members of the church taking in the situation appealed to the American Baptist Home Missionary Society for aid and obtained it. I was appointed a missionary and served the Society for two years, receiving for the first year $200.00 and for the second year $100.00. From this time the church became independent of outside help. Although the little church was comparatively poor in finances, yet they were liberal in their gifts for foreign and home missions, one year donating $91.50.

After I became well acquainted with the people and conditions of the field, I found that I could not reach the many people in the country about the city with the gospel message, and I determined to carry the message to them by holding services in School Districts, where a school house was opened for me in one of these districts, I held a service Sabbath afternoon every two weeks. This was in Le Beouf Township where I was enabled to form a branch church. Winter months I held protracted meetings in school houses, in most cases with excellent results. I found that many people had, in many instances, erroneous views of Baptist doctrine; views that created a prejudice against us, that was preventing the growth of the church, and was unpleasant to meet in the social life of the community. This lead me to preach a series of doctrinal sermons setting forth Baptist views of Christian teaching, upon the Church, the Gospel Ordinances, and the history of these doctrines which Baptists now believe.

This series of sermons gave the Baptists a much better standing before the people, but of course aroused some opposition.

During my pastorate, there was a slow growth of membership, but the loss by death and removals were very many. I had many funerals and a fair share of the weddings. All in all, my labors at Union City were a great pleasure to me. I had a faithful and loyal co-operation of all the church members, and peace and brotherly love, without any serious discord, continually prevailed.

The last years of my work on this field present nothing aside from the common experiences of a pastor's life. At times I felt that my work was drawing near the close, that it would be better for the church to have a change of pastors. At last Providence presented the occasion, but brought upon me the great sorrow of my life.

DEATH OF MY FIRST WIFE.

On the 15th of September, 1870, at our home in Union City, after a few days sickness, my precious wife passed from the scenes of this life to her eternal home. She was rendered unable to communicate her feelings while I was away from home to a public meeting. In this condition I found her upon my return. As I shall write a tribute to her memory for this book I shall omit all that might be said here.

RESIGNATION FOLLOWED.

My blessed wife's death, indicated to me, that it was plainly my duty to close my labors on this field. So, at the end of a pastorate beginning May 1, 1865 and continuing to the last Sabbath of September, 1870. I closed my labors and immediately broke up house-keeping, and in a few days was on my way to Rochester, N. Y., to enter the Middle Class at the Theological Seminary.

THEOLOGICAL SEMINARY COURSE.

I took the two year course, then allowed to men who were not College graduates. The course included a full course in Systematic Theology, Greek, N. T. Exegesis, Church History and Pastoral Theology. My previous studies in Greek enabled me to enter the class in Greek Exegesis.

This Seminary Course made up a certain fraction of my loss of a College education. The venerable Dr. Ezekiel G. Robinson, D. D., LL. D., was the President of the Institution and Prof. of Theology. The venerable Dr. Horatio B. Hackett, D. D. was Professor of Greek Exegesis and Dr. Bucklin, Professor of Church History. Under the instruction of such men of great ability and learning, the profit I received can never be estimated. At the very beginning of this three-fold course of instruction, my mind began to open to new truths and divine realities which hitherto I had only dimly seen as "through a glass darkly," but now the shadows began to flee away, my mental horizon was broader, my mind cleared of many misconceptions and errors and established in the truth.

PREACHING AT NIAGARA FALLS.

During the second year of my studies at Rochester I supplied every Sabbath the Baptist Church of Niagara Falls, which was without a pastor. This work commenced Nov. 19, 1871. I was now on my second year at Rochester. The Summer vacation had been spent in Ionia County, Michigan, visiting my wife's sister, Mrs. Rev. A. Cornell, whose maiden name was Catharine Mason of Ripley, N. Y. Rev. Cornell was the pastor of the Baptist Church at Smyrna, Mich. Through his influence I secured a position as a pulpit supply for the Baptist Church at Portage, Ionia Co., where I preached twice each Sabbath from the 1st of July to the last of August, 1871. The Portage Church gave me a call to become their pastor when I had finished my Seminary Course. This I did not accept, as duty led me to accept a call from the Baptist Church of Niagara Falls.

PASTORAL WORK AT THE FALLS.

My pastorate at Niagara Falls commenced the first Sabbath of July, 1872. In coming to this field, I was led by a deep conviction that I ought to try to aid the Baptist Church to maintain its visibility and secure a healthy growth. I rejected a call from the First Baptist Church of Portland, Oregon, to enter upon this field. My immediate predecessor was Rev. Mr. Barnes who had closed his work here about two years before my pastoral work commenced. They had maintained an excellent Sabbath School and their weekly prayer meeting. However, during all my work here, there were few conversions and but two baptisms. The Church seemed to have reached a dead line in its growth, and no further progress was visible. I labored on till the Spring of 1874.

EXTRA WORK AT LOCKPORT.

By invitation of the Baptist Church at Lockport, Niagara Co., N. Y., I assisted their acting pastor, Rev. Robert Hull, then a student in the Seminary at Rochester, in a series of extra evangelical meetings commencing the last week of January, 1874, and continuing for nine weeks. I preached during these meetings every week-day evening except Saturday. We had large congregations, and the interest and fruits may be estimated by the number of conversations. I recorded in my Pastor's Journal, March 15th, 1874, the following:

"During the past week I have continued my labors at Lockport. About seventy have been baptized, and more are awaiting baptism. The meetings have been glorious in their results."

CALL TO NORTH EAST, PA.

In my Journal, Feb. 22, 1874, I recorded "Have received a call from the Baptist Church at North East, Pa., and accepted it, expecting to begin my labors the first Sabbath of March next." For about four months previous to receiving this call, I was becoming more and more dissatisfied with the results of my work at the Falls. I upbraided myself, much more than I found fault with the church. It seemed evident to me, that both for the good of the church as well as for myself, a change was necessary; hence the acceptance of the call from North East. I had now served the church as a supply and as pastor about two and a half years. I had been treated so kindly by the church, that I left as one who parts from dear friends.

SETTLED AT NORTH EAST.

My work on this field began March 1, 1874. At once there were omens of good fruit. I had larger congregations than the average on any former field. Before six months had passed I began to realize that there were elements of discord in the Church, that would certainly weaken if not destroy my influence for usefulness. Toward the close of the year these elements became an open and radical opposition. I determined, after much anxious prayer, that I could not face such strong opposition, so I resigned and at the end of thirteen months service closed my work. The bitter disappointment I experienced, the distrust of my brethren which was created in my heart, nearly drove me out of the ministry. It was all too dark and sad to recall or record. My pastorate ended the 27th of March, 1875.

RETURNED TO THE FALLS.

As the Falls church was without a Pastor, I returned to them and served them again as a pulpit supply till the month of July.

SETTLEMENT AT PANAMA, N. Y.

The Harmony Baptist Church of Panama, Chautauqua County, N. Y., extended me a call, and I entered upon work there the first Sabbath in August, 1875. This settlement proved to be a very happy and successful one for me. I had a church membership of strong, devoted and consecrated men and women. The venerable Rev. Alfred Wells was my predecessor, and his labors and his greatly lamented death, had prepared the hearts of church members and the people, for a gracious revival of religion. This came in the winter following my settlement. We commenced extra evangelical meetings the first week of January, 1876 and held them four week-day evenings each week, with two services on the Sabbath day, for eleven weeks. At these services I preached short sermons, led the singing, and conducted the service of prayer and exhortation. Scarcely had the meetings been fairly begun, before there was evidence of the presence of the Holy Spirit in quickening and converting power. Heads of families, strong men and women, and many young men and women, began to enquire "Men and brethren, what shall we do to be saved?" The whole community was moved by an irresistable power.

BAPTISMS.

It was confidently believed that over seventy-five were converted to Christ. Of this number in the months of January, February and April I baptized twenty-nine. Later additions brought the number up to thirty-four. A number of converts united with the Presbyterian and M. E. church.

The above records the most gracious revival of all my pastoral labors. I had no assistance in the work. My work continued at Panama for five years, closing the last Sabbath in July, 1879. I can truly say that in all respects the work and its fruits was most encouraging and delightful, and leaves on my mind most precious memories of many dear brethren and sisters, so many of whom have long since gone to their eternal reward. They were "faithful unto death" and now have received the "crown of everlasting life."

SECOND MARRIAGE.

While at Panama on the 20th of Dec. 1876, I married Mrs. Mary Cornelia Moore Cook, daughter of David and Beda Sperry Moore, and widow of Philander Cook, one of the successful business men of Chautauqua County. For six years I had lived a widowed life, which can be truthfully called a homeless life. This marriage has proved an unspeakable blessing to me, giving me a faithful wife and a delightful, happy home. Mrs. Tennant is a member of the Presbyterian Church and very loyal to her faith.

After our marriage, we lived at Panama up to the time of the closing of my labors there in the summer of 1880, the last Sabbath of July.

After closing my work at Panama I went to Point Chautauqua on Chautauqua Lake for a month's vacation, waiting meantime for an opening on some other field. The field I was looking for was one where the church needed a new house of worship. While at Chautauqua I met Rev. J. B. Olcott of East Aurora,

Erie Co., N. Y.   He was in search of a man to become pastor
of the Baptist Church at that place.   I engaged to visit
the Church and did so, and preached to them two Sabbaths,
Aug. 8th and 15th, 1880.   The Church there needed a new house
of worship.   They gave me a call to become their Pastor.   I accepted on the condition that they would join their efforts with
mine in erecting a new church building.   This was agreed to, and
I was to commence my labors as soon as I could make arrangements to move my household goods.

SETTLED AT EAST AURORA.

On the third Sabbath of Sept. 1880, I preached my first sermon as their Pastor.

Now came the long severe tug of christian warfare.   As soon
as I commenced agitating the question of building, I found the
entire Board of Trustees were radically opposed to any effort of
this kind.   As there were five strong men on the Board what
could I do?   Nothing unless there could be a change in the per-
sonel of this Board.   The majority of the members favored
building.   I suggested to the church that we re-organize the In-
corporate Body under the new trustee law passed in 1876 by the
New York State legislature for the benefit of the Baptist churches
of the State.   This propositon was endorsed by a large majority of the voting members of the Church and congregation.   Steps
were at once taken to effect this change.

THE RE-ORGANIZATION.

At a special meeting called for this purpose, the re-organization
was effected, and three of the strongest business men of the
Church and congregation were chosen as a new Board of Trustees—Dr. Horace Hoyt, Hon. Seth Fenner and Hon. James D.
Yeomans.

SUBSCRIPTIONS STARTED.

After some delay the three Trustees headed the subscription
with $500.00 each.   From this time on the subscriptions were
added till $5000.00 was pledged.   Then work was commenced.
The old Church was moved on to the back end of the lot and excavating was commenced May 1st, 1883.   The venerable deacon
Calkins moved the first hsovel full of earth in excavating.   May
31st, the masons commenced on the wall and the corner stone
was laid June 25th with appropriate ceremonies and an address by
Rev. E. B. Olmsted, Pastor of the Baptist Church at Arcade, N.
Y.

THE BAPTIST CHURCH OF EAST AURORA,
ERIE COUNTY, N. Y.

Built during the pastorate of Rev. A. M. Tennant, under the
direction and supervision of the Board of Trustees, Dr. Horace
Hoyt, Hon. Seth Fenner, Hon. Jonas Dallas Yeomans, and dedicated to Divine Service June 12, 1884.

CHURCH DEDICATION.

The work of construction went on without any set-back. No words can set forth the deep interest I felt in the work. This was what I had been praying for, and now I could see the answer to my prayers rising up before my eyes.

On June 24th, 1884, the Dedicatory Services were held. The edifice was all new and beautiful, having bent seats and a floor inclined toward the pulpit, a gallery in the front part and a prayer room under it. The edifice was all the Church desired or needed. The opposition that was at first aroused now subsided, and a general good will prevailed among the members of the Church.

As I am not writing the history of the Baptist Church of East Aurora, all I need further to say is that the church cost in all $7662.73. At the close of the dedicatory service there was a balance unpaid and unprovided for of $1376.20. Nearly all the money raised on subscription, was obtained by my individual effort. In this God answered my prayers. But strange to say, in all the newspaper reports, not one syllable was written concerning the efforts of the Pastor, nor was he recognized at all, in all that was done or said at the dedicatory services. But God knows what a burden I carried on my heart and hands, and I shall not be forgotten when the rewards are distributed.

After the dedication, now occurred what so often does occur; the church had a new house of worship, now there must be a new pastor to fill the pews. Although a vote was taken to renew my call for another year, the sentiment among a few leading members that a change of pastors would be better for the church, led me to make my resignation final which I did and closed my labors Sept. 14th, 1884, having served as pastor for four years.

I resolved now to have a few months respite from pastoral work. We rented rooms, moved out of the parsonage, and remained in East Aurora until the following Spring.

During this winter vacation I assisted a few weeks Rev. Syse at Strykersville, N. Y., in a series of meetings and preached in different places as opportunity afforded.

Early in the Spring of 1885 I received a call from the Baptist Church at Westfield, Chautauqua County, N. Y. This call I accepted.

SETTLED AS PASTOR AT WESTFIELD.

May 1, 1885 I commenced pastoral work at Westfield, N. Y. I entered upon the work here with much fear and trembling for I was undecided as to whether I was the right man for the place. This fear passed when I found I was receiving a very hearty and earnest co-operation of all the church members. We lived till the Spring of 1886 in a rented house on Union Street.

In the Fall of 1885 Mrs. Tennant went to California to spend the winter with her sister, Martha, Mrs. Morgan, at Oakland. This was a delightful experience for her. Early in this winter, I purchased a house and lot on South Portage Street. Upon Mrs. Tennant's return we moved into this home of our own, the first owned since our marriage. This was in the Spring of 1886.

· The Westfield Church being weak in finances, appealed to the New York State Baptist Convention for aid. This was granted. I was appointed their missionary with a pledge of $100.00 for the first year; for the second year the aid was $50.00.

LECTURE ON PROHIBITION.

During the months of September and October, 1885, I lectured on temperance and the prohibition of the liquor traffic, advocating the necessity for a political party whose principal object was the total destruction of this wicked traffic. I did not hesitate to arraign the old political parties as secretly or openly supporting the iniquitous business. I delivered that Fall twenty-three lectures in different places in Chautauqua County where friends interested in the cause invited me to speak. This lecture course, gave me great satisfaction, and created for me many political enemies. I wrote articles for a third party paper, "The Agitator" published in Jamestown, N. Y. For these articles I got most warmly scored by old party papers particularly those supporting the Republican Party. All this gave me supreme delight. You know, when you fire into a flock of birds, the birds that flutter have been hit. I was glad to witness the fluttering and the return fire caused no bleeding wounds.

All my life before the public, I have been an uncomprising enemy of the sale and use of strong drinks, and never hesitated to condemn it from the pulpit when occasion required. I could here relate many pleasing incidents in connection with my work along this line, but all cannot be related in an article that must be limited in length.

MY WORK AT WESTFIELD.

The limited means of the Baptist Church forced me to resort to some manual labor for the support of my family, so, by the aid of my faithful wife, I purchased sixteen acres of land and set all out to grapes except about three acres. Nearly half of this land might properly be called unimproved, as it was swampy and stony. Here there was work. But I was enabled to preach two sermons every Sabbath, and after the first year, every other Sabbath three sermons, one at an out station.

In the summer of 1891 I purchased, with my nephew, Moses D. Tennant, seventeen acres of land. This I plowed over in the Fall and in the Spring of 1892 it was all planted to Concord grapes. Thus I had about twenty-six acres of grapes to cultivate and harvest, when all had come to bearing. This meant hard work for me and plenty of it. None the less, my pastoral work continued. My father used to say "You can't kill a Tennant with hard work." When the grapes were harvested and sold, then from the 1st of November to the 1st of April of each year I was at liberty to give my time to preparing sermons and to pastoral visitation.

The first weeks of January of each year extra meetings were held, always with good results in the quickening of the spiritual life of the church members, and usually in some conversions.

RESIGNATION.

Thus my work continued in the church and on the farm until the Spring of 1891, when I resigned my pastorate and closed my labors the last Sabbath in August, 1891.

WORK AT MAYVILLE.

In the Spring of 1897 I visited the Baptist church at Mayville, the County seat of Chautauqua County. I found it utterly destitute. no preaching, no week-day prayer meeting, nor Sabbath School. At the close of the morning service, I called the few members present together, and boldly offered to them my services for one year without any pay, only the church board must board myself and horse over the Sabbath day. On these terms I worked the first year, preaching to them twice each Sabbath.

The second year the work continued and I received $3.00 a week and my board over the Sabbath. In the winter of this year the Mayville church released me from the 1st of December, 1897 to the 1st of April, 1898.

SUPPLIED AT RIPLEY.

On the 1st of December, 1897, to the 1st of April, 1898 I supplied the pulpit of the Baptist church at Ripley, N. Y. This was my old home town, and I had excellent congregations morning and evening every Sabbath.

Returning again to my work in Mayville, I undertook to raise about $300.00 on subscription for re-roofing and repairing their house of worship. I obtained pledges enough to enable them to venture on making needed repairs. This they undertook and carried through after the close of my labors the last Sabbath in August, 1899. From that time to the present, 1915, the church has had almost contiuous pastoral service, and their work has not ceased for a single month.

A REVIEW AND SUMMARY.

The years and months of my labors in the Christian ministry are as follows:

At Clymer, N. Y., from May 1st, 1863, two years.

At Union City, Pa., from May 1st, 1865, five years and 5 months.

At Niagara Falls as supply, from Nov. 19, 1871, seven months.

At Niagara Falls as pastor, from Jul. 1, 1872, 1 year and 8 months.

At North East, from Mar. 1, 1874, 13 months.

At Niagara Falls as supply, from Apr. 15th, 1875, 3 1-2 months.

At Panama, N. Y., from Aug. 1, 1875, 5 years.

At East Aurora, N. Y., from Sept. 22, 1880, 4 years.

At Westfield, N. Y., from May 1, 1885, 6 years.

At Mayville, N. Y., from May 1, 1897, 1 year and 8 months.

At Ripley, N. Y., from Dec. 1, 1898, 4 months.

At Mayville, N. Y., from Apr. 1, 1899, 4 months.

At Portage, Mich. in the summer of 1871, 2 months.

The full time of my services as pastor and supply is only twenty-eight years and six months.

MARRIAGES CELEBRATED.

I have kept in my Pastor's Journal the names of all persons at whose marriage I have officiated, and the year, month and day of each marriage. The entire number is one hundred and sixty-one.

FUNERALS.

I have also kept nearly a complete record of funerals at which I have been called to officiate. These aggregate two hundred and sixty-three. There are a number of funerals that I was called to, which I have not recorded. These would make the full number about two hundred and seventy-five.

BAPTISMS.

At Clymer, N. Y., while pastor...................... 3
At Clymer, N. Y., after series of meetings............... 9
At Union City as Pastor 20
At Niagara Falls, N. Y., as Pastor...................... 2
At Panama, N. Y., as Pastor 35
At Findley Lake, N. Y., as assistant.................... 4
At Busti, N. Y., as assistant 5
At Westfield, N. Y., as Pastor.........................18
                                                        —
    Total number of Baptisms.........................96

This record of Baptisms should shame me into the deepest penitence and humility. The only consolation I can derive from the fruits of my labors computed by the number of baptisms I have administered, is from the known fact, that the number of conversions under my ministry has been more than the number of baptisms, and that I have worked hard all my life to do my whole duty as pastor.

During the twenty-eight years work I have preached on an average, including extra meetings and out stations, about three sermons each Sabbath, making in all four thousand three hundred and eighteen discourses. Included in these is a series of thirty-one discourses on the Life of Christ; nine discourses on the Life of St. Paul; two on the Parables; a series on the Biblical History of the Jews; a series of discourses on the Doctrines of the Gospels as believed and advocated by the Baptist denomination, including a history of these doctrines.

I wrote out the history in full of three Baptist Churches, the East Aurora, the Panama and the Westfield. I prepared and preached a series of sermons on the Second Coming and Millenial Reign of Christ; another on the Doctrine of Creation, including a Refutation of False Theories concerning creation, and defending the Biblical History. All these series of discourses called for much diligent research and study and many days of writing.

If this auto-biography was for the public to read I would not be guilty of so much apparent egotism in going thus far into some of the details of my life work. But all this is written for reading by relatives and personal friends.

Having reached that age when farm work was too heavy for me, I completed the sale of all the balance of my farm, sold my home on South Portage Street at Westfield, fitted up a home at Silver Creek, N. Y., and moved there in the month of November, 1909, with the fond hope of casting off all worldly care and spending the balance of my days in reading, writing, and preparing my soul for the last great change.

WHAT I BELIEVE.

I believe the Christian Scriptures are the word of God; that by them "men of old spake as they were moved by the Holy Spirit;" that there is no real discrepancy between their teaching, when rightly interpreted, and the most advanced teaching of modern science; that indeed science assists in the correct interpretation of the word, and that without this aid the words of the Bible could not be correctly understood.

I believe in the Eminency of God in nature; that His pres-

ence is everywhere, and that natural forces, material and spiritual, are the creation of His wisdom and power, and continue to
exist by the perpetual exercise of His power. I believe that we
must distinguish between the essence of the Divine Being and
the substance of matter as the Creator and the created cannot be
of the same substance.

I believe that God subsists in three persons having one nature,
and are co-equal in all their attributes, the Father, Son and Holy
Spirit. I believe that the Son of God took to Himself a complete
and perfect Human Nature and dwelt upon earth, and that He
took this nature for the purpose of saving man from his sins;
that this salvation is provided in His life and sufferings as a vi-
carious sacrifice for sin. I believe that this salvation is offered
to all the human race, on the conditions of repentance, faith and
obedience.

I believe in the immortality of man's soul; that he will have a
self-conscious existence after the dissolution of the mortal body,
and this consciousness of existence does not cease for any period
of time after death.

I believe that the righteous will be rewarded with eternal life
solely as a free gift of God's gracious favor and not as merited
by personal virtue or by good works.

I believe the wicked will suffer punishment in the future state
of existence, because the sins of their earthly life are continued
in their life after death; that the duration of their punishment
co-exists with the continuance of their sinning from a free choice
and from a degree of unholy satisfaction therein.

I believe in the resurrection of the bodies of the just and the
unjust and in a general judgment. I believe in the second coming of our Lord to this earth in His glorified body, and at this
coming the destiny of all human souls of the vast generations of
men will be forever determined and fixed. As a preparation for
that great and notable day of the Lord the souls of sinful men
must be quickened into a holy spiritual life by the Holy Spirit,
and such only will be permitted to enter heaven. Formal professors will be excluded.

With a correct interpretation of the words "The Holy Catholic Church" and the words "He descended into hell," I accept
the Apostles Creed as a true epitome of Christian doctrine.

In closing this auto-biography I wish to say to all my friends
and relatives, when I have passed away from earth, do not think
of me as lying in a dark cold grave, but rather hope for me, that
through grace and grace alone I have been permitted to enter
through the gates of the celestial city, there to meet my blessed
Savior and the dear ones who have gone before me and to await

the coming of those I have left on earth. This is my faith and my glorious hope.

"I know not the hour when my Lord will come,
To take me away to his own dear home;
But I know that His presence will lighten the gloom
And that will be glory for me,
And that will be glory for me."

MEMORIAL TRIBUTES.

DIVISION II.

REV. GEORGE SAWIN AND HIS WIFE, BETSEY TENNANT.

In the family record, in Part 2, Chapter Second, will be found recorded the births, marriage and deaths of Rev. George Sawin and his wife, Betsey Tennant. The writer of this Memorial was well acquainted with his uncle and aunt, and it gives him great pleasure to contribute something to reveal to others, who may have never seen or known their lovely characters, and to perpetuate their memories. What has been previously written in the family record need not be repeated here.

Two nobler spirits could not be named. If there is any special meaning to the word "Christian," they possessed the very best elements of such a character. Uncle George was more impulsive in his temperament, but he always controlled his impulses as he was thoroughly conscientious and had a well balanced mind and sound judgment. Aunt Betsey was mild, even-tempered, everyday-alike in her life and spirits. Both became members of the Baptist church of Ripley, N. Y., and passed into the church triumphant in the fullness of a christian faith and hope, and a ripened christian experience.

The writer has had a correspondence with Deacon R. P. Bennett, a member at this date, January, 1913, of the Baptist Church of Springfield, Otsego Co., N. Y. He has been a member of this church for forty years and a deacon for twenty years. He examined the church record and finds that Rev. Geo. Sawin was ordained to the gospel ministry April 21, 1819. As he was the immediate predecessor of Rev. David Tennant who was ordained as pastor on the first Wednesday of March, 1823, we conclude, that the services of Rev. Sawin continued to about this time, which would make about four years service in all. He and his wife came to the Baptist Church of Ripley, N. Y., with letters from the Baptist Church of Springfield, N. Y. The family moved from Otsego Co. to Chautauqua in 1832. The records of the First Baptist Church of Ripley show that Rev. Sawin became its Pastor in 1834 and served the church till 1837. He was succeeded in the pastorate by his brother, Rev. John Sawin.

Rev. Sawin's sermons were usually expository. The last sermon the author remembers hearing him preach was on "Christ in Prophecy." It was marvelous for its grasp of the subject, for its many scripture quotations from memory, and its poetical imagery. The writer has recalled the impressions of that discourse for many years. Uncle George was in the congregation when the writer preached his first discourse in the Baptist Church

WM. WILSON SAWIN
Born August 25, 1888

on Ripley Hill. His venerable form was an inspiration to the young preacher, as he tried to speak upon the theme, "God, the Support and Defense of the Church."

The writer remembers well the last visit he made his uncle George. His venerable form was lying peacefully on his death-bed, waiting for the summons of the Master and Savior to call him to his blessed reward, his eternal home. "With a low, trembling voice but with perfect clearness and composure, he repeated, word for word, the following beautiful hymn, from the Psalmist, No. 835.

"How sweet and awful is the place,
    With Christ within the doors,
While everlasting Love displays
    The choicest of her stores;

While all our hearts and every song,
    Join to admire the feast;
Each of us cries with thankful tongue,
    Lord, why was I a guest?

Why was I made to hear thy voice,
    And enter while there is room,
When thousands make a wretched choice,
    And rather starve than come?

'Twas the same love that spread the feast
    That sweetly forced us in;
Else we had still refused to taste,
    And perished in our sin.

Pity the nations, O our God;
    Constrain the world to come;
Send thy victorious word abroad
    And bring the strangers home.

We long to see thy churches full,
    That all the chosen race
May, with one voice and heart and soul
    Sing thy redeeming grace."

These may be considered the last words of this venerable and honored saint, before the crown of glory was placed upon his head, and the palm of victory in his hand.

His death took place at his home on Ripley Hill at the age of 73 years, 3 months and 13 days. His beloved wife died on her 71st birthday, at the same place May 31st, 1860.

"There is a place of sacred rest,
    Far, far beyond the skies,
Where beauty smiles eternally
    And pleasure never dies;—

My Father's house, my Heavenly Home,
    Where "many mansions" stand,
Prepared by hands divine, for all
    Who seek the better land."

"In that pure home of tearless joy,
    Earth's parted friends shall meet,
With smiles of love that never fade,
    And blessedness complete.

There, there are sounds unknown,
    Death frowns not on that scene,
But life, and glorious beauty shine
    Untroubled and serene."
                                        —*Selected.*

REV. JOHN SAWIN.

The writer of this Genealogy did not at first purpose to extend his work beyond the limits of those families or individuals which were related by consanguinity to his parents, but the Rev. John and George Sawin who were brothers and men of remarkable personality and who married sisters of the author's mother, Delinda Tennant, he considered it a privilege and duty to make special mention of these uncles, to give a brief sketch of their lives and characters in a Memorial Tribute.

Rev. John Sawin was born in the Township of Willington, Folland Co., Connecticut, on the 10th of April, 1786. At the age of eleven, in 1797, the family moved to Washington County, N. Y., and afterwards to Stark Township, Herkimer Co., N. Y.

Mr. Sawin's early life was spent on a farm. He secured, however, a good common school education, but having a bright mind and being ambitious to get a higher education than the District School offered, he applied himself to other branches of learning in which he made rapid advancement. He soon became qualified to teach and for several years taught in District Schools.

Early in life he made a public profession of faith in Christianity and joined the Baptist Church. While occupied in teaching he was a diligent student of the Sacred Scriptures and of Christian theology, availing himself of such works as those of Scott and Andrew Fuller and other great theologians. His piety and learning and mental ability was readily recognized by his Baptist brethren and so a council was called by the Baptist Church of Exeter, Otsego Co., N. Y., and he was there ordained a Baptist minister. The family moved to Springfield in 1828. Before leaving Herkimer Co., he made the acquaintance of Miss Orrel Tennant. This happy acquaintance resulted in their marriage at Stark, Herkimer Co., N. Y. June 25th, 1813. Mrs. Sawin was born at Springfield, Otsego Co., N. Y., April 28, 1793. Being married and ordained to the Christian ministry he now devoted his time and talents to this greatest of callings.

In the year 1887 occurred the Centennial of the organization of the Baptist Church of Springfield, Otsego Co., N. Y., the church having been organized in 1787 five years after the close of the Revolutionary war. In an edition of "The Freedmen's Journal" published at Cooperstown, Otsego Co., N. Y., on June 24th, 1887, a full account is given of this Centennial celebration. A History of the Baptist Church was prepared and read. In this History are the names of all the pastors, deacons, trustees and clerks who had served the church during its first hundred years of history. Rev. W. Farman was the first pastor, closing his labors in 1800. "From 1821 to 1855, thirty-four years, this church had twelve pastors, namely, Rev. Daniel Putnam one year, David Tennant two years; Jacob Knapp five years; John Sawin three years." This extract shows that John Sawin was the seventh pastor of the Baptist church of Springfield, N. Y., and that he succeeded the noted evangelist, Jacob Knapp, and served the church three years from 1828. This brings the time of his service down to near 1832 when the family moved to Ripley, Chautauqua Co., N. Y.

Having settled in Ripley he still continued preaching. His income from such service was very inadequate for the support of his large family. He purchased a farm and this helped supply the family. Mrs. Sawin, the faithful wife, was a woman of remarkable energy, tact, and courage. The spinning wheels were kept busy; the loom was kept banging and hundreds of yards of linen and woolen goods were manufactured for home consumption. One of the older daughters was a seamstress who could cut and make garments for the family. All worked and rendered what help they could.

This preaching and farming Rev. Sawin continued at Ripley from 1832 to 1846. He was pastor of the Baptist church at Ripley, N. Y., from 1837 to 1840. During this time four daughters were born, the youngest of this large family of thirteen children. Now great changes took place in this history of this remarkable family.

In 1846, on the 19th of Feb. Rev. Sawin and three of the children started with a team and a covered wagon for Wisconsin, then a territory. Before reaching Erie, Pa., there had fallen a heavy snow compelling them to change from wheels to sled shoes. Thus rigged they went on, arriving at their destination in Walworth County, Wisconsin the 19th of March. Alvin, the oldest son, had preceded them, going with his sister, Ann Eliza and her husband, Mr. Gott, immediately after their marriage in 1842.

This first visit of a part of the family was only to spy out the land. Mr. Sawin remained only till about the first of May when he returned by the lake route to New York State, arriving at home on the 7th of May. Preparations were now made for the moving of the entire family to Wisconsin. On the 10th of June, 1846, they bade their old friends and neighbors of Chautauqua good bye and started from Erie, Pa., up the lake to Racine, Wisc., and from there on to Walworth County.

For a short time they stopped at the home of the daughter, Mrs. Gott. Soon they found a vacant residence and moved into it and there lived for six months.

Mr. Sawin was looking for a farm. He finally located one in Green Co., Wisc., and purchased 175 acres. On this farm he built a new and comfortable home. As the sons grew into manhood they wanted more land so forty acres more were purchased making a farm of 215 acres. On this land prosperity came to the family such as they had never before experienced.

Rev. Sawin, however, did not lose his interest in the cause of Christ. He served as pastor of the Rutland church for many years, besides holding services and preaching in log school houses located many miles apart. He maintained family worship in the reading of the Scriptures and prayer.

Mrs. Sawin during all these years was a faithful helper in all her husband's labors. Her great energy and untiring love of work kept the wheels of industry constantly in motion at her home. She was a genial, happy spirit which no amount of care or burden bearing could crush or becloud. Her christian influence in the home directed and moulded the character and lives of

PROF. ALBERT MONROE SAWIN
Born April 3, 1858

her children so that not one of this large family went astray to bring a shadow of disgrace upon themselves or the family, but lived honorable, pure and upright lives such as are always ornaments and benedictions to society and the world.

Rev. Sawin in the later years of his life was led to believe in the possibility and actuality of communications with departed human spirits. Such had been made to members of his family so he believed. The writer does not know that his uncle accepted in full the teachings of modern spiritualism, but presumes that he only went so far as to believe in spirit communications, still adhering to the teachings of the sacred scriptures on fundamental evangelical doctrines.

After many years of labor and burden bearing Mr. Sawin's health began to give way. The physician who rendered medical treatment pronounced the disease "hardening of the arteries." No medical skill could save him from the final results. As death approached he had some strange and remarkable visions of spirit beings. On the 19th of March, 1866, at the advanced age of 79 years, 11 months and 9 days, at Brooklyn, Wisc., this servant of God fell asleep in Jesus. Having fought the good fight and kept the faith, henceforth there is laid up for him a crown of righteousness which the Lord, the righteous Judge, will give him in the great day. His faithful and beloved wife survived him until the 5th of Aug. 1873, when, at the same place, she was called home to her eternal rest and reward.

"Servant of God well done;
Rest from the loved employ;
The battle fought, the victory won,
Enter thy Master's joy.

Tranquil amid alarms,
It found him on the field;
A veteran slumbering on his arms
Beneath the red-cross shield.

The pains of death are past;
Labor and sorrow cease;
And life's long warfare closed at last,
His soul is found in peace.

Soldier of Christ well done;
Praise be thy new employ;
And, while eternal ages roll,
Rest in thy Savior's joy."

—From the Psalmist.

MOSES ASEL AND DELINDA TENNANT.

By Their Son, Albert.

In the family genealogy of this book will be found a record of the ancestors of my parents, the place and dates of their birth, and mention made of their brothers, sisters and children. This Memorial Tribute is written to express not only the sweet memories of the writer, but also to voice the sentiments and feelings of all their children, the living and the dead.

We children would be cruelly ungrateful and wanting in all the elements of human kindness and natural affection if we did not appreciate what our parents have done for us, not only in bringing us into being, but in ministering to our bodily wants, in loving efforts to make our home life happy and blest, and in helping and encouraging us to make the best possible use of our time and the gifts of mind and heart with which nature had endowed us. Considering the hard and ceaseless struggle for existence, for food, raiment and shelter, it is a marvel of industry, of practical wisdom and skill that enabled them to do for their children, aside from feeding and clothing them, as much as they did.

From our earliest childhood their vigilant care anticipated every want of their chlidren, and they spared neither body or mind in their unremitting efforts to meet all our necessities. It was toil early and late to support their family. Our mother scarcely ever retired before ten or eleven o'clock and after a hard day's work the evening was spent in knitting stockings and mittens, or in making or mending garments. It was no small task to do the knitting for so large a family and no stockings, mittens, or garments of any kind were ever bought and brought in for family use. All were made from the flax and the wool raised on the farm, and spun and woven by willing hands. The writer remembers of seeing the walls of the kitchen of the old log house filled as closely as the large bunches could hang of yarn made ready for the loom.

That old loom banged away day after day and sometimes late in the evening, to bring forth the cloth for clothing the family. All woolen goods designed for dressing was taken to the mill of Hezekiah Mason for that purpose. We children never lacked for proper clothing summer or winter. We always had decent clothes to go to school or to church and never went to bed hungry or slept cold at night for the lack of bed clothing.

As the writer looks back over those early days of the family existence, he can but wonder how so much could be accomplished to support so large a family. He remembers well how all the older children worked with willing hands. The two oldest brothers, Alvin and Delos, and two older sisters, Eliza and Julia, worked to help the parents in caring for and supplying the wants of the family.

Our parents were not indifferent to the education of their children. All had a good common school education and four of the children became teachers in early years. No excuse but sickness would be taken as reasons for remaining a single day from school, summer or winter. We took our dinners with us, which consisted many times of a lusty slice of Johnny cake, a doughnut and an apple. The cold winter weather never kept us from school for, were we not all as hearty as white beans? The writer well remembers of wading over snowdrifts four or six feet deep to school. This was work and fun combined. Our parents had but little schooling when young, and they saw and felt the great need of children receiving an early education, at least in the common branches of learning.

Our parents were not indifferent to the religious education of their children. They both made a public profession of their faith in Christ the Lord, and united with the Baptist church of Springfield, Otsego Co., N. Y., while in their youth, father was baptized Sept. 15th, 1811, while under ten years of age, by Rev. Phineas Holcom, pastor of the church, and mother was baptized Nov. 2nd, 1818, being a few days over 16 years and 6 months old. When they moved to Chautauqua Co., both received letters of dismissal and recommendation from the Springfield church. Father's letter was dated March 9th, 1833, and mother's letter was dated April 14th, 1833. On these letters they were received into the fellowship of the Baptist church of Ripley, N. Y. We see in the above record, found in the Springfield Baptist church book that our parents began the christian life in early life, and maintained a worthy standing in the christian church in subsequent years. We children were all regular attendants upon church service and Sabbath school; no excuse for remaining at home was allowed, this was the unchangeable order of the family.

As the happy result, all but two professed faith in Christ the Lord in early years, one of the two here excepted, in later years made a like profession. All united with the Baptist Church of Ripley, N. Y.

Our father was a man of excellent natural ability. In his boyhood days he was an athlete and fond of sports and had the reputation of being quite a wild boy.

He was very sympathetic in his nature, easily wept when his emotions were wrought upon. In prayer, public or private, the tears would often flow down his cheeks while he was addressing

the throne of grace.   At Ripley he received from his fellow citizens the honor of representing them on the Board of Supervisors for six years, as follows: 1843, 1844, 1845, 1847, 1848 and
1853.   He served with ability and fidelity.   The writer remembers how he worked over the town tax-roll.   On one of these
occasions the boy got noisy in the room where his father was at
work.   His mother said to him "Albert, you must keep still.
If father makes mistakes he may be sent to jail."   Albert was
quiet the rest of the day.

Our father was deeply interested in the cause of temperance.
He lectured when called upon, and one of the political causes
of his repeated election on the Board of Supervisors was his
firm stand against the sale and excessive use of strong drink.

Although far from being independent in his finances, he gave
$100.00 toward the building of the Baptist house of worship on
Ripley Hill.   He was afterwards, although against his strong
protest, elected deacon of the Church.

Our mother was in some respects of a different temperament
from our father.   She was a person of remarkable nerve, always calm and deliberate under the most trying circumstances.
The writer has heard her say that if it was necessary she could
assist a surgeon at any time to amputate a leg or arm or perform
any kind of a surgical operation.   She had a strong physical con-
stitution and could endure much hard work.   With little early
education she was a constant reader of the Bible and religious
works.   It was in this way she spent her leisure hours.   She
used but little time in visiting and entertaining.   Indeed her life
was too full of family cares and duties to use time in social affairs.   She was very even and unchangeable in her religious
feelings and convictions.   Her faith in the Bible as the Word of
God was unwavering and without any shadows of doubt.

In the management of her children she was kind and firm.
Indeed, the writer does not remember a single instance of dis-
obedience on the part of either of us children to our mother's
commands or request.   The writer recalls an instance when he
had been in the ministry for a few years and was past thirty
years of age.   He was at his parents home on a visit.   The fire
got low in the stove and mother said "Albert, go and bring in
some wood for the stove."   Did Albert hesitate?   Not a moment.   It was obedience and no thought of anything else.   And
why should I have felt too old or too big to obey my mother?
She knit all my woolen and cotton socks till I was nearly forty
years old.   I protested but she would do it.

It makes no abatement of our love and regard for the dear
memory of our mother that she was not highly educated nor

made any pretentions to high social standing among the wealthy and influential. We know what labors she wrought, what burdens of anxious care she carried for so many years for her large family of children. We see in our own lives in our maturer years the impress of her life, love and devotion to her children. Her anxiety that we should make no great mistakes in life and fall the victims to direful temptations, was a powerful influence to keep us from surrendering to evil passions and making shipwreck of our lives. We should not, we would not, dishonor our parents and bring shame and grief to their hearts, whose very life blood had been shed for so many years to shield us from evil and build up our characters into a true and noble manhood and womanhood.

It is not strange that children thus protected, guided and inspired should revere the name of father and mother whose lives have been consecrated to the well-being of their children.

In concluding this Tribute the writer does not care to shadow the triumphant entrance of his parents into the Higher Spirit Life by speaking of their physical sufferings at the time of their departure. Our father died at his home in Ripley, N. Y., on the 1st of November, 1876, with all his children and their mother at his bedside. He said to us just before his departure, "What can a man do in such a condition as I am in, without a hope in Jesus Christ." In this hope he fell asleep in Jesus, at the age of 74 years, 10 months and 8 days.

Our mother lived till the 3rd of February, 1893, when at the age of 90 years, 10 months and 8 days, she also passed into the Spirit Life.

"Why do we mourn departing friends,
Or shake at death's alarms,
Tis but the voice that Jesus sends
To call them to His arms.

Why do we tremble to convey
Their bodies to the tomb?
There the dear flesh of Jesus lay
And scattered all the gloom.

The graves of all the saints He blest,
And softened every bed;
Where should the dying members rest
But with their dying Head?

Thence He arose ascending high,
And showed our feet the way;
Up to the Lord our souls shall fly
At the great rising day.

Mrs. Ellen Mason Tennant.

By Her Husband.

I have already recorded in the family genealogy my marriage to Ellen Mason, third daughter of George and Jane Gardner Mason of Ripley, N. Y., March 24th, 1859. This tribute to her memory is given to make known more fully her character and life and to express in loving words my appreciation of her real worth and of the wealth of goodness, purity, love and piety which were the predominant elements of her superior character.

I find it difficult to express in moderate terms what to me seems to be superior to all ordinary characters and which was true of her in any just estimate of her strong, beautiful and pure nature and life.

She inherited from a long line of ancestors elements of mind and heart that were most pronounced and striking in their development. We mention first her bright intellectual faculties. In her school life astromomy and mathematics were her favorite studies. Nothing pleased her more than the solving of abstruse and difficult problems. She also delighted in tracing out the various constellations on the map of the starry heavens. She numbered the stars and called them by name. She had an excellent memory that readily recalled to mind what she had learned or produced by the processes of her own reasoning.

She commenced teaching in early life. She taught the large Village school at Ripley composed of fifty or sixty scholars. Although small in stature and weight, she had that strong genial personality that commanded respect and honor, and that easily enforced obedience to the rules of the school so necessary for the maintenance of good order. Her scholars obeyed her commands from love and fear combined. They knew that she was deeply interested in their welfare, in their advancement, in their studies and in their forming true and noble characters. Back of all her intellectual and moral qualities was her sincere and devout religious life which made its pure and powerful impression upon what she was and all that she did.

The period of her teaching was shortened by her failing health, yet she pursued her studies and extensive reading, attended a select school in her home Village and so kept her mind in active use. While a young girl she read through every volume in the Village library, containing works on ancient and modern history, the history of the United States, the writings of Benjamin Franklin, the lives of Geo. Washington, LaFayette, Marion, Wm. Penn, General Daniel Boone and many other works

MRS. ELLEN MASON TENNANT
First Wife of Rev. A. M. Tennant
Born November 12, 1832   Died September 15, 1870

which I do not recall. She was not a careless reader. She read for information and her ready memory retained a large part of what she read. Religious works especially interested her. The Life and Times of Martin Luther, the Rise of Papacy, the History of the Martyrs, and many devotional works as Baxter's Saints Rest, Bunyan's Pilgrim's Progress, Edwards History of Redemption, were among her favorites. Before her marriage at the age of twenty-six she had read the Bible through nine times by course, most of this reading being done at her secret devotions.

When I commenced my home studies in preparation for the Christian ministry I had no concordance, no library to help me. My wife's memory was my concordance. I had only to give an idea of the passages of Scripture I wanted to find and soon she would be able to locate them.

Mrs. Tennant was converted to the Christian faith in early life. From childhood she had been taught to believe the Bible to be the word of God, but she had not given the love of her heart to the Lord Jesus and taken him as a personal Savior. It would seem incredible that a person of her temperament and disposition would have any heart struggles, any deep convictions of sin, or any strong rebellion against yielding to the call of God. In relating her own experience she told of the conflict in her heart when the Lord Jesus knocked at the door for entrance. However, she was sweetly compelled to yield to the great joy and satisfaction of her soul.

After conversion she united with the Baptist Church of Westfield, N. Y., and there retained her membership until after our marriage and my settlement at Clymer, N. Y., as pastor, when our membership was transferred to the Baptist Church of that Village.

Mrs. Tennant's change of heart and life was inwardly to her as great as if she had been outwardly very sinful. From this time on, her beautiful life flowed in a deeper, broader and purer current than ever before. Nature and grace combined to make as perfect a life as human nature is susceptible of reaching in the earthly state. She held constant and intimate communion with divine and heavenly things. The Church, the Bible and Christian conversation and activities were her supreme and constant delight. She ate of the Bread and drank of the Water of Life freely. Gospel sermons were always a feast to her. Her knowledge of the sacred scriptures greatly increased her interest and profit in the preaching of gospel truths.

At the time of our marriage I was engaged in farming. Mrs. Tennant wanted to be a farmer's wife and did not want to be a

pastor's wife.   Her father was a farmer and all connected with
farm life appealed to her.   Its out-door work, its communion
with the beauties and wonders of Nature, its freedom from commercial conflicts and competition, its humble and unpretentious
social aspects appealed to her love of the beautiful, and her dis-
regard for worldly honors or distinctions led her mind to choose
a quiet retired and unpretentious farmer's life.

Notwithstanding these desires and preferences when convinced
it was my duty to enter the work of a pastor she yielded without
complaint and advised me to do my duty as I felt was required
of me.

Before this experience came to her, the insidious work of an
incurable disease began to lay its heavy burden upon her.   It
was a curvature of the spine which slowly crippled her for life.
She was so far paralized that she could only take a few steps by
being supported.   She could do no kind of work although she
was able to feed herself while at the table.   For eight years before her death she could neither dress or undress herself.

Now came the great trial of her faith.   Could she be patient
and trustful when the hand of God was upon her in affliction?
Could she say "Not my will but thine, O Father, be done?"
Never was there a more decided proof that God's promises will
never fail his children, than was manifested in her experience.
Her life was constantly radiant with sunshine and peace and
hope.   Not a cloud of doubt or fear or complaining cast a
shadow over her mind or heart.   Cheery, happy and joyous her
blessed life flowed on like a calm and peaceful river whose banks
are decorated with beautiful trees and fragrant flowers while
above and around birds of paradise were filling the air with
their enchanting songs.

Every effort was made to effect a cure.   One of her sisters in
the Spring of 1853 went with her to Dr. Trale's Institute in
New York City.   There she was treated for eleven weeks with
no beneficial results.

I had accepted a call to the pastorate of the Baptist church of
Clymer, N. Y., and while she was gone I moved our goods from
Ripley on to that field.   After the eleven weeks had passed I
went to New York to bring her home.   Before starting homeward we took a trip to Coney Island and spent the day.   Her
sister Frank and other friends were with us.   On our homeward
trip we went up the Hudson River to Albany.   Neither of us
had ever set our eyes on the magnificent scenery through which
that renowned river flows.   To say that we enjoyed the trip only
half expresses our delight.   We were enthusiastic admirers of

the grandeur of the natural scenery which floated by us as we floated up the river.

Mrs. Tennant had the happy faculty of winning to herself many friends. Her acquaintances became at once warm friends. She always threw a cloak of charity over the weaknesses and faults of others, and always saw something to be admired and loved in all persons with whom she became acquainted. She was always a welcome guest in the homes of church members and neighbors. She was an easy and ready talker but would never engage in neighborhood or town gossip. She would always give a religious turn to conversation when she could do so with courtesy.

I will here relate two instances which occurred while we were living at Union City, Pa. A Methodist sister had become greatly depressed in mind concerning her christian experience. She come to doubt whether she was really a christian or not. Clouds of despair would shadow her mind and heart for weeks at a time. She had heard about Mrs. Tennant, how cheerful and happy she was in her almost helpless condition, and resolved to make her a visit. This was made and the result was told to me on a visit I made at her home. She said, "Since my visit with Mrs. Tennant the clouds which had obscured and darkened my mind and heart so long have all passed away and the blessed sunshine of God's love in Christ has lighted up my mind and comforted my heart."

Another instance was that of a wealthy lady of high social standing who was greatly troubled with doubts concerning the Christian religion and the Bible. This lady visited Mrs. Tennant and this was the happy result. She said "When I saw Mrs. Tennant so helpless with no hope of a cure and yet so cheerful and happy and all because God was fulfilling His blessed promises to her as she said, how could I any longer doubt the truthfulness of the Bible or the reality of the christian religion."

Such instances might be multiplied of her great usefulness in ministering light, hope and comfort to other hearts by her strong faith, her firm grasp upon christian truth and her beautiful sunny life, when from a human view of things it might have been expected that weakness and nervous suffering would crush out of her heart and life all hope, peace and joy.

It was never a burden but always a pleasure for her family and friends to minister to her wants. Never a word of murmuring or complaint fell from her lips. When epilepsy seized upon her, caused by the curvature of the spine effecting the brain, she suffered greatly from nervousness and muscular contortions. For the four last years of her life this epilepsy continued, with a slowly increasing severity. Her sufferings were painful to witness but how much more painful to endure? Did she complain that God was dealing unkindly with her? No. She never seemed to have a thought or feeling against the Divine Hand that suffered these sad things to befall her.

It might have been expected that epilepsy would produce loss of memory and weakness of the mental faculties. But she was mercifully preserved from such effects and her mind was clear and active up to the last few hours of her life on earth.

Some portions of the Bible were her special favorites from which she made most frequent quotations. The 1st and 23rd Psalms; the 41st and 53rd chapters of the prophesy of Isaiah; the 14th and 17th chapters of John's Gospel and the two last chapters of Revelation were among her favorites.

The year before her death she commenced keeping a diary. This little booklet is worth its weight in gold to those who loved her. A few days before her death I was called away to a meeting of the Baptists of the Oil Creek Association. Upon my return home she barely recognized me. I saw at once that the end was approaching. All was done that could be done for her. As the moment of her departure drew near I took her hand in mine and held it until the end came. Now on the wings of the spirit as it left the body she passed into the realm of spirit-life where bodily ills no more afflict and confine the movements of the soul. Now was realized with her the fulfillment of those many precious promises with which she was so familiar and upon which her heart found sweet repose for so many years.

"In my Father's house are many mansions. If it were not so I would have told you. I go to prepare a place for you, and if I go and prepare a place for you, I will come again and receive you unto myself, that where I am there ye may be also."

John 14: 1st and 2nd

It was Mrs. Tennant's wish that she be buried beside her father and mother in the cemetery at Ripley, N. Y. So the funeral was held in the Presbyterian Church at that place, the Rev. Lyman Fisher, pastor of the Baptist church at Westfield, N. Y. preached the sermon, and the beautiful form was laid away to await the resurrection of the just.

I had placed upon her tomb-stone these words: "Blessed are the pure in heart for they shall see God."

Alvin Jewett and Delos Gibson Tennant.

In the genealogy of Moses Asel and Delinda Tennant, found in Part III, Chapter IV, Division I, may be found the record of the births, marriages and deaths of these two brothers, oldest children of their parents. What is there recorded need not be repeated, hence in this Memorial reference will be made to the personal characteristics of these brothers, together with a brief sketch of their life-work and the changes of place and circumstances that transpired after their marriage and settlement in life.

Both brothers were born in Springfield, Otsego County, N. Y., Alvin on September 18th, 1821, and Delos on July 2nd, 1823, making a difference in their ages of one year, nine months and fourteen days. Both brothers came with the family in the Spring of 1833 to Ripley, Chautauqua County, N. Y. At this time Alvin was some over eleven years of age and Delos was nine years. Both were healthy strong boys, and at this early age were able to help much in farm work. Both were ambitious and willing to take hold of any kind of manual labor that boys could do. At the time the family arrived at Ripley there were the parents, one grandmother, three sons and three daughters, making a household of nine persons to support. All that were old enough to do any kind of work had to contribute what they could for the care, support and comfort of the family.

For the first few years after they arrived at Ripley, the family had no permanent abiding place. In another article, the writer has given the changes of residence that took place during these years. During this period three children were born, Albert, Ellen and Fannie. At the close of this period, which extended from the Spring of 1833 to the birth of the daughter, Fannie, February 18th, 1838, nearly five years, the parents purchased a farm of one hundred acres on Ripley Hill. This gave the family the first permanent home in Chautauqua County. This farm had a house on it of logs with a framed lean-to on the west side having two rooms and a pantry between them.

In this house the youngest child of the family, John Asel, was born. A large portion of the farm was heavy timber land. This had to be cleared for the production of crops, and this furnished plenty of hard work for the two oldest boys. As years advanced with them they soon became strong to swing the axe, the cradle, the scythe and the hoe. Delos was especially skillful with the axe, as he had the strength of a giant to swing it.

After clearing the land, wheat, oats, barley, corn, flax and potatoes could be raised. Pasture and meadow land kept a few

cows, a flock of sheep, a yoke of oxen and a span of horses.
There was always fed and fattened four hogs which were usually butchered just before the winter came on. They were kept
till they weighed from three hundred and twenty-five pounds to
four hundred and twenty-five pounds each. All this pork was
salted down for family use. If any of it was sold it went as
salted pork. At this period in the family history, but little
money was in circulation. But taxes and interest on the farm
debt had to be paid in cash. Black-Salts was the only farm product that could be sold for cash. So a big leach was made into
which ashes were gathered and leached for the lye, which was
boiled down into black-salts used for manufacturing saleratus
and other products. Delos was the ready captain of this important industry. All day and late in the night he built the fires
under the large iron kettles to boil out cash to pay taxes and interest on the farm debt. In the house the spinning wheels and
the loom were kept busy weaving both woolen and linen fabrics
for family wear. Grandmother Morse, our father's mother,
was skillful with the loom, and produced beautiful woolen coverlids and table linen, some samples of which still remain in the
possession of members of the family.

This first period of a permanent farm life continued to the
Spring of 1842, when the first break in the family circle took
place in the marriage and departure of Brother Delos.

MARRIAGE OF DELOS.

Sally Eliza Sawin, a daughter of Col. Ethan Sawin, who was
a near neighbor, was the bride of Delos. They were married
at her home on Ripley Hill, March 1st, 1842. She was in all
respects a worthy, intelligent young woman, of strong and determined personality, with a willing heart and ready hand to take
hold of life's duties with courage and steadfastness of purpose.
She had an active mind, a kind, generous and sympathetic heart.
Suffering of any kind always touched the depths of her nature.
She would do and give beyond her real ability to help her friends
or neighbors in distress of poverty or sickness. There seemed
no limit to her unselfish emotions. Her influence in the
Church, in the family, and in the community, was always in the
line of doing good to others, and in seeking to make them prosperous and happy. Those who only knew her in the declining
years of her life could not know and appreciate her real ability
and worth when she was in the prime of her womanhood.

Immediately after their marriage they moved on to a small
farm on the Lake Shore Road located in the northeast corner
formed by the terminus of a cross road leading from the main or

Buffalo Road in East Ripley Village to the Lake Shore Road. Ethan Allen's residence was directly across the street on the west side from their first home. The first year Delos raised a fine crop of oats and sold them for thirteen cents a bushel; corn was twenty-five cents a bushel and wheat fifty cents. All their household goods were loaded on to a sleigh box when they moved. The writer well remembers this as he saw them start off from the old home. Delos and his wife commenced life, as to finances and conveniences for living, at the lowest round of the ladder.

They remained at this first place of settlement but one year; then moved on to the Webster farm about two miles eastward on the Lake Shore Road. This change of residence gave them a more productive farm to work and a better house to live in, and was the beginning of their financial prosperity.

They remained on this farm till 1850, when they moved to Ripley Village. Delos purchased the undivided half of the Shaver farm located on the north side of the Buffalo or Main Road, for $1200.00. The deed was dated Jan. 8th, 1850. This property was sold and Delos purchased 36 acres on the west side of the Ellis farm. On this property he built a new house of good size and with many conveniences. Here the family lived for many years. Two children, Caroline and Moses Delos, had been born to them. Prosperity now waited at their doorway. More land was purchased on the side hill west of the Wattlesburg Road. Finally the Ellis farm was sold and a home was purchased on Railroad Street in Ripley Village, just north of the Lake Shore depot. This purchase furnished the family with an excellent home all the remainder of the lives of the parents and their daughter, Caroline, Mrs. Crandall. On this place, at this date, 1914, their grandson and his family, Jay Crandall, have their home. At this place Delos died in the year 1905, and his beloved wife in 1908.

In this Memorial we mention Delos and his family first as he was the first to marry and leave the old home. Alvin remained at home till he past twenty-six years of age.

ALVIN'S MARRIAGE.

Emorette Wattles was the oldest daughter of Gerdon H. and Lucreatia Phelps Wattles. She and Alvin were married at her home in Wattlesburg, Ripley, N. Y., September 27th, 1847. In the Spring of 1848 father took the Anson Goodrich farm located in West Ripley Village of his widow on shares, and moved on to the place the same Spring. Father had built a new frame house on his hill farm and now left it for Alvin and his wife, who

worked the farm on shares. He gave Alvin a span of young
horses, a harness and wagon and some farming tools for his four
years' service at home after he was twenty-one years old. This
was the only way to reward him for his faithful service. At this
time all the older children had married and left home except the
three youngest, Albert, Fannie and John. Grandmother Morse,
father's mother, went to Michigan and spent about two years
with her daughters, at this time leaving only a family of five
during the two years residence on the Goodrich place. When
the family at the end of the two years moved back on to the
hill farm, grandmother Morse returned from Michigan, and
Alvin and his wife moved on to a farm they had purchased, located in South Wattlesburg on the west side of the road just south
of the John Newbury farm. This change was made in the
Spring of 1850. Alvin and his wife were now on a farm they
owned. Their father Wattles gave them five hundred dollars
toward purchasing this land. Now they had a good start in the
world, and the prospects were bright for those times of early
settlement.

Now, after two years another move was made. Father sold
his hill farm to Rev. Ira Stoddard, then Pastor of the Baptist
Church located in Wattlesburg. He gave possession in the
Spring of 1852 and moved to East Ripley Village on to a farm
of eighty two acres that he purchased of Mr. Curtis. A cross
road extended diagonally through this land from the Buffalo to
the Lake Shore Road. Alvin and his family still lived on his
hill farm till the Spring of 1872 when he sold out and took Deacon Lyman Gate's farm on shares. This land was near to the
Curtis place, on the south and west. Alvin and father were now
located near each other. Delos and family were also located in
Ripley Village.

In the Spring of   father purchased of the heirs of widow
Ellis, her eighty acres of land lying on the immediate west side
of the Curtis farm. The west part of this land was sold to Delos, and on the front of the east part, father built a nice frame
house for his son Albert (the writer) and his first wife, Ellen
Mason, to occupy after their marriage on March 24th, 1859.
This building was an ell part with an excellent cellar under it.
It was constructed with the design of building to it on the west
side, an upright story and a half addition which would constitute
the main part of the structure. In this ell part, the son Albert
and his first wife lived from the Fall of 1859 to the Spring of
1863, when they moved to Clymer, N. Y., and he settled there
as Pastor of the Baptist Church.

Now, another movement took place, the son, John, was married and he and his wife moved into the home on the Curtis

OLD HOME, RIPLEY HILL

farm with his parents. Brother John always said he would never leave his father and mother. But they wanted a better home to live in and they were able to create it. The upright part to the new house on the Ellis farm was built, and father and John moved into the new house. Meantime the east part of the Curtis farm was sold to Alvin, and he and his wife moved into the old home. This change took place in 1864 or 1865.

On the Curtis farm Alvin and his wife lived for many years. When age began to weaken his physical ability, farming was too heavy work for him. He thought best to sell his farm of about thirty-five acres, and purchase another home in the Village. This was accomplished and he located a home on Main Street in the east part of the Village. Subsequently this was sold and a home purchased on Railroad Street, just south of the Railroad tracks, where he lived the rest of his life and where his widow now lives at this date, May 1914. Alvin died at this home in Ripley Village, January 16th, 1897, at the age of seventy-five years, three months and twenty-eight days.

Between these two brothers there was much similarity and some dis-similarity in their personal characteristics. Both had only a common school education which fitted them for the ordinary practical duties of life. Both were very kind-hearted, industrious, and strongly attached to their friends. Both were brought up to respect the ordinances of religion, to attend public worship, and to observe the principles of good moral teaching. Alvin publicly professed his faith in Christ and Christian Doctrine and united with the Baptist Church of Ripley by baptism. He retained his identity with the Church till his death. Delos inclined to the belief in the final salvation of all men. But his religious sentiments, to outward appearance, had but a slight hold upon his heart and life. Still he had no fear as he was brought in his last sickness face to face with death and future realities. For a time during the pastorate of Rev. Barris, he was leader of the Presbyterian Church choir and a regular attendant upon its service. The writer of this memorial believes that his brother had deep unexpressed convictions of truth that must have led him to a humble confession of the sins of his life, and to a secret reliance upon Christ, the Savior, for his salvation. His perfect calmness and reconciliation in the approach of death leads to such a hopeful and charitable view of his last days on earth. "Hope rises eternal in the human breast," is the great consolation of human life. It gives assurance that the sins and imperfections of human life on earth, are canceled and lost from view by the supernal radiance and glory that shines in beams of Infinite Divine Love from the cross of Christ the Savior of the World.

My two brothers lead strenuous lives of toil and hardship to the very end, and there must be held in store for them in the great hereafter, some reward however undeserved, that grace will bestow when the drama of life is ended and the curtain falls that conceals from view all earthly scenes and realities.

The following poem entitled "Rousseau's Hymn," written in 1775, by J. J. Rousseau, the author, quotes as expressing the hopes he fondly entertains concerning his two brothers mentioned in this humble Memorial Tribute.

ROUSSEAU'S HYMN.

When the mists have rolled in splendor
From the beauty of the hills,
And the sunshine warm and tender,
Falls in kisses on the rills.

We may read love's shining letter
In the rainbow and the spray;
We shall know each other better,
When the mists have rolled away.

If we ere in human kindness,
And forget that we are dust;
If we err in human kindness,
When we struggle to be just;

Snowy wings of peace shall cover
All the anguish of today;
When the weary watch is over,
And the mists have rolled away.

When the mists have risen above us,
As our Father knows his own,
Face to face with those who love us,
We shall know as we are known;

Low beyond the orient meadows
Floats the golden fringe of day;
Heart to heart we'll bide the shadows
Till the mists have rolled away.

OLIVE ELIZA TENNANT.

A Memorial Tribute by Her Brother, Albert Milton Tennant.

Our sister was the fourth child and oldest daughter of her father's family. She was born in Springfield, Otsego Co., N. Y., Aug. 5, 1827, and died at the home of her daughter, Kittie Belle, Mrs. William Stanton, at Ripley, Chautauqua Co., N. Y., Feb. 26th, 1906. She married Henry Shaver at Ripley Village Sept. 24, 1844. She was given the full name of her mother's next older sister, Olive Eliza Tennant, who married Rev. David Tennant.

Eliza came with the family from Springfield, N. Y., in the Spring of 1833, being at the time five years and almost ten months old. At this age she had not commenced her school life, hence her school days were all passed at Ripley, N. Y. She had only a common school education. Whatever may have been her ambition to get a higher education, the opportunity was denied her by conditions that could not be overcome. However, she obtained a good education by making use of the privileges she had.

In early girlhood she was healthy and strong. As the family were poor, she with all the other children were brought up to work. She learned to cook, sew, knit and spin. At the age of eleven years her mother gave her and her sister Julia about two years younger, the task of spinning a run of linen or woolen yarn each day and help about the housework. Each had a large spinning wheel, and before this they tread back and forth each day until their task was accomplished. Both loved to work and so their tasks were performed with willing hands and happy hearts. When the spinning was done then followed the indoor or outdoor sports. Their sister, Wealthy and myself joined in these sports. Out in the pasture a little way east of the old loghouse was a stream of water that seldom if ever was dry. Across this stream a large tree had fallen. The branches had been cut off and the body served as a bridge during times of high water. On this tree bridge we children used to run back and forth, balancing ourselves carefully lest we fall into the water. This was a circus and a menagerie combined, the children being the live animals. The bridge was in commission for many years. Just below it the horses and cattle were watered summer and winter. Tripping across this stream was not our only sport. The barn with its big beam, its ladder, its broad scaffolds, its girts and beams, furnished a place for venturesome walking, climbing and racing. Boys and girls shared alike in gymnastics and athletics. "Ring around Rosy, a pocket full of posies" was often sung when all joined hands and circled about. "Kitty, kitty wants a corner" was another play.   All stood in some corner and when the leader pronounced the words each would rush to get into the other's corner.   A child's play, to be sure, but we were all children.   If city people and their families flatter themselves that they have a monopoly of all the sports and fun in the world, we who have been brought up on a farm in country life, can certify that they are much mistaken, and can assure them that rural life furnishes the freest, cheapest, healthiest and happiest sports, and in them the children have the lion's share.

Sister Eliza was a great help to our mother not only in housework but in the care of the younger children.   I well remember how afraid I was of thunder storms and how at one time sister took me on her lap when a storm was rising in the northwest and putting her hands over my ears she said "The thunder won't hurt you, hear it? what grand music it is."   Yes, I heard it, but it wasn't grand music at all, it was just plain thundering thunder, and that was all there was of it.   But sister helped me bear it with her soothing words.

Thus in many ways sister Eliza helped so much in lifting the burden of care and labor from the heart and hands of our mother.   Now, at the age of 78 years, the memory of the early days comes back to me, bringing flood-tides of light and joy, and filling my heart with gratitude and praise to the Divine Father that I had such kind parents, such loving sisters and genial brothers to make my childhood days so pleasant.   A happy childhood is the richest and noblest inheritance the life of man on earth can inherit.   It sheds a benediction upon advancing years and brings a fortaste of future heavenly joys.

I have already mentioned sister Eliza's marriage.   She was but seventeen years old when this great event of her life took place.   Her sister, Julia, younger by a little over two years, was married at the same time.   As their husbands were brothers, they went in together to keep the Shaver Hotel at Ripley, N. Y. In this business they continued a few years.   After the death of her husband's father who was familiarly called "Uncle Hank," that part of his large farm lying south of the Main road in Ripley Village and extending south and immediately west of the road leading from the Village to the side hill road, fell to his son Henry.   The old homestead was located on the west corner where this road terminated in the Main road, and on the northeast corner of the farm.   On this farm and on the site of the old homestead, a new house was built where sister Eliza and her husband had a home till the time of their deaths, he having died in 1889 and she in 1906.

Our sister was in all respects a true and faithful wife, a kind and devoted mother.   If she failed at all in the management of her children and household affairs, it was on the side of patience and indulgence rather than too much strictness and severity. She enjoyed seeing her family happy and contented in their home life and to this end she turned all her thoughts and energies, but she was too conscientious on all moral questions to approve of conduct, pleasures and indulgences that lead to looseness of character, to corrupting associations, to vile habits or to excesses of any kind that might end in the sacrifice of virtue, honesty, purity, or usefulness in the lives of her children. If they all heeded her example and instruction they could not fail to become ornaments in the home life, models in the social life, useful in the industrial life, and worthy citizens of the State.

In early life she made a public profession of her faith in christianity and was received by baptism into the fellowship of the Baptist Church of Ripley, N. Y. From this time to her death she never wavered in her faith, nor deviated in her christian walk. Her pathway was "that of the just that shineth more and more to the perfect day." She was liberal in her views of christian doctrine, yet a firm believer in the inspiration and authority of the Christian Scriptures. To her the Holy Bible was God's book.

Mr. Shaver, her husband, during the gold hunting excitement went to California to seek his fortune. It was a worthy and honorable endeavor but failed of the end sought. Upon his return home he took up again his farming and labored faithfully to support his family which he dearly loved. He slowly added to his accumulations so that at the time of his death in 1889 he left them with an excellent productive farm, a good new home and everything necessary for their support and comfort. His loss was very great to his wife and family.

A second great sorrow of our sister came when her oldest child, Harriet Eliza, was taken from her by death Dec. 10, 1900. I have mentioned her death in the family record. It is sufficient now to say that her loss was a crushing blow upon her mother and her brother and sisters and relatives. This daughter had a business ability that made her a great assistance to her mother in the care of the family and maintenance of their home after the death of the husband and father.

Through all these trials sister Eliza's faith in God's love and goodness never forsook her. She was the same patient, trustful and hopeful soul.

Her son Charles married in 1879. He soon built him a new house just west of the old homestead. In a few years three children were born to this son, each and all of whom were greatly beloved by their grandmother. Their mother was like an own daughter to her husband's mother and all in all the two families blended together as one family in love and mutual helpfulness.

Sister Eliza spent much of the last months of her life at the home of her daughter Kitty, Mrs. Stanton. While making this winter's visit she was taken with her last sickness which terminated in death Feb. 26th, 1906.

With wonderful patience, faith and hope and a longing to be delivered from pain and suffering she yielded to the call of her Lord and Savior to enter her heavenly home, her eternal rest. "Blessed are the dead that die in the Lord."

MEMORIAL POEM.

On the hills of Otsego, a star once arose,
  To shed its soft light on a cottage below,
Where a beautiful babe had just then been born,
  To fill parent's hearts with love all aglow.

She was the fourth child that came to that home;
  Three brothers before her their visits had paid;
All the more was she welcomed for what that home lacked
  Was a precious home idol, a sweet baby maid.

The star lingered long on that bright happy night,
  To give the dear babe a glad welcome to earth;
'Twas a prophecy sure of a good useful life,
  That a star did appear on the night of her birth.

That prophecy proved true; in the oncoming years,
  When womanhood bloomed from this little child's life;
And the babe that was born became a wife and a mother
  To bless her dear home with the lives of four others.

Years come and go, and the night is fast passing
  When the stars shine the brightest on earth's broad expanse;
For the Sun of a Day that is never to end,
  Dims the light of earth's star as it rises perchance.

The earth star that heralded that sweet babe's coming,
  Gives place to the Sun of an immortal day;
Its promise of life was now fully fulfilled;
  As its mission was finished, it now fades away.

MRS. JULIA EMMA TENNANT SHAVER.

By Her Son, Prof. Frank Shaver.

The subject of this Memorial Tribute was the daughter of Moses Asel Tennant and Delinda Tennant, his wife, and granddaughter of John Tennant and Elizabeth Loomis Tennant, his wife. She was born in Springfield, Otsego Co., N. Y., January 26, 1829.

A long line of Christian ancestry from the Loomis family on one side and the Tennant family on the other, has brought to the subject of this sketch a fullness of capabilities rarely seen in one person. Her intense love of natural beauty gave her full appreciation of the beautiful when at five years of age she, with her father's family moved from Otsego Co. to Ripley, Chautauqua Co., by way of the Erie Canal to Buffalo, N. Y., a time of the year when nature displays the beauties of field and garden, orchard and meadows of central New York. Her trip on Lake Erie from Buffalo to Barcelona during which a terrible storm was encountered, furnished a series of nature wonders that deeply impressed her young heart and life. The family settled on Ripley Hill at Wattlesburg. She soon began to feel the impulse of her inherited spirit force and wished to do something for herself, and her strong resolve won her parents' reluctant consent that she might begin teaching in public schools before she was fourteen years of age. That she succeeded at this early age is evidence of her ability. She passed an examination for a teacher's certificate under the Commissioner, David Shaver, and her brightness, efficiency and capacity for devotion so impressed this serious philosopher that he resolved to make her his wife.

In a letter written at Valparaiso, Ind., July 28, 1844, where he had gone to purchase a home, Mr. Shaver refers to her as "of intelligent turn of mind, of philosophical views, modest deportment, and personal beauty, and what adds charm to it all is an affectionate and confiding heart." This sentiment culminated in their marriage on September 26, 1844 at the Shaver Hotel which her father had rented. The double marriage of herself to David Shaver and her older sister Eliza to Henry Shaver, his brother, was followed by a joint proprietorship of the hotel where their first experience in housekeeping occurred.

She was not sixteen years old until the following January. That they could run a hotel at that tender age is additional evidence of their inherited capability and efficiency.

Marriage and motherhood always develop the latent faculties of women's nature. The death of little Alice, her first born, who lived only about a year, and died under circumstances that seemed preventable, tested to the full her mother heart and her faith in God in bereavement and suffering. Two more children were born while they were living in the home that was deeded to them by Henry J. Shaver in 1846. Subsequently this property was sold and Mr. Shaver purchased a farm of Alexander Cochrane in 1854. At this home three boys were born, making five children over whom she had a mother's tender and thoughtful care. Added to this care were the duties of home tailoring, a dairy, bees, fruit and orchard. All these cares and duties she carried along with lightness of heart, with song and cheerful countenance that banished doubt and worry, and taught what all believe in theory, that God is love. Her generous impulses inclined her to minister aid to her neighbors in times of sickness. She kept medicines and a book of instructions and it was a common occurrence t osee her go with these to her neighbors, to the bedside of the sick and suffering to give aid and relief.

The testing of strength is in time of discipline when children with strong wills have declared war. She could control, yet made the child see the hurt in the heart of affection. We children could always find shelter in times of storm and balm for our pains, courage for our despair, and this continued to her last year.

The writer recalls her devotion, faith and loyalty when others were false in many cases in the experience of her children and friends. She would always make a defense for any accused when the proof was positive. It was hard for her to believe evil of anyone. Her own honest heart caused her to see others with like purpose and she saw all that was good and fair. The writer had the special opportunity of a closer life with his mother during several summers at Chautauqua Lake where she became interested in C. L. S. C. Her interest at this time of life, past fifty-five, her eagerness in study after the activities of her strenuous early life, and when the loneliness of widowhood came to her, plodding alone over the books, her girlish glee at receiving the diploma, all showed forth the abounding ambition to gain knowledge of the wonders of the world.

Her religious life became manifest in an early conversion and membership in the Baptist Church in Ripley, N. Y. Through her purity and faith her husband united with the same church. She was in advance of her times in her liberal views on religious matters. Though a Baptist she worshipped with the Methodist when there was no Baptist Church and had her children attend the Episcopal Sunday School during one Summer. She saw the good in all denominations. She led in the idea of making home a place for entertainment and amusements. She consented to the introduction of games considered in that day forbidden and she lived to see the wisdom of her choice as the forbidden games became tiresome when they were not forbidden.

She was not a suffragist yet her wish was dominant over all her sons and her memory is an inspiration to lofty purposes and noble endeavors.

She rests in a sweet memory of a life full of good works, a character that was sunshine in its contagion and an intelligence that made few mistakes. If the mothers of America could all be of her spirit and intelligence the Republic would grow in power, in righteousness and in devotion to human betterment until the end of history.

DAVID SHAVER.

The ancestors of David Shaver were from German stock coming from the Rhine province and settling in Cobbleskill, Schoharie Co., N. Y. in 1711. His grandfather, John H. Shaver of Cobbleskill, married Marie Brook and eight children were born in Schoharie Co. One son, Henry J. Shaver, moved to Oneida Co. about 1806 and bought a farm near Lowell where nine children were born. The sixth child was David, born May 26, 1816. He was delicate and did light work about the house, was fond of books, became a drummer boy in a Militia Company of old training days. In 1834 his father moved his family to Ripley (or Quincy as it was then) starting in November in four wagons drawn by ox teams. They followed the public roads stopping over night at taverns and arriving at Ripley, settled in the Fairchild home which soon became the permanent home.

The farm of 161 acres on which the house stood, was bought from Fairchild by Henry J. Shaver Jan. 26, 1835. David fitted himself for a teacher. While teaching in Wattlesburg district he met Julia Tennant as a pupil. Later he became Town Supervisor of Schools and in this capacity examined teachers and issued certificates. Among the candidates was Julia Tennant to whom he granted a certificate as teacher. In 1844 he drove from Ripley to Valpairaiso, Ind., taking twelve new farm wagons tandem and selling to farmers in Indiana. Writing under date of July 28, 1844 he refers to a farm of 105 acres that he had recently purchased and asks for advice as to time of moving to take possession. Malaria caused him to give up the plan, and selling his farm in Indiana he returned to Ripley and was married September 26, 1844 to Julia E. Tennant.

In writing to his wife June 11, 1865, who had gone to Wisconsin to visit friends after twenty-one years of married life, he calls her his "wife, tried and endeared." These words show his tenderness and affection in domestic life. He was devoted to his children with a love as deep as it was unpretentious. In religion he cared more for the essentials of Christian morals than for the dogmas of the Church. He united with the Baptist Church after he was married. He had an extensive reading and knowledge of literature and history, especially the didactic poets. He could call to use quotations in conversation or discussion. He grasped the principles underlying state and political parties and cared more for those principles than the party. By training, a Democrat, he became a follower of Lincoln. Prudent in business, clean in all his thoughts and acts, he was of that class of citizens that render Republics safe. Intelligent and loyal to his country, progressive in church affairs, tender but firm in home life, public spirited in all civic reforms, he has left a memory of a peerless life as an inheritance to his family and the generation in which he lived.

MRS. FANNIE OLIVA TENNANT (MASON) HOUGH.

By Her Brother, Albert Milton Tennant.

We cannot write a memorial of sister Fannie without having our mind more or less influenced by the last scenes of suffering which closed her earthly career. It is always well if we can close our eyes to the ills of life, cease looking upon its dark side and gather into our thoughts things which gladden the heart and bring sunshine and beauty into the life. It is enough to say that her sufferings from physical causes were very great and her friends well knew that only death could bring relief. This came on the 11th of January, 1913 when her weary but triumphant spirit took its departure from its earthly tabernacle and soared away to the realms of spirit life. Had she lived to the 18th of February, 1913, she would have been 75 years old.

All the early and middle portion of her life was passed in the town of Ripley, Chautauqua County, N. Y., where she was born Feb. 18, 1838. She was not a strong vigorous child and her mother had to favor her in many ways till she grew into young womanhood, calling upon her to do light work only. In after years she became stronger and was able to do heavy work but always with care and prudence lest she overworked.

Notwithstanding all the draw-backs her life has been a life of toil and burden bearing. It has all been limited to household duties and the care and training of her children. She had a good, common-school education and could assist her children in their study of the rudiments of learning. The record of her marriages and that of her two sons and their children can be found in the family records of her parents and their descendants and need not be repeated here.

Sister Fannie was in her temperament kind hearted, even tempered, social, confiding and charitable. In early life she united with the Baptist church at Ripley, N. Y. She was a member of this church till after her second marriage when she united with the M. E. Church of Fredonia, N. Y. which became her place of residence, and where she lived till the time of her death.

After her first marriage she and her husband settled on a farm located on the lake shore road north and east of Ripley Village. Here the family lived for a few years, when the farm was sold and another farm purchased on the Main road west of Ripley Village. Here the family lived for a few years when another change was made, this farm was sold and another purchased on the lake shore road west and north of Ripley Village. On this farm the family lived till after the death of her first husband, George Mason, which took place May 23, 1887.

The loss of her first husband was a sad bereavement. He was the father of her children, had been a faithful and kind husband, intelligent and industrious, and always furnished for her a pleasant happy home. His death was unexpected as he was only in middle life and apparently had the promise of many years. I well remember the words of my sister when I met her for the first time after her husband's death. She burst out crying and exclaimed, "Now I am a widow." This was her second great sorrow, the other being the loss of an infant daughter. At the time of his father's death his son, Charles, had passed his 19th birthday the 22nd of Oct. 1886, and Eugene, the younger brother, had passed his 15th birthday in July 27, 1886. The sons were now old enough to assist much in the farm work. This relieved their mother and lifted from her much of the burden and care of the farm.

Two years and six months passed when sister married Eugene Hough. Now a complete change in our sister's circumstances in life took place. Mr. Hough was a very kind and generous hearted man. He purchased the farm on the lake shore road and purchased a home for himself and family at 27 Green St., Fredonia, N. Y. In this home sister's family was now settled for the rest of her life. Mr. Hough was a photographer and started the business in Fredonia, N. Y. He taught his step-son Charles the art, who succeeded him in the business and has continued in it down to this date, 1913, at Fredonia.

Years passed on and again our sister was left a widow by the death of her second husband which has been heretofore record-ed. By his kindness and generosity toward a maiden sister, Mary Hough, and his brother, Sylvester and his family, these had a home with sister Fannie for many years after the husband's death. Indeed at her home three of her husband's relatives, two sisters and a brother, died. The care of these in their last sick-ness was cheerfully shared with other members of the family by sister Fannie. Her kind forgiving spirit overlooked all un-pleasantness that arose from time to time in the family circle.

All her lifetime our sister had been a singer. All the Ten-nant family could sing from childhood. Sister had a clear, sweet voice that made her a pleasant companion among the young people of her early society. Some of the songs which were her favorites I recall. One was "A Life on the Ocean Wave, a home on the rolling deep." Another was

"The sea, the sea is the place for me,
With its billows blue and bright;
I love its roar as it breaks along the shore,
And its pleasures to me are a delight.

Then hurrah for the foaming wave,
Hurrah for the bold and the brave,
For the ever ever free, for the ever ever free,
Hurrah for the glorious sea."

These and other beautiful songs she used to sing at home and with her young companions. Her social nature and musical gifts seemed to keep her young, for her voice had a charm after she was seventy years old.

Our sister lived to see her two sons grow up into an honorable manhood and a successful business life. Both married into the same family. The younger brother graduated from the Acade-my at Westfield, N. Y., and from Cornell University, at Itha-ca, N. Y. This son entered the Patent Office department at Washington, D. C., studied law, was admitted to the Bar, and after receiving an honorable degree he resigned his position in the Government service, formed a partnership with another patent lawyer, and is now and has been for several years doing an extensive and prosperous business in Washington, D. C.

From a human view it would seem that such a life and char-acter as our sister always maintained should continue on earth

indefinitely. But Infinite Love and Wisdom has decreed other-
wise. From the beginning of her last sickness, sister Fannie anticipated her own death. For a short time her mind was gloomy
from the effects of the disease that was preying upon her body.
This passed away and a calm and peaceful spirit prevailed to the
end. She said to me "Peace in the blood of Jesus." That faith
in Christ that she had for years entertained asserted its divine
right to fill her heart with heavenly peace and hope during the
last weeks of her life on earth. In this peace she fell aselep in
Jesus Jan. 11, 1913, at her pleasant home in Fredonia, N. Y.

On the 13th of the same month a funeral service was held at
her home conducted by her pastor, Rev. C. G. Farr of the M.
E. Church. She was buried in the beautiful cemetery at Ripley,
N. Y. on the Mason lot beside the grave of her first husband.

Henceforth there is fulfilled to her the Savior's promise,
"And if I go to prepare a place for you
I will come again and receive you unto myself,
That where I am there ye may be also."
—John's Gospel 14:3

MY PEACE I LEAVE WITH YOU.

Tis the peace of a faith that is true and strong,
That guides us in safety life's journey along,
Which lights up our path in the wilderness road
And points the lone pilgrim to his heavenly abode.

Tis the peace of forgiveness by God's pardoning love,
Through the blood of the Savior sent down from above,
To purchase redemption for souls that are lost
An bear in His body our sins on the cross.

Tis the peace of acceptance when God makes it known,
That we are His children His loved and His own;
And gives us to feel in the depths of the heart,
That nothing shall tempt us from Him to depart.

Tis the peace o fadoption when God by His grace,
When the soul dead in sin now ceases its strife,
And battles no more against truth and free grace,
But yields to the call for the heavenly race.

Tis the peace of adoption when God by his grace,
Makes His children the heirs to a heavenly place,
An inheritance incorruptible that fades not away,
Where the river of life flows, through an endless day.

Tis the peace of communion when the soul mounts away,
And abides with the Father and Son every day;
In His bosom of love it finds a sweet rest
While it leans so confidingly on Jesus' own breast.

Tis the peace of a hope that never shall fail,
That anchors the soul within the bright veil;
A hope that the world cannot give or destroy,
For it promises the soul an eternal joy.

Lord, for such peace I earnestly pray,
That its fountains may flow in my heart every day;
When death's shadows are over me cast,
And the scenes of the earth are forever passed,
Then visions of glory before me will glide,
And I'll awake in His likeness forever satisfied.

JOHN ASEL TENNANT.

By His Brother, Albert Milton Tennant.

John Asel Tenannt died at the Hamot Hospital in Erie City, Aug. 13th, 1906, at the age of 67 years, 2 months and 13 days.

In writing this Memorial Tribute to his memory, it would not be strange, if my language to the reader seemed untruthful and overdrawn. No person ever knew another better than I knew my brother. I was just enough older than he to be able to see and appreciate the true elements of his nature and character. We lived under the same roof till he was past twenty years of age and I was past twenty-four, there being four years, nine months and thirteen days difference in our ages.

From his childhood to mature manhood he was a good boy and a good man. He never sowed any wild oats and consequently had no wild oats to harvest. He was remarkably even tempered and well balanced without being dull and morose. He could stand up for his rights without passion or excitement. His firmness might easily have been misunderstood as stubbornness or wilfullness. What he did not want to do or thought it wrong to do, he would not do. So he could not be easily led astray by evil associates. He seemed never to be even tempted to do evil.

Temptation seemed never to have any power over him. Lust, profanity, obscenity or even rudeness and roughness had no place in his nature. When he mingled with other children in sports he was lively, free and joyous, without being coarse, rough and disagreeable. At home, at school, at work or play, he was the same even-tempered, calm and happy child. These natural characteristics never changed when he grew into manhood and had to face the sterner realities of life. All these elements were strengthened by age and contact with the world, so they formed a strong and noble manhood that could resist the evil, cling to that which was good, and sow the seed and reap the harvest of a successful and useful life.

On the 29th of June, 1850, being just past 11 years of age he was baptized into the fellowship of the Baptist church of Ripley, Chautauqua County, N. Y., being 11 years old on the 30th of May the preceding month. Outwardly his christian profession made but little change in his life. He had been brought up to go to church and Sabbath School. Now, however, his heart entered upon the duties of life with a religious zeal and devotion which continued through the future years. As his father was a farmer John never tried to shirk his duties. He was always at home, always ready to perform any task that was allotted to him. The writer can truthfully say that his brother John never ran away from work to play as boys and young men at home so often do.

In the spring of 1852 the family moved from Ripley Hill to the Village then called Quincy, and settled on a farm purchased of a man by the name of Curtis, and located on the north side of the main road in the east part of the Village. This farm needed many improvements and brother John being 14 years old in May of that year, helped a great deal in the work of improvements, in picking up stone, cutting down and piling for burning the brush and small trees.

At this time all the older chidren were married and had started homes of their own, leaving only Fannie, John and myself with our parents. We had a team of horses, three or four cows, a flock of sheep, some hens and pigs, and raised corn, oats and winter wheat. There was a small orchard that furnished plenty of fruit, without spraying, every year. I taught school winters and worked on the farm the rest of the year. Every year improvements were made, heavy pasture land, rough and stony, was broken up and planted, the first year to corn and the next year sowed to oats and the third or fourth the patch thus prepared was seeded and turned into meadow. In six years we had fine meadows and plenty of good pasture.

A widow by the name of Ellis owned 80 acres of beautiful land lying beside our 65 acres on the west. There was not a foot of waste land on the entire farm. Mrs. Ellis died and father bought this farm but sold brother Delos thirty-five acres of it. The remaining thirty made a splendid addition to our farm.

On March 24, 1859, the writer of this Memorial married. Father proposed to build me a home on the farm purchased of Mrs. Ellis. This was finished, and in the month of October, 1859, my wife and I moved into our new home.

In four years from this date in the Spring of 1863 I left farming and settled as pastor licentiate of the Baptist church of Clymer, Chautauqua County, N. Y.

Before this event the great change took place such as should take place in the life of every young man who desires to make the best of his own life and confer the greatest possible good upon the world of mankind. On the 20th of October, 1862, brother John was united in marriage to Miss Julia Ann Adams, youngest daughter of Harry and Laura Pride Adams of Ripley, N. Y. This was a happy event in the lives of these two young people. They soon went to live with his parents in the old house on the Curtis farm and afterward in the new house on the Ellis farm, which was enlarged in the summer of 1863.

Brother John and his wife lived with his father and mother for about thirty years till both had passed away. Our father died November 1, 1876 and our mother Feb. 3, 1893. After the death of Harry Adams at Ripley, N. Y., Oct. 15, 1883, his widow came to live with her daughter. Here she had a happy home till her death, April 24, 1886.

Brother John had only common school privileges for an education, having never entered a High School or College. He was ambitious to get a better education than common schools then offered and this he could get by studying at home. He was soon able to teach a select school and this he did before he was eighteen years of age. This school was conducted in the old Ellis house before it was torn down to give place to a new structure. This was his first teaching. In subsequent years he taught the District School at the time Prof. Alanson Wedge taught the High School of Ripley Village. He afterwards succeeded Prof. Wedge as Principal of the High School. After marriage he and his wife taught the High School at Brocton, N. Y., during the winter of 1864 and 1865. His teaching in all extended through a period of about twelve years, including a period before and after his marriage.

Time passed on. The east half of the Curtis farm was sold to brother Alvin. The small new home built for myself and wife was enlarged and remodeled and all made suitable for a farm-house with adequate accommodations. This was in 1863. In the Spring of 1863 John purchased of father twenty acres of the thirty acres of the Ellis land. He supplemented farming by engaging in the peano and organ trade which added to his income and assisted much in lifting his indebtedness incurred by his purchase of land.

During these years of toil brother John was a constant attendant upon church service. He had for twenty years the superintendency of the Presbyterian Sabbath School, for many years was leader of their Choir. During these years he organized singing classes usually for the winter months, thus teaching the young people the rudiments of music and this greatly helped in maintaining choirs in the churches. For all this service he only had for remuneration the proceeds of a public concert at the end of the term of teaching.

On May 18, 1871 there came a new joy to my brother and his wife in the birth of their first born, a son, whom they named Frederick Adams Tennant. In temperament and disposition the son was much like his father, always a good child, never sowed any wild oats and when he grew into manhood he devoted his energies to self improvement. His father furnished means for his education at an Academy and at College so he was amply fitted for a position of honor and trust which he subsequently found in a position in the Patent Office department of the Government at Washington, D. C. Afterward he became a patent lawyer.

The Baptist church of Ripley township of which brother John was a member, was organized when most of its membership lived on the hill. Its worship was conducted for a number of years in the school-house of the Wattlesburg district. When its members became financially able, a house of worship was built on the northwest corner of land then owned by Col. Ethan Sawin. In a few years the membership of the church was so reduced in numbers by deaths and removals that it was impossible to support a pastor. A few families had moved to Ripley Village or vicinity and this reduced the attendance at the church gatherings till at last Baptist services ceased all together. Meantime Baptists at the Village and vicinity increased in number till at last they came together, a few members in good standing in the church, renewed their covenant with each other and proceeded to receive into their communion such other Baptists as held good letters and those who wished to join the church on profession of their faith in Christ and former baptism. This meeting was held June 27, 1891 in Stanton's Hall. Thus a small and enthusiastic membership was gathered. For a time they worshipped in Stanton's Hall. Soon, however, they settled a pastor, Rev. G. F. Woodbury, and commenced agitating the question of building a house of worship at Ripley Village. They were successful. They built a new house of worship during 1892 and the Spring of 1893, which was dedicated June 27, 1893. This house is of brick, of modern style inside and outside, with a gallery on two adjacent sides and a prayer room in front of the audience room. It has an inclined floor, bent seats, and a platform for a choir in front of the audience room.

I have reviewed the revivifying of the Baptist church of Ripley, its growth and progress, because brother John had a leading and conspicuous part in this period of its history. He was superintendent of their Sabbath School, leader of their choir, a deacon, trustee and a zealous devoted church member. He contributed a large sum for the building of the new church edifice.

Brother John was liberal in his doctrinal belief but his liberality never carried him into a denial of the authority or inspiration of the Christian Scriptures. The Bible to him was God's revelation to man of God as Creator, Ruler and Law-giver, and in Christ, the Lord, as Savior and Redeemer from sin of all men who would accept a free and full salvation.

For a number of years our brother suffered with granulated eyelids. He had the granules removed a few times. At last ulceration took place in both eyes. He went to the Hamot Hospital of Erie, Pa., to receive treatment. On the morning of Aug. 13, 1906, after a treatment in his room by his nurse, he arose and was in the act of dressing himself when he suddenly fell to the floor. The nurse heard the fall, hastened back to the room, but our dear brother John had heard his Savior's call "It is enough, come up higher, enter thou into the joy of thy Lord."

No pen or human tongue can describe the tidal wave of sorrow that swept over the hearts of his devoted and faithful wife and son and all other members of the family. His son Frederick was at the time of his father's death in Washington, D. C. Previous to the death of his father he had lost by death his lovely wife while still in the prime of young womanhood. Her maiden name was Evalena Bell Mason, daughter of Oscar and Flora Bell Mason of Ripley, N. Y. She died at Ripley, Dec. 30, 1896. For the son and husband this was a double portion of bereavement and sorrow when his father was so suddenly taken away. Let us not despair when such waves of sorrow sweep over our souls; rather let us count it all joy when we become partakers of the sufferings of Christ for our sakes, who was "wounded for transgressions and bruised for our iniquities."

The Ripley community deeply lamented our brother John's death. For years he had assisted in the support of their churches, was called upon to furnish singing at their family funerals, and was in many ways a useful and honored citizen and to many a personal friend. He died at the Hamot hospital in Erie, Pa.

Brother John's funeral was held at the new home that he had purchased located directly across the street from the old homestead. His pastor, Rev.   of the Ripley Baptist Church conducted the services. The burial was in the beautiful Ripley cemetery on the Tennant lot where there had been previously erected a beautiful monument of Scotch granite.

> "And I heard a voice saying unto me, Write Blessed
> are the dead which die in the Lord from henceforth;
> Yea, saith the Spirit that they may rest from their la-
> bors, and their works do follow them."
>
> Rev. 14:13.

MEMORIAL POEM.

Our dear brother John, you have gone to your rest,
  Your voice now mingles with the songs of the blest;
Fain would we call thee back to our arms,
  And greet thee, and love thee, with your strong manly charms.

Oft do we shed the hot flowing tear,
  And wonder if possible you are not near;
  Sweet memory brings you so near to the heart,
  That we cannot endure to have you depart.

It seems as if death again had stepped in
  And stirred the deep fountain of grief within;
Yet we know it is better, far better for you
  To be with your Savior, His face now to view.

Would we deprive you of heavenly joys?
  Or stain your white robe with earthly alloy?
Nay, better to wait till we go where you are,
  Than to wish you back here,—far better by far.

So let us take up our everyday tasks,
  Be loyal to Christ, this is all that He asks;
Then when life on earth ends and eternity is nigh
  We will meet you in heaven, bidding earth a good bye.

We hope you didn't know when you went away,
  What a void was left in our hearts every day;
How the loved ones you left were crushed by the blow,
  The depths of whose sorrow God only could know.

If permitted, come often to these earthly scenes,
  And visit your loved ones if only in dreams;
We'll welcome your coming by day or by night,
  We'll sing the old songs with heavenly delight.

If you cannot come here, then watch for our coming,
  On the King's Highway we surely are running;
And by grace we will win, and the Goal we will gain,
  With the King in His Beauty forever to reign.

WILLIAM SELDEN TENNANT.

A Memorial Tribute.

The subject of this Tribute was a son of Moses Selden Tennant and Mary Jane Billings Tennant. He was born at Camden, Lorain Co., Ohio, Feb. 7, 1842. He married Miss Mary Josephine Sutton at Flint, Mich., Aug. 15, 1865. Their family record will be found in this book among the descendants of Selden Tennant and Lydia Allen Tennant who were the grand-parents of William Selden Tennant. After the death of his wife the grandfather moved from   New York State, to Camden, Lorain Co., Ohio, with his family in the year 1846 and purchased a tract of land.

Mr. Tennant's earliest years were spent on the farm. But the farm life was not that which was most congenial to his taste nor did it furnish impetus to his rising ambition to enter upon a vocation in which his mental powers could be employed and his acquisitions in the knowledge of men and human affairs could be used for the good of society and the world. So in early years he sought and obtained, by diligence and perseverance in study, that education which would prepare him for the position and occupation which his aspirations led him to choose. In early life he was graduated from Oberlin College, Ohio.

In 1862 Mr. Tennant came to Flint, Mich., and was chosen Superintendent of the Public Schools. The following Spring he went into the army of the United States as Paymaster's Clerk. At the end of this service he returned to Flint only to enter upon a College Course at the Michigan University at Ann Arbor where he was graduated from the Law Department March 29, 1865. On July 12th of the same year he was admitted to the Bar. He was in Gov. Fenton's law office at Flint until the Spring of 1866 when he went to Saginaw City to finish a term as Superintendent of Schools. After a service of three months he entered into partnership in law with Mr. D. W. Perkins at Saginaw.

His duties in the law office brought him before his fellow citizens as a lawyer of ability worthy of recognition. He had a pleasing address, a well balanced judgment, an analytical mind that could easily sift the chaff from the wheat in the testimonies that would be presented in Court, a conscientiousness that would not justify evil and wrong, nor overlook the principles of right and justice. His thorough knowledge of law and its forms and methods of procedure in the Courts fitted him for the high position to which he was finally called.

In 1874 when the Hon. John Moore retired from the bench of the Circuit Court of Saginaw, Mich., Mr. Tennant was appointed as his successor to serve the balance of the term. At the end of the term his ample fitness for this high office was justly recognized and rewarded by his election to the same office. His district comprised the Tenth Judicial District of Michigan.

As Circuit Judge he served his fellow-citizens for six years from 1874 to 1880.

Mr. Tennant was very social in his nature as the following facts abundantly prove. Soon after his settlement at Saginaw City he united with the Saginaw Valley Lodge of Free and Accepted Masons and afterwards took Knight Templar and Scottish Rite degrees. He was a charter member of the Saginaw Council of the Royal Arcanum and took great interest in its organization, and also helped to organize the State Council, and was the first delegate to the Supreme Council. In 1882 he was elected to the Supreme Regency as 4th Supreme Regent. He tions and at one time was a member of the Knights of Pythias. was much interested in other fraternal and benevolent organiza- He also helped to organize the order of the Royal League.

We have now to relate a sad and mysterious providence, the mystery of which can only be revealed when ternity discloses the strange events of time. In the midst of a high and noble career which had not reached but only anticipated the zenith of its glory, this useful citizen, this noble soul, was stricken down and his lifework ended. While attending the Supreme Council of the Royal Arcanum at Richmond, Va., he met with an accident by falling which resulted in a severe injury to his head.

It was three or four years before the seriousness of this injury appeared in paresis of the brain, the effect of which was mental debility.

Before this accident Mr. Tennant had retired from all official duties in the practice of law. Now all mental labor ceased and he had only to wait for the slow but certain approach of the end of his noble and useful life.

All his family relations had been truly ideal. His mother, wife and children were living at the time of his departure into the spirit ilfe. He was mourned by the citizens of his city and county, by many warm-hearted personal friends and by a devoted family. How often in man's earthly life is he called to face mysteries he cannot solve and concerning which he can only say in the language of the hymnist.

> "Judge not the Lord by feeble sense
> But trust him for his grace;
> Behind a frowning providence
> He hides a smiling face."

Mr. Tennant's death took place at Pontiac, Mich., Feb. 13th, 1897. His funeral was largely attended by citizens and friends. It was conducted under the auspices of the Masonic Order. The President of the Saginaw County Bar Association, Mr. L. T. Durand, appeared before Judge Wilber, and after appropriate remarks moved the adjournment of the Court till after the funeral services, which motion was affirmed by the Court. This shows his standing before the members of the Bar.

Followed by many mourning friends and his bereaved family, the mortal remains of Judge William Selden Tennant was consigned to the grave in the beautiful Oakwood Cemetery at Saginaw City to await the resurrection of the just to life and immortality.

JOHN HARRIS CHAMPION.

A Memorial Tribute.

The author of this work wrote to the editor of the Owasso Free Press, and obtained the following excellent tribute to the memory of Dr. John Harris Champion published in its issue of Aug. 14th, 1895. We quote in full:

Dr. John H. Champion expired at his residence in this city, 407 North Washington street, Tuesday morning, August 13, 1895, aged 80 years and 8 months. He had been an invalid for over seven years; for two weeks past he had failed perceptibly, but was confined to his bed only four days, and the release from life came without a struggle. He was a prominant citizen and a staunch, aggressive Democrat, and before his health failed was active in city, county and state politics—always as a patriotic politician, not as a wire-puller.

John Harris Champion was born in Starkville, Herkimer Co., N. Y., December 13, 1814. At the age of seventeen years he commenced teaching school in his native village. He chose the medical profession and entered the medical department of Hobart College, Geneva, N. Y., from which he was graduated in 1841. In 1842 he was married to Caroline C. Fowler, of Oriskany Falls, N. Y., who survives him. He leaves no children. He practiced his profession thirteen years, but its duties proved too severe for his health, and in 1854 he removed to Adrian, Mich. There he became connected with the Watchtower, a daily and weekly Democratic newspaper, first as editor and later as one of its proprietors. In May, 1866, having some property interests in Shiawassee county, he removed to Owasso, and in the autumn of that year purchased a half interest in The Owasso Press, then published by Messrs. Green and Lee. A few months later his sister-in-law, Mrs. Jane A. Church, purchased the remaining interest, and the firm became J. H. Champion & Co.

Mr. Champion loved newspaper work. He devoted his life to the building up of his paper. His whole soul was in it, his pride was in its success. Under his management The Owosso Press was raised to a high position among the best country newspapers of the state. His close application of business unnerved the system, and in February, 1888, he had an attack of nervous prostration which confined him to his home six weeks. He recovered sufficiently to ride daily to his office on a tricycle and to attend to some light duties, but he was a constant sufferer from vertigo which incapitated him for his former work. The additional labor thrown upon his partner was too heavy and September 4, 1890, the plant was sold to the present proprietor, H. Kirk White. But Mr. Champion never lost interest in his beloved Press. Since he left business, a period of nearly five years, he has never failed to make his trip on his tricycle to this office on Wednesdays to get his Owosso Press in advance of the regular delivery, except when unavoidably prevented from going.

John H. Champion was always a Democrat. He cast his first presidential vote for Martin Van Buren, and ever afterward adhered to the Democratic party as the party for the people, never wavering or losing courage through all its dark days. During his entire newspaper work, covering nearly thirty years, his paper was always staunchly Democratic, and he fought for clean politics.

The growth and prosperity of Owosso were dear to Mr. Champion's heart, and he always gave encouragement to every worthy enterprise. He took great interest in the Ladies' Library from the organization of the Association, and the columns of The Press were always free to everything which could promote its advancement and aid the struggling women in their work.

A striking characteristic of Mr. Champion was his high moral standard of character, and he bore out that standard in his own life. He hated duplicity and loved honesty for its own sake. He will be remembered for sound judgment and integrity of character wherever he was known. Although not a communicant in the Episcopal church he loved its service, and for the past forty years he has been a steady supporter of that church and has served on the vestry of Christ Church, this city.

Mr. Champion leaves four sisters, three in the State of New York and one in Ohio.

The funeral will take place Friday, at 2 o'clock, p. m., from the residence, under the auspices of the Masonic fraternity, Rev. Sherwood Roosevelt officiating.

JAMES FRANCIS PHILLIPS

and

MRS. FANNIE LUCY MILLER PHILLIPS.

James Francis Phillips,, the seventh child and fourth son of William and Olivia (Tennant) Phillips, was born at Pontiac, Oakland County, Michigan, July 28th, 1843.

In his boyhood days he attended what was locally known as the Kessley School, till he reached young manhood, and gained a good education. He was a farmer's son, and remained with his parents up to the time of his marriage. He was of a happy disposition and contributed much to make home a happy place to live. He was fond of reading and music was always a great delight, as he had a fine tenor voice and made good use of it in social circles, at home and in Church service.

It was at the religious services held in a local school house that he made the acquaintance of Miss Frances Lucy Miller. He was then about nineteen years old. They attended a singing school, he was the leading tenor and Miss Miller the leading soprano. In social affairs young Phillips was among the leaders, and often was called upon to serve on committees relating to social and other affairs. The friendly associations between Mr. Phillips and Miss Miller, which were so mutually congenial, ripened into pure and ardent love, and finally lead to their happy marriage. This took place in the Township of Burton, Genesee County, Michigan, March 18th, 1863.

As Mrs. Phillips was an only daughter of her parents, and her help in the house and her husband's help on the farm was very much needed, they remained with her parents for twelve years. During this time the family attended the Methodist Protestant Church. Mr. Phillips was elected Superintendent of the Sabbath School and served them acceptably for four years. By this appointment and service is shown the standing and influence of Mr. Phillips in the Church and community. No one can truthfully estimate what great good was the fruit of these four years of faithful Christian work. May we not hope that much fruit unto Eternal Life was then gathered.

After the death of Mrs. Phillips' mother, the family moved to Owosso, Shiawassee County, Michigan. Here Mr. Phillips purchased a farm of which he was very proud, as it was, in all respects, an excellent property.

During this period of their lives thus far related, six children had been born to them. The record of the births and marriages of these children may be found in Part III, Chapter IV, of this book. They lived and labored together for about six years on the Owosso farm. But Mr. Phillips' health began to fail, and he was compelled to make a change of business and location. So the family moved from Owasso to Bancroft, Michigan, where they lived for three years. From Bancroft they moved to Saginaw, Michigan, and from Saginaw to Bay City, Michigan.

At this City Mr. Phillips engaged in such light work as he could find to do, and being industrious and of a social genial nature, he had no difficulty in finding all the work he was able to do. So he was successful in getting for himelsf and family a comfortable support. He employed help in his business. He had a place furnished him for the tools he used in his business. This place was called for many years the "Phillips Room." He became widely known in the City, formed many pleasant acquaintances, and had many special social favors bestowed upon himself and wife by friends and citizens.

At Bay City, Mr. Phillips and his son Selden Tennant Phillips, built a fine house for the family. This house was beautiful in design and finish. The grounds on which it was located were well cultivated and planted with ornamental shrubbery, vines and flowers, with a small plot of land left for a garden. All seemed to give promise for a permanent happy home. But alas! how little do mortals know what changes a Divine Providence has decreed for them. The following story is told by Mrs. Bessie (Phillips) Baisley, a daughter of Mr. and Mrs. Francis James Phillips. This is the story:

Cleantha Phillips DeHart, a sister of Francis James, came with her two twin granddaughters, Lela and Lola Perry, to Bay City to visit her brother, James, and the two girls' great uncle. The Sunday following their coming, Mr. and Mrs. Phillips' son, Selden Tennant from Saginaw City came to pay a visit to his father and mother and the family. Here was now gathered a loving family group. As all were good singers it was proposed to sing the old song "Grand Father's Chair is Vacant." On this day the son and his family returned to their home. The following day Mr. Phillips took a day off from his work and he and his family and the other guests went to the beach of the lake at Bay City and spent the day in pleasant recreations. Upon returning home from their pleasant trip Mr. Phillips went to his barn to look after his horses. At the door of one of the stalls, while he was carrying a pail of water, he fell to the floor, and died immediately. Grandfather's chair was vacated, but a seat among the heavenly choir was at the same time occupied, and a life that has no end commenced, and a song was sung with a celestial voice, whose music shall never grow faint or cease. "And they sang a new song, saying, Thou art worthy to take the book, and to open the seals thereof; for Thou wast slain, and hast redeemed us to God by thy blood out of every kindred, and tongue, and people, and nation; And hast made us unto our God kings and priests." Rev. V :9 & 10.

After the death of Mr. Phillips, his wife, now widowed, spent her remaining years with her children. She outlived her two daughters, Susie Olivia and Floy Esther, by a few years, the former passing before her mother in 1902, and the latter in 1907.

Mrs. Phillips was a person of deep sympathies and of genial nature; and as she was industrious she aided her children at their homes when with them, and rendered them and their children tender care and sympathy in times of sickness or trial. Toward the last of her life, for over a year, she had failing health which weakened her body and mind. At last the end came, and with her daughter, Bessie (Mrs. Baisley,) at whose home she had been living for a number of years, and her son Selden by her bedside, she calmly slept the sleep of death on the early morning of September 3rd, 1913, at her son's home in Saginaw, Michigan.

It has already been stated in the history of her husband's family, that Mrs. Miller was born in St. Lawrence County, N. Y., May 13th, 1847. She was aged sixty six years, three months and twenty days at her death. She had survived her husband for twelve years. Her remains were taken to Bay City, Michigan, and buried beside her husband.

> Rest weary soul, on the bosom of Love,
>   Life's battle is ended forever;
> The victory is won, the crown has been given,
>   And a union is formed that time cannot sever.
>
> Though separated here for a very brief time,
>   True hearts will yet meet in a happy reunion;
> Drawn by the love that bound them on earth,
>   They'll find in Heaven a sweeter communion.

WILLIAM JEWETT HASTINGS.

The subject of this Memorial Tribute was a son of Henry Hastings and his wife, Esther Olivia Phillips, second child and oldest daughter of William Phillips and his wife Olivia Tennant.

He was born near Flint, Genesee Co., Mich., Dec. 11th, 1852. The maiden name of his great-grandmother was Sarah Selden Jewett who married as her third husband Moses Tennant, Sr., by whom she had four children, Lucy, Olivia, Moses, Asel and Esther.

Mr. Hastings early childhood was spent in Michigan on a farm. He had only the opportunities which the farm life afforded the early settlers of that state.   At his birth-time nearly sixty years ago, much of the territory that is now containing rich farm lands and many beautiful and thriving Villages and Cities, was a "waste howling wilderness" inhabited by Indians and beasts of the forests.   But his parents determined to give their children all the advantages available for education in the rudiments of learning as preparatory for higher advancement and for honorable and useful lives.   Their children were sent to the district school and their school life was supplemented by careful, wise and prudent home training such as parents who take pride in their children's attainments would naturally give.   So Mr. Hastings was in no sense a neglected child in his youth.   These early impulses manifested their good effects in subsequent years in the truly noble and manly life and character which he attained in his maturity.

His education however was not confined to the curriculum of the common school.   His fortune was cast in Cincinnati, Ohio where he had the advatages given to students for higher education.   There he attended the city High School which afforded those better advantages which make for greater mental development and larger acquisitions in the natural sciences and current literature.   Mr. Hastings made the best use he could of these opportunities for a broader education.   He realized however, that school life is only a preparatory stage from which a young man must graduate into a higher and more useful business life.

Mr. Hastings did not attempt to fit himself for a profession. He might have done this for his natural abilities would have justified him in the undertaking.

Now came the period when the young man contemplated settling in life and making for himself a home with its comforts, advantages and ties of friendship and love.   Just at this turning time many young men have faltered, wandered, fallen and made sad wrecks of themselves and their fortunes.   Young Mr. Hastings took the wiser, safer and better course.

Having made the happy acquaintance of Miss Alice Margaret Allen of Tescott, Kansas, they were united in marriage at her home in Tescott on the 10th of February, 1886. The happy life which followed this union of two hearts and lives proved the wisdom of their choice. With sweet harmony and love they ministered to each other's happiness, co-operated in all life's plans and labors, and when children were born to them, home joys were made more joyful, home ties strengthened, and mutual burden bearing lightened all their labors and sweetened all their comforts.

Now Mr. Hastings had reached the noontide of manhood. Now he proved to his family and to the world the elements of strength, of nobility, of wisdom and kindness which were born into his nature and purified by his firm religious faith.

After their marriage Mr. and Mrs. Hastings commenced house-keeping on a farm. Two years later they moved to Topeka, Kan., where they lived for two years. He was employed by the City Trolley Company. From Topeka they moved to Grass Lake, Mich., and remained there for about two years, he working on a farm. Now the family go back to Kansas, to Ottawa County, and a year later to Ossawatomie, Kansas, where he was employed by the Missouri Pacific Railroad for about six years as machinist. At this time his health failed and the family moved onto a farm in Ottawa Co., Kansas, where they lived for six years, then moved to Kansas City, Kan.

About seven years before his death he united with the Christian Church. He was active in the church work as far as his strength would allow. He was an everyday christian, setting an example for his family, the Church and his acquaintances. He was a diligent reader of books, but toward the last days of his life the Holy Scriptures were his choice for reading.

After a life of industry and purity in the fulness of a strong and unwavering faith, Mr. Hastings passed into the Spirit life at his home in Kansas City on the 22nd of Feb. 1912.

No writer can adequately describe in words the sadness and desolation produced by the breaking of family ties when they are strengthened and purified by love. Before such sorrow we sit in holy silence and think only of the mystery of death, the uncertainty of life, and the promises and hopes of the future beyond the grave. Shall we see our loved ones again? Shall we meet them and hold sweet converse with them?

> "Shall we meet beyond the river
> Where the surges cease to roll?
> Where in all the bright forever
> Sorrow ne'er shall press the soul?"

The answer comes through faith to every christian's heart.

"We shall meet beyond the river,
    By and by, by and by;
And the darkness shall be over,
    By and by, by and by;

With the toilsome journey done
And the glorious battle won,
We shall shine forth as the sun,
    By and by, by and by.

There our tears shall all cease flowing,
    By and by, by and by;
And with sweetest rapture knowing,
    By and by, by and by;

All the blest ones who have gone
To the land of life and song,
We with shoutings shall rejoin,
    By and by, by and by."

JOHN FULLER HASTINGS.

The family connections and the dates of the birth and death of John Fuller Hastings may be found in the family record in Chapter III of this Book.

Mr. Hastings was in poor health for many of the last years of his life. He had been an active, progressive business man, thoroughly awake to the responsibilities of life and conscientiously performing his part in the home as a husband and father, and in society as a citizen.

Soon after his marriage to Elizabeth Davison he was taken with the asthma, from which he suffered more or less the rest of his days, and which at last brought him under the shadow of death. Finding that he must have outdoor work, he took a position as fireman and was soon promoted to the position of engineer on the Baltimore and Ohio and Southwestern Railroad which position he held for eighteen years. Soon his health would not permit him to do heavy work. At this crisis the burden of life was then taken up by his family and carried on successfully. This continued until they were enabled to build for themselves a home in the City. Three years after this home was built Mr. Hastings and his father, Henry Hastings, died at this home, the father preceding the son by nine months.

Mr. Hastings was an honored member of the Order of Free and Accepted Masons, taking within one or so of the last degrees of the Order, the thirty-second degree. He was highly respected and much beloved by his fellow citizens and neighbors.

His family relations were ideal. His wife writes to the author "Our home life was beautiful in its fullest sense. He realized he could never get well, so every effort was put forth to educate our children so they might be able to support the home when he was gone. He lived as though each day might be his last, and he desired no one to remember anything unkind or ungenerous of him when he was gone. We love his memory."

The above facts reveal many qualities of true manhood which are worthy of commendation and imitation.

There was manifested in Mr. Hastings' life great moral courage. He would not yield to adversity until ill-health actually compelled him. Many men would have given up the struggle long before. Courageously he held his post of duty until the last of serviceable strength was exhausted. Then his wonderful patience under suffering is worthy of remark. He could not have been so reconciled to his lot had he been without a strong faith in a wise and beneficent Providence who determines our lives and destiny. He who can "kiss the rod that smites him" and can say in his heart "Not my will but Thine be done," must possess a faith.

" —that will not shrink,

Though pressed by every foe,
That will not tremble on the brink
Of any earthly woe."

We discern in Mr. Hastings a strong personality that asserts itself when the exigencies of life demand that a man should have self-reliance, strength and perseverance. These elements predominate in a man who ventures upon positions of trust where his own life and that of others are endangered.

Mr. Hastings was a man of deep sympathies. He could not consider his own well-being and happiness without an equal regard for the well-being of others. This is shown in the most tender love he had for his family, and also in the fraternal relations which he sought with his fellow citizens. It was not in his heart to stand aloof from the world of mankind as if he himself were not human. He could only be himself when he was a man among men.

The long period in which he must have anticipated the end of life, could not have been passed with such courage, calmness and hope without deep religious feelings and convictions. Back over such a life memory lingers in pleasure, however much the heart is broken with the sadness of separation. Such a life contains in itself the promise and hope of immortality.

Toward the close of his life Mr. Hastings saw that he had not reached the height of his early ambition. We do not say that he thought that his life had been a complete failure, only he had not accomplished what he desired. It is not strange that such were his reflections when failing health had robbed him of the strength to do what his ambition longed to accomplish.

The following beautiful lines quoted in a letter to the writer by Mrs. Hastings expresses the feelings of his heart as he looked back over the past:

"My struggling soul may never gain the prize it covets so,
It may not reach the gates of Paradise at sunset's glow,
But I have faith that in the shadows blue at set of sun
I shall be judged by what I've tried to do, not what I have done."
Surely such faith and humility can never lose its reward.

At the funeral there was a large attendance of citizens, neighbors, fraternal brothers, and railroad employees. Thus passed from earth a noble spirit, a generous, sympathetic and affectionate soul that disease and bereavement and disappointment could not crush or embitter.

The Revelator declares: "These are they who coming up through much tribulation and sorrow, have washed their robes and made them white in the blood of the Lamb."

PART FIFTH

Immigration of Tennant Families to America
ANCESTRAL HISTORY
IMPORTANT LETTERS

Organization, Phillips and Tennant Reunion
Interesting Addresses

POEMS BY THE AUTHOR
—and—
CLOSING PRAYER

DANIEL TENNANT OF WATERVILLE, N. Y.

HIS FAMILY, DESCENDANTS AND ANCESTORS,

—BY—

WILLIS H. TENNANT, OF BUFFALO N. Y.

BROTHERS NEWTON P. TENNANT, MARVIN G., ORREN L., and the writer, WILLIS HALE TENNANT, are descended from a long line of ancestors, all prominent New England families of early American history, viz: The Tennants, the Hales, the Leeches and the Mathers. The Tennants and Leeches having emigrated from Scotland.

DANIEL TENNANT, our father, was born at Waterville, Oneida County, N. Y., June 17th, 1802. He was a son of Daniel and Martha Hale Tennant, who was born near Norwich Ct., about 1762. He was a son of Caleb Tennant, born near Norwich Ct., about 1715, who was a son of Daniel Tennant born at Kings Town, Rhode Island, about the year 1685. This Daniel Tennant was a son of Alexander Tennant hereafter referred to, who emigrated from Scotland and who lived at Rock Hill, R. I., as long ago as 1675.

He was raised a farmer, but at the age of 22 years, he was employed to care for, and drive a three horse team between Utica and Albany, a distance of 96 miles hauling whiskey (which was about the only surplus product of the early settlers of that locality), for shipment down the river; and hauling westward from Albany, merchandise which came up the river for distribution through the interior of the state. The next two years he worked on farms by the month. One year he received but $8.00 per month or 30 cents per day, and his board. In 1825, he worked on a farm in Genesee County. The following Spring he started on foot for the wilds of Chautauqua County. His traveling outfit consisted of a bag thrown over his shoulder, in which were a boiled ham, loaves of bread and a table knife. Each day he traveled as far as he could, and slept where night overtook him, but not always under the most desirable circumstances. Arriving at Hartfield, a little settlement near the northeastern shore of Lake Chautauqua late in April, he concluded to rest for a day or two. Before resuming his journey, however, he had purchased a farm having a small clearing upon it, near the Hartfield settlement and Lake Chautauqua. Here he took up his bachelor home. In the following Fall, his brother Austin came on from the east, and soon purchased Father's interests in that farm, which at the present time (1915) is known as the Ecker Farm. Soon after selling, father went to what is known as the Beech Hill section, about three miles from Hartfield and five miles from Mayville, N. Y., and bought a heavily timbered tract of land, inhabited by wolves and other wild animals. In April 1827 he went upon it, cut away some underbrush, erected a rude hut, using earth and brush for a roof, and with a quantity of straw for a bed, he began clearing this wild land and turning into farmland. Soon after, Richard Leech became one of his pioneer neighbors. Two or three years later, Mr. Leech's sister Hephzabah M. Leech came from Deep River Ct., to visit him. Father met her and in due time (March 14th, 1832,) they drove to Westfield, N. Y., a small settlement six or seven miles distant, in a rude home-made sled drawn by an ox-team, and were married. This wild land farm became their home for the remainder of their lives. Father died there in February, 1890, nearly 88 years of age; and nearly sixty-four years after the purchase of the same. The old farm is now owned by his grandson Levant O. Tennant, a son of Orren L. Tennant, and in a few years the same will have been owned by the Tennant family and known as the Tennant Farm for a full century.

HEPHZABAH LEECH-TENNANT, our mother, was born in what is now Erie County, N. Y., January 7th, 1807. She was the daughter of Richard Leech, who was born at Lyme Ct., December 25th, 1774, and Hephzabah Mather of Deep River Ct., who was born February 4th, 1776. After the death of her father, (grandfather Leech), at what is now Buffalo, N. Y., mother returned with grandmother and her brother Richard M., to Deep River Ct. Later she went to Chautauqua County, N. Y., and there met and married our father, Daniel Tennant, with whom she lived until the time of her death July 30th, 1874, at the age of nearly 68 years. She was the mother of six sons and one daughter, three of whom died in infancy. She was a member of the Baptist Church of Mayville, N. Y., and here let me add, no better woman ever lived.

Father's and Mother's family consisted of six sons and one daughter. All were born on the farm five miles northeasterly of Mayville, N. Y. The daughter and two of the sons died in infancy. The others were:

NEWTON P. TENNANT, born June 10th, 1833. He married Martha Jane Baker at her home near Janesville, Wis., about 1861. He returned to Chautauqua County, N. Y., and engaged in farming. In 1868 he moved with his family in a "Prairie schooner" wagon, to the town of Coloma, Waushara County, Wis., and purchased a wild farm, then 40 miles from a post office. A railroad was built through that locality afterwards, and a village sprang up within a mile of his farm. He became a prosperous farmer and died there, February 1st, 1903. His wife died a short time thereafter.

Newton Tennant's children were Lillian, born in Chautauqua County April 26th, 1863. She married Warren A. Baker and lived near Hundock, Wis. with her husband until her death, March 12th, 1915. She is survived by her husband, four children, Omri H., Hazel D., Earle S., and Lester W. Emma R., born in Chautauqua County, May 4th, 1864, died February 28th, 1912. Mary J., born in Chautauqua County, March 30th, 1866; Richard L.., born October 26th, 1869 (Wis.) married ———— ————, who died leaving her husband alone surviving her. Willis H. born (Wis.) April 9th, 1872, never married and died March 11th, 1915; Louise, born (Wis.) July 6th, 1875, died unmarried, March 28th, 1895; Cora B. Holmes, born (Wis.) May 4th, 1877; Lizzie H. Hamilton, born (Wis.) May 26th, 1880; Ella M., born (Wis.) October 8th, 1882, died unmarried, January 28th, 1900; and Ida B. Cotton born (Wis.) April 3d, 1895.

MARVIN G. TENNANT, born August 11th, 1836; farmer by occupation, married Miss Malvina ———— near Janesville, Wis., in 1863. He returned to Chautauqua County, N. Y. Later he returned to Wisconsin and located in the town of Coloma, near his brother Newton, where he resided until his death, May 1st, 1874. One son Emory Tennant, survived him, who married in 1904 and moved to Everson in the State of Washington, where he is now living. He has three daughters.

ORREN L. TENNANT was born September 9th, 1846. By occupation is a farmer and resides at Mayville, N. Y. His first wife was Helen A. Casselman; and their family consisted of five daughters and one son; Bertha A., born October 7th, 1875, married William Garfield; Ethelyn G., born December 4th, 1877, married Wilber A. Crane; Milissa H., born June 16th, 1879, married Monroe Skillie; Libbie G., born April 26th, 1881, married John M. Eckman and Levant O. Tennant born March 7th, 1883, married Mary A. Tanner, born September 30th, 1885, whose family consists of four daughters: Ethelynd M., born November 30th, 1906; Gladys H., born December 20th, 1908; Alice L., born January 12th, 1911; and Lottie J., born July 19th, 1913.

Orren L.'s second wife was Elizabeth Lowden. By her he has no children. In 1890 Orren L. purchased the old Beech Hill farm, which father purchased from the Holland Land Company in 1826. In 1909, he sold it to his son, Levant O., who now owns and occupies the same as his home.

WILLIS H. TENNANT, the writer of this sketch, was born on the home farm in the town of Chautauqua, N. Y., April 20th, 1854; was educated at the "Beech Hill Corners" school; in the Mayville Union School and Painsville Commercial College. To attend school at Mayville he was obliged to travel on foot ten miles per day between the old farm and the

Mayville school house, altogether upwards of 1750 miles; and over country roads which in the winter and spring time, can better be imagined than described. He followed farming and teaching country school until he was 22 years of age. Soon thereafter, December 18th, 1876, he began reading law in Mayville, at the same time paying for his board, working about one of the village hotels. He was admitted to the Bar and licensed to practice before the courts of the New York State at Syracuse in January 1880; was licensed to practice before the U. S. District and Circuit Courts in 1881, and before the U. S. Supreme Court in 1906. In 1884, he married DeEmma Von Valkenburgh, a daughter of Henry Von Valkenburgh, and Ruth Kelsey-Von Valkenburgh, and resided in Mayville, N. Y., and practiced his profession there until December 1909; when he moved with his family to Buffalo and continued the practice in that City. They have three children; Henry F., born March 5th, 1886; Mary V., born December 10, 1889; and Ruth A.,. born May 14th, 1892 While living in Mayville, N. Y., he was Supervisor of the town of Chautauqua, President of the Village, and of the Board of Education for a term of years. One of the great improvements of the State of New York which he advocated from its inception to its completion was the building of the Barge Canal system. In 1905 and 1906, he held the office of Deputy Attorney General of the State of New York during the term of Attorney General Julius M. Mayer of New York.

HENRY F. TENNANT was educated in the Mayville High School and was graduated from the same in 1904. In September of the next year, he entered Cornell University, selecting the Law and language course. In language he specialized in Spanish and French. While in the University he was elected a member of the Psi U., fraternity. He passed the state bar examination at Rochester in January 1909, and soon thereafter was admitted to the Bar of New York State. He finished at the University in June, 1909, receiving the degree L. L. B. In September following, he began practicing law with his father in Mayville, N. Y., and continued to Buffalo in 1910, the firm name being Tennant & Tennant. He entered the diplomatic service as assistant to the Secretary of Legation at Lisbon, Portugal, in October 1910. He was appointed Third Secretary of Embassy at Mexico City in October 1912. In February, 1913, he was appointed Second Secretary of Embassy at Mexico City, and held that office during, and some time after the Revolution which overthrew President Madero. He was appointed Secretary of Legation at Caracas, Venezuela, in August, 1913, and was hastily sent to that city on the U. S. Cruiser "Des Moines" upon the breaking out of the Venezuelan Revolution at that time. While there, he was

Charge d' Affaires for some months.   In January, 1914, he was appointed Consul General and Secretary of Legation at San Salvador C. A., where he went soon after the confirmation of his appointment.   He is now Charge d' Affaires at San Salvador, On May 29th, 1915, he married Miss Paulita Mejia (Ma-he-ah), at San Salvador, C. A., daughter of Hon. Frederico Mejia, for many years Salvadorian Minister to the United States, residing in Washington, D. C.

MARY TENNANT.   Educated in Mayville High School and Brenau College-Conservatory, Gainsville, Ga., specialized in voiec culture and later became a contralto singer of note.

RUTH TENNANT.   Educated in Mayville High School and Select School for Girls, Buffalo, N. Y.

DANIEL TENNANT, our grandfather (son of Caleb) was born near Norwich, Ct., in 1762.   Later, at the age of 18, he enlisted in Col. Canfield's regiment and became one of the Revolutionary Army.   He was at West Point at the time of the treason of Arnold, and saw the cannons of the Americans spiked to destroy their usefulness, preparatory to the surrender of that fort to the British.   After the war, he returned to Norwich Ct., and some years later met, eloped with and married Martha Hale.   Grandfather was a shoemaker by trade.   Later they settled at Waterville, Oneida County, N. Y., where they lived and reared a family of four children, two sons and two daughters: Orilla, who died young and unmarried; Austin, born April 4th, 1799; Daniel (our father) born June 17th, 1802, and Betsey, who married, but died leaving no children.   In 1827 his wife having died a short time before, grandfather left Waterville, N. Y., and went to live with his sons Austin and Daniel, who had located near Hartfield, Chautauqua county, the year before.   With them he made his home until he died, which was in 1850, at the age of nearly 88 years.

Grandfather was a cousin of Hon. Moses Asel Tennant, who at the time of his death, Nov. 1st, 1876, and for 47 1-2 years prior to that time had resided at Ripley, Chautauqua county.   During the years grandfather lived at Hartfield, he and his cousin Moses A., exchanged visits from time to time.   Grandfather was a good walker for a man of his years, and usually traveled on foot, when making his visits at Ripley, a distance of 15 miles.   Grandfather was a member of the Presbyterian church.   He is buried in the Mayville cemetery, where an appropriate headstone marks his resting place.

MARTHA HALE TENNANT, our grandmother, mentioned above, was born near Covington Ct., about 1772.   She married Daniel Tennant, was the mother of two sons and two daughters; was a member of the Presbyterian church of Waterville, N. Y.,

and died at that village in 1825 or 1826. She was a daughter of
Dr. Hale who was an uncle of Nathan Hale. Dr. Hale was born
in Beverly, Mass., about 1725. He was a son of Samuel Hale
born at Beverly, Mass., in April 1684, who was a son of John
Hale of Beverly, Mass., was born about 1636, who was a son of
Robert Hale who came to America in 1630 or 1631. The Rev.
Edward Everett Hale, former Senator Eugene Hale of Maine,
and other distinguished Americans of that name, were descended from the line of Samuel, John and Robert Hale. Grandmother
was cousin of Nathan Hale, who was captured by the British
within their lines on Long Island in 1776, and who was later convicted as an American spy, and executed by them.

RICHARD LEECH, our grandfather on mother's side, was born
of Scotch ancestry at Lyme, Ct., December 25th, 1774. He married Hephzabah Mather November 27th, 1799, and soon thereafter settled on what was then a wild west farm, at what is now
known as Cold Springs, in the City of Buffalo, N. Y., where
three children were born: Elisha E., born September 2nd, 1800,
and who died December 9th, 1802; Richard M., born May 30th,
1803, and who died at Mansfield, Ohio, December 5th, 1861,
leaving two sons and one daughter, all of whom died without
children. Grandfather Leech had been elected a member of the
New York State Legislature, a few days before his death. He
was buried in what is now Buffalo, N. Y., but where is not
known.

HEPHZABAH MATHER LEECH, our grandmother on mother's
side, was born at Deep River Ct., February 4th, 1776, married
Richard Leech of Lyme Ct., November 27th, 1799. After the
death of her husband in November 1813, she returned to Deep
River Ct., with her two children, Richard and Hephzabah. Both
later went west and located at what is known as Beech
Hill near Hartfield, Chautauqua County, N. Y. After her return to Deep River Ct., grandmother Leech married a Mr. Marvin, a brother of Capt. Dan Marvin of Deep River Ct., with
whom she lived until her death August 19th, 1847 at the age of
72 years. Her husband, Mr. Marvin followed her by death, 16
days later, September 4th, 1847. Grandmother's sister Huldah
married Capt. Dan Marvin. Grandmother was a sister of Joseph Higgins Mather and the daughter of John Mather of
Lyme Ct., who was a son of John Mather Sr., who was a son of
Joseph Mather, who was a son of Richard Mather, who was a
son of Timothy Mather, who was a son of Rev. Richard Mather,
who was a son of Thomas Mather, born in England, and who
was a son of John Mather who also was born in England. (See
Mather Geanealogy in Hartford, Ct., Library).

AUSTIN TENNANT, (uncle of the writer, and son of Daniel Tennant of Waterville, N. Y.) was born at that place in April 1799. He was well educated and taught school both in that locality and in Chautauqua county. He went from Waterville to Hartfield, N. Y., in the Fall of 1826, and in the following Spring married Laura Morgan, a daughter of Amos Morgan, who was the father of Amos and Harvey Morgan, later of Buffalo. He united with the Baptist church of Mayville, N. Y., and was chairman of the building committee that erected the present church in that village in 1834. Concerning his family and other incidents of the lives of his father, the writer has the written statement of his oldest son Amos H. Tennant, made in March, 1912, as follows: "By his first wife my father had three children Amos H. born at Hartfield April 1st, 1828; James H., born in December 1829, and Sarah born in 1833. His first wife Laura Morgan Tennant died in March 1834. In April 1835 father married Eliza Dibble, by whom he had eleven children. After living with his second wife at Hartfield for a few years, father sold his farm and moved to Ashtabula, Ohio, where he purchased another farm, upon which he lived until the time of his death, in 1892, at the age of 93 years. His children by his second wife were Laura who married, but died without children; Jarius, who a few years ago was living unmarried in southern S. Dakota; Edgar, who became a physician, finally went to California, where he died, leaving no wife or children. Rebecca married a Mr. Cole, lived and died on father's farm at Ashtabula, O., leaving two sons and two daughters; John died leaving neither wife or children; the next was a boy who lived but a week; Henry, is living in Kansas, a prosperous farmer; with a nice family. Eugene, a lad of 14, lost his life in a fire which destroyed the family home at Ashtabula; Delia, who married Andrew Jackson, has two sons and a daughter; there were two more boys who died while infants.

JAMES H. TENNANT, my own brother, died at his home in Houston, Texas, in 1906 or 1907 at the age of 77 or 78 years. He was a prosperous businessman throughout his lifetime. He left two sons, George Boyce Tennant, who lives in Brooklyn, N. Y., and Joseph A., who lives with his mother at Houston. My sister, Sarah A. never had any children

AMOS H. TENNANT, oldest son of Austin Tennant, was born at Hartfield, N. Y., April 1, 1828. Of himself and family he says: "My first wife was Amelia Newton. By her we had five children, all of whom died in childhood. She died in 1864. My second wife was Polly A. Platner, by whom we had two children, one son and one daughter: James Austin Tennant, who is now living unmarried at Sedall, Ill., and Armelia who first married George Creaser, by whom she had four sons. Her second husband was Albert Sprague. By him she has no children. She now lives in Cleveland, Ohio.

"Grandfather Daniel lived with my father most of the time he lived in Chautauqua county and died at our home in January, 1850. He lived there from the time of my birth until I left home in 1848 at the age of twenty years, when I went to Jamestown to learn the blacksmithing trade, which I did. Grandfather used to tell me much about his experiences in the Revolutionary war. He told me he was present at West Point at the time of the treason of Arnold, and saw them spiking the American cannon with rat-tail files. He said his wife was a cousin of Nathan Hale whom the British captured and executed as a 'spy', that grandfather spoke of him when talking of him as "my wife's cousin." He said Hale had a large hollow ball in which he inserted a finely written sketch of what he had learned as a spy, and when arrested he swallowed it. He was forced to take an emetic and reproduce it, and that was the evidence that caused his conviction.

Grandfather and the Hon. Moses A. Tennant of Ripley were well acquainted and were accustomed to visit each other, exchanging visits usually once each year. Grandfather was a great walker, and usually went on foot to Ripley. They called each other cousins and talked about their families. Grandfather was a shorter man than Moses A. The last time I saw Moses A. was at our house in the Fall before I went to Jamestown in 1848; excepting, that he with one of his sons attended grandfather's funeral in January 1850. On one occasion when Moses A. was visiting grandfather at Hartfield, Moses said to him: "Dan, from what we know of the Tennants they are just good, every day people. We never have heard of any of them being president or in prison."

That in the opinion of the writer, is as true today as then—75 years ago. The Tennants, so far as known, have been people of good habits, industrious, self supporting, reasonably prosperous, temperate, law abiding and law sustaining."

AMOS H. TENNANT, who furnished the narrative above quoted, died at his home in Mayville, N. Y., April 15th, 1912, at the age of 84 years, and his wife, Polly A., died just a week later.

GEORGE BOYCE TENNANT, son of James H. Tennant, born December 6, 1863. Eentered U. S. Naval Academy at Annapolis from Michigan, class of 1885. From among many distinguished engineers, he was selected to superintend the construction of Machinery Hall for the Centennial Exposition at Chicago in 1893. He married Miss Viola Parish. They have two children, Philip Tennant, born January 12th, 1887 and Louise Tennant, born December 2nd, 1889. Their home is at Amburg, Va.

JOSEPH A. TENNANT, second son of James H. Tennant, was born at Houston, Tex., November 27th, 1888. Educated at University of Texas, 1910, A. B.; Massachusetts Institute of Technology, 1913, S. B., Elec. Eng. Fraternities: Theta Xi and Phi Beta Kappa. He married Miss Lucile Borden, University of Texas, 1913, B. A., member of the Kappa Kappa Gamma Sorority. Their home is at Houston, Tex.

ALEXANDER TENNANT, mentioned above, and a native of Scotland, who is said to have been a strict Presbyterian, emigrated to America and lived in Kings Town, R. I., in 1675, with his wife, whose name was Prudence. They had four children, Hannah, born 1680 who never married; Daniel, born 1685, who married Ann Green; John, born 1689, who married Martha Remington; and Abigail, who married Samuel Tefft. Daniel, (the son of Alexander) lived in Rock Hill, R. I., had two sons, Caleb (born 1730) and Samuel. Both CALEB and SAMUEL migrated to Connecticut and lived in Bozrah, near Norwich, Ct.

JOHN TENNANT, born 1689, the second son of Alexander, migrated to and lived in New London, Ct., and, it is believed, was the ancestor of Charles L. Tennant (who married Elizabeth Deckwith), and who with his brother, Timothy Tennant, and their families migrated with ox-teams from New London, Ct., to Bethany, Wayne County, Pa., crossing the Hudson River on their way at Newburg, immediately after the closing of the Revolutionary War. The name of the father of Charles L. and Timothy is not known to the writer. Hon. Horace G. Tennant of Schoharie, N. Y., descended from this line.

Reference to the map of the State of Connecticut discloses therein a town in New London County by the name of Bozrah. Adjoining this is the town of Norwich in which the county seat of New London County is located. A few miles from Bozrah to the west, is the town of East Hadlen. Here in this immediate locality Caleb and Samuel, sons of Daniel Tennant, of Rhode Island, located and reared their families. How many children they had is not known by the writer with the certainty that could be wished. It is certain that one had a son by the name of Daniel. He was the paternal father of the writer, and was born in 1762 and lived near Norwich, Ct., until he was eighteen when he joined Colonel Canfield's militia regiment at Norwich, Ct., in 1779 or 1780. He is understood to have been the son of Caleb.

MOSES A. TENNANT of Ripley, N. Y., and he were personal friends while living in Chautauqua County between 1830 and 1850. They said they were cousins and visited each other as such. Grandfather Daniel was born in 1762 and Moses A. about

1800.   Thus, it appears that grandfather was one generation
ahead of Moses A., and therefore probably they were not first
cousins.   Moses A.'s father, Moses Tennant, married Betsey
Tennant and had four children, Selden, Betsey, Polly and David,
before he married Sarah Jewett Shaw about 1792; and therefore
he was probably born about 1760, and was about the same age as
grandfather.   If his son, Moses A., and the writer's grandfather
were second cousins, then Daniel of Norwich, Ct., and Moses
were first cousins.

Who was Betsey Tennant, the wife of Moses Tennant?   The
writer cannot answer the question except to say that his father,
Daniel Tennant, born in 1802, said his father; Daniel, had a sister
Betsey and a daughter Betsey.   It is therefore possible that
grandfather's sister Betsey, became the wife of Moses Tennant.

Who was the father of Moses Tennant?   This is not known
for certain, but it is understood he was Samuel Tennant, a son
of Daniel of Rhode Island, who later migrated from Bozrah,
New London County, Ct., and settled at or near Springfield ,Ot-
sego County, N. Y., where he lived the remainder of his life.

The records of the Revolutionary War disclose that grandfather, DANIEL TENNANT, enlisted as a private in Colonel Canfield's regiment, organized at Norwich, Ct., in 1779 or 1780, and
was at West Point in 1781.   CALEB TENNANT was a corporal in
Captain Hale's regiment organized in 1776.   JOHN TENNANT
was a lieutenant in Captain Eliphlet Horn's company of Minute
Men of East Hadden, Ct., and REV. WILLIAM TENNANT of
Greenfield, Ct., was chaplain for Mott's and Swift's regiment.
JOHN TENNANT, above referred to, married Elizabeth Loomis
and became the father of Delinda Tennant, who married Moses
A. Tennant of Ripley, N. Y.

LETTER FROM AMOS H. TENNANT.

The following letter is published in this genealogy for the reason that the writer's grandfather, Daniel Tennant, and Moses Tennant, Sr., the father of Moses Asel Tennant, were first cousins. The letter speaks for itself.

STATEMENT OF MR. AMOS TENNANT,
MAYVILLE, MARCH 12TH, 1909.

My name is Amos H. Tennant. I was born at Hartfield, Chautauqua County, N. Y., April 1st, 1828. My father's name was Austin Tennant, who resided on the farm just east of the 3-corners on the roads leading from Hartfield to Jamestown, Stockton and Sinclairville, and on the Sinclairville road, on the farm now owned by Ernest W. Ecker. My father, Austin Tennant, was a son of Daniel Tennant, who was born in Connecticut about 1762, and entered the Continental Army (Col. Canfield's Regiment) at Norwich in that State, at the age of 18 years; and was at West Point at the time of Arnold's treason. My father was born at Waterville, N. Y. (Oneida County) in April, 1799. His only brother was Daniel Tennant, who came to Hartfield in the Spring of 1826, and bought the farm above mentioned. In the fall of 1826 my father came and bought out Daniel and he, Daniel, went up on what is known as Beach Hill, in the northeast part of the town and purchased what has been since known as the Tennant farm and lived there until he died in 1890 at the age of 88. In January, 1827, Daniel went back east to Waterville, N. Y., and brought my grandfather, Daniel Tennant, back with him and he (grandfather) lived with my father and Daniel, until he died in January, 1850, at our house near Hartfield, at the age of 87 years. I lived at home with father and grandfather from infancy to November, 1848, when I went to Jamestown to learn the trade of blacksmithing with William Broadhead; with whom I lived and worked for two years and a half. During my boyhood I knew Mr. Moses A. Tennant who lived at Ripley, N. Y. He was accustomed to come to our house once a year, usually in the fall, stay the day, make a visit and generally took back a quantity of apples, as we had a very good orchard, for that period in the early history. Grandfather used to go to Ripley once a year and return the visit of Moses, and usually stayed a day or two, as he usually walked, he being a good walker, for a man of his age. He and Moses seemed well acquainted with each other, and called each other cousins. They

stated that their fathers were brothers. I do not remember the
name of grandfather's father's name, but it almost seems that it
too was Daniel. Grandfather was a shorter man than Moses.
Moses was rather a tall man, and grandfather was about 5 feet
and 9 or 10 inches in height. The last time I saw Moses was at
father's house visiting grandfather in the fall of 1848 before I
went to Jamestown; excepting, that he, Moses, came with one of
his sons to attend grandfather's funeral in January, 1850. I returned to Jamestown and never saw Moses after the day of the
funeral. Grandfather used to tell me time and again about his
war experiences, and much in detail about what occurred at West
Point where he saw, among other things the execution of
Arnold's order to spike the cannon, using rat-tail files, driving
them in the vent or thumb-hole and breaking them off in there.

Grandfather married a Hale girl, who was a cousin of Nathan
Hale, whom the British caught in New York and executed as a
spy before the capture of Andre. Grandfather said that when
the British caught Nathan Hale he had a hollow ball, and he
swallowed it, and then they gave him medicine that made him
vomit it up, and inside of that was a letter very completely written, which told the story of his work as a spy, and convicted him
of being a spy. The ball was as large as it was possible for a
man to swallow. I think grandmother's first name was Arrillia
or Orilla. Father had one other girl (Betsy) who came here and
married; first, a man at DeWittville by the name of Job Toby;
their house took fire and they got Betsy out, but her husband per-
ished in the flames; after a while she married a man by the name
of Haskins, and after a while he moved from Busti and went to
Pennsylvania, I think to Crawford County, where he died, and
after that she married a man by the name of McClintock. She
died about 35 years ago. She never had any children. My father's sister, Aurilla, died when she was quite young. She never
came to Chautauqua County. My father's family consisted of his
first wife who was Laura Morgan, daughter of Russell Morgan.
She was a sister of Amos Morgan and Harvey Morgan, and several other brothers of Buffalo, N. Y. I was named after Amos
Morgan. Father had three children by his first wife. Myself,
James H. and Sarah A. James is dead and Sarah is living, I
think in Erie, Pa., at this time. She was born in August, 1833.
Sarah Ann never had any children. James left two children,
George Boyce Tennant of Brooklyn and Joseph who now lives in
Houston, Texas. My mother died in March, 1834. In April,
1835, father married again to Eliza Dibble. By her he had 11
children: Laura Tennant married and died without children.
Jarius, who if living, is in Southern Dakota; I think he never
married. Edgar Tennant became a physician, and finally went to

California. He had one child, who died. He left no wife or children. Rebecca, who married a Mr. Cole and lived and died at Ashtabula, Ohio, leaving two girls and two boys who now live at or near Ashtabula. John died without being married or leaving children. The next was a boy who lived only about a week. Henry, who lives in Kansas, or did the last I knew of him. Have not heard from him personally, but his sister, Delia, told me a few years ago that he was living in Kansas and had a good farm and a nice family. Eugene was next, who was burned to death at the age of 14 when their home was destroyed at Ashtabula. Then there was Delia, who married Mr. Jackson and they had three children, two sons and one daughter. There was another who died when a baby or when very young—his name was Peter. And still another who died young.

I married for my second wife Anna P. Platner by whom I had two children, Austin and Armelia—who married George Creaser for first husband, and Albert Sprague for second husband. My first wife was Armelia Newton. She died in the spring of 1864— March. By her we had five children, all of whom died in childhood. My father, Austin Tennant, died in 1892, 93 years of age, at Ashtabula, Ohio.

AMOS H. TENNANT.

(Amos H. Tennant died at his home in Mayville, Chautauqua County, N. Y., April 15, 1912. His beloved wife survived him but one week, and died at the same place April 22, 1912. Their remains were buried in the beautiful cemetery at Mayville.)

MOSES ASEL TENNANT FAMILY

EARLY SETTLEMENT AT RIPLEY.

Upon the arrival of the family at Ripley, N. Y., in the Spring of 1833, they moved into a two-room log house located south of what was known as "Palmer's Gulf" and on the west side of the Wattlesburg Road, on a farm afterwards known as the "Connelly" farm. Rev. John Sawin's family had already settled in a log house on the east side of the road, located nearer the Gulf. This property was afterwards owned by Platt Webster, and here his family lived for a number of years up to the time of the death of Mrs. Webster.

The Tennant family lived at this first place of settlement for about two years. Here the first child born in Chautauqua County was added to the family group. This child was the author of this Genealogy, born August 7th, 1834.

From the above named place the family moved into a log house located west of the Wattlesburg road but north of Palmer's Gulf fully a half mile. Here the eighth child was born, a daughter who was named Ellen Delinda. She died in infancy. Her birthday was October 20th, 1836.

The next move was to the side-hill road into a house located on the southeast corner of the junction formed by the Wattlesburg and side-hill roads, and afterwards owned and occupied by a family named Alford.

The third movement of the family was to Ripley Village, then named Quincy, into a frame house located on the north side of the Buffalo Road and just east of where the Wattlesburg road terminates. This was the Joseph White property. Across the street was the reisdence of Henry Shaver, Sr., familiarly known as "Uncle Hank." At this home the ninth child was born, a daughter named Fannie Oliva, February 18th, 1838.

During this year, 1838, the old home on Ripley Hill was bought of a Mr. Tupper. The farm contained one hundred acres. The south west corner of which was a little east of where the Baptist Church is now located. It extended back nearly three-quarters of a mile and the extreme north end was north of the south branch of the twenty-mile creek. About forty acres of the front part of this farm was cleared and converted into meadow and pasture land. Some of the rest had been "slashed" and the balance was a heavy forest of hemlock, beech, maple, basswood and birch, very few elm and no whitewood. In a large measure the hemlock prevailed. The house was built of logs with two rooms and a frame leanto on the west side with two rooms and a small pantry between. Here our brother John, the youngest and tenth child of the family, was born May 30th, 1839.

On this farm the family lived until the Spring of 1844 when another move was made to Ripley Village, and the family went into the Shaver Hotel. This move did not prove profitable nor satisfactory. In September of this year the two oldest sisters, Eliza and Julia, were married, and immediately afterwards the family moved back to the old farm leaving the two married sisters with their husbands to occupy and keep the hotel.

It was during the period from 1838 to 1844 that a large portion of the farm clearing took place. It was not however, completed; much work remained to be done.   When the family returned to the old farm in the Fall of 1844 it was somewhat diminished in numbers by marriage.   The oldest son Alvin was at home and work went on at good pace.   The family kept a small dairy of four or five cows and a flock of sheep from fifty to one hundred.

During the years of 1845 and 1846 a new frame house was built and the old log house was taken down.   The oldest son, Alvin, was married September 26th, 1847.   Now another move was made.   Our father took the Anson Goodrich farm in West Ripley Village on shares and in the Spring of 1848 the family moved to the Village again.   The son Alvin and his wife moved into the new house on the old farm.

The Goodrich farm consisted of eighty acres on the Main Road and one hundred acres on the side-hill road.   We kept thirteen cows and about one hundred sheep.   The writer was thirteen years old past.   The older children were all married and gone from home and only the three younger left.   We occupied and worked this farm for two years.   Again in the Spring of 1850 the family moved back into the new house on the old farm where they lived until the Spring of 1852.   This Spring our father sold the old farm on the hill to Rev. Ira Stoddard and purchased the Edmund Curtis farm in East Ripley Village, and the family moved on to it.   This farm consisted of about eighty-two acres, divided obliquely by a road leading from the Main to the Lake Shore road.   Here the family lived until after the marriage of the three youngest children.   In the year 1855 or 1856 father bought of the heirs of a Mrs. Ellis eighty acres of land lying west of the Curtis farm and adjoining it.   He sold thirty-five acres of this to brother Delos.   After my marriage in the Spring of 1859 father built for me and my wife a little home on the front of the forty-five acres he retained.   In this home we lived till the Spring of 1863.

In the Spring of 1863 I entered upon the work of the Christian ministry at Clymer, N. Y., and moved to that village the same Spring.

Brother John and his wife moved into the house of his parents on the Curtis farm, in the Spring of 1863, after their marriage in September, 1862.   From this time on, during the life time of our parents, brother John and his wife lived with them.

The following changes were made in the sales of property by the family.

Delos purchased the undivided half of the Henry Shaver farm located north of the Main Road for twelve hundred dollars. The deed was dated January 8th, 1850.

Father bought of Edmund Curtis a farm of eighty-two acres in the Spring of 1852. Deed dated February 6th, 1852. Afterwards he bought of the heirs of the widow Ellis eighty acres of land located on the west side and adjacent to the Curtis farm. This was a beautiful farm. The purchase was made in the year 1856 or 1857. Father sold off from the west side of the Ellis farm, thirty-five acres to Delos. On this purchase Delos built a fine house that made his family an elegant home. Subsequently he sold twenty acres of this purchase to George Mason for ten hundred and fifty dollars. This twenty acres was the east part of the thirty-five acres of the Ellis property he had purchased. The deed was dated May 1st, 1862.

George Mason sold this twenty acres to John for ten hundred and fifty dollars, subject to a mortgage of two hundred dollars. The deed was dated February 24th, 1863.

In the Spring of 1863, father sold to Alvin all that part of the Curtis farm located east of the cross road leading to the lake. This included about thirty-five acres. This was the year of my settlement at Clymer, Chautauqua County, N. Y., as pastor of the Baptist church. I moved out of the new house father had built for me. In the year 1863 father finished the house by building the upright part, a story and a half on the west end of the ell part. This now made a commodious home for father and John, now one family. Subsequently the ell part was enlarged by the addition of the second story and a back kitchen. In 1864 father sold to John four acres of the Ellis farm for two hundred and seventy-five dollars, deed dated April 1st, 1864.

Alvin lived on the property he bought of father from the Spring of 1863 to the Spring of 1890, twenty-seven years. He was now too old to work a farm, so he sold out the thirty-five acres to Mr. Crocker and son. The deed was dated May 1, 1890. In 1900 Mr. Crocker sold this property to the Wiley family for six thousand dollars. The deed was dated April 29th, 1900.

Brother John bought of Mr. Tarbox a house and lot located directly across the Main Road in East Ripley Village from the old home. Here he lived at the time of his death, August 13th, 1906. At the time of his death he owned all that had not been sold of the Ellis farm, and of the Curtis farm west of the Cross road leading to the lake, and in addition a portion of the Ethan Allan farm, including about   acres, located on the Lake Shore road. He had set out to grapes about sixty-five acres of his farm. His widow and his son Frederick now (1914) own this land and obtain from it an annual income of about four thousand dollars. John was the wealthiest member of the Tennant family at his death.

In this article the writer has indicated some of the changes made by the Tennant family at Ripley in residence and property ownership. This will be interesting only to future generations. For future generations is this work prepared and published and not so much for present generation, to whom the above mentioned facts may be familiar.

THE PHILLIPS AND TENNANT REUNION, 1912.

The following paper was read by its author, Mrs. Josephine M. Tennant of Saginaw, Mich., at the reunion held at the home of Mr. and Mrs. Ellis Perry of Bridgeport Township, Saginaw Co., Mich., on August 7th, 1912. The author of this Genealogy was present at this gathering. He ventures to publish it, notwithstanding the complimentary references to himself. The names found in this paper are names of families related to each and descendants of a common parentage.

AUGUST 7th, 1912 REUNION.

"There comes a time whate'er betide, when every man and woman must lay aside their sceptred pride and just be nice and human." So, when asked to "prepare something for this occasion" we threw every obstacle aside and prepared the following story, combining names as best we could so far as we knew them.

August 7, 1912 brought a meeting of interested ones to the pleasant home, whose Tennants proved a royal host and hostess. Some came on the inter Reuben; some walked; others in conveyances reminding us of Mother Shipton's famous prophecy in the year 1485, that " carriages without horses should go—" These auto satisfy the lords of creation. John Rhoda grey nag whose Mary pranks caused to Holden in Ernest. William said: "When you get home you give him Jessie." On reaching the stable we heard the call, "Phil, Lipsy is lame, better take him to a Black-Smith. Don't ride him. He will be Leadbetter having nothing to Carrie. Among the guests was a famous writer, Milton by name; not the author of Paradise Lost, but of past and present periods, tracing each generation of the Tennant family

back to Darwin. He is very Frank in his statements and in his
own De(ar)Hart Perryshes the idea of our being descendants
of the monkey tribe, even tho some of us Everettempt Jimnastics.

Today is the birthday of our Emmanent cousin.
"Oh be thou blest with all that Heaven can send,
Long health, long life, long pleasure, and a friend."

Our latest Poet with the very uncommon name of Smith entertained us delightfully with a Poem written especially for the
occasion. Royalty too was present in the person of an Earl
from Co. Kent, Ireland.

The table was Georgeously arranged with different flowers and
the cloth was Huckinstead of Damask, filled with the good things
provided for the feast. Harriet more than her share. Anxiety
was felt lesther appetite should prove too much for her. We had
Blackberries, Raspberries, and Kingsburys. The apples unfor-
tunately were water coraed, but we Etta lot of them.

Hollenbeckoned to Bessie and gave her a SMcLeod enough to
be heard for some distance. He being a great Joeker. We bade
our Host and Hostess Goodbye, thanking them for their generous hospitality, and started for our homes, stopping on our way
to Sarah-nade Emily and Florence.

This red-letter day will long be remembered for the festivity
and meeting of friends old and new, every one of them being
jolly good Fellows.

This part of the address was made in the presentation of a
birth-day present to the author. The present was "Travels in
Holy Land by Van Dyke."
Mr. President:

One year ago a stranger came within our gates, one of our
kindred. We gave him a hearty welcome and the glad hand of
fellowship, accepting his right to be one of the tribe. Today he
is with us again. We are glad to greet him and hope that so
long as he can he will join us annually in our reunions. For
many years he gave of his time and talent to minister unto an
appreciative people, work well done. He with his good wife are
quietly passing their days amid pleasant surroundings. The poet
Bobbie Burns, described their present life in his touching poem.

"John Anderson, my John,
We've climbed the hill together,
And many a happy day John
We've had with one another.

Now we must totter down John,
But hand in hand we'll go,
And sleep together at the foot,
John Anderson, my jo."

Today we celebrate the birthday of our guest, uniting in a gift as a slight token of our love and good wishes. When you return to your home beside the Silver water, as you read its pages, our forms, our faces, the words of good cheer, shall pass before you like a dream, so we shall be held in memory dear, as we shall hold you in our heart of hearts.

"The sweetest music ever heard.
The sweetest perfume ever stirred,
Cannot compare with this dear word,
The simple sweet, "God Bless you."

A POEM.

The following poem was read at this Reunion by Mr. William Smith, the Author. It chimed in most pleasantly with many other delightful things which all enjoyed on this occasion.

Mr. Chairman, allow me to make intimation,

We're here in response to your kind invitation.
But I've no intention to make a sensation
    By what I am going to say;
Yet, I'm glad to be here this joyous occasion

    On this our reunion day.
The family I see here is well represented,
    Surveying the company this I commented:
Apparently prosperous, happy, contented,

    And this I remark by the way:
And I hope that our friendships more closely cemented
    By this our reunion day.
We're men representing every profession,

    A lawyer to help us to get in possession;
A minister also to give us expression,
    Or keep us from going astray;
But we've no intention to make a confession,

    On this our reunion day.
We've mechanics, a postman, engineers, farmers,
    All peaceable citzens, none are alarmers,
If I am not led astray.

Our wives and our sweethearts they are the charmers,
On every reunion day.
We've Perry and Leadbetter, Covert, Dehart,
These names are familiar we have them by heart.

A Simons, Van Curran, and Brown he's a plumber,
And Potter and Bradley and Harry the drummer.
A butcher we have but no Killings allowed,
And Comstock, and Jacobs, and builder McLeod.

A doctor that punches but revenge will not harbour,
And Farwell and Hastings and Perry the barber.
And Charley tho fat he can run like the dickens
And Jewet is also a farmer of chickens.

And Holenbask, Kingsbury, Hackans and Auton,
But we lack a policeman to handle the baton.
A Rice and a Kent, a Wentworth and Russell,
And some that I mention are men of some muscle.

We all know the Philipses, Carry the Tennant,
But we haven't forgotten a judge that was Lennant
But ladies it's easy for us to surmise,
Our success is due to your enterprise.
The meeting this year I am free to confess
And we'll join in pronouncing a splendid success.

The following is a Letter addressed to his sister, Wealthy by the author, and was read at a family reunion held at the home of her oldest son, Gurdon M. Wattles of Buffalo, N. Y., on the 25th of December, 1912. The poem contains the names of her husband, Erbin Cone Wattles and the given names of all her children and grand-children, both of the living and the dead.

A CHRISTMAS GREETING.

Dear Sister Wealthy, tis Christmas time now,
And we must renew our most solemn vow
To be loyal and true to our Savior and King,
Who suffered and died, salvation to bring

To souls that are sinful and under the ban
Of God's holy law, once given to man.
He arose from the dead and ascended on high,
That sinners unworthy to God may draw nigh.

'Tis a time for rejoicing and giving of gifts
To friends and to loved ones, to the needy adrift
Over life's stormy sea, and who may be tossed
On unfriendly shores, most helpless and lost.

Since August 24th, in 1830, eighty-three years
Have passed over your life, and now there appears
Bright visions of glory as by faith you now see,
The end of this life, the dawn of eternity.

Many years ago, to you grace was given,
To forsake the vain world and gain treasures in heaven;
And now you await God's promise to test,
That his faithful children shall enter His rest.

Your life has been checkered with pleasure and sorrow,
Not knowing what next might happen tomorrow.
'Twas 1845 in the month of October,
On the 22nd day (it was not a day over),

When Erbin C. Wattles led you forth to the altar
Of marriage; your heart did not falter,
Though young as you were you performed all your part,
For love lightened your burdens and strengthened your
    heart.

Soon there came to your home a treasure most meet,
'Twas the boy Gurdon so handsome and sweet.
His high brow and bright eyes revealed at a glance
What he could do in the world only give him a chance.
Time goes on, and soon there came to your home

The dear darling Sara, whom now you bemoan;
She could not stay long, a few years were all,
When she passed into heaven at the Good Shepherd's call.
Then Bert and Jay B. followed soon by their birth,

To make your home cheerful and gladden the earth.
These sons and their wives made a happy home circle,
Where harmony and love each heart did encircle.
Soon grand-children came to fill up the ranks,

And brighten your life with their innocent pranks.
There were Frank, Maud and Fred, May, Eddie and Jay,
And Raymond and Florence to make home more gay.
Other grand-children came to add to the list,

And round up the circle and perfect your bliss.
There is Elizabeth and Gurdon and Frank,
And dear little Alice to fill up the ranks.
Richard, Louise and Martha must stand in their station

For they count two apiece in the family relation.
May Louise and Frank Truman Rawlings,
Are a worthy addition to the roll we are calling.
One other child we must not forget,

She is lively and cheerful; her name is Janet.
So quick are her thoughts, so lively her pace,
She seems the same time to be twice in a place.
In our thoughts, if we roam, wherever so far,

We must not forget sweet baby Dunbar;
God loved him so well that he took him up home
To live with the angels near by the White Throne.
Dear Sister, I must close this letter to you,

Tis my warm Christmas Greeting with love pure and true.
If you reach the bright goal toward which we are running,
Look out at the window and watch for my coming.
Our sun is fast setting, it will not be long,

Before we shall join that blest happy throng.
We'll join with the saints in that holy land,
Our robes washed white in the blood of the Lamb.

THREE SCORE YEARS AND TEN.

From the top of the Mount of Vision,
Looking two ways o'er the scenes,
Backward to days of my childhood
Forward for the fruit of my dreams.

Can I say that life is worth living?
That its treasures are dross and not gold?
Or can I believe that its riches,
Are greater than yet has been told?

With me the Fates have dealt kindly,
I have nothing of which to complain;
My trials are sanctified blessings,
Enriching me only with gain.

My mistakes have been many, no doubt,
My sins pain my heart with regrets,
But God, who graciously loves me,
Forgives me and comforts me yet.

No virtue have I to commend me,
My goodness no better than rags
To cover my guilt and defend me,
When Justice no longer shall lag

But draws his swift sword to strike me
And make me His victim by right.
I flee to the Cross for defense,
And know I am safe from His might,

So, when time brings about that Great Day
When all Souls in judgment must stand;
If I will but trust God's mercy
He will place me at His right hand.

The past is now left behind me,
Its record I cannot now change;
The future looms brightly before me,
In visions of Heavenly reign.

Earth fades from view looking forward,
Its pleasures no longer invite;
My soul has fixed its dominion
In realms of immortal delight.

So, I face the future with calmness,
My victory over death and the grave
Is assured to me by my Savior,
Who suffered and died to save

Sinners like me from destruction,
And bring them to glory at last,
When He makes up His bright jewels
To adorn His rich crown at last.

MY FAREWELL.

Dear nephews and nieces and cousins,
I bid you a kindly farewell;
The shadows of death draw near me,
Just when I shall go I can't tell.

I sit on the bank of the river,
The Ferryman bends to his oar;
I wait his strokes on the life-boat,
As it nears the evergreen shore.

"Shall we gather at the River
    Where bright angel feet have trod;
With its crystal tide forever
    Flowing by the throne of God.

Yes, we'll gather at the River
The Beautiful, the beautiful river,
Gather with the saints at the river,
That flows by the throne of God."

Rev. Robert Lowry, 1864.

MY PRAYER.

(ORIGINAL)

At Thine Altar Lord I bow,
. Here to pay my solemn vow;
That henceforth my life shall be,
Consecrated, Lord, to Thee.

Let me not from Thee astray;
Keep me in the narrow way;
Save me from the World's alloy,
Fill my heart with peace and joy.

When I tread o'er Jordan's wave;
May my hope on Thee be stayed;
Since my Savior's gone before,
LAND ME SAFE ON CANAAN'S SHORE.

SUPPLEMENT

Full Catalogue of Families
Named in the Genealogy

LIST OF NAMES IN PART FIRST.
FIRST GENERATION.

I.   John Tennant and Elizabeth Loomis.

SECOND GENERATION.

II.   1. Alfred,   2. Betsey,   3. Orrel,   4. Alvin Loomis,
5. Olive Eliza. 6. Delinda, 7. Clairisa.

THIRD GENERATION.

III.   Children of Betsey Tennant and Rev. George Sawin.
1. Olive Eliza, 2. Maria Edna,   3. William Orlando.

FOURTH GENERATION.

IV.   Children of Olive Eliza Sawin and Platt Webster.
1. Helen M.,   2. Maria Emma.
V.   Children of William Orlando Sawin and Jane Bacon.
1. Frank Benjamin,   2. Bernice Augustus,   3. George
William.

FIFTH GENERATION.

VI.   Children of Helen M. Webster and Lorenzo Sawin.
1. Ida Adell,   2. Emma Grace.
VII.   Children of George William Sawin and Margaret Wilson, his first wife.
1. Nellie,   2. William,   3. Ruth.
A son born to Byron Kester and Ruth Sawin September 22,
1915.
Minford George Kestor.
By his second wife, Mary Maud Carr.
1. George Arland,   2. Bernice Helen,   3. Milton Orlando,   4. Mary Grace.

SIXTH GENERATION.

VIII.   Children of Nellie Sawin and Lewis Delos Lull.
1. Raymond Sawin Lull, 2. Infant son.

The above named descendants number as follows:

Children 3
Grand Children 5
Great-grand-children 9
Great-great-grand child 1
                                              ——
    Total 18

Including parents and grand-parents there are six generations.

Descendants of Orrel Tennant (Second child of John Tennant
and Elizabeth Loomis), and Rev. John Sawin.

THIRD GENERATION.

I.   Children.

1. Aurilla,   2. Ann Eliza,   3. Alvin, 4.   Clarissa,   5.
David M.,   6. Ethan,   7. Lucinda,   8. Lorenzo,   9.
Mary Jane,   10. Marinda,   11. Murinda,   12. Eleanor.
13. Juliette.

FOURTH GENERATION.

II.   Children of Ann Eliza Sawin   and   Nathaniel William
Gott.

1. Emma Augusta,   2. William Watson.

III.   Child of Clarissa Sawin and Albert Tillinghast.

1. Ella Florine.

IV.   Children of Ethan Philander Sawin and Harriet Lucina
Tupper.

1. Albert,   2. Charles.

V.   Children of Lorenzo Sawin and Helen Webster.

1. Ida Adell,   2. Emma Grace.

VI.   Children of Mary Jane Sawin and John J. Montgomery.

1. Orrel Marie,   2. John Eugene,   3. Kittie Adell.

VII.   Children of Eleanor Matilda Sawin and Anson Baldwin.

1. David,   2. Myrtle,   3. Llewellyn,   4. Jay, 5.
Jennie,   6. Zala.

VIII.   Children of Julia Ette Sawin and Charles Mortimer
Smith.

1. Flora,   2. Charles.

Total of Fourth Generation 18.

FIFTH GENERATION.

IX.   Child of Emma Augusta Gott and Henry Erdley.

1. Emma Eliza Erdley.

X.   Children of William Watson Gott and Emma Hicks.

1. Mabel, 2. Irene, 3. Nina Belle, 4. Ellis.

XI.   Children of Albert Monroe Sawin and Josephine Alice
Hall.

1. Lester,   2. Genevieve,   3. Ruth,   4. Ethel.

XII.   Children of Ida Adell Sawin and Frank Hyne.

1. Ray,   2. Hugh,   3. Grace.

XIII.   Children of John Eugene Montgomery and   Kate S.
Starkweather.

1. Alvin,   2. Caryl,   3. Lyell.

XIV.   Child of Kittie Adell Montgomery and Edward R.
Ellis.

1. Mary Adell Ellis.

XVI. Child of Myrtle May Baldwin and Edgar Myers Cole.
1. Donald Baldwin Cole.
XV. Child of Jennie Ella Baldwin and Fred Burr Hartfield.
1. Hazel May Hartfield.
XVI. Children of Zala Sawin Baldwin and Nora G. Haynes.
1. Percy, 2. Eunice, 3. Esther.
XVII. Child of Flora D. Smith and George O. Gordon.
1. Doris Mildred Gordon.
XVIII. Child of Dr. Charles Mortimer Smith and Jennie M. Frantz.
1. Ruth E. Smith.
Total of fifth generation, 23.

SIXTH GENERATION.

XIX. Children of Emma Eliza Erbley and Chester Mayhew.
1. Henry, 2. Wallace, 3. Willard.
XX. Children of Mabel Elizabeth Gott and Rev. Harland Chester Logan.
1. Eveline, 2. Ruth, 3. Margaret, 4. Gordon Donald.
XXI. Child of Mary Adell Ellis and Harvey Wall.
1. Fred Ellis Wall.

TOTALS.

Children 13
Grandchildren 18
Great-Grandchildren 23
Great-Great-Grandchildren 8

Total descendants 62

With grand parents and parents the descendants include six generations.

THIRD GENERATION.

I. Descendants of Alvin Loomis Tennant, oldest son of John and Elizabeth Loomis Tennant, by his first wife, Eliza Ann Thompson.
1. Harriet Amanda, 2. Alfred, 3. Milton.
By his second wife, Sophronia G. Kelley.
1. Eliza.

FOURTH GENERATION.

II. Child of Alfred Tennant and Cornelia Hixon.
1. Alice Tennant.
III. Children of Eliza Tennant and Willard F. Plate.
1. Willard, 2. Cora, 3. Nora, 4. Charles.

Number of descendants:

Children 4

Grandchildren 5

Total 9

Including with parents and grandparents four generations.

The descendants of Olive Eliza Tennant, third daughter of John Tennant and Elizabeth Loomis, may be found recorded under the name of her husband, Rev. David Tennant, in Part II, Chapter Fifth.

Descendants of Delinda Tennant, fourth daughter of John Tennant and Elizabeth Loomis, are recorded under the name of her husband, Moses Asel Tennant, in Part III, Chapter Fifth.

Descendants of Clarissa Tennant, daughter of John Tennant and Elizabeth Loomis, and wife of Henry Gay.

THIRD GENERATION.

I.   Their children.
1.   Laura Ann,   2.   Ira,   3.   Francis,   4.   Alonzo.

FOURTH GENERATION.

II.   Children of Laura Ann Gay and Isaac Palmer.
1.   Galen,   2.   Alice,   3.   Clara,   4.   Frank,   5.   Etta.
III.   Children of Ira Gay and Diana Mason.
1.   Edith,   2.   Bertha,   3.   Cassius.
IV.   Children of Francis Henry Gay and Martha L. Clark.
1.   Claribell,   2.   Henry Frank.
V.   Children of Alonzo Gay and Maria Josephine Shiller, his second wife.
1.   Clarence,   2.   Earl,   3.   Gilbert,   4.   Ira.

FIFTH GENERATION.

VI.   Children of Galen Eugene Palmer and Martha Cook.
1.   Grace,   2.   Earl,   3.   Ira,   4.   Frank,   5.   Ray, 6.   Norris.
VII.   Children of Alice Elizabeth Palmer and Horace Eugene Sawin.
1.   Laura May,   2.   Lee Willis.
VIII.   Children of Clara Augusta Palmer and John Newbury.
1.   Bertha,   2.   Julia,   3.   Rush,   4.   Alice.
IX.   Children of Frank Henry Palmer and Nellie Lentz.
1.   Laura F. Palmer.
X.   Children of Etta Estella Palmer and John Philpott.

1. Chester, 2. Frank, 3. An infant son, 4. John, 5. Myrtle.

XI. Children of Edith Mason Gay and Allen Prince Bartlett.
1. Gay, 2. Allen, 3. Fanny Edith.

XII. Children of Bertha Rosina Gay and Moses H. Smith.
1. Jay, 2. Ira, 3. Guy.

XIII. Children of Cassius Mason Gay and Julia I. Fessendon.
1. Byron S., 2. Norman H., 3. Ira F., 4. Edith A., 5. Bertha A., 6. Cassius Mason.

XIV. Children of Clarabell Gay and George Sprague Bright.
1. John Gay Bright.

XV. Children of Henry Frank Gay and Mary Agnes Crocker.
1. Carleton, 2. Frank, 3. Robert.

XVI. Child of Earl Alonzo Gay and Carrie Pepper.
1. Romona Lillian Gay.

SIXTH GENERATION.

XVII. Children of Earl Eugene Palmer and Emma Jane Porter.
1. Floyd. 2. Ira. 3. Ray.

XVIII. Children of Laura May Sawin and Burdette Phillips.
1. Alice. 2. Raymond.

XIX. Children of Lee Willis Sawin and Emma Morgan.
1. Albert, 2. Jennie, 3. Laura, 4. Frederick.

XX. Children of Bertha Alice Newbury and George R. Russell.
1. Velma Jessie Russell.

XXI. Children of Julia Etta Newbury and Herman Ruch.
1. Clara, 2. John.

XXII. Child of Allen Prince Bartlett and Lena Rowley.
1. A son.

XXIII. Children of Fanny Edith Bartlett and Dr. Fred Conley Rice.
1. Laura 2. Allen, 3. Edith.

XXIV. Children of Jay Gay Smith and Maud Whitman.
1. Byron, 2. Lessie, 3. Naomi.

XXV. Children of Ira R. Smith and Flossie Hall.
1. Edgar, 2. Ira, 3. Raleigh, 4. Bertha, 5. Grace, 6. Mildred.

XXVI. Children of Guy Moses Smith and Mabel Ross.
1. Ruth, 2. Irma.

Number of descendants are as follows:

Children 4
Grandchildren 14
Great-grandchildren 35
Great-great-grandchildren 27

Total 80

LIST OF PARENTS, GRANDPARENTS AND CHILDREN NAMED IN PART SECOND.

FIRST GENERATION.

I. Moses Tennant, Sr., and his wife, Betsey Tennant.

SECOND GENERATION.

II. 1. Selden, 2. Betsey, 3. Polly, 4. David.

THIRD GENERATION.

I. Children of Selden Tennant and Lydia Allen .
1. Moses, 2. Ruben, 3. Betsey, 4. Allen, 5. Lydia, 6. David, 7. Hannah.

FOURTH GENERATION.

II. Children of Moses Selden Tennant and Mary Jane Billings.
1. William, 2. Celeste.
III. Children of Betsey Tennant and Charles Kingsbury.
1. Selden Bingham, 2. Lydia Jane, 3. Alice, 4. Evangeline, 5. Charles, 6. James, 7. Amy.
IV. Children of Lydia Tennant and David Myron Tennant.
1. Mary Ann, 2. Alfred Myron, 3. Eleanor Lydia, 4. Selden David, 5. Hiram Adelbert.
V. Children of David Russell Tennant and Melita Burpee.
1. Franklin Russell, 2. Emily Dorinda, 3. Ellen Arminda, 4. Clara Melita, 5. George William, 6. Mary Almina.
VI. Children of Hannah Tennant and Moses Holcomb.
1. Elida, 2. Oliva, 3. Truman, 4. George, 5. William Page, 6. Fred Grant.

FIFTH GENERATION.

VII. Children of William Selden Tennant and Mary Josephine Sutton.
1. William, 2. John, 3. Daisy, 4. Frank, 5. Sidney.
VIII. Children of Selden Bingham Kingsbury and Hulda Corning.

1. Nathan, 2. Elizabeth, 3. Frederick, 4. Helen, 5. Ross.

IX. Children of Lydia Jane Kingsbury and Jerome Culver.

1. Roy, 2. Guy.

X. Child of Alice Kingsbury and Mr. Huckins.

1. Seth G. Huckins.

XI. Child of Charles Henry Kingsbury and Rena Abbott.

1. Helen Kingsbury.

XII. Children of James Dayton Kingsbury and Mary Alida Abel.

1. James, Jr., 2. Ora Louise, 3. Fred, 4 Ralph Abel, 5. Raymond, 6. Selden, 7. Martin.

XIII. Child of Amy Kingsbury and Edward W. Marsh.

1. Alice Ernestine Marsh.

XIV. Children of Mary Ann Tennant and Orlando Brownell.

(See list of the descendants of Rev. David Tennant. In the same list may be found the descendants of Alfred Myron, Eleanor Lydia, Selden David, and Hiram Adelbert Tennant.)

XV. Children of Franklin Russell Tennant and Ella Damon.

1. Eugene, 2. Roy, 3. Ray, 4. Clayton, 5. Frank.

XVI. Children of Emily Dorinda Tennant and Albert Kennedy.

1. Mabel, 2. Clarence, 3. Alberta.

XVII. Children of Ellen Arminda Tennant and Herbert H. Howe.

1. Myrtie, 2. Lena, 3. Grace, 4. Maud.

XVIII. Children of Clara Melita Tennant and Frileto Hebart Bronson.

1. Rosella Adelia Brown.

XIX. Children of George William Tennant and Mattie Gifford.

1. Ernest, 2. Albert, 3. Arthur, 4. George, 5. Ada 6. Emma.

XX. Children of Elida Holcomb and Henry Breckenridge.

1. Mattie, 2. Earl.

XXI. Children of Oliva Holcomb and Derastus Brown.

1. Nettie, 2. Charles, 3. Albert.

XXII. Children of Truman Holcomb and Clara Campbell.

1. Mamie, 2. Frank.

By second wife, Mrs. May Whitney, a daughter.

1. Leita Louise Holcomb.

SIXTH GENERATION.

XXIII. Children of John Selden Tennant and Sarah Olive Banard.

1. John Selden, 2. Florence Banard.

XXIV. Child of Nathan Corning Kingsbury and Lillian Blanche Prescott.

1. Eleanor Kingsbury.

XXV. Child of Helen L. Kingsbury and Capt. Charles Frederick Humphrey.

1. Elizabeth Humphrey.

XXVI. Child of Ross Selden Kingsbury and Josephine Elliott.

1. Priscilla Kingsbury.

XXVII. Children of James Dayton Kingsbury, Jr., and Mary Susan Gallup.

1. Dorothy Alida, 2. Marion Judith.

XXVIII. Children of Ora Louise Kingsbury and Ezra Durham Smith.

1. June Ernestine, 2. Beatrice Rea.

XXIX. Child of Roy Russell Tennant and Mattie Eastman.

1. Alice Amelia.

XXX. Children of Ray Damon Tennant and Etta Histed.

1. Hulda Alberta, 2. Gertrude Louise, 3. Gilbert Lawrence.

XXXI. Children of Clayton Franklin Tennant and Eva Madill.

1. Ellen Louise, 2. Dorothy Eveline.

XXXII. Children of Lena Ellnora Howe and Robert E. Lance.

1. Sidney Herbert, 2. Iona Ellnora.

XXXIII. Child of Grace Ellen Howe and Abraham Burton Cashner.

1. Gerald Burton Cashner, 2.. Ralph Herbert Cashner.

XXXIV. Child of Maud Lula Howe and Roy H. Eggleston.

1. Thelma Ellen Eggleston.

XXXV. Children of Arthur Sidney Tennant and Dora Allison.

1. Albert Lee, 2. Arthur Perry.

XXXVI. Child of Mattie Breckenridge and Robert Johnson.

1. Leon Johnson.

XXXVII. Child of Nettie Brown and Mr. W. F. Sump.

1. Florence Stella Sump.

XXXVIII. Children of Albert Brown and

1. Kathryn, 2. Charles.

XXXIX. Children of Mamie Holcomb and Charles Bartles.

1. Clara, 2. Ora C., 3. Lulu, 4. Roy, 5. Glenn, 6. Fay, 7. Clifford, 8. Myrtle.

XL. Children of Frank M. Holcomb and Lulu Whitson.

1. Mildred, 2. Welma, 3. Donald, 4. Doris, 5. Dale, 6. Fred W.

The descendants of Selden Tennant and his wife, Lydia Alden, are included in the above list except the children and

grand children of his daughter, Lydia, who married David Myron Tennant, a son of Rev. David Tennant. (See descendants
of Rev. David Tennant, found in Part II, Chapter 5, of this
book.) The descendants of Lydia Tennant by her husband,
David Myron Tennant, number twenty-eight. These added to
those recorded among the descendants of Rev. David Tennant
make the total number of the descendants of Selden Tennant
one hundred and forty-nine. A summary here follows:

Children 7
Grandchildren 26
Great-grandchildren 49
Great-great-grandchildren 39

Total 121
Descendants of Lydia Tennant................ 28

Grand Total 149

Descendants of Betsey Tennant, oldest daughter of Moses
Tenant, Sr., and his wife, Betsey Tennant, and her husband,
Sterlin Way.

THIRD GENERATION.
I. Children of Betsey Tennant and Sterlin Way.
1. Lucy Ann, 2. Maria, 3. David S., 4. Martin,
5. Dulcena, 6. Elizabeth, 7. Eli.

FOURTH GENERATION.
II. Child of Lucy Ann Way and Dr. William Way.
1. Helen Maria Way.
III. Children of David Sterlin Way and Margaret Elizabeth
Mosher.
1. David Watson, 2. Lucy Emily, 3. Eli Sylvester.
IV. Children of Martin Way and Ruth Ely.
1. Mary, 2. Richard, 3. Heman, 4. Lydia, 5. Will
Burt.
V. Children of Dulcena Way and Delos Nicholson.
No report.

FIFTH GENERATION.
VI. Child of David Watson Way and Maria E. Stanbro.
1. Orville David.
VII. Children of Lucy Emily Way and Martin Julett Doo-
little.
1. Manley Freeman, 2. Marion Martin.
VII. Children of Eli Sylvester Way and Margaret Mosher.
By first marriage.

1. Adah Venett,   2.   Nellie De Ette.
By second marriage.
1.   Alice Merton Way.
X.   Children of Mary Maria Way and Harry Van Horn.
1. Lena,   2. Ruth,   3. Lizzie,   4. George,   5, Allie,
6. Reuben,   7. Echna.
XI.   Child of Richard S. Way and Gertrude S. Small.
1.   Edith Way.
XII.   Children of Ely Herman Way and Flora Heckerman.
1.   Pearl Way,   2.   A son who died in infancy.
XIII.   Children of Will Burt Way and Maude Rathburn.
No report.

SIXTH GENERATION.

XIV.   Child of Orvill David Way and Ida Viola Tompkins.
1.   Carl Watson Way.
XV.   Child of Ada Venett Way and Munson Enoch Himes.
I.   Robert Himes.
XVI.   Children of Edith Way and Floyd Burst.

No report.

Children . . . . : 7
Grandchildren 9
Great-grandchildren 15
Great-great-grandchildren 2
                                                                                    —
Total descendants 33
Including parents and grand parents there are six generations.

DESCENDANTS OF
REV. DAVID TENNANT AND OLIVE ELIZA TENNANT
THEIR CHILDREN.

I.   THIRD GENERATION.

1.   Alfred Augustus,   2.   Leventia,   3.   Harriet Eliza,
4. David Myron.

FOURTH GENERATION.

II.   Children of Alfred Augustus and Fannie Louisa (Wheeler) Tennant.
1.   Harriet Stanley,   2.   Francis Augustus,   3.   Olivia
Sarah.
III.   Children of Harriet Eliza Tennant and Sylvester Covil.
1.   Sylvester Covil.
IV.   Children of David Myron Tennant and Lydia Tennant

1. Mary Ann, 2. Alfred Myron, 3. Eleanor Lydia, 4. Selden David, 5. Hiram Adelbert.

FIFTH GENERATION.

IV. Children of Harriet Stanley Tennant and Abram Jewett Champion.

(See descendants of John and Lucy Tennant Champion.)

V. Children of Francis Augustus Tennant and Elva Rosetta (Corbin) Tennant.

1. Frank, 2. Olivia, 3. Belle, 4. Joseph, 5. Harriet.

IV. Children of Olivia Sarah Tennant and Samuel Emlen Comfort.

1. Frances Elizabeth, 2. Olive Sarah.

VII. Children of Mary Ann Tennant and Orlando Bunnell.

1. Eli Granger, 2. Charles Orlando.

VIII. Children of Alfred Myron Tennant and Mary Jane Schafer, his first wife.

1. Eva Josephine, 2. Myron J.

By his second wife, Carrie Estelle Smith.

1. Belle, 2. Julia, 3. Dorothy, 4. Alfred.

IX. Children of Selden David Tennant and Anna Cuddeback, his first wife.

1. Jessie, 2. Nellie, 3. Charles, 4. Myrtie, 5. Archie, 6. Ray.

X. Children of Hiram Adelbert Tennant and Mary J. Short.

1. Floyd Adelbert, 2. Jeness Emily, 3. Bernice Wilberta, 4. Leventia Grace.

SIXTH GENERATION.

XI. Descendants of Harriet Stanley Tennant and Abram Jewett Tennant. (See descendants of John and Lucy Tennant Champion.)

XII. Children of Frank Adelbert Tennant and Mary Caroline Parry.

1. Edward Augustus, 2. Elva Bernice, 3. Esther Jane.

XII. Children of Olivia Aileen Tennant and Edgar Mauier Williams.

1. Emily, 2. Anabelle, 3. Charles.

XIII. Children of Belle Tennant and Thomas Joseph Laycock.

1. Doris Elizabeth, 2. Francis Ellsworth, 3. Edgar, 4. Elva Josephine, 5. Frank Maxwell, 6. Rosemary Ruth.

XIV. Child of Olive Sarah Comfort and Alfred E. Difford.

1. William B. Difford.

XV. Children of Eli Granger Bunnell and Minnie Edna Eurst.

1. Leah May,   2. Orlando Alphens,   3. Lila May,   4. Luana Julia,   5. Lila Edna,   6. William Eli,   7. Florence Minnie,   8. Died in infancy,   9. Died in infancy.

XVI.   Children of Charles Orlando Bunnell and Verne Beatrice Saxton.

1. Leslie Charles,   2. Howard Melville,   3. Rosetta.

XVII.   Children of Belle May Tennant and Herbert C. Snow.

1. Winifred Belle,   2. Shirley Elizabeth.

XVIII.   Children of Myrtie E. Tennant and Charles W. Dunham.

1. Adah Elizabeth,   2. Ruth Myrtie.

XIX.   Child of Floyd Adelbert Tennant and Mabel Hardy Wilson.

1. Florence May.

Number of descendants:

Children 4
Grandchildren 9
Great-grandchildren 25
Great-great-grandchildren 30
                                                                          —
Total 68

Including parents and grandparents these comprise six generations.

REMARKS.

In the catalogue of the descendants of Moses Tennant, Sr., and his wife, Betsey Tennant, the names of the children of their third child and second daughter, Polly, who married a Mr. Howard do not appear. After much correspondence, the record of their family could not be obtained by the author of this Genealogy. The author has been informed that they had a son who died in his youth. He also has been told that they had a daughter, but her name could not be obtained.

LIST OF DESCENDANTS OF
SARAH SELDEN JEWETT AND NATHANIEL BAKER,
HER FIRST HUSBAND.

SECOND GENERATION.

I.   One child, a daughter, Sarah Baker.

THIRD GENERATION.

Child of Sarah Baker and Mr. Whipple.

II.   A son, Timothy Whipple.

LIST OF DESCENDANTS OF
SARAH SELDEN JEWETT AND ISAAC SHAW,
HER SECOND HUSBAND.

SECOND GENERATION.

I.   One child, a daughter, Deborah Shaw.

LIST OF DESCENDANTS OF
DEBORAH SHAW BY CALVIN GIBBS,
HER FIRST HUSBAND.

THIRD GENERATION.

I.   Children of Deborah Shaw and Calvin Gibbs.
1. Orton,   2. Charlotte,   3. Clarissa,   4. Graham,
5. Eliza,   6. Julia,   7. Monroe.

FOURTH GENERATION.

II.   Children of Charlotte Gibbs and Jonathan Green.
1. A son,   2. A daughter, Zipha.
III.   Children of Clarissa Gibbs and Austin Jones.
1. Euseba,   2. Eliza.
IV.   Children of Graham Gibbs and a daughter of Alvin and Minerva (Phelps) Lewis.
1. Charles,   2. Emma.

FIFTH GENERATION.

V.   Children of Charles Gibbs and Eva L. Davis.
1. Eddie,   2. Harry,   3. Minerva,   4. Amelia.

SIXTH GENERATION.

VI.   Children of Eddie Charles Gibbs and Julia Ann Welch.
1. Robert,   2. Alma,   3. Alice,   4. Charles.
VII.   Child of Harry Gibbs and his wife, whose maiden name has not been given to the writer.
1. Harry J. Gibbs.
VIII.   Children of Amelia Maria Gibbs and Oscar Julius Lare.
1. Alice,   2. Horatio,   3. Paul,   4. Howard W.,
5. Charles,   6. Gladys,   7. Ruby.

The above completes the list of the descendants of Deborah Shaw and Calvin Gibbs so far as the writer was able to obtain them. It is very incomplete and contains only a part of these descendants; entire families are left out of this list because the names of children and grandchildren could not be obtained.

The above list comprises:

Children 7
Grandchildren 6
Great-grandchildren 4
Great-great-grandchildren 12
                                                             —

Total 29

They include six generations. By her second husband, Mr. Marvin, Miss Shaw had a son named John Marvin, who died when but seven years old. His name makes the number thirty.

List of the descendants of Moses Tennant, Sr., and Mrs. Sarah Selden Jewett Shaw, his second wife, and her third husband named in Part III, and arranged according to their generations.

FIRST GENERATION.

I.   Moses Tennant, Sr., and Sarah Selden Jewett.

SECOND GENERATION.

II.   1. Lucy Selden Tennant, 2. Olivia Tennant, 3. Moses Asel Tennant, 4 Esther Tennant.

DESCENDANTS OF
LUCY SELDEN TENNANT AND JOHN CHAMPION

THIRD GENERATION.

1. Eliza Ann,   2. Moses.   3. John Harris,   4. Lucyette. 5. Abraham Jewette, 6. Caroline I., 7. Esther, 8. Dan Nelson, 9. Caroline, 10. Ruth.
Total, 10.

FOURTH GENERATION.

IV.   Children of Eliza Ann Champion and Horatio Beals.
1. Mary,   2. Lucinda,   3. Horatio,   4. Avoline,   5. Caroline.
V.   Children of Lucyette Champion and Asa Potter.
1. Juliet,   2. Helen,   3. Abbie,   4. Abraham,   5. Mary, 6. Annie.
VI.   Children of Abraham Jewett Champion and Lanah Maria Miller.
Of the first marriage.
1. Francena,   2. Adelia,   3. Lavina,   4. William,   5. Kendrick, 6. LaClaire, 7. Maxwell.
Of the second marriage.
1. Llewellyn,   2. Jewett,   3. Ralph Waldo,   4. Arthur, 5. Merrill.

VII.   Child of Esther Champion and Frederick Lenardson.
1,   Frederick Lenardson.
VIII.   Children of Ruth Ann Champion and Jonathan Wight Clough.
1. John,   2. Joseph,   3. Ephraim,   4. Carrie,   5. Clara,
6. Solon.   7. Henry,   8. Almon,   9. Lucyette,   10. Ruth.
Total,   4 of the Fourth Generation.

FIFTH GENERATION.

IX.   Children of Mary Eliza Beals and Henry Clarke.
1.   Zechariah,   2. Ella,   3. Clayton,   4. Emma,   5. Henry.
X.   Children of Lucinda Rovanda Beals and James W. K. Loomis.
1.   Carlton,   2. Arthur,   3. Earl,   4. Dan,   5. Victor,
6. Albertus,   7, Charles.
XI.   Children of Avoline Cornelia Beals and Henry Harding.
1. Carrie,   2. Frederick,   3. John,   4. Henry,   5, Carlton.
XII.   Children of Caroline Amelia Beals and Harvey Frederick Wilcox.
1. Ida May.   2. Elvina Avaline,   3. Eunice Ann.
XIII.   Children of Juliette Potter and William Henry Tiffany.
By first marriage.
1. Emmett,   2. Mann.
By second marriage to Ryman Van Evera.
1. Potter Van Evera.
XIV.   Children of Abbie Mahala Potter and Adrian Emmett Wallace.
1. William,   2. Charles,   3. Victor.
XV.   Child of Abraham Charles Potter and J. Louise Meisinger Potter.
1. Carlton Ames Potter.
XV.   Children of Mary Emma Potter and Dr. Edward Carleton.
1. Spencer.   2. Mary,   3. Mabel,   4. Bertha.
XVI.   Children of Francena Louise Champion and Bradley Gilman Stanley.
1. Carl,   2. Alcesta.
XVII.   Children of Adelia Jewett Champion and Dr. Sanford Monroe Clark.
1. Lanah,   2. Jay,   3. Dorman.
XVIII.   Children of Lavina Alcesta Champion and Henry Vrooman.
1. Edward Ernest,   2. Adelia Janet.
XIX.   Children of William John Champion and Emily Pigot, his first wife.

1. Maud,   2. Frances,   3. William.
By his second wife, who was Susan (Barber) Champion.
1. Charles,   2. George,   3. Bessie,   4. John Wesley.
XX.   Children of Kendrick Abram Champion and Anna Enora McIntyre.
1. Amelia,   2. Grace,   3. Earl,   4. Cathran,   5. Pearl, 6. St. Clair.
XXI.   Children of LaClair Smith Champion and Julia Etta Conklin.
1. Florence, 2. Laura, 3. Cesta, 4. John.
XXII.   Children of Llewellyn Earl Champion and Martha Miser, his first wife.
1. George Earl Champion.
XXIII.   Child of Fullman Merrill Champion and Olive Emma Scott Champion.
1. Constance Ydeomie Champion.
XXIV.   Children of John Morton Clough and Alice Smith.
1. Solon, 2. Samuel, 3. John, 4. Amos, 5. Nelson.
XXV.   Children of Joseph Hamilton Clough and Rachel Priscilla Frier Clough.
1. Rose, 2. Frederick, 3. Jennie, 4. Jonathan, 5. Amelia, 6. Matilda, 7. Myra, 8. Ephraim, 9. Emma, 10. Florence, 11. Earl.
XXVI.   Children of Ephraim Theodore Clough and Esther Viola Wibber Clough.
1. William,   2. David.
XXVII.   Children of Carrie Mariah Clough and William Horace Wilcox.
1. Ella,   2. Oliver,   3. Florence.
XXVIII.   Child of Henry Jewett Clough and Martha Gundry Clough.
1. Fulton Clough.
XXIX.   Children of Ruth Ann Clough.
By her first husband, William Kimball.
1. Helen Juliett Kimball.
By her second husband, William Franklin Scott.
1. Jessie Kirby,   2. Wade Hamilton Scott.
Total of Fourth Generation, 82.
Total of Fifth Generation, 85.

SIXTH GENERATION.

XXX.   Children of Ella Ann Clark and Charles C. Holden.
1. Anna, 2. Addie, 3. James.
Children of Clayton Beals Clark.
Had two children by his first wife. No names given of wife or children.

XXXI. Children of Henry Worthington Clark and Josephine Elizabeth Pelon.

1. Ida, 2. John, 3. Maud, 4. Frank, 5. Clayton, 6. Louie.

XXXII. Children of Carlton Jewett Loomis and Carrie Kuney Loomis.

1. Lotta, 2. Rodney, 3. Emily, 4. Gerald.

XXXIII. Children of Arthur Herbert Loomis and Ida Cornelia Jennings.

1. Lee C., 2. Inez Irene.

XXXIV. Children of Earl Dan Loomis and Lina Pritchard Loomis.

1. Glenn, 2. Leta Belle.

XXXV. Children of Victor James Loomis and Mary Louise King Loomis.

1. Harold, 2. Cameron, 3. Donald, 4. Kenneth.

XXXVI. Children of Albertus Chester Loomis and Cora R. Wilcox Loomis.

1. Eleanor May, 2. Myron Albertus.

XXXVII. Child of Ida May Wilcox and Oliver McPhail.

1. Ethel May McPhail.

XXXVIII. Children of Elvina Evaline Wilcox and Charles Harrison Nettleton.

1. Minnie, 2. Gertrude, 3. Earl.

XXXIX. Children of Eunice Ann Wilcox and Sanford Asaph Graves.

1. Verice, 2. Harvey, 3. Richard.

XL. Child of Emmett Tiffany and Evelyn Brown.

1. Harriet Tiffany.

XLI. Children of William Adrian Wallace and Anna (Bernard) Wallace.

1. Adrian, 2. Carlton, 3. Louie, 4. Raymond, 5. Milton, 6. Milford, 7. Bernard, 8. Juliet, 9. Anna.

XLII. Children of Victor Morean Wallace and Edna Adelia Rudy.

1. Edith, 2. Mabel, 3. Helen, 4. Victor, 5. Frank, 6. Chester, 7. Edna, 8. Donald.

XXLIII. Children of Dr. Spencer Carleton and Ernesta Stephens Carleton.

1. Baldwin, 2. Ernest.

XLIV. Children of Bertha Carleton and Wilbur Abbott Welch.

1. Oliver, 2. David, 3. Barbara, 4. Madaline, 5. Paul.

XLV. Children of Carl Stanley and Estella Hunt.

. 1. Helen, 2. Mary Francena.

XLVI. Child of Lizzie Alcesta Stanley and Walter Scott Colvin.

1. John, 2. Nizel Colvin.

XLVII. Children of Lanah Augusta Clarke and Miles A. Kahle.

1. Lulu, 2. Rozella, 3. Clarke James, 4. William Henry, 5. Nelson.

XLVIII. Children of John Jay Clarke and Alta Crockett.

1. Sanford, 2. Mabel, 3. Pearl.

XLIX. Child of Frances Amy Champion and William Eli Frisbie.

1. Frances Lillian Frisbie.

L. Child of Bessie Olive Champion and Herbert Fred Hopkins.

1. Stanton Hopkins.

LI. Child of Florence Champion and Ray Caset Smith.

1. Vivian Smith.

Total, 72.

SEVENTH GENERATION.

LII. Children of Anna Holden and Robert McKay

1. Elaine C., 2. Sarah H., 3. Louise A., 4. Charlotte E., 5. John Angus.

LIII. Children of Addie Holden and Charles E. Pratt.

1. Margaret, 2. Robert, 3. Mabel.

LIV. Child of James Holden and Minnie Marlin.

1. Ethel May Holden.

LV. Children of Lotta Lucinda Loomis and Edward Moran.

1. Mignon, 2. Charlotte, 3. Carlton.

LVI.. Child of Emily Jessie Loomis and Frederick Louis Shultz.

1. Frederick Louis Shultz.

LVII. Child of Lee C. Loomis and Sarah Fidelia Burham Loomis.

1. Charles Donald Loomis.

LVIII. Children of Leta Belle Loomis and Irving J. Hewes.

1. Vida, 2. Clarence, 3. Lulu, 4. Dorothy.

LIX. Child of Dr. Earl Howard Nettleton and his wife.

1. A son who is at Gangton, South Dakota.

LX. Children of Lulu Adelia Kahle and Asbury Loar.

1. Roland, 2. Maria.

LXI. Child of Rosezella Kahle and Russell B. Crockett.

1. Ruth. 2. Miles Willard.

LXII. Child of Clarke James Kahle and Wilhelmina Shephard (Cogwin) Kahle.

1. Charles Miles Kahle.

LXIII. Child of Sanford Monroe Clarke and his wife. Name not reported.

1. Kenneth Sanford Clarke.

LXIX. Children of Mabel Clair Clarke and Fred Petee.

1. Howard,   2. Wanda.

Seventh Generation, 27.

This finishes the list of the descendants of John Champion and Lucy (Tennant) Champion, numbering as follows:

Children 10
Grandchildren 34
Great-grandchildren 82
Great-great-grandchildren 72
Great-great-great-grandchildren 27

Total descendants 225

The author does not claim that the above list is absolutely complete. The reader, who may have personal knowledge of the families who constitute the descendants of John Champion can supply the deficiencies and so make up a full list. The author has done his best to make the list complete, but realizes his failure because he could not find, after much correspondence, the sources of any further information.

Including the parents and grand-parents there are seven generations recorded.

With the parents and grandparents the descendants comprise six generations.

[Descendants of Olive Eliza Tennant and of her sister, Delinda Tennant, are listed under the names of their husbands, Rev. David Tennant and Moses Asel Tennant, in another part of this catalogue.]

DESCENDANTS OF
OLIVIA TENNANT AND WILLIAM PHILLIPS.
THIRD GENERATION

1. William Jewett,   2. Esther,   3. John Galusha,   4. Andrew Jackson,   5. Sarah,   6. Cleantha,   7. James, 8. Mariah.

FOURTH GENERATION

I. Children of Williaim Jewett and Nancy Holden Phillips:

1. Otto Francis,   2. Louisa,   3. George,   4. William Holden.

II. Children of Esther Phillips and Henry Hastings:
1. George, 2. Frank, 3. William Jewett, 4. John Fuller.
III. Children of John Galusha Phillips by his first wife, Lydia Morrison:
1. Austin.
By his second wife, Amanda Darrow, 2. Delaski. 3. Hortens, 4. Elizabeth.
   IV. Children of Andrew Jackson Phillips and Emily Blackmer.
1. Elvira Olivia, 2. Edison Jay.
V. Children of Sarah Phillips and Gibbons Wentworth.
1. Emma, 2. Amanda, 3. Mary, 4. Elvira.
VI. Children of Cleantha Phillips and Gilbert DeHart.
1. Elsie Olivia, 2. Lewis, 3. William, 4. Herbert, 5. Gilbert Edison, 6. Juliette.
VII. Children of James Francis Phillips and Lucy A. Miller.
1. James B., 2. Selden Tennant, 3. Susie Olivia, 4. Floy Esther, 5. Bessie V., 6. an infant.
VIII. Children of Mariah Phillips and John Vankuren.
1. Rose Zella, 2. An infant, 3. Emma, 4. Ireka, 5. Mary, 6. Olivia, 7. Andrew, 8. Edward, 9. James.
Total Fourth Generation, 39.

FIFTH GENERATION.

IX. George Phillips. He died unmarried.
X. Children of Holden Phillips and Ida Conger.
1. Bessie, 2. Elvira, 3. Jewett.
XI. Children of George Hastings and Sophia Glidden.
1. Alice, 2. Jessie, 3. George, 4. Wilmot.
XII. Children of Frank Hastings and Jessie Weston.
1. Julianna Maria, 2. Frank Weston.
XIII. Children of William Jewett Hastings and Alice Margaret Allen.
1. Anson, 2. Charles, 3. William.
XIV. Children of John Fuller Hastings and Elizabeth Davison.
   1. Esther, 2. Carolyn, 3. Fuller, 4. Leslie, 5. Bessie.
XV. Children of Elvira Olivia Phillips and Roscoe Leadbetter.
1. Helen, 2. Edison, 3. Charles Curtis.
XVI. Children of Horace Edison Jay Phillips and Rosa Tuttle.
   1. Jay, 2. Gertrude, 3. Ora.
XVII. Children of Amanda Wentworth and Walter Eugene Covert.

1. Harry Wentworth Covert.

XVIII. Children of Mary Wentworth and Seth Farwell.

1. Edith, 2. Ethel, 3. Austin, 4. Margurite, 5. Gertrude.

XIX. Child of Elvira Wentworth and Frank Albert Burleson.

1. Fred Wentworth Burleson.

XX. Children of Elsie Olivia DeHart and Adoniram Perry.

1. Clyde, 2. Lynn.

XXI. Children of William Jewett DeHart and Cora Smith.

1. Ellis, 2. Elbert, 3. Vern, 4. William.

XXII. Children of Herbert Cornelius DeHart and Frances Dorr.

1. Florence, 2. Gilbert, 3. Willis, 4. Cleantha, 5. Dorothy, 6. Ruth.

XXIII. Children of Juliette DeHart and Ellis Perry.

1. Lulu, 2. Lola, 3. Arthur, 4. George.

XXIV. Children of Selden Tennant Phillips and Anna Agnes Darling.

1. Bessie, 2. James, 3. Mariah.

XXV. Child of Susie Olivia Phillips and William Plumstead.

1. Susie Irene Plumstead.

XXVI. Children of Floy Esther Phillips and Archie Potter, her first husband.

1. Fannie L., 2. Leola D.

XXVII. Children of Floy Esther Phillips and John Schell, her second husband.

1. John Phillips, 2. Floyd Selden.

XXVIII. Child of Bessie B. Phillips and Henry J. Baisley.

1. Floy Alpha.

XXIX. Children of Rose Zella VanKuren and Ransom E. Rogers.

1. David L. Rogers.

By second marriage to Mr. Burroughs, three children who died in infancy.

XXX. Children of Emma VanKuren and Albert Erastus Wait.

1. Della, 2. John.

XXXI. Children of Ircha VanKuren and Myrtle Sherman.

1. Vilbert, 2. Nina, 3. Ernest, 4. George, 5. Alice, 6. Andrew.

XXXII. Children of Mary Vankuren and John Albert Wait.

1. Della, 2. John.

XXXIII. Children of Olivia Nancy Vankuren and Horatio Bidwell Wait.

1. Ethel,   2. Ruby,   3. Mary,   4. Esther.

XXXIV. Children of Andrew Jackson Vankuren and Martha (Copince) Vankuren.

1. William,   2. Oliver,   3. Eunice,   4. Delos,   5. Beatrice,   6. Hattie,   7. Andrew,   8. Harry.

XXXV. Children of Edward Vankuren and Tryphema Tulet.

1. Roy,   2. Addison.

Total Fifth Generation, 83.

SIXTH GENERATION.

XXXVI. Children of Bessie Phillips and Claud Isaac Anton.

1. Dorothy,   2. Phillips George.

XXXVII. Child of Elvira Phillips and John Burton Gidley.

1. Jane Louise Gidley.

XXXVIII. Children of Julianna Hastings and Arthur Clemens Crowther.

1. Artha,   2. Julianna,   3. Ellison,   4. Enid,   5. Ada, 6. Joseph,   7. May DeVerne,   8. Bryce Carrol.

XXXIX. Children of Frank Weston Hastings and Marguretta F. M. Sellick.

1. Henry James,   2. Weston Hastings.

XL. Children of Charles Curtis Leadbetter by his second wife.

1. Charles Austin,   2. Katharine Grace.

XLI. Children of Clyde Perry and Aura Louise Brastal.

1. Dana,   2. Bertha Edna,   3. Anna Cora.

XLII. Children of Lynn Perry and Jennie Wilson.

1. Kenneth,   2. Madaline Beatrice.

XLIII. Child of Lola Perry and George P. Simmons.

1. Silvia E. Simmons.

XLIV. Children of David Rogers and Maud Hartwick.

1. Mary Jane,   2. Zella May,   3. Charles David, 4. Asa Ransom,   5. Ralph Edward.

XLV. Children of Della Wait and Byron Jenkins.

1. Neil,   2. Lee.

Total, Sixth Generation, 28.

Descendants of Sarah Selden Jewett and her third husband, Moses Tennant, Sr., by her daughter, Olivia Tennant, wife of William Phillips, number as follows:

```
Children . . . . . . . . . . . . . . . . . . . . . . . . . . . . . . . . . .  8
Grand-children . . . . . . . . . . . . . . . . . . . . . . . . . . . . .39
Great-grandchildren . . . . . . . . . . . . . . . . . . . . . . . .83
Great-great-grandchildren . . . . . . . . . . . . . . . . . . .28
                                                          ———
    Total . . . . . . . . . . . . . . . . . . . . . . . . . . . . . . .158
```

Including parents and grandparents there are six generations.

DESCENDANTS OF
MOSES ASEL TENNANT AND DELINDA TENNANT,
(HER MAIDEN NAME).

THIRD GENERATION.

Their children.
1. Alvin, 2. Delos, 3. Selden, 4. Eliza, 5. Julia,
6. Wealthy, 7. Albert, 8. Ellen, 9. Fannie, 10. John.

FOURTH GENERATION.

I. Child of Alvin Tennant and Emerett Wattles.
1. Alvin Jewett Tennant.
II. Children of Delos Tennant and Sally Eliza Sawin.
1. Caroline, 2. Moses Delos.
III. Children of Olive Eliza Tennant and Henry Shaver.
1. Harriet, 2. Charles, 3. Catharine, 4. De Ette.
IV. Children of Julia Tennant and David Shaver.
1. Alice, 2. Ellen, 3. Frank, 4. Frederick, 5. Emerson, 6. Dwight.
V. Children of Wealthy Tennant and Erbin C. Wattles.
1. Gordon, 2. Sarah, 3. Bert, 4. Jay B.
VI. Children of Fannie Tennant and George Mason.
1. Charles, 2. Sarah, 3. Eugene.
VII. Child of John Tennant and Julia Adams.
1. Frederick Adams Tennant.

FIFTH GENERATION.

VIII. Children of Jewett Tennant and Carrie Brown.
1. Emma, 2. Leah, 3. Mable, 4. Alvin.
IX. Child of Caroline Tennant and Ahija Jay Crandall.
1. Jay Crandall.
X. Child of Moses Delos Tennant and Helen Smitih.
1. Arthur Smith Tennant.
IX. Children of Charles Shaver and Priscilla Elliott.
1. Sarah, 2. Ada, 3. Harold.
XII. Children of Frank Shaver and Floretta Lewis, his first wife.
1. Bertha Shaver.
By his second wife, Miss Myrtie Culver.
1. Winifred, 2. Carlton.
XII. Children of Frederick Shaver and Amy Robsart Ries.
1. May Belle, 2. Maud, 3. Gladys, 4. Grace, 5. Dorthea, 6. Phillips, 7. David, 8. George.
XIII. Children of Emerson Shaver and Cora Bennett.
1. Helen Belle, 2. Roy Bennett.
XIV. Children of Dwight Shaver and Jennie Moorehead.
1. Carol, 2. Rolla.

SIXTH GENERATION.

XIII.   Child of Leah Tennant and William Elmer Stout.
1.   Margaret Tennant Stout.
XIV.   Children of Mabelle Tennant and Roy Duane Adams.
1.   David Tennant Adams,   2.   Kathrine Tennant Adams.
XV.   Children of Jay Crandall and Carrie Ludlow.
1.   Darwin,   2.   Edna,   3.   Harold.
XVI.   Child of Arthur Smith Tennant and Grace Skinner.
1.   Arthur Skinner Tennant.
XVII.   Children of Helen May Belle Shaver and William Edward Ferrell, her first husband.
1.   Dorothy Maybelle Ferrell.
By her second hsuband, Herman Gilbertson.
1.   John Randolph Gilbertson.
XVIII.   Child of Roy Bennett Shaver and Jessie Bedford.
1.   Horner Bedford Shaver.
XIX.   Children of Frank Wattles and Alice Weller.
1.   Elizabeth,   2.   Gordon Weller,   3.   Frank Erbine,
4.   Alice Kathrine.
XX.   Children of Maud Wattles and Benjamin Hawkins.
1.   Richard Wattles,   2.   Louise Florence,   3.   Martha.
XXI.   Children of Mary Lucretia Wattles and Richard Rawlings.
1.   Mary,   2.   Louise.
XXII.   Children of Raymond Wattles and Lucilla Dunbar.
1.   Harris Dunbar Wattles,   2.   Erbin Dunbar Wattles.

The descendants of Moses Asel and Delinda Tennant are enumerated as follows: Children, ten—five sons and five daughters.   Grandchildren, twenty-one—thirteen sons and eight daughters.   Great-grandchildren, twenty-four—eleven sons and thirteen daughters.   Great-great-grandchildren, twenty — ten sons and ten daughters.   Total descendants, seventy-five.

The above computation was made in December, 1913, and includes with parents and grandparents, six generations.

A list of the descendants of Esther Tennant, youngest daughter of Moses Tennant, Sr., and his wife, Sarah Selden Jewett, and wife of David Hollenbeck.

THIRD GENERATION.

I.   Their children.
1.   Sarah,   2.   Ellen,   3.   Dolly Jane,   4.   William,
5.   Georgiana.

FOURTH GENERATION.

II.   Children of Sarah Olivia Hollenbeck and George Robertson.

1. Maria,   2. Lewis,   3. David,   4. Ovid.

III. Children of Dolly Jane Eliza Hollenbeck and John Wright.

1. Esther,   2. George,   3. Emma.

IV. Children of William Warren Hollenbeck and Amarilla Theresa Hewett.

1. Jetora,   2. Jenora,   3. David,   4. Tennant,   5. Lila, 6. T. D. (No names, just the letters),   6. Bertha Mae.

V. Children of Harriett Georgiana Hollenbeck and Edward Elon Fellows.

1. Newell,   2. Rhoda,   3. Edna,   4. Clara,   5. David, 6. Cora,   7. Edwin,   8. Hattie,   9. Nellie,   10. Jessie, 11. Bessie.

FIFTH GENERATION.

VI. Children of Marie Robertson and Willard Mackey, her first husband.

1. George Mackey,   By her second husband, Mr. Henry Mitchell.   2. Alfred,   3. William,   4. Ernest,   5. Mary, 6. Edward,   7. Charles.

VII. Child of Esther Wright and Elbert C. Harvey.

1. Emma L. Harvey.

VIII. Child of George David Wright and Miss Nellie Wright.

1. Florence Georgia Wright.

IX. Children of Jetora Hollenbeck and Noel C. Miller.

1. Lillie,   2. Dennis,   3. Perry,   4. Harold,   5. Noel.

X. Children of Bertha Mae Hollenbeck and D. J. Lorne McColl.

1. Ilah Mae,   2. Rena Charlotte,   3. James Lorne.

XI. Child of Newell H. Fellows and Nellie Godfrey.

1. Celia May Fellows.

XII. Children of Rhoda Ann Fellows and William A. Brown.

1. Herbert,   2. Harriett,   3. Esther,   4. Willie.

XIII. Child of Cora Ette Fellows and William Duncan McLeod.

1. Edna Evelyn McLeod.

XIV. Children of Edwin Warren Fellows and Rose May Jones.

1. Harriett Edwina,   2. Newell Edwin.

XV. Child of Jessie Ketchum Fellows and Everett M. Russell.

1. Warren E. Russell.

XVI. Child of Bessie Ketchum Fellows and Mr. A. Earl Kent.

1. Junier Lewis Kent.

SIXTH GENERATION.

XVII.   Children of Emma L. Harvey and Dr. Ernest Emerson Rice.

1.   Esther,   2.   Pauline.

XVIII.   Child of Florence Georgia Wright and William Benjamine Plumb.

1.   Billy Plumb.

XIX.   Children of Celia Mae Fellows and William H. Miller.

1.   Althea Lucille,   2.   Ruth Ellen.

XX.   Child of Herbert Brown and Edith Haufe.

1.   Sidney Brown.

The descendants of the above list number as follows:

Children 5
Grandchildren 25
Great-grandchildren 27
Great-great-grandchildren 6
                                                                          —
    Total 63

Including parents and grandparents there are six generations.